Transactions of the RHS (2022), **32**, 1–4
doi:10.1017/S0080440122000123

INTRODUCTION

An Anniversary and New Departure: *Transactions,* 1872–2022

Emma Griffin

Department of History, University of East Anglia, Norwich, Norfolk NR4 7TJ, UK
Email: E.Griffin@uea.ac.uk

On 26 November 1872, members of the Royal Historical Society gathered for their annual meeting at the Scottish Corporation Hall, off Fleet Street, London. The Society was marking its fourth anniversary since formation, and was delighted to have recently received recognition 'as "Royal" by Her Majesty the Queen'. A buoyant annual report described a year of 'extraordinary' growth and change, which included the election of 158 new Fellows and of a popular new president. The minutes of the meeting also drew attention to the Society's recent and successful foray into the publishing sphere, noting the 'general satisfaction with the first volume of the Society's Transactions' which had recently been circulated to the membership.[1]

This publication was not, strictly speaking, the first occasion on which scholarly papers read to the Society had been made available in print.[2] It did, however, mark the beginning of a more ambitious and structured approach to the Society's publishing programme. In an editorial preface by Charles Rogers, the Society's founder and self-styled 'historiographer', volume 1 of the *Transactions of the Royal Historical Society* promised 'the recovery, from recondite sources, of materials which might illustrate the less explored paths of national and provincial history'. The volume opened with an article by the Cork-based historian Louis de Vericour on 'The Study of History' which lamented the 'absence of historical studies in British education' and argued for the subject's 'dignity and pre-eminent utility ... as a regulator of the human mind and as a teacher of Christian morality'.[3] Members' warm reception of this first volume of *Transactions*, as recorded on 26 November 1872, led the Council to 'recommend that a volume of Transactions should be printed annually'.[4]

---

[1] Royal Historical Society archive, RHS 1/1/1, fol. 73. The new president was the former prime minister, first Earl Russell, elected in November 1871.

[2] Royal Historical Society archive, RHS 1/1/1, fols. 41 and 57.

[3] Louis Raymond de Vericour, 'The Study of History', *Transactions of the Royal Historical Society*, first series, 1 (1872), 32.

[4] Royal Historical Society archive, RHS 1/1/1, fols. 73–4.

A century and a half later, *Transactions of the Royal Historical Society* is still going strong. Appearing fourteen years before the *English Historical Review*, and twenty-three years ahead of the *American Historical Review*, *Transactions* was a pioneer of the modern scholarly journal for history, and is the longest-published English-language historical journal still in existence. Since 1872, 145 volumes (including this one) have appeared across six series. This longevity should not obscure the precariousness of the journal's opening decades. As historians of the Society have noted, its early volumes were patchy in terms of academic distinction and there were breaks in publication, with no volumes appearing in 1875, 1879, 1883 and 1887–8.[5] These years were also administratively difficult given the dominance of Charles Rogers, who had become an increasingly divisive figure.

With Rogers's departure, the journal's fortunes began to improve. The Society's growing professionalisation in the late nineteenth and early twentieth century was evident in the improving quality, ambition and regularity of its journal. These years featured research articles by the likes of Oscar Browning, Charles Oman and C. H. Firth, and publication of occasional studies on 'The Progress of Historical Research'. Presidential Addresses were first published from 1893, and articles by university-based presidents – including Adolphus Ward (1900), George Prothero (1902–5) and T. F. Tout (1926–9) – made interventions on the scope, vitality and practice of the historical discipline. From 1899, winners of the Society's annual Alexander Prize had their essays published in *Transactions*, the first being Frances Hermia Durham, winner of the inaugural award for 'The Relations of the Crown to Trade under James I'. As Ian Archer has recently shown, annual publication of winning essays significantly raised the profile of women authors in the early volumes of *Transactions*, with female scholars being recipients of the Alexander Prize on eight of twelve occasions to 1917. But prize-winning was not the only route by which women historians were able to publish in *Transactions*. Having presented her research as a paper, in 1895 Alice Law became the first woman to have a full article published in the journal.[6] There followed a steady rise in the number of women whose work appeared in *Transactions*, gathering pace in the second decade of the twentieth century, when one-fifth of contributors were women, and peaking at two-fifths in the 1920s.[7] Subsequent developments

---

[5] On the early publishing history of *Transactions* see Alexander Taylor Milne, *A Centenary Guide to the Publications of the Royal Historical Society, 1868–1968* (1968); J. W. Burrow, 'Victorian Historians and the Royal Historical Society', *Transactions*, fifth series, 39 (1989), 125–40; Ian Archer, '150 Years of Royal Historical Society Publishing', *Transactions*, sixth series, 28 (2018), 265–88. Since 1888, the journal has seen continuous annual publication, with the exception of 1938.

[6] Alice Law, 'The English *Nouveaux-Riches* in the Fourteenth Century', *Transactions*, second series, 9 (1895), 49–73. A graduate of Cambridge and an early contributor to the *Victoria County History*, Alice Law was elected a Fellow of the Society in February 1910.

[7] Archer, '150 Years', 276–7. The subsequent sharp decline in women's representation is one manifestation of a pattern witnessed in the academic historical profession during the mid- and later twentieth century, as discussed by Carol Dyhouse, *No Distinction of Sex? Women in British Universities, 1870–1939* (1995) and Laura Carter, 'Women Historians in the Twentieth Century', in *Precarious Professionals: Gender, Identities and Social Change in Modern Britain*, ed. Heidi Egginton and

in the journal's history include the publication, since 1969, of the Society's annual Prothero Lecture,[8] and proceedings of conferences organised by the Society on topics such as 'Christian Life in the Later Middle Ages' (1991), 'The Eltonian Legacy' (1997), 'Oral History, Memory and Written Tradition' (1999), 'Architecture and History' (2003) and 'Elizabeth I and the Expansion of England' (2004). Throughout *Transactions'* first 150 years, articles have reflected changing priorities in historical research. The past decade alone is witness to a marked increase in articles situated beyond Britain and Europe, and focused on global connectivity, as well as (among other areas) histories of the body, disability, ethnicity, gender, materiality, selfhood, and studies of digital, interdisciplinary or community-based historical practice.[9] Contributions to this current volume likewise offer studies of, among others, Black history, environmental history, public history, and the intersection of historical research and the creative arts.

As an anniversary, November 2022 provides us with an opportunity to mark the origin, development and contribution of *Transactions*. At the same time, November 2022 is also an important point of departure for the journal and its future contribution to historical communications.

This year's volume signals a number of important changes to the aims, authorship and format of the journal. Until now, all articles published in *Transactions* have been read, by invitation, at meetings of the Society, prior to their publication in article form. This changed in 2021, since when the Society has welcomed submission of articles from historians worldwide, many of whom will not have opportunity to present their research as a Society lecture or conference paper.[10] The current volume is the first to include submitted articles, appearing alongside versions of RHS Lectures presented in 2021. In opening up the journal in this way, we seek to make *Transactions* more accessible to historians at all career stages, to those working collaboratively, and for practitioners in sectors beyond higher education. It's our hope that publication of the 2022 volume encourages many more researchers to submit their work for review.

This year's volume also sees important changes regarding editorship. From 2022, *Transactions* is edited not, as previously, by members of the Society's Council but by an appointed team of historians with responsibility for the journal's academic content and intellectual development. Earlier this year, the

---

Zoë Thomas (2021), 263–86. The level of women's representation in *Transactions* in the 1920s (40 per cent of articles) has not been matched since (being 26 per cent for 2000–9 and 32 per cent for 2010–19), though 51 per cent of articles for 2020–2 are wholly or jointly written by women authors.

[8] This latest volume includes an article version of Robert Frost's 2021 Prothero Lecture, 'The Roads Not Taken: Liberty, Sovereignty and the Idea of the Republic in Poland-Lithuania and the British Isles, 1550–1660', delivered on 2 July 2021.

[9] A complete listing of *Transactions* articles, 1872–2022, is available via the Cambridge University Press Cambridge Core platform https://www.cambridge.org/core/journals/transactions-of-the-royal-historical-society/all-issues; a print list of articles to 1968 is available in Milne, *Centenary Guide*, pp. 81–137.

[10] An initiative proposed and enacted by Professor Andrew Spicer, the Society's literary director, 2015–21.

Society chose Dr Harshan Kumarasingham and Dr Kate Smith as the new editors of *Transactions*, supported by recently created UK editorial and international advisory boards. In consultation with these historians, the editors are currently rethinking aspects of the journal. This includes presentation of work in a wider range of formats (going beyond the traditional article type), and encouraging submissions that explore new research, methodologies, multidisciplinary perspectives, and historical practice both in higher education and cognate sectors. The outcomes of these changes will become increasingly apparent from next year and thereafter, as the new editorial structure takes hold. In addition, *Transactions* has a new look and design, with use of a cover image to highlight one of the articles in this year's collection.[11] Now published in paperback print, from 2022 new *Transactions* articles are accessible – via Cambridge University Press's 'FirstView' – weeks after acceptance, compared to the months that often elapsed before the annual November print publication.

These changes are in line with wider, ongoing work at the Royal Historical Society to make the RHS as responsive, engaging and meaningful as possible to a broad membership, while also remaining true to the scholarly standards that have long characterised the Society's activities, including publishing. In a final innovation for this 150th year, Fellows and Members of the Society are now able to access the journal's complete online archive – comprising 145 *Transactions* volumes and a sequence of more than 2,200 articles, which began, in 1872, with Louis de Vericour's call to study history. In a year that's both an anniversary and new departure, we hope to encourage discoveries from the journal's rich past and provide new opportunities to shape its future.

---

[11] This year's cover image, a watercolour by an unknown Burmese artist (*c.* 1895), was chosen to accompany Jonathan Saha's article: 'Accumulations and Cascades: Burmese Elephants and the Ecological Impact of British Imperialism'.

Cite this article: Griffin E (2022). An Anniversary and New Departure: *Transactions*, 1872–2022. *Transactions of the Royal Historical Society* **32**, 1–4. https://doi.org/10.1017/S0080440122000123

Transactions of the RHS (2022), **32**, 5–23
doi:10.1017/S0080440122000111

PRESIDENTIAL ADDRESS

Writing about Life Writing: Women, Autobiography and the British Industrial Revolution

Emma Griffin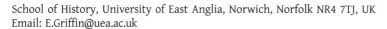

School of History, University of East Anglia, Norwich, Norfolk NR4 7TJ, UK
Email: E.Griffin@uea.ac.uk

Abstract

Few historical problems have attracted so much attention over so many years as the social consequences of the British industrial revolution. For the most part, historians presumed that working people produced very little historical evidence that could be used to contribute to our understanding. However, projects to catalogue and encourage the use of the nation's scattered, yet extensive, archive of working-class autobiography have revealed that such evidence does, in fact, exist. The insertion of working-class autobiography helps to offer a new perspective, one which suggests a more positive interpretation of industrial life than historians have usually been willing to admit. Yet there remains a problem with the archive. During the industrial revolution, life-writing was a male art form. Women only started writing autobiographies in any number around 100 years after the conventional periodisation of the industrial revolution. This article surveys the autobiographical writing during and after the industrial revolution – around 1,000 items in all – in order to rethink the relationship between economic growth and social change. It confirms that industrial growth improved the position of working men in society, but concludes that female perspectives on this change are far more ambivalent.

Keywords: standard of living; autobiography; industrial revolution; women; working class

As the moment when one small, European nation entered decisively down the path to modernity, the industrial revolution has rightly attracted considerable reflection and attention. Those living through the industrial revolution may have lacked our modern vocabulary and understanding of the transition, but they were certainly aware of the unprecedented economic change that was occurring, and the question of how this change was altering the texture of life for the population attracted wide and lively interest. By the middle of the nineteenth century a debate about the 'Condition of England' had taken shape.[1] Political economists, poets, novelists and philosophers all contributed, and, despite considerable heterogeneity in their views, writers from across the political spectrum frequently turned to the concepts of loss and decline in order to make sense of their changing world.[2] John Stuart Mill's view sums up the position of many. He concluded that society's mechanical inventions had done no more than 'enable a greater proportion to live the same life of drudgery and imprisonment'.[3]

Just as those living through the industrial revolution were interested in unpacking its social consequences, so too have been subsequent generations of historians. Throughout the late nineteenth and early twentieth centuries, a succession of influential writers – Arnold Toynbee,[4] Sidney and Beatrice Webb[5] and John and Barbara Hammond[6] – tackled the social and cultural significance of Britain's industrial revolution, and by the middle of the twentieth century the Condition of England question – now restyled the 'Standard of Living Debate' – had attracted the attention of some of the most influential historians in a generation.[7] Yet despite the passage of time, the arguments penned by academic historians had much in common with the pessimistic interpretation of earlier commentators, emphasising the myriad ways in which industrialisation destroyed older and happier patterns of life, and describing the industrial revolution as a fundamentally deleterious event in the lives of the working poor. And although tempers have cooled since the heyday of the standard of living debate in the 1970s, interpretations have moved on far less.[8] In the past fifty years, the

---

[1] Early discussion begins with T. Robert Malthus, *An Essay on the Principle of Population; or a View of its past and present Effects on Human Happiness; with an Inquiry into our Prospects respecting the Removal or Mitigation of the Evils which it occasions* (1803); David Davies, *The Case of the Labourers in Husbandry Stated and Considered* (1795); Frederick Morton Eden, *The State of the Poor: A History of the Labouring Classes in England, with Parochial Reports*, ed. A. G. L. Rogers (1928).

[2] William Wordsworth, 'Outrage done to Nature', from *The Excursion* (1814); William Blake, 'And did those feet in ancient time', from *Milton: A Poem* (1804–8); Benjamin Disraeli, *Sybil, Or the Two Nations* (1845); Charles Dickens, *Hard Times* (1854); William Cobbett, *Rural Rides* (1830). See also Friedrich Engels, *The Condition of the Working Class in England*, ed. David McLellan (Oxford, 1993), 16. Though note also a few dissenting voices, for example, Andrew Ure, *The Philosophy of Manufactures* (1835).

[3] John Stuart Mill, *Principles of Political Economy*, ed. W. J. Ashley (1909), 751.

[4] Arnold Toynbee, *Lectures on the Industrial Revolution of the Eighteenth Century in England* (1884), 84.

[5] Sydney and Beatrice Webb, *The History of Trade Unionism* (1898).

[6] J. L. Hammond and Barbara Hammond, *The Village Labourer* (1911), *The Town Labourer* (1917) and *The Skilled Labourer* (1919); J. L. Hammond, 'The Industrial Revolution and Discontent', *Economic History Review*, 2 (1930), 215–28.

[7] See the essays by Ashton, Engerman, Gilboy, Hartwell, Hobsbawm and Thompson in *The Standard of Living in Britain in the Industrial Revolution*, ed. Arthur J. Taylor (1975). See also, especially, E. P. Thompson, *The Making of the English Working Class* (Harmondsworth, 1976).

[8] C. H. Feinstein, 'Pessimism Perpetuated: Real Wages and the Standard of Living in Britain during and after the Industrial Revolution', *Journal of Economic History*, 58 (1998), 625–58; S. Nicholas and D. Oxley, 'The Living Standards of Women in England and Wales; 1785–1815: New Evidence from Newgate Prison Records', *Economic History Review*, 49 (1996), 591–9; Roderick Floud *et al.*, *The Changing Body: Health, Nutrition, and Human Development in the Western World since 1700* (Cambridge, 2011); Hans-Joachim Voth, 'The Longest Years: New Estimates of Labor Input in

literature on working-class living standards has continued to grow steadily and now encompasses a far wider range of arguments and evidence than ever before; yet the pessimistic view that the world's first industrial revolution brought nothing but stagnant, possibly declining, living standards to the first generation of workers who lived through it continues to dominate scholarly understanding of this historical moment.[9]

The pessimism that has surrounded interpretations of working-class life during the period of industrialisation forms a marked contrast to those of working-class experiences during the later nineteenth century. Whereas nostalgia for a simpler, purer, happier life is the hallmark of discussion about the industrial revolution, contemporary commentators and later historians have both taken a much more upbeat view of living standards down to the end of the nineteenth century. All the standard economic measures – gross domestic product, gross national product, real wages – indicate steady rises throughout the nineteenth century.[10] As a result, we are left with a two-part interpretation of the impact of industrialisation on the working poor, which describes the first generation as having experienced this as a time of dislocation and declining living standards. Meaningful gains for working people, we are told, only started to trickle through to subsequent generations later in the nineteenth century.

At the same time as the literature on working-class living standards, both during and after the industrial revolution, has grown, so too has scholarly interest in working-class autobiography as a historical source. With the compilation of John Burnett, David Vincent and David Mayall's invaluable and much-used finding aid, *The Autobiography of the Working Class: An Annotated, Critical Bibliography*, in the 1980s, it became possible for historians to identify the themes of individual autobiographies as well as to track down copies of the autobiographies in question.[11] It is therefore little surprise that the use

---

England, 1760–1830', *Journal of Economic History*, 59 (2001), 1065–82; I. Gazeley, and S. Horrell, 'Nutrition in the English Agricultural Labourer's Household over the Course of the Long Nineteenth Century', *Economic History Review*, 66 (2013), 781–2; R. C. Allen, 'The High Wage Economy and the Industrial Revolution: A Restatement', *Economic History Review*, 68 (2015), 1–22.

[9] I discuss this more fully in Emma Griffin, 'Diets, Hunger and Living Standards during the British Industrial Revolution', *Past & Present*, 239 (2018), 71–111,

[10] C. H. Feinstein, *National Income, Expenditure and Output of the United Kingdom, 1855–1965* (Cambridge, 1972); R. C. O. Matthews, C. H. Feinstein and J. C. Odling-Smee, *British Economic Growth, 1856–1973* (Oxford, 1982); N. F. R. Crafts and Terence Mills, 'Trends in Real Wages in Britain, 1750–1913', *Explorations in Economic History*, 31 (1994), 176–219; Gregory Clark, 'The Condition of the Working Class in England 1209–2004', *Journal of Economic History*, 58 (2005), 1307–40; Stephen Broadberry, 'Relative Per Capita Income Levels in the United Kingdom and the United States since 1870: Reconciling Time-Series Projections and Direct Benchmark Estimates', *Journal of Economic History*, 63 (2003), 852–63; Stephen Broadberry and Alexander Klein, 'Aggregate and Per Capita GDP in Europe, 1870–2000: Continental, Regional and National Data with Changing Boundaries', *Scandinavian Economic History Review*, 60 (2012), 79–107, table 3; Nicholas Crafts and Terence C. Mills, 'Six Centuries of British Economic Growth: A Time-Series Perspective', *European Review of Economic History*, 21 (2017), 141–58.

[11] John Burnett, David Vincent and David Mayall (eds.), *The Autobiography of the Working Class: An Annotated, Critical Bibliography* (3 vols., New York, 1984–9). See also David Vincent, *Testaments of*

of working-class autobiography as source material has grown substantially over the past forty years.[12] Yet despite the existence of these two large literatures – concerned with working-class experiences of economic change on the one hand and working-class autobiographies on the other – there have been relatively few attempts to bring them together. My research over the past fifteen years has been focused on precisely this endeavour and forms the focus of this paper.

Burnett *et al.*'s *Bibliography* is comprehensive, but when I began my project on working-class life in industrialising Britain, in the mid-2000s, I noticed that the listings for the region in which I was based, Norfolk, were surprisingly sparse, so I made a speculative trip to the Norfolk Record Office to search for autobiographies that the original compilers might have missed. An item in their catalogue listed simply as 'Memoirs of John Lincoln' looked promising.[13] The condition of John Lincoln's memoirs was too poor to be made available in the reading room, but the archivist pointed me towards the microfilm drawers and readers and advised me to access it there. And although both Lincoln's handwriting and the microfilm format made for a difficult day's reading, the rich content of this unknown autobiography more than compensated for these inconveniences. This single source spoke to a host of questions concerning autobiography, working-class life and the social consequences of industrialisation, and is worth exploring in some depth.

The author of the Memoirs was a man called John Lincoln. The eighty pages of Lincoln's notebook, written in the 1830s, are fragile and torn, filled with the untidy hand of a self-taught writer. The closely written, margin-less pages remind us that Lincoln lived at a time when paper was a precious commodity. They comprised what he called his 'simple Naritive', a detailed account of his

---

Radicalism: Memoirs of Working Class Politicians, 1790-1885 (1977); John Burnett (ed.), *Useful Toil: Autobiographies of Working People from the 1820s to the 1920s* (1974); John Burnett (ed.), *Destiny Obscure: Autobiographies of Childhood, Education and Family from the 1820s to the 1920s* (1982).

[12] The literature here is large and growing. For some examples, see M. Roper, 'Re-remembering the Soldier-Hero: The Psychic and Social Construction of Memory in Personal Narratives of the Great War', *History Workshop Journal*, 50 (2000), 181–220; Jonathan Rose, *The Intellectual Life of the British Working Classes* (New Haven, 2001); Carolyn Tilghman, 'Autobiography as Dissidence: Subjectivity, Sexuality, and the Women's Co-operative Guild', *Biography*, 26 (2003), 583–606; Jane McDermid, 'The Making of a "Domestic" Life: Memories of a Working Woman', *Labour History Review*, 73 (2008), 253–68; Keith Gildart, 'Mining Memories: Reading Coalfield Autobiographies', *Labor History*, 50 (2009), 139–61; Laura Ugolini, 'Autobiographies and Menswear Consumption in Britain, c. 1880–1939', *Textile History*, 40 (2009), 202–11; Lucy Delap, *Knowing Their Place: Domestic Service in Twentieth-Century Britain* (Oxford, 2011); Jacob Middleton, 'The Cock of the School: A Cultural History of Playground Violence in Britain, 1880–1940', *Journal of British Studies*, 52 (2013), 887–907; Julie-Marie Strange, *Fatherhood and the British Working Class, 1865-1914* (Cambridge, 2015); Fanny Louvier, 'Beyond the Black and White: Female Domestic Servants, Dress and Identity in France and Britain, 1900–1939', *Cultural and Social History*, 16 (2019), 581–602.

[13] Norfolk Record Office: John Lincoln, 'Memoirs of John Lincoln', MC 2669/29, 991X9. Also of interest in the Norfolk Record Office are John Hemmingway, 'The Character or Worldly Experience of the Writer from 1791 to 1865', MC 766/1, 795X5; Samuel Huggins, 'Some Short Account of the Birth Life Conversation Travels and Christian Experience of Samuel Huggins Primitive Methodist Preacher', FC 17/148.

life from his earliest childhood recollections (he was born in 1777) to the present.[14]

John was born, he tells us, into a single-parent family. He left home at the age of seven (not unusual for a fatherless child) and moved around a succession of 'live-in' positions as an outdoor agricultural servant and as an indoor servant and valet for the following fifteen years. It was in one of these situations, at Wingfield Castle in Suffolk, that he learned to read and write. At the age of twenty-one he took a place as a footman with a clergyman in Oxborough, Norfolk. And there he got on very well and 'became acquainted' with the cook, Ann – an excellent cook but a woman with 'a hot and Violent Temper – she was a very stout person and ten years older than myself'.[15] Within little more than a year, Ann was pregnant. According to Lincoln, his employer and his friends all warned him not to marry, but he would not listen. He went ahead with marriage (though was soon wishing he had 'followed their advice, and never married'). Just five short months later, Ann presented John with a son, but in the winter she took ill. Weeks later she lay dead. John removed his son to a second nurse, but the child's pitiful life was cut short at eighteen months.[16] Two years had passed since John had married. Both his wife and son had died and John, as he laconically observed, 'was far from being happy'.[17]

But life moved on. Two years later, John had another pregnant girlfriend, and once again was contemplating marriage. In sharp contrast to the usual desires of unmarried women in her predicament, however, John's new girlfriend seemed to care little for John's suggestion of marriage. She denied she was pregnant and brusquely terminated the relationship.[18] Unable to persuade her otherwise, John moved away. But marriage remained on his mind, and a few years later he once more 'began to think of trying another partner for life'.[19] He met a suitable young woman and although John said little about their courtship it was clearly conducted along similar lines to his previous two. His new wife gave birth to their first child just four months after the wedding. During the course of their marriage, she bore ten children in all. The memoirs provide scant detail about the nature of their married life (he did not even note her name) or the fate of their children (from the baptisms registers we learn that her name was Sarah; the parish registers also reveal the family suffered at least one infant death that was not mentioned in the memoir[20]). After his marriage, John's memoirs wander on to other themes and he returns to family matters only sporadically and inconsistently.

Family, both the one he was born into and the one he created, forms the foundation of John Lincoln's life story, but the matter of earning a living

---

[14] Lincoln, 'Memoirs', 82.

[15] *Ibid.*, 10

[16] *Ibid.*, 13

[17] *Ibid.*

[18] *Ibid.*, 23.

[19] *Ibid.*, 27

[20] At least this seems a reasonable inference given that John and Sarah gave the name Elizabeth to a daughter in 1826 and again in 1830. See Norfolk Record Office, Oxborough Baptism Registers, 1813–1998, PD 139/56.

also occupies considerable space and attention. Information about John's struggles to find work and on his experience of different positions is threaded through his life story. As a young man in rural East Anglia, for example, his jobs included minding horses, harvesting, well-digging, driving a 'Mail Cart', managing a garden, ploughing, and working as a footman.[21] In 1807, when he received a letter from a friend who had moved to Woolwich and had found work at the Royal Arsenal, John was offered the opportunity to leave behind the rural life. Lincoln left without hesitation. He had no reason to regret his decision. At the arsenal 'the work was very Light and the pay very good,' and at one point his earnings rose as high as 38 shillings a week.[22] But regrettably for Lincoln the good times did not last. Following the peace with France in 1814, the government downscaled production at Woolwich and Lincoln was laid off. He moved back to Norfolk, but returned to Woolwich soon after in the hope of a new opening at the arsenal. The opening did not materialise, so a disappointed John returned to Norfolk once again, abandoning all hope of work at the arsenal and settling down to life as an agricultural day-labourer, his paltry earnings eked out by a small dole from the parish.[23]

John's autobiography provides rich detail for any historian interested in family or work during the industrial revolution, but it is important to recognise that whilst these themes may interest us, they never formed the 'point' of John's autobiography. John wrote about the material and emotional aspects of his life simply in order to contextualise and explain his spiritual journey. The defining event in John's life was his religious conversion, and midway through his autobiography John turns his attention to this. It forms the bulk of the narrative thereafter. He describes how the dull services of the Church of England had done nothing for him. As he explains, he liked to sing, but in alehouses not churches. In any case, during much of his life John was so poor that he lacked the respectable Sunday clothes that the Church's clergymen expected of their flock. And then, at some point in 1816, John began to turn the matter of religion over in his mind. The lady of the village bought him a nice Bible and prayer book and his master provided him with some 'tidy Cloaths', so he decided to go to church on Sunday – though he did so, he confessed, more from 'curiosity and Pride' than from any religious conviction. Once there, however, the minister touched 'my eyes, my ears, my heart'.[24] He started to attend weekly services. His religious commitment grew and within a few years he had begun to preach the occasional sermon. Then, back in Oxborough where he had embarked on married life with the stout and hot-tempered Ann many years ago, he opened his 'humble Cottage' as a meeting house, determined 'to bring the inhabitants of Oxborough under the sound of the Gospel'.[25]

---

[21] Lincoln, 'Memoirs', 15–25.

[22] Ibid., 27.

[23] Ibid., 28–34.

[24] Ibid., 50-2.

[25] Ibid., 80

It is worth emphasising how far John had moved away from the expectations of a working man in rural Norfolk when he opened the doors of his cottage and began preaching the Gospel to his neighbours. A man like Lincoln was not supposed to teach the Gospel. John fathered his first child out of wedlock. His second son was illegitimate. His third child was also conceived before marriage. John Lincoln did not conform to the Church's notions of sexual propriety and respectability. John was also a poor man. He was poor at his birth and remained poor throughout his life, never rising above his station as a day labourer, living from one day to the next through the labour of his hands and frequently unable to earn enough to support his family decently. In fact, that 'humble Cottage' that he turned into a preaching house was not his at all. It was provided by the parish as his income was too low and too precarious for him to provide lodging for his family without their help. Yet here he was: not sitting in the pews designated for the poor at the back of the parish church, listening to a religion that taught the poor will always be with us, but standing at the front, delivering his interpretation of God's teaching. In all, it is a very far cry from the dark interpretation of the industrial revolution that has dominated historical writing on the topic for the past seventy years. It is not that John did not suffer loss, hardship and poverty on a scale difficult to comprehend from a modern perspective. He did. The point, rather, is that in casting his eye back over his life, John did not accord particular significance to any of this. John did not regard himself as a victim, ground down by the march of mechanisation. He thought of himself as a preacher, playing an important role in bringing the word of God to his neighbours. This may not fit with the dark interpretation of British industrialisation that initially commentators, latterly historians, have consolidated over the past 200 years. But as a working man who himself lived through the industrial revolution, it is an important perspective and one that merits further consideration.

John Lincoln's autobiography is but one historical source, and few historians would venture bold generalisations on the basis of a single source. But since the publication of Burnett *et al.*'s *Bibliography*, historians have been able to work at scale. Their listing, if not complete, is certainly wide-ranging, and that makes it possible to move beyond the individual stories contained in the chance finds of particular archives and to consult the sources more widely. The *Bibliography* lists more than 300 autobiographies written by working people alive during the industrial revolution, and a systematic reading through this material helps us to establish which parts of John Lincoln's – or any other writer's – life story are unusual, and which are more typical.[26] And a careful reading of the full collection of autobiographies certainly throws up some surprises for historians familiar with the standard account of declining living standards during the industrial revolution.

A number of observations stand out. Firstly, and perhaps most importantly, industrial employment pushed up male wages in a meaningful and significant way. Lincoln's comment about working in the munitions factory – the 'pay

---

[26] I develop this argument more fully in Emma Griffin, *Liberty's Dawn: A People's History of the Industrial Revolution* (New Haven, 2013).

[was] very good' – was not an exception; it was repeated by others.[27] A favourable comparison with the low pay and grinding hard work of agricultural labour was frequently drawn, whereas positive depictions of rural life were almost entirely absent.[28] Furthermore, the autobiographies (as Lincoln's implied) suggested that there was something else at stake. Poverty forced the hand of our writers in other walks of life. The decision to marry, the timing and content of their sexual lives – such things could be controlled to some degree by more powerful neighbours when a couple's outlook for raising their children by their own labour was poor.[29] And the same was true in the sphere of belief and ideas. How did a man challenge the religious or political views of his employer when that was the only person with the means to feed his family? The autobiographies reveal that low rates of pay in non-industrial areas obviously meant low incomes, but they also suggest that low incomes restricted the personal and political expression of the labouring poor.[30] And it is perhaps here that we see most clearly the grounds for emphasising the ways in which the industrial revolution enhanced rather than destroyed patterns of life. Critics will argue that the material gains for most families were meagre. Given the absence of robust information about wages and living costs for this period, definitive answers on this point are likely to elude us. We do, however, have a substantial body of autobiographical writing that provides a working-class perspective on work, wages and experience during the industrial revolution, and collectively this writing suggests that moving to cities and industrial areas brought male workers higher wages and considerably more freedom and autonomy both with respect to work, and to the things they could do outside work. This is not to suggest that the autobiographical collection provides a simple, linear account of social progress. Undoubtedly, working-class writers described complex and untidy lives, irreducible to one common theme or overarching narrative. Yet taking the autobiographical literature as a whole, the evidence is reasonably clear. From the perspective of the working men, industrial employment carried a number of advantages over the rural and pre-industrial alternatives that had traditionally been their lot.

The views of the autobiographers might be quite consistent, but this still leaves us some way from certainty about the fate of working-class experiences

---

[27] For example: Charles Campbell, *Memoirs of Charles Campbell, at Present Prisoner in the Jail of Glasgow* (Glasgow, 1828), 23; Samuel Catton, *A Short Sketch of a Long Life of Samuel Catton Once a Suffolk Ploughboy* (Ipswich, 1863), 4; Benjamin Shaw, *The Family Records of Benjamin Shaw, Mechanic of Dent, Dolphinholme and Preston, 1772-1841*, ed. Alan G. Crosby, Record Society of Lancashire and Cheshire, vol. 13 (1991), 45.

[28] George Mitchell, 'Autobiography and Reminiscences of George Mitchell, "One from the Plough"', in *The Skeleton at the Plough, or the Poor Farm Labourers of the West: with the Autobiography and Reminiscences of George Mitchell*, ed. Stephen Price ([1875?]), 96–108; Isaac Anderson, *The Life History of Isaac Anderson. A Member of the Peculiar People* (n.p., 1896), 8.

[29] Griffin, *Liberty's Dawn*.

[30] For example: Joseph Mayett, *The Autobiography of Joseph Mayett of Quainton, 1783-1839*, ed. Ann Kussmaul (Buckinghamshire Record Society, 23, 1986), 69–73; James Murdoch, 'Autobiography', in his *The Autobiography and Poems of James Murdoch* (Elgin, 1863), pp. 1–17.

at large. Thoughtful historians rarely accept documentary evidence at face value, and the gulf between the accounts of modern historians on the one hand and those of working-class writers on the other ought to give us pause for thought. Indeed, the limits of life-writing as a historical source have attracted considerable attention in recent years, as the growth of interest in life-writing that has occurred since the publication of the *Bibliography* has gone hand in hand with careful reflection about how historians can make best use of this material.[31] There is no need to retread the detail of those debates here. The sheer size of the literature is testimony to historians' faith in their ability to navigate the challenges of working with autobiographical evidence. There has, however, undeniably been a preference in favour of deep-reading strategies of individual works over wide reading across the full corpus.[32] After all, it is pointed out, the great majority of working people did not write an autobiography. Those who did had both the desire to write their story and the ability to do so, and these two qualities necessarily make them highly atypical of working-class people in general who had neither the wish nor the means to write. In consequence, there remains some scepticism about our ability to move from the particular to the general and a reluctance to engage with the autobiographical archive as a whole.

It is true that the overall number of autobiographies that have survived is small, and legitimate to consider the extent to which this small body of writing can 'speak' for working people more generally. There is no obvious solution to this problem, though it is of course worth bearing in mind that there is nothing unusual about historians working with collections of sources that are much smaller than the populations they wish to study. At the same time, it is worth wondering why these questions have attracted such detailed investigation, whilst other features of the autobiographical archive have escaped scrutiny. Indeed, it is striking that across a large, thoughtful and complex literature about autobiography as a historical source, very little attention has been paid to the complicating fact of gender.

This oversight is yet more remarkable when the gender imbalance of the sources is considered. Figure 1 visualises the growth of autobiography during

[31] In addition to the references in note 11, see also Nan Hackett, 'A Different Form of "Self": Narrative Style in British Nineteenth-Century Working-Class Autobiography', *Biography*, 12 (1989), 208–26; Regenia Gagnier, *Subjectivities: A History of Self-Representation in Britain, 1832–1920* (Oxford, 1991); Carolyn Steedman, *Past Tenses: Articles on Writing, Autobiography and History* (1992); Trev Lynn Boughton, *Men of Letters, Writing Lives: Masculinity and Literary Auto/biography in the Late Victorian Period* (1999); Chris Waters, 'Autobiography, Nostalgia, and the Changing Practices of Working-Class Selfhood', in *Singular Continuities: Tradition, Nostalgia, and Society in Modern Britain*, ed. George K. Behlmer and Fred Marc Leventhal (Stanford, 2000), 178–95; Sidonie Smith and Julia Watson, *Reading Autobiography: A Guide for Interpreting Life Narratives* (Minneapolis, 2001); James Treadwell, *Autobiographical Writing and British Literature* (Oxford, 2005); David Amigoni (ed.), *Life Writing and Victorian Culture* (Aldershot, 2006); Kevin Binfield, 'Ned Ludd and Labouring Class Autobiography', in *Romantic Autobiography in England*, ed. Eugene Stelzig (Farnham, 2009), 161–78.

[32] Helen Rogers and Emily Cuming, 'Revealing Fragments: Close and Distant Reading of Working-Class Autobiography', *Family and Community History*, 21 (2018), 180–201. The sole exception is Jane Humphries, *Childhood and Child Labour in the British Industrial Revolution* (Cambridge, 2010).

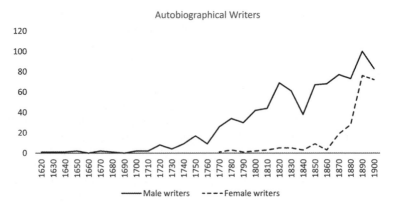

Figure 1. Autobiographies by sex, 1620–1900.

this period of industrialisation, and it breaks down the composition of writers by sex. The graph plots the date of birth of the writers, not the writing of the autobiography, which could occur anywhere between forty and eighty years later. It demonstrates a neat synchronicity between the onset of industrialisation in the late eighteenth century and an increase in male autobiographical writing. The number of writers continues to grow throughout the nineteenth century, but the rate of growth after about 1830 is less dramatic. The writing of autobiographies by women follows a very different path. Throughout most of the eighteenth century there are virtually no women that we could classify as working-class who have left behind an autobiography. There is a very small cohort of women born in the last quarter of the eighteenth century who wrote an autobiography, but the numbers are much lower than they are for men. It is not until around 1870 that the number of female writers starts to rise, and by the end of the nineteenth century the gender imbalance has narrowed considerably.

This is not to suggest that historians have been unaware of the dearth of female autobiographies. This has, of course, been widely recognised – and regretted – and feminist historians have displayed considerable imagination and ingenuity in exploiting the smaller corpus of writing by women that does exist.[33] The point rather is that scholarly analysis of women's writing tends to remain siloed from the rest of the archive. Female-authored autobiographies are used to explore specific aspects of the history of women's lives rather than to shed light on topics of broader interest, such as the fate of

---

[33] Tess Cosslett, Celia Lury and Penny Summerfield (eds.), *Feminism and Autobiography: Texts, Theories, Methods* (2000); Susan Zlotnick, *Women, Writing, and the Industrial Revolution* (Baltimore, 2001); Kelly Mays, 'Domestic Spaces, Readerly Acts: Reading(,) Gender, and Class in Working-Class Autobiography', *Nineteenth-Century Contexts*, 30 (2008), 343–68; Florence S. Boos, *Memoirs of Victorian Working-Class Women: The Hard Way Up* (Basingstoke, 2017); Penny Summerfield, *Histories of the Self: Personal Narratives and Historical Practice* (Abingdon, 2018); McDermid, 'Making of a "Domestic" Life'; Louvier, 'Beyond the Black and White'; Tilghman, 'Autobiography as Dissidence'.

working-class living standards during the industrial revolution. Gender imbalance at the heart of the archive has never been used to problematise the use of working-class autobiography as source material. Nor have historians argued that over-representation of male voices and views might introduce a significant distortion into the narratives we derive from autobiographical records.

Indeed, it is worth underscoring that the omission of female voices goes beyond the autobiographical material. Since the inception of interest in the social consequences of industrialisation, the debate has overwhelmingly been produced by men rather than women. The Victorian commentators who helped to shape the Condition of England question were almost all men. And the historians, starting with Toynbee, running up through E. P. Thompson and Eric Hobsbawm and beyond, who authored the Standard of Living Debate were men as well. By the 2000s, women historians too were writing about working-class life during the industrial revolution, and whilst they often argued for great attention to the role and experiences of women and children, this fresh perspective did not dismantle the pessimism that pervaded accounts of the period.[34] In reality, the frameworks for understanding this historical moment had by this time become fairly firmly fixed and largely had been constructed by men looking at evidence about men. The more recent insertion of the evidence from working-class autobiographies has offered a genuinely working-class perspective and has clearly been instrumental in suggesting that the views of elite and middle-class commentators might be in need of revision. But it has not solved the problem of a long-standing omission of female voices and of the consequent risk that experiences and perspectives that are uniquely male are represented or understood to be universal and to speak to more general truths.[35]

There is, of course, no simple way of correcting this omission. Historians have not neglected female autobiographies through lack of interest or care. As we can see from the graph, the sources simply are not there for the period of industrialisation and earlier. We can, however, learn more about the experiences of women by shifting our focus forward to the Victorian and Edwardian periods. Once again, the *Bibliography* provides a roadmap. This indicates the existence of almost 700 autobiographies written by individuals born into impoverished, working-class families in Britain between 1830 and 1903, and therefore describing childhoods from the start of Queen Victoria's reign in 1837 down to the outbreak of World War I.[36] Around two-thirds were written

---

[34] Maxine Berg, 'What Difference Did *Women's Work* Make to the Industrial Revolution?', *History Workshop Journal*, 35 (1993), 22–44; Sara Horrell and Jane Humphries, 'Old Questions, New Data, and Alternative Perspectives: Families' Living Standards during the Industrial Revolution', *Journal of Economic History*, 52 (1992), 849–80; Katrina Honeyman, *Women, Gender and Industrialization in England, 1700–1870* (Basingstoke, 2000).

[35] Humphries addressed the under-representation of female-authored autobiographies by omitting analysis of them altogether. Yet the fact that the resulting account does not sustain broad arguments about wider working-class experiences is never acknowledged in her work. See Humphries, *Child Labour*.

[36] I discuss the archive more fully in Emma Griffin, *Bread Winner: An Intimate History of the Victorian Economy* (New Haven, 2020).

by men and one-third by women. These authors' memories do not extend so far back as the industrial revolution, but they do capture a host of information around the same spheres of wealth, welfare, experience and opportunity. The existence of records written by both men and women also permits us to question the overlap between the two – and, more generally, the extent to which male writers accurately represent the female experience.

Let us proceed once again through the use of example. Consider, then, Molly Murphy – a suffragette, nurse, mother, Socialist and autobiographer.[37] Molly is not only a fascinating individual in her own right, but is also one of a handful of women married to men who also wrote an autobiography. The existence of two life stories, one written by each partner of a marriage, thus enables us to address a raft of additional questions about the role of gender in shaping both autobiographical and historical narratives.

Molly Murphy was born in Leyland, Lancashire, in 1890, the eldest daughter in a family of seven children. And like most autobiographers, she started her life story with her parents – or, more accurately, with her father, Julius Morris. And in this she was far from unusual. Many elements of a writer's childhood were determined by the presence (or not) of a father, the extent of his earnings, and his willingness (or not) to share his income with his family. Little surprise, then, that fathers loom large in the sources.

Extracting the details about Julius Morris from Molly's writing produces an account of the benefits that industrial work brought to workers that chimes very neatly with those written by earlier male writers. Julius Morris was born in London but living in Lancashire and working as a cutter in a rubber factory by the time of his marriage to Molly's mother in 1886. According to both Molly's autobiography and the census which provides information corroborating her account, Julius was doing well through the 1880s, rising from rubber-cutter to factory foreman by 1891. Molly recalled living in an unusually large house at this time and remembered her early years as a period of relative affluence. Not only was Julius Morris earning well, like many Victorian men he had a range of interests and leisure pursuits outside the spheres of work and family. In Julius's case, his interest was his factory's union: he was not just a member, he was a leader and in the early 1890s led a strike for higher wages, though unfortunately the strike was not successful, and in a fit of indignation he resigned his position as a foreman, declaring that 'Never again will I be a bosses man.'[38]

Julius was born in the 1860s, yet as an adult man he described a life that has striking similarities to those of the first generation of industrial workers born a century earlier. These included the opportunity of work that paid beyond a bare subsistence and which contained an element of skill and the possibility of advancement; the chance to get involved in other political or intellectual causes; and the enjoyment of some agency with respect to who he agreed to work for and the terms under which he would work.

---

[37] Molly Murphy, *Molly Murphy: Suffragette and Socialist*, with an introduction by Ralph Darlington (Salford, 1998).

[38] *Ibid.*, 5–6.

But in Molly's eyes, it all looked rather different. As she wrote (in reference to her father giving up his management position to go back to work on the bench): 'That sounds very fine and noble, but coming from a man with a family of six to provide for, it was just silly.'[39] Julius's union activity brought an end to the family's period of affluence, and indeed was the beginning of the end for the Morrises' marriage – the family downfall and separation were both described in some detail by Molly. Within a few years, Julius was living away from the family, the family had moved from the big house and Molly's mother was trying to balance wage-earning with the responsibility for seven children. From her perspective, and from that of all seven children, there was very little advantage to the higher wages and greater autonomy that Julius Murphy had enjoyed as a skilled, industrial worker.

Molly, perhaps unsurprisingly, having witnessed the breakdown of her mother's marriage and the heavy burden of seven children at close hand, was in no hurry to tie the knot herself. As she explained, she 'wanted to be a nurse and not a housewife'. During her teens she dabbled with the suffragette movement and in her twenties fulfilled her dream of training and working as a nurse. At the age of thirty, however, knowing that if 'I was ever going to get married I should not delay much longer', she married Jack Murphy, a rising star in the British communist movement, and another autobiographer.[40] As a significant political figure in his own right, most of Jack's autobiography was preoccupied with his own endeavours.[41] But Jack had once been a child and like Molly, and most other autobiographers, he started his life story there. And it is striking that Jack too knew all about growing up in a family without a reliable breadwinning father. Jack's father, John Murphy, was an ironworker, and as such engaged in relatively skilled and well-paid, industrial labour – he earned 24 shillings a week and often had the possibility of overtime. But as Jack explained, a hefty deduction from this wage had to be made for 'his beer money', which left 'not much' for a family of four.[42] As for the overtime, Jack described its consequences as follows:

[extra hours] did not bring many blessings to our house. On the contrary, they meant an increase in the worries associated with dad's heavier drinking at the week-ends. It certainly brought a little more money into the house; but the joy of the 'extras' was somewhat short-lived. Usually they were used to clear off the debts incurred by some spell of recklessness on my father's part.[43]

It is striking that Molly and Jack, though raised in very different families in different parts of England, both shared the experience of growing up in a household without a reliable, male wage, but they are, of course, just two

---

[39] *Ibid.*, 6.
[40] Murphy, *Molly Murphy*, 64–7.
[41] J. T. Murphy, *New Horizons* (1941).
[42] *Ibid.*, 17.
[43] *Ibid.*, 18–19.

individuals amongst a much larger collection of writers. Since the publication of the *Bibliography*, however, it has been possible for us to query the autobiographical literature at scale. Over 600 men and women raised in a working-class family in the Victorian and Edwardian periods have written an autobiography. Some had lost their father through death or desertion during their childhood, yet this still leaves a large collection of almost 500 records permitting us to probe the typicality, or otherwise, of Molly and Jack's stories. And the figures make for sobering reading. The stories narrated by Molly and Jack, in which fathers were able to earn a relatively good wage but made decisions that left their family without, were far from rare. Reading across the entire collection, fewer than one-half of writers provide unambiguous evidence that their father was working steadily and sharing all his earnings with his family. For many men, high wages were a temptation and a distraction, and the value of a high wage could look very different from the perspective of children to that of the man who earned it. Even worthy causes, such as politics, unions and churches, were liable to drain money from the family budget.[44] Furthermore, the Victorian city was teeming with a wide range of less worthy causes. Autobiographers recalled fathers prioritising spending on clubs,[45] horses,[46] betting matches[47] and women[48] over their wives and children. And alcohol. More than anything else, pubs and alcohol were a drain on family budgets.[49] Jack Murphy was not uniquely unfortunate in having a father who liked to spend his earnings on drink. He is just one example of a large group of working-class autobiographers raised in a household where the man's enhanced earning capacity was spent on alcohol rather than on contributing to a meaningful uplift in the family's living standards.

It is interesting to compare how the evidence from Victorian writers sits alongside that produced by the earlier generation of working men alive during the industrial revolution. Without a doubt, that earlier literature provides far more evidence about some forms of masculine behaviour than others. The kind of worthy political agitation that occupied Julius Morris also occupied a large space in the earlier autobiographical material, whereas stories of drunken binges such as those of Jack Murphy were largely (though not wholly)

---

[44] Elizabeth Oakley, 'The Autobiography of Elizabeth Oakley, 1831–1900', *Norfolk Record Society*, 56 (1993), 113–50, at 143; John Allaway, untitled, in *Breakthrough: Autobiographical Accounts of the Education of Some Socially Disadvantaged Children*, ed. Ronald Goldman (1968), 1–18, at 5–6; Kate Taylor, unpublished autobiography, in *Destiny Obscure*, ed. John Burnett, 301–9, esp. 305.

[45] Joseph Stamper, *So Long Ago* (1960), 42, 106–7.

[46] Vere W. Garratt, *A Man in the Street* (1939), 4–6.

[47] Mary Gawthorpe, *Uphill to Holloway* (Penobscott, ME, 1962), 21–2, 26, 36; [Joseph Sharpe], *Dark at Seven: Life of a Derbyshire Miner, 1859-1936, Told by Joseph Sharpe*, ed. Nellie Connole (York, 1988), 1.

[48] Ernie Benson, *To Struggle Is to Live: A Working Class Autobiography*, I (Newcastle, 1979), 51–2; [Rosa Lewis], *Queen of Cooks - and Some Kings (the Story of Rosa Lewis)*, ed. Mary Lawton (New York, 1926), 4; Gawthorpe, *Uphill to Holloway*, 21–2, 26, 36; V. S. Pritchett, *A Cab at the Door. An Autobiography: Early Years* (1968), 67.

[49] For a few examples, see Leily Broomhill, 'In Memory of My Mum', in *Like It Was Yesterday: Childhood Memories*, ed. Daphne Chamberlain (1989), n.p.; Alice Foley, *A Bolton Childhood* (Manchester, 1973); A. S. Jasper, *A Hoxton Childhood* (1969), 40, 51; Bishopsgate Institute Library, London: Arthur Harding 'My Apprenticeship'.

absent. It is not simply that worthy causes make for a more edifying life story; there is also the material fact that heavy drinking was incompatible with long life. Indeed, Murphy's father himself died young owing to a mix of heavy drinking and heavy labour, leaving not much opportunity for an end-of-life auto-biography.[50] Unhealthy and difficult lives were far less likely to produce an autobiography, and it is important to recognise this as a structural omission from our archive of first-person narratives.

Clearly, however, skilled and sensitive reading of the kind that historians are trained in permits us to address these kinds of omissions. Male writers living through the industrial revolution may not have written much on the themes of heavy drinking and of men (and their families) failing to flourish in the new industrial era, but these themes are not altogether absent from the archive. It is rather that we tend to learn about them through the eyes of other family members. The men writing during the industrial revolution revealed how higher wages offered them a degree of agency and autonomy in their life. Later autobiographers writing about their fathers captured the same phenomenon, but they also reveal that agency and autonomy could be experienced in ways that were harmful as well as beneficial.

The evidence in the Victorian autobiographies helps us to reinterpret the social consequences of the industrial revolution and warns us against general-ising from the male perspective they provide. But writers such as Molly and Jack are not useful simply as ciphers for their fathers' generation. They also produced a rich seam of evidence for their own times. Indeed, there is a vast number of potential topics that their writing addresses, but in the space remaining here let us look at the thing that had originally brought Molly and Jack together – politics.

Since the late eighteenth century, the combination of industrial work, high wages and city life had provided a growing number of working men with the possibility of entering the political sphere. With a generation of women start-ing to write autobiographies at the end of the nineteenth century, it becomes possible to ask if working women were now starting to participate in the nation's political process too. Politics was a major preoccupation for both Molly and Jack throughout their lives and provided both of them with the motivation for writing an autobiography. Their writing thus provides a good starting point for larger questions about the gendered nature of political engagement in the early twentieth century.

The difference in opportunity for Jack and for Molly is very clear. After his challenging childhood, Jack went on to become a leader of the British com-munist movement. Shortly after starting work, he joined his local union. Within the space of a few years, Jack's union membership developed into a full-time position as a political agitator and Jack remained continuously active in the labour movement throughout his adult life. Molly, as the eldest daughter of a fatherless family of seven children, had always enjoyed far less freedom of action. After her parents' separation, Molly had spent her childhood and ado-lescence preoccupied with domestic duties and only got involved in politics –

---

[50] Murphy, *New Horizons*, 18–20.

she joined her local branch of the Women's Social and Political Union (WSPU), a militant suffragette movement – once her younger siblings grew older and her 'household duties had lessened'. But Molly's work for the WSPU was unpaid and her immersion in the suffrage movement proved to be an interlude of around eight years. When the First World War brought an end to her local committee's activities, she redirected her energies to getting her training as a nurse.[51] That, followed by her subsequent marriage to Jack and motherhood, brought a hiatus to her political activism of more than ten years. Jack's biographer describes him as 'one of the most important self-educated worker-intellectual figures of the early twentieth century British revolutionary socialist tradition', but no such claims could be made of Molly.[52] As Jack's star rose in the 1920s, Molly 'was a full-time housewife bringing up their son'.[53] It was only once their son had reached an age where Molly felt able to entrust him to other care-givers that she re-entered the political sphere, though always in a supportive, and unpaid, capacity and never in a way that rivalled that of her husband. As children of late Victorian Britain, there was much that Jack and Molly had in common; but as adults attempting to engage in the political sphere, the role of gender ensured sharply divergent experiences.

Jack and Molly Murphy were but one married couple, but the advantage of the *Bibliography* is that it allows us to consider a sample of over 600 working-class men and women and to question whether their experiences speak to wider truths about the gendered nature of political opportunities. A careful examination of the larger sample confirms that they do. Consider first the 450 autobiographies written by men. Of this group, fifty-seven had become MPs. A further forty had played a significant role in national, as opposed to local, organisations. This group of forty includes men such as Joseph Burgess, a founding member of the Labour Party;[54] Tom Mann, leader of the London Dock Strike of 1889 and secretary of the Independent Labour Party;[55] and Harry Pollitt, leader of the Communist Party of Great Britain – as well of course as Jack Murphy, another leader of the British Communist Party.[56] Most of these men held paid positions in the organisations they were involved in; and a majority have entries in the *Oxford Dictionary of National Biography*. Aggregating these forty and the fifty-seven MPs, it is seen that almost 100 male autobiographers held formal positions of political power, whether inside or outside the Houses of Parliament. Alongside these men were many more who testified to engagement on a more local level.[57]

The global picture of political engagement for our 200 women autobiographers is dissimilar in several respects. Only thirty-four of the female writers mentioned any kind of engagement with a political organisation at all, and

[51] Murphy, *Molly Murphy*, 5–63.
[52] See Ralph Darlington's editorial introduction to Murphy, *Molly Murphy*, ii. See also his biography: Ralph Darlington, *The Political Trajectory of J.T. Murphy* (Liverpool, 1998).
[53] Murphy, *Molly Murphy*, iii.
[54] Joseph Burgess, *A Potential Poet? His Autobiography and Verse* (Ilford, 1927)
[55] Tom Mann, *Tom Mann's Memoirs* (1932).
[56] Harry Pollitt, *Serving My Time: An Apprenticeship in Politics* (1940).
[57] Griffin, *Breadwinner*, 264–7.

these women described very different patterns of involvement. Just four of the female autobiographers had become MPs: Margaret Bondfield,[58] Bessie Braddock,[59] Jennie Lee[60] and Ellen Wilkinson, all of them representing the Labour Party.[61] A further twelve, whilst never serving as MPs, nonetheless made a sustained contribution to political life on the national stage. These twelve include women like Helen Crawfurd, suffragette, pacifist and prominent figure in the Communist Party; Elizabeth Andrews, suffragist, leading figure in the women's branch of the Labour Party; and Jessie Stephen, militant suffragette, union organiser for domestic workers and political agent for the Labour Party. All received national recognition for their work and are honoured with an entry in the *Oxford Dictionary of National Biography*. The remaining cohort were women like Molly, who had engaged with politics but on a smaller, more local scale, and in ways that did not earn them either an income or national recognition.[62]

It is also significant that this generation of female writers was born many decades after the industrial revolution. This generation of female autobiographers was born a full century after working-class men first started describing their forays into the political sphere, and yet the women were still largely unable to make meaningful inroads into the nation's political life. Their experiences reinforce once again that the social history of the industrial revolution is deeply gendered and suggest a new way of thinking about the limits of autobiographical evidence. For the most part, historians have fretted that autobiographers tend to have achieved success in life and that this success makes them poor witnesses of the lives and experiences of working people more broadly. Yet across the whole of the autobiographical canon, around 1,000 items in all, and spanning the period during and after the industrial revolution, there is strong evidence of a positive correlation between industrial work and male autonomy. The problem with the autobiographical archive is both simpler and more complex than historians have imagined. The major drawback with these records is that prior to around 1870, autobiographical writing was produced almost exclusively by men, and men cannot speak for women.

This central problem – that women's and men's experiences are distinct – is even manifest in the creation of the autobiographical archive. We have already observed that men began writing autobiographies many decades before women and that the generation of women born around the turn of the nineteenth century was the first to produce autobiographies in any number. Even at this point, however, significant differences between the sexes persist. Consider again the production of the autobiographies of our married couple, Molly and Jack Murphy. Jack wrote his autobiography when he was in his

---

[58] Margaret Grace Bondfield, *A Life's Work* ([1949]).

[59] Jack and Bessie Braddock, *The Braddocks* (1963).

[60] Jennie Lee, *To-morrow Is a New Day* (1939). See also Patricia Hollis, *Jennie Lee: A Life* (2014).

[61] Ellen Wilkinson, untitled, in *Myself When Young by Famous Women of Today*, ed. Margot Asquith, Countess of Oxford (1938), 399–416. See also Laura Beers, *Red Ellen: The Life of Ellen Wilkinson, Socialist, Feminist, Internationalist* (Boston, 2016).

[62] See also, Griffin, *Breadwinner*, 264–7.

early fifties. It was published by Bodley Head in 1941 and reprinted the following year. It is listed in the *Bibliography*, available in several libraries and for sale on various bookselling sites. By contrast, Molly's autobiography was written towards the end of her life – it has even been suggested that Jack ghostwrote it for her. At any rate, no publisher was found for it during her lifetime, and it is only thanks to the efforts of her son and the historian Ralph Darlington that it was ever published at all. It is not listed in Burnett *et al.*'s *Bibliography* and is not easy to find. It was a pure stroke of luck that I spotted it whilst browsing the local studies shelves of Sheffield Central Library, and I only managed to locate a copy by contacting Ralph Darlington and buying it from him personally as it was not for sale on Amazon or any other bookseller's site.[63] For a host of reasons, therefore, it is far easier to get hold of a copy of Jack's autobiography than it is Molly's.[64]

And like so many of Jack and Molly's stories, what is true for them is true for many others too. The permanency and findability of Jack's writing compared to the fragility of Molly's were not quirks unique to them. There are more general features of the entire autobiographical archive.[65] Well over half of the autobiographies written by men were published by a national press during the author's lifetime. They have been catalogued, recorded in the *Bibliography* and are relatively easy to obtain from libraries and second-hand booksellers. By contrast, fewer than 20 per cent of the women's autobiographies were published by commercial presses. Even where female autobiographies were published, they were often printed by a small, local history society, sometimes as a stapled pamphlet rather than a bound book, and although such records are more likely to survive than handwritten documents, they are still difficult to locate.[66] 'Amateur' history of this nature does not generally end up in academic libraries or bibliographies, and although some have been deposited at the British Library, they have never been catalogued or recorded as female autobiography, and can therefore be virtually impossible to find. It is little surprise then that men's stories have so long dominated our understanding of working-class life. It is not simply that men wrote more autobiography; their writing was also more likely to be published and catalogued, and it is therefore much easier for historians to find. In effect, the dominance of male voices is a structural feature of the archive just as it was a structural feature of British society throughout this period. As a result, we work with an archive that disposes us to provide universalising accounts of human experience on the basis of work written by men.

---

[63] A particularly serendipitous discovery given that Sheffield is the only public library in the UK that has the book sitting on its open shelves.

[64] Compare also with the experiences of Philip and Ethel Snowden; though both were politically active, only Philip wrote an autobiography: Philip Viscount Snowden, *An Autobiography* (2 vols., (1934).

[65] Griffin, *Breadwinner*, 8–23.

[66] For a few examples, see Ada Matthews, *Recollections of Life in Shepherds Bush* (c. 1989); Gertie Mellor, *Gertie's Story: Memories of a Moorland Octogenarian*, ed. Betty Gouldstone (Hollinsclough, 1994); Edith Pratt, *As If It Were Yesterday* (Huntingdon, 1978).

In drawing attention to the limitations of the autobiographical archive, my intention is not to dismiss its use, but rather to encourage more careful reflection on the consequences of its limitations. Certainly, inserting the writing of working-class men into debates about the social consequences of the industrial revolution has enhanced our understanding. Over a period of many years, this debate has spawned a very large literature and tended towards a pessimistic interpretation, but discussion has proceeded without the inclusion of the considerable body of autobiographical material written by working men. The insertion of that material provides a rather different account of the industrial revolution, and teaches us that working men who lived through industrialisation viewed the period as one of optimism and opportunity. This may jar with our preconceptions, but it is nonetheless a perspective that requires serious engagement.

At the same time, however, using women's life-writing provides a very different account again, and turns us back once more to more pessimistic terrain. It is not that women's writing disputes the gains that were made by men. In fact, their writing powerfully confirms that industrial employment did offer men higher wages, and that that in turn offered them greater power and autonomy in their non-working lives. It is rather that in a world in which work, wealth and resources are shared unequally by men and women, gains made by men cannot be straightforwardly presumed to have also been beneficial for women. Bringing in women's stories does not just add depth and colour to our understanding of the social impact of the industrial revolution; it fundamentally changes it. Above all, the inclusion of women's writing teaches us that whilst male voices may be dominant, the male experiences they describe are not universal. And this is a lesson for all historians. Omissions in the archive are a hazard for all; grasping the nature and consequences of those omissions is the pathway to the historical pasts we seek to understand.

Acknowledgements. An earlier version of this article was first presented as the annual lecture from the President of the Royal Historical Society, 25 November 2021.

Cite this article: Griffin E (2022). Writing about Life Writing: Women, Autobiography and the British Industrial Revolution. *Transactions of the Royal Historical Society* **32**, 5–23. https://doi.org/10.1017/S0080440122000111

Transactions of the RHS (2022), 32, 25–45
doi:10.1017/S0080440122000093

ARTICLE

The Making and Breaking of Kinetic Empire: Mobility, Communication and Political Change in the Eastern Mediterranean, c. 900–1100 CE

Catherine Holmes

Faculty of History, University of Oxford, Oxford, UK
Email: catherine.holmes@univ.ox.ac.uk

Abstract

This paper applies the concept of 'kinetic empire' to the eastern Mediterranean world in the tenth and eleventh centuries. The term 'kinetic empire' is borrowed from Hämäläinen's analysis of the eighteenth- and nineteenth-century north American Comanche Empire. It refers to the way in which trans- and supra-regional power could be created, expressed and enforced through mobile means. The article focuses primarily on the role of mobility in the expansion of the Byzantine Empire between c. 900 and 1050, but also makes comparison with the contemporaneous Fatimid caliphate and other regional polities which we might usually regard as sedentary states. Recovering the role of the kinetic not only extends our understanding of the modalities of power in this crucial region of the medieval world, it also allows us to question the nature and degree of transformation wrought by mobile newcomers, such as Normans, crusaders and Turks in the later decades of the eleventh century. In this sense of developing and exploring concepts useful for the study of the transregional in premodernity and questioning standard periodisations, this article is also a practical exercise in medieval global history.

Keywords: kinetic; empire; Byzantium; Fatimid

Global history has been one of the most influential but also the most contested forms of historical enquiry in recent decades. For enthusiasts, a global approach provides the potential to rethink geopolitical frameworks and standard periodisations; for sceptics, the gains are few, particularly if the conceptual tools associated with the global entail the erosion of specific detail and precise context.[1] As a medievalist and a Byzantinist, I have been enthused by global

---

[1] The literature promoting a more global approach to history is vast: important advocates are Kenneth Pomeranz, 'Histories for a Less National Age', *The American Historical Review*, 119 (2014), 1–22, and Richard Drayton and David Motadel, 'Discussion: The Futures of Global History', *Journal of Global History*, 13 (2018), 1–21; sceptical voices include David Bell, 'This Is What

approaches which privilege comparative study and the identification of connections across geographies, but I recognise that many pressing questions remain. Is 'medieval' too irredeemably Eurocentric for the analysis of pre-modern history on a transregional scale?[2] Were the defining characteristics of the 'global' in the medieval world similar to those detected in later contexts, or were they unique? Do concepts used to interrogate global phenomena in more recent centuries have much power when applied to earlier periods?[3] Debates about terminology and scope are, of course, important. But nuanced answers to such large-scale framing questions require the exploration of concrete case studies as well as abstract conceptualisations. And the potential of global history will only become evident if the deployment of concepts across space and time results in new ways of thinking about familiar topics; and if periodisations and standard geopolitical units of investigation are indeed challenged and reinvented.[4]

In this paper, I attempt to provide one such practical exercise with broader implications, focusing on a concept which current research suggests has traction for global history of all periods, including the centuries between *c.* 500 and 1500 CE. That concept is mobility.[5] My aim is to explore the implications of understandings of mobility in one relatively modern historical and geographical context – eighteenth- and nineteenth-century north America – for the study of another world region in a much more remote period, the eastern Mediterranean in the tenth and eleventh centuries. In making my case, I seek to break down the concept of mobility, conscious of the critique that global paradigms can be so capacious that they lose explanatory power. That we need to be alert to the different shades and forms inherent in the broad category of mobility is, for example, a point emphasised by Christopher Atwood in his analysis of the thirteenth-century Mongol Empire. As Atwood notes, the mobility of Mongol *qans*, measured in terms of their seasonal itineracy, the size of their camps and the routes they followed, was rather different to the quotidian movements of the steppe nomad pastoralist communities.[6] Following Atwood's lead, my paper does not try to elide all forms of mobility, but instead

---

Happens When Historians Overuse the Idea of the Network', *New Republic* (October 2013); Stuart Alexander Rockefeller, '"Flow"', *Current Anthropology*, 52 (2011), 557–78.

[2] For scepticism about the appropriateness of 'medieval' for regions outside western Europe, see Daniel Martin Varisco, 'Making "Medieval" Islam Meaningful', *Medieval Encounters: Jewish, Christian, and Muslim Culture in Confluence and Dialogue*, 13 (2007), 385–412; and Anthony Kaldellis, *Byzantium Unbound* (Leeds, 2019), 76–92. For the problems as well as the potential associated with global approaches to the medieval, see Kathleen Davis and Michael Puett, 'Periodization and "The Medieval Globe": A Conversation', *The Medieval Globe*, 2 (2016), 1–14; Catherine Holmes and Naomi Standen, 'Introduction: Towards a Global Middle Ages', in *The Global Middle Ages*, ed. Catherine Holmes and Naomi Standen, *Past & Present* supplement 13 (Oxford, 2018), 15–20; Geraldine Heng, *The Global Middle Ages: An Introduction* (Cambridge, 2021).

[3] Holmes and Standen, 'Introduction: Towards a Global Middle Ages', 1–3.

[4] Heng, *Global Middle Ages*, 11–53.

[5] Naomi Standen and Monica White, 'Structural Mobilities in the Global Middle Ages', in *Global Middle Ages*, ed. Holmes and Standen, 158–89.

[6] C. Atwood, 'Imperial Itinerance and Mobile Pastoralism: The State and Mobility in Medieval Inner Asia', *Inner Asia*, 17 (2015), 293–349.

focuses on just one facet: the way in which trans- and supra-regional power could be created, expressed and enforced through mobile means – a facet of mobility I refer to as 'kinetic empire'.

In discussing 'kinetic empire' I am exploring ideas developed by Pekka Hämäläinen in his examination of the indigenous Comanche Empire in the south-west of North America in the eighteenth and nineteenth centuries. For Hämäläinen, the Comanche polity was a kinetic empire in the sense that it was a nomad power regime which revolved around 'a set of mobile activities: long-distance raiding, seasonal expansions, trans-national diplomatic missions, semi-permanent trade fairs, recurring political assemblies and control over shifting economic nodes'.[7] At this point, I should make it clear that I am not arguing that all the principles and structures that Hämäläinen identifies were visible in the high medieval eastern Mediterranean; to suggest that would be unhelpfully reductive. Instead, in elaborating what *was* kinetic about this medieval example, I develop two broad points which take inspiration from Hämäläinen's work on the Comanches. First, that thinking about kinetic power allows us to expand the ways in which empire as a diachronic historical category is conceptualised; and second, that thinking about empire in an 'expanded and more elastic form' can, perhaps paradoxically, allow us to gain more analytical precision.[8] In this second sense, I argue that distilling out evidence for kinetic empire in this particular medieval context can shed new light on a crucial watershed period in medieval Eurasian history.

It is something of a commonplace among medieval historians that in the half-century between *c.* 1050 and *c.* 1100 the geopolitics of the eastern Mediterranean region were completely transformed, as two sedentary empires suddenly came under immense political and military pressure from a variety of highly mobile newcomers.[9] The sedentary empires in question were Byzantium in the north, with its capital at Constantinople, and the Fatimid (Shia) caliphate in the south, with its capital at Cairo. Among the mobile and predatory newcomers were Latins, especially Normans, from the north and west who were joined later by crusaders, and Turks from the east, although we should always be aware that the ethnic descriptors I use here are very general labels of convenience under which nestled an enormous variety of different groups. In the short term neither Byzantium nor the Fatimid caliphate was immediately destroyed by these newcomers. Indeed, it proved to be the case that the recent arrivals were able to convey some temporary benefits to existing regimes, as when the passage of the armies of the first crusade in the late

---

[7] P. Hämäläinen, 'What's in a Concept? The Kinetic Empire of the Comanches', *History and Theory*, 52 (2013), 81–90, at 85; see also *idem*, *The Comanche Empire* (New Haven, 2008).

[8] Hämäläinen, 'What's in a Concept?', 83.

[9] M. Brett, *The Rise of the Fatimids: The World of the Mediterranean and the Middle East in the Fourth Century of the Hijra, Tenth Century CE* (Leiden, 2001), 15–16, makes a similar point with reference to the entire Mediterranean, but with a primary focus on the Fatimids; for the twin threat of Turks and Normans to Byzantium in the later eleventh century, see also Anthony Kaldellis, *Streams of Gold, Rivers of Blood: The Rise and Fall of Byzantium, 955 A.D. to the First Crusade* (New York, 2017), especially at 228.

1090s enabled Byzantine forces to regain some ground in coastal Anatolia lost to the Turks during the previous decades.[10] Nonetheless, it is clear that the military and political weather of the eastern Mediterranean was irrevocably changed in the longer term by the presence of these mobile newcomers. During the twelfth and early thirteenth centuries, these two empires with their carefully curated ceremonial centres were taken over and radically refashioned by rulers whose political culture derived much from the religio-social structures and political symbolisms of the warlord migrants of the eleventh century. Between 1169 and 1171 the Fatimid caliphate was dismantled by Saladin, a Kurdish commander whose career was shaped by the military power structures associated with the Turkish warlord regimes of twelfth-century Syria and Mesopotamia; in 1204 the sack of Constantinople by the armies of the fourth crusade shattered Byzantium irrevocably.[11]

Such a chronology obviously includes much oversimplification, and one could argue that the extent of the transformation wrought by the Latins and Turks requires nuance. It is clear, for instance, that incoming peoples and the regimes they established actively borrowed from the political cultures of those they either replaced or rivalled. The Latin emperors of Constantinople chose to adopt the dress and insignia of the former Byzantine emperors; Saladin and his family invested heavily in the built environment of the Fatimid city of Cairo.[12] But in this paper, my focus is not on the ways in which the political culture of incomers with kinetic power came to be legitimised in more local contexts. Instead, my concern is with the period *before* incursions from Turks and Latins became so destabilising for this region. Above all, I consider the ways in which the kinetic was *already* an integral ingredient in the exercise and creation of power in the eastern Mediterranean in the century *before* 1050, a period when both Byzantium and the Fatimid empires were not weakening and contracting but were instead apparently stable and even expanding. I suggest that this kinetic dimension to regional power stemmed partly from the fact that some of the newcomer peoples and practices so visible after 1050 were already present in the eastern Mediterranean region. From the tenth century onwards this region was becoming increasingly locked into a series of wider geographies through which kinetic people and their goods were liable to travel, forming the kinds of 'circuits' that Jonathan Shepard has suggested saw many from northern and western Europe move south-eastwards to take up military service and engage in

---

[10] Peter Frankopan, *The First Crusade: The Call from the East* (2012).

[11] Anne-Marie Eddé, *Saladin* (Paris, 2008) [Eng. tr. published in 2012]; Michael Angold, *The Fourth Crusade: Event and Context* (Harlow, 2003).

[12] On the Latin emperors: Teresa Shawcross, 'Conquest Legitimised', in *Byzantines, Latins, and Turks in the Eastern Mediterranean World after 1150*, ed. Jonathan Harris, Catherine Holmes and Eugenia Russell (Oxford, 2012), 181–220; on Ayyubid and Mamluk patronage of Cairo, Carole Hillenbrand, *The Crusades: Islamic Perspectives* (Edinburgh, 1999); Laila 'Ali Ibrahim, *Mamluk Monuments of Cairo* (Cairo, 1976). For the relationship between the Fatimid caliphate and Ayyubids (and later the Mamluks) concerning the use of architecture and ceremonial to express power and legitimacy, see R. Stephen Humphreys, 'The Expressive Intent of the Mamluk Architecture of Cairo: A Preliminary Essay', *Studia Islamica*, 35 (1972), 69–119.

trade.[13] But the argument I advance here is not simply that there were more kinetic newcomers in the eastern Mediterranean region in the century and a half up to 1050, but that the creation, sustenance and communication of power by the so-called sedentary empires into which these newcomers moved was *already* strongly kinetic.

The crucial point, then, is that it was the so-called sedentary empires themselves which demonstrated kinetic attributes from as early as the tenth century rather than simply the more obviously kinetic new arrivals. If viable, this insight has two notable implications: first, for the way in which we think about military and political frontiers in this region; and second, for how we interpret the incursions into the eastern Mediterranean by mobile newcomers in the later eleventh century and the regional political reordering which those invasions are said to have precipitated.

In unravelling the kinetic, my principal focus is on Byzantium, a polity and territorial empire of considerable antiquity. Members of the political and intellectual elite who produced the written records so crucial to understanding the history of this empire regarded themselves as Romans.[14] In the Constantinopolitan focus of so many of their writings, the Byzantines can appear to be the ultimate, stay-at-home sedentary imperialists, with many famously reluctant to countenance the indignity of exile on government service in the provinces or at the frontiers.[15] Such a political culture may seem a very unlikely candidate for scrutiny at a kinetic level. However, some recent research has begun to connect issues of mobility to the governance of the Byzantine Empire. Monica White has commented on the ways in which predictable patterns of movement were built into the structures and operation of the thematic (provincial) armies of Byzantium in the later seventh to mid-tenth centuries, particularly the routine practice of mustering and reviewing provincial troops at fixed gathering points, a practice which inevitably required individual soldiers, *stratiotai*, to travel.[16] The realities of the movement of people, products and information have also been integral to other

---

[13] J. Shepard, 'Storm Clouds and a Thunderclap: East–West Tensions towards the Mid-Eleventh Century', in *Byzantium in the Eleventh Century: Being in Between*, ed. Marc D. Lauxtermann and Mark Whittow (Abingdon, 2017), 127–53.

[14] Helpful introductions to Byzantine politics and governing structures of the tenth and eleventh centuries are Mark Whittow, *The Making of Orthodox Byzantium, 600-1025* (Basingstoke, 1996), especially chs. 9–10; Michael Angold, *The Byzantine Empire: A Political History*, 2nd edn (New York, 1997), 1–170. How the Roman identity of the Byzantines should be interpreted in this period is a matter of debate: see Ioannis Stouraitis, 'Roman Identity in Byzantium: A Critical Approach', *Byzantinische Zeitschrift*, 107 (2014), 175–220, who interprets 'Roman' in terms of a political identity for a multi-ethnic elite; and Anthony Kaldellis, *Romanland: Ethnicity and Empire in Byzantium* (Cambridge, MA, 2019), for whom 'Roman' is more of a widely shared, almost national, identity.

[15] Margaret Mullett, 'Originality in the Byzantine Letter: The Case of Exile', in *Originality in Byzantine Literature, Art and Music*, ed. A. R. Littlewood (Oxford, 1995), 39–58, although as Mullett points out, many writers invoking the topos of exile could also promote the interests of the localities to which they were sent; see also *eadem*, *Theophylact of Ochrid: Reading the Letters of a Byzantine Archbishop* (Aldershot, 1997), 247–77; Dimitri Obolensky, *Six Byzantine Portraits* (Oxford, 1988), 34–82.

[16] Naomi Standen and Monica White, 'Structural Mobilities in the Global Middle Ages', in *Global Middle Ages*, ed. Holmes and Standen, 176–80.

analyses of sociopolitical and cultural relations in Byzantium. For instance Anthony Kaldellis describes the waves of provincials in the tenth and eleventh centuries who regularly went to seek their political fortunes in Constantinople, still susceptible to the magnetic attraction that service to the emperor in the capital had exercised over provincial elites since late antiquity.[17] Implicit in work done on Byzantine letter writing and the lead seals which authenticated letters is a sense that long-distance communication of information was integral to the sociability and political culture of the governing elite.[18]

In these senses then, there are many ways in which mobility can be studied in relationship to the operation of power in Byzantium. However, what I want to stress here are *other* aspects of the kinetic, those which did not rely on routine forms of movement and communication rooted in much earlier medieval traditions of governance. Above all, I am interested in how the kinetic was expressed and utilised in the dynamic expansion of Byzantium between the mid-tenth and mid-eleventh centuries, a period often regarded as the highwater mark of the medieval empire, when the territorial frontiers were restored in regions of the Balkans, Syria and Mesopotamia which the Byzantines had vacated several centuries earlier.[19]

In making this primarily Byzantium-based case I draw some parallels with the Fatimids of Egypt, a neighbouring power with imperial credentials, which was encountered with ever increasing frequency by the Byzantines across the tenth and eleventh centuries. In comparison to Byzantium, the Fatimids can seem like relative newcomers. Their geopolitical prominence in the Mediterranean only began in the early tenth century and from an original power base located somewhat further west, in modern-day Tunisia. When the Fatimids arrived in Egypt in 969, they did so as self-proclaimed caliphs, their Shia regime differentiating itself clearly from the Sunni Abbasid caliphs of Baghdad.[20] However, they serve as a very useful point of comparison to Byzantium, in part because their control of Egypt made them simply the latest in a series of independent-minded regional regimes which governed the eastern Mediterranean in a type of modus vivendi with Byzantium: earlier examples included the ninth-century Tulunids, and the tenth-century Ikshidids,

---

[17] Kaldellis, *Streams of Gold, Rivers of Blood*, 5; on the attractions of Constantinople to provincials in late antiquity see Peter Heather, 'New Men for New Constantines? Creating an Imperial Elite in the Eastern Mediterranean', in *New Constantines*, ed. Paul Magdalino (Aldershot, 1994), 11–44.

[18] Margaret Mullett, 'Writing in Early Medieval Byzantium', in *The Uses of Literacy in Early Medieval Europe*, ed. Rosamond McKitterick (Cambridge, 1990), 156–85; Jean-Claude Cheynet and Cecile Morrisson, 'Lieux de trouvaille et circulation des sceaux', in *Studies in Byzantine Sigillography*, ed. Nikolaos Oikonomides (Washington, DC, 1990); Peter Frankopan, 'The Workings of the Byzantine Provincial Administration in the 10th–12th Centuries: The Example of Preslav', *Byzantion*, 71 (2001), 73–97; Jonas Nilsson, 'Aristocracy, Politics and Power in Byzantium, 1025–1081' (D. Phil. thesis, Oxford University, 2017).

[19] Jonathan Shepard, 'Equilibrium to Expansion (886–1025)', in *The Cambridge History of the Byzantine Empire, c. 500–1492*, ed. Jonathan Shepard (Cambridge, 2008), 493–536.

[20] Brett, *Rise of the Fatimids*, 269–316; *idem, The Fatimid Empire* (Edinburgh, 2017); Paul E. Walker, *Exploring an Islamic Empire: Fatimid History and Its Sources* (2002).

whom the Fatimids replaced.[21] In common with (perhaps even drawing some inspiration from) Byzantium, the Fatimids invested much time and resource into developing and sustaining a very elaborate ceremonial focused on a purpose-built capital city.[22] But they also represent an interesting point of comparison in that, as we shall see, their rise to prominence in North Africa and their eventual seizure of power in Egypt relied extensively on the mobilisation of various forms of the kinetic.

One further framing point: I should also make it clear from the outset that in invoking the kinetic I am not trying to suggest that the expansion and consolidation of imperial power in either the Byzantine or Fatimid cases owed nothing to traditional sedentary modes of governance: the collection of taxes by an imperial bureaucracy from an agrarian peasantry; the use of taxation to pay professional armed forces, including navies; the use of written records to govern the distribution and allocation of resources. All of these aspects of power mattered. But what I do want to suggest is that these modes existed in a complex relationship with the kinetic, and that the presence and importance of that kinetic is something which has all too often been overlooked.

In the case of Byzantium the reason why a kinetic dimension to empire has been overlooked is not hard to detect. This is because the imperial expansion of the tenth and early eleventh centuries has usually been analysed in terms of the acquisition, control and exploitation of territory. Central to this scholarly preoccupation have been contemporary administrative sources produced in Constantinople such as banqueting lists and military handbooks that focus on official hierarchies, and the lead seals struck by civil and military officials appointed by the emperor. Both types of evidence have been scrutinised to describe the apparent creation and management of new territorial divisions, particularly those associated with the frontiers.[23] Historians of the evolution of the Byzantine frontier differ in their sense of how intensively that administrative imprimatur was applied in practice, with some arguing for an intense roll-out of a centralised administration and others suggesting that there was more devolution to local agents.[24] But what both approaches have in common

---

[21] For precursor regimes in Egypt, see Thierry Bianquis, 'Autonomous Egypt from Ibn Tūlūn to Kāfūr, 868–969', in *The Cambridge History of Egypt*, I, ed. Carl Petry (Cambridge, 1998), 86–119.

[22] Paula Sanders, *Ritual Politics and the City in Fatimid Cairo* (Albany, 1994); Irene A. Bierman, *Writing Signs: The Fatimid Public Text* (Berkeley and Los Angeles, 1998); Jenny Rahel Oesterle, *Kalifat und Königtum: Herrschaftsrepräsentation der Fatimiden, Ottonen und frühen Salier an religiösen Hochfesten* (Darmstadt, 2009).

[23] J. B. Bury, *The Imperial Administrative System in the Ninth Century: With a Revised Text of the Kletorologion of Philotheos* (1911), was a foundational study; for change in the tenth and eleventh centuries, see Nikolaos Oikonomides, *Les Listes de préséance byzantines des IXe et Xe siècles* (Paris, 1972); idem, 'L'Évolution de l'organisation administrative de l'empire byzantin au XIe siècle', *Travaux et Mémoires*, 6 (1976), 125–52; also relevant Whittow, *Making of Orthodox Byzantium*, 96–133, 193; J.-C. Cheynet (ed.), *Le Monde Byzantin II. L'Empire byzantin (641–1204)* (Paris, 2006), 125–74.

[24] A more maximalist approach is taken by Oikonomides, 'L'Évolution de l'organisation administrative de l'empire byzantin', and James D. Howard-Johnston, 'Crown Lands and the Defence of Imperial Authority in the Tenth and Eleventh Centuries', *Byzantinische Forschungen*, 21 (1995), 76–99; for the involvement of local agents, see Vera von Falkenhausen, *Untersuchungen über die*

is the degree to which they interpret the exercise of power in terms of the sedentary state; that is to say in terms of the organisational logic of Constantinopolitan bureaucrats, or at least in terms of what modern historians assume the logic of Constantinopolitan bureaucrats to have been. But adopting this approach means ignoring a number of aspects of the extension and application of Byzantine governance which can certainly be equated with empire building, but which were not necessarily about permanent control of territory and the direct imposition of the administrative machinery of the sedentary state. Many of these aspects were kinetic, and tend to be more visible in narrative sources rather than administrative ones, especially texts written by those on the receiving end of Byzantium's kinetic power.

One of the most striking aspects of the Byzantine kinetic in this period was the empire's propensity for engaging in long-distance campaigns which had little to do with establishing permanent military bases or new settlements, but which were instead about making hitherto distant and even invisible imperial power suddenly very present. This effect was achieved either by imperial armies resorting to unexpected and extreme violence, in the form of punitive raiding; or by conducting something akin to an imperial triumph, which enabled emperors or their commanders to engage in ceremonies of subjugation. Lightning strikes from distance include land raids against the emirates of Dvin in Armenia in 922 and 928 and Edessa in 944. Against Dvin in 928, the Byzantines took with them the shock technology of Greek fire which could be blasted out of handheld devices.[25] Meanwhile, even those military emperors of the third quarter of the tenth century who took some interest in permanent territorial occupation and the creation of pliant frontier client states, such as Nikephoros Phokas and John Tzimiskes, still used raiding as a means to that objective. The incursions which preceded the fall of Antioch in 969 are a prime example.[26] Even in these years of permanent conquest, long-distance raids beyond the frontiers which had little territorial ambition also occurred, as with the attack on Damascus in 975 by John Tzimiskes which resulted in a one-off tribute payment.[27] Nor does the advancing of direct

---

byzantinische Herrschaft in Süditalien vom 9. bis ins 11. Jahrhundert (1967), 84–7; P. Stephenson, Byzantium's Balkan Frontier (Cambridge, 2000); Catherine Holmes, Basil II and the Governance of Empire, 976–1025 (Oxford, 2005), 299–447.

[25] For Dvin in 922, see Stephen of Taron, The Universal History of Step'anos Tarōnec'i. Introduction, Translation and Commentary, tr. Tim Greenwood (Oxford, 2017), 221–2; for Dvin in 928, see Ibn al-Athīr, in A. A. Vasiliev, Byzance et les arabes II: La Dynastie Macédonienne (867–959), Deuxième partie: Extraits des source arabes, tr. (French) Marius Canard (Brussels, 1950), 150; for Edessa, see Ibn al-Athīr, in Byzance et les arabes II, 156–7; Yahya ibn Sa'id al-Antaki, 'Histoire', ed. and tr. (French) I. Kratchkovsky and A. Vasiliev, Patrologia Orientalis, 18 (1924), 730–2.

[26] John Skylitzes: Ioannis Skylitzae Synopsis Historiarum, ed. Hans Thurn (CFHB v, Berlin and New York, 1973), 267–73; tr. John Wortley, John Skylitzes, A Synopsis of Byzantine History 811–1057 (Cambridge, 2010), 256–62; Leo the Deacon: Leonis Diaconi Caloënsis Historiae Libri Decem, ed. C. B. Hase (Bonn, 1828), 70–83; tr. Alice-Mary Talbot and Denis F. Sullivan, The History of Leo the Deacon (Washington, DC, 2005), 119–34.

[27] Yahya ibn Sa'id, 'Histoire', Patrologia Orientalis, 23 (1932), 368–9; Marius Canard, 'Les Sources arabes de l'histoire byzantine aux confins des Xᵉ et XIᵉ siècles', Revue des Études Byzantines, 19 (1961), 293–5.

territorial control seem to have been the principal concern of Basil II, Tzimiskes's successor as emperor. In the first of his eastern campaigns, in 995, Basil crossed Anatolia in little over two weeks appearing unexpectedly in northern Syria at the start of spring, with the ambition of scaring off a Fatimid army which was threatening Antioch, while disciplining the commander at Antioch who had suffered an unexpected defeat the previous year.[28] A second imperial raid, in 999, again provoked by Fatimid attack, entailed the emperor raiding the Syrian coast as far as Tripoli and Beirut, before withdrawing for the winter to the plains of Cilicia (around Tarsos), and then unexpectedly changing direction to put in an appearance in the Armenian borderlands at Tao, where a local ruler had recently died leaving Basil as his heir. But what is striking about the events of 999–1000 is how little territory was permanently occupied, with most of Basil's energies going first into raiding, and then, into a long tour of the frontier region, when client rulers, Muslims as well as Christians, received titles and salaries.[29] Even in a longer eastern campaign of 1021–3, when one purpose was to secure the Tao legacy, many aspects of Basil's campaign resembled a raid rather than a planned territorial conquest. We are told that contemporaries were taken by surprise when Basil chose to march towards Tao rather than down into Syria. And once a handful of fortresses had been reoccupied, Basil did not tarry but instead kept marching as far east as Lake Urmia in western Iran, a campaign which was perhaps intended to rival the expeditions of the seventh-century emperor Herakleios.[30]

One could perhaps argue that Basil's raiding in the east was too infrequent to justify the term 'kinetic empire'; and one could argue that it was in fact Bulgaria which interested Basil the most, and where he worked in a more piecemeal but consistent way to advance his empire, until in 1018 the Byzantines were able to absorb the Bulgarian state; and then, over a number of decades, the indigenous Bulgarian governing system was gradually replaced with Byzantine officials and structures. In fact, the state of the evidence does not really allow us to say all that much about how warfare was conducted across Bulgaria in Basil's reign. Where such evidence does exist (in the rather muddled text of the later eleventh-century historian John Skyliztes), it appears

---

[28] Yahya, 'Histoire', *PO*, 23 (1932), 442–4; Alexander D. Beihammer, 'Muslim Rulers Visiting the Imperial City: Building Alliances and Personal Networks between Constantinople and the Eastern Borderlands (Fourth/Tenth–Fifth/Eleventh Century)', *Al-Masaq*, 24 (2012), 164.

[29] Yahya, 'Histoire', *PO*, 23 (1932), 457–61; Stephen of Taron, *The Universal History*, 306–11; Aristakes of Lastivert, *Récit des malheurs de la nation arménienne*, tr. M. Canard and H. Berbérian according to the edn and tr. (Russian) by K. Yuzbashian (Brussels, 1973), 2–6; Holmes, *Basil II*, 475–81.

[30] For this campaign see Robert Thomson (tr.), *Rewriting Caucasian History: The Georgian Chronicles* (Oxford, 1996), 281–4, 374; Aristakes of Lastivert, *Récit des malheurs*, 11–21; Yahya ibn Sa'id, 'Histoire', *Patrologia Orientalis*, 47 (1997), 459–63, 467–9; Skylitzes, *Synopsis*, 366–7; tr. Wortley, *John Skylitzes*, 346–7; Holmes, *Basil II*, 482. For Herakleios's campaigns in this region see James Howard-Johnston, *The Last Great War of Antiquity* (Oxford, 2021), chs. 7 and 9. Indeed it is possible that Basil's own reputation as a raider in the east may have inspired his own successors to seek to emulate him, as with Romanos III's ultimately unsuccessful campaign against Aleppo in 1030 (Yahya, 'Histoire', *PO*, 47 (1997), 493–501).

that small-scale campaigns to seize particular fortified targets may have been the bread and butter of Balkan fighting: hardly kinetic empire or even kinetic warfare.[31] Yet even here, the kinetic, in the shape of long-distance raids, does still seem to have played a role. For instance in 1002 Basil is said to have marched well beyond Byzantine-held territory, up to the middle Danube at Vidin, and then to have raided deep within the territory of his Bulgarian rival Samuel, around Skopje in Macedonia.[32] Somewhat later after the rather sudden and mysterious Bulgarian capitulation to Byzantium in 1018, the surrenders of royal princes and local commanders were taken publicly by the emperor in something like a grand tour of the Balkans. This imperial peregrination included the surrender of much gold from Samuel's stores at Ochrid, and culminated in an imperial entry back in Byzantine-governed territory in Athens.[33]

Indeed, other aspects of Byzantium's long-term military engagement with the Balkans evoke the kinetic. It is possible that Basil II's striking of a trade deal in 992 with the still rather obscure power of Venice was partly about gaining a naval ally who might present the Bulgarian rulers with problems in the Adriatic.[34] Other neighbours with access to ship power were regarded as useful allies by the Byzantines at the same time, above all the Rus from settlements such as Kyiv on the Dnieper. Their military involvement with Byzantium is particularly well recorded for Basil II's reign, since it was a detachment of Rus troops who helped to defend the emperor against the serious rebellion led by two of his most senior generals: Bardas Phokas and Bardas Skleros. In return for these troops, the ruler of Kyiv, Volodymyr, received Basil's sister Anna as a bride, and took on Orthodox Christianity. This deal, however, was built on an evolving tradition across the tenth century by which troops from Rus campaigned with Byzantine armies, or on behalf of Byzantium, as far west as Italy, and as far east as Georgia and Syria as well as against Bulgaria.[35] Their naval expertise was integral to a very big campaign against Crete in 949, which was one example of a campaign where territorial reconquest does seem to have been expected, even if the campaign ended in failure.[36] But, Crete may be an exception which proves a rule: for there were many other engagements when Byzantine kinetic power at sea was involved where the principal objective appears to have been a display of the raw

---

[31] Stephenson, *Byzantium's Balkan Frontier*, 59–79; idem, *The Legend of Basil the Bulgarslayer* (Cambridge, 2003), 1–48; Holmes, *Basil II*, 394–428.

[32] Skylitzes, *Synopsis*, 346; tr. Wortley, *John Skylitzes*, 328; Holmes, *Basil II*, 414–18; Stephenson, *Byzantium's Balkan Frontier*, 65.

[33] Skylitzes, *Synopsis*, 357–64; tr. Wortley, *John Skylitzes*, 338–44; Holmes, *Basil II*, 421, 501.

[34] A. Pertusi, 'Venezia e Bisanzio nel secolo XI', repr. in *Storia della civiltà veneziana*, ed. V. Branca (3 vols., Florence, 1979), I, 195–8; Donald Nicol, *Byzantium and Venice: A Study in Diplomatic and Military Relations* (Cambridge, 1988), 39–40.

[35] Holmes, *Basil II*, 510–15; Simon Franklin and Jonathan Shepard, *The Emergence of Rus, 750–1200* (New York, 1996), 160–8.

[36] Constantine VII Porphyrogenitus, *The Book of Ceremonies: With the Greek Edition of the Corpus Scriptorum Historiae Byzantinae (Bonn, 1829)*, tr. Ann Moffatt and Maxeme Tall (Canberra, 2012), 664–7.

power and resources of the empire rather than territorial occupation. Into this bracket might fall the naval support the Byzantines provided to multi-party alliances of Mediterranean Christians which attacked Muslim enclaves on the Garigliano river near Rome in 915, and at Fraxinetum, near Marseille, in 941–2.[37] Perhaps most intriguing of all is the expedition of 935 which was sent to southern Italy to bring the rebellious Lombard princes of Benevento and Salerno to heel, in which imperial officials employed portable wealth, above all silks, to persuade local allies to fight on their behalf. This campaign force included a small detachment of elite troops from as far away as Rus and central Asia to impress locals in Italy with the Byzantines' access to specialist fighting manpower.[38]

Another aspect of Byzantine military endeavour integral to kinetic empire is revealed when the objectives, or at least the acquisitions, of many campaigns are registered: in short when we realise how important were movable goods and people to the Byzantines, as well as the places (in Pekka Hämäläinen's terms, the 'nodes') where goods and people could be exchanged. Thus, the main result of the raid against Edessa in 944 was not control of territory but instead a relic-cum-ikon (the face-of-Christ handkerchief known as the *Mandylion*).[39] This was just one of many different relics which were taken back to Constantinople during the later tenth century.[40] One purpose to this sacred capital transfer may have been to increase the spiritual arsenal which protected the emperor, palace and capital. But interestingly such sacred capital could itself play a kinetic role: we know for instance that ikons were taken into battle against both domestic and external enemies by Basil II, including on long-distance raids.[41] We also know that holy water, extracted by contact with relics in the capital, was transported from Constantinople in order to bless the troops before their campaigns.[42] Meanwhile, relics exported from Constantinople were a tried and tested means by which to attract the loyalty and service of peoples and rulers on the empire's periphery and well

---

[37] Luigi Andrea Berto, *Christians and Muslims in Early Medieval Italy: Perceptions, Encounters and Clashes* (Milton, 2019), 5 (for Garigliano); Paolo Squatriti, *The Complete Works of Liudprand of Cremona* (Washington, DC, 2007), 181 (for Fraxinetum).

[38] Constantine VII Porphyrogenitus, *Book of Ceremonies*, 660–2.

[39] Whittow, *Making of Orthodox Byzantium*, 321; Averil Cameron, 'The History of the Image of Edessa: The Telling of a Story', *Harvard Ukrainian Studies*, 7 (1983), 80–94; Meredith Riedel, 'Demonic Prophecy as Byzantine Imperial Propaganda: The Rhetorical Appeal of the Tenth-Century Narratio de Imagine Edessena', *Fides et Historia*, 49 (2017), 11–23.

[40] Whittow, *Making of Orthodox Byzantium*, 352.

[41] Basil II carried an ikon of the Virgin into battle against the rebel general Bardas Phokas in 989 (Michael Psellos, *Chronographie*, ed. Emile Renauld (2 vols., Paris, 1967), i, 10; E. R. A. Sewter (tr.), *Fourteen Byzantine Rulers: The Chronographia of Michael Psellus* (1953), 36); in the final campaign of his reign against the Georgians, he carried the *Mandylion* (Thomson (tr.), *Rewriting Caucasian History*, 284). Later eleventh-century emperors carried ikons of the Virgin into battle: see Bissera V. Pentcheva, *Icons and Power: The Mother of God in Byzantium* (University Park, PA, 2006), 75–103.

[42] Eric McGeer, 'Two Military Orations of Constantine VII', in *Byzantine Authors: Literary Activities and Preoccupations: Text and Translations Dedicated to the Memory of Nicolas Oikonomides*, ed. John W. Nesbitt (Leiden, 2003), 132–3; for Greek text see R. Vari, 'Zum historischen Exzerptenwerke des Konstantinos Porphyrogennetos', *Byzantinische Zeitschrift*, 17 (1908), 78–84.

beyond. And, of course, it was not necessarily just the sacred goods themselves which could move, but also the people able to create and interpret the sacred: thus, the tenth and eleventh centuries were striking for the circulation of Byzantine craftsmen, especially mosaicists to decorate new churches in locations such as Venice and Kyiv, as well as mosques in the case of the Umayyads of al Andalus.[43]

While the mobilisation and transfer of the sacred was integral to the conduct of military campaigns and the sealing of political alliances, more mundane circulation was also integral to Byzantium's kinetic empire. Narratives of the Byzantines' eastern campaigns stress with great frequency the imperial armies' acquisitions of booty, prisoners of war and slaves. When the mid-tenth-century emperor Constantine VII Porphyrogenitus was exhorting his troops, for instance, he invoked the example of a provincial naval commander who raided deep within the frontier emirate of Tarsos (in modern southern Turkey). The emperor reminded his audience not of territory gained but of the 'huge number of Tarsiots taken prisoner'.[44] By the reign of John Tzimiskes (969–76) so many prisoners were being taken in raids that legislation was introduced to regulate their sale and the taxes owed to the state by the purchasers of the enslaved.[45] And half a century later, during Basil II's last great eastern campaign, the imperial armies wintered at Trebizond on the Black Sea, a noted entrepôt, where many prisoners of war were sold as slaves; these prisoners were almost certainly Georgians, fellow Christians.[46]

The capture, sale and ransoming of captives, many of whom must have been women, is evidence for the very tangible impact that kinetic empire could have on contemporaries who suddenly found themselves in the path of the highly mobile Byzantine forces, whether large field armies or small raiding parties. But integral to kinetic empire in the Byzantine case was also an element of the intangible, an elusive quality which was nonetheless rooted in real-world events and must have had very real-world consequences. What I have in mind here is the degree to which Byzantium's practice of kinetic empire relied on the creation and transmission of stories about the empire and its powers. When historians focus on Byzantium as a place of stories for wider consumption, it is generally on tales generated about the luxuries and improbabilities of the imperial court in Constantinople; or about the sacred complexes of the imperial city, above all the church of Hagia Sophia, which famously left Rus

---

[43] Helen C. Evans and William D. Wixom (eds.), *The Glory of Byzantium: Art and Culture of the Middle Byzantine Era, A.D. 843–1261* (New York, 1997), 282–3, 408, 434, 438.

[44] The naval commander in question was Basil Hexamilites (McGeer, 'Two Orations', 130–1).

[45] Eric McGeer, *Sowing the Dragon's Teeth: Byzantine Warfare in the Tenth Century* (Washington, DC, 1995), 365–8.

[46] Aristakes of Lastivert, *Récit*, 16; one of the main objectives of embassies moving between Byzantium and the Islamic world, including between Byzantium and the Fatimids, was the redeeming of prisoners, some of whom remained in captivity for many years: Hugh Kennedy, 'Byzantine–Arab Diplomacy in the Near East from the Islamic Conquests to the Mid-Eleventh Century', in *Byzantine Diplomacy*, ed. Simon Franklin and Jonathan Shepard (Cambridge, 1992), 137–9; Yvonne Friedman, *Encounter between Enemies: Captivity and Ransom in the Latin Kingdom of Jerusalem* (Leiden, 2002), 33–47.

visitors unsure of whether they were in heaven or on earth.[47] In short, about the stories of a sacred and stable centre which the Byzantines wished the outside world to see as a conduit between the mundane and the supernatural. These stories about a stable centre were of course themselves kinetic as their appearance in texts as diverse as the embassy reports of the Italian envoy Liudprand of Cremona, the prisoner narrative of Harun ibn Yahya and a variety of entries in the *Russian Primary Chronicle* indicates.[48] But these were not the only stories which circulated. Just as relevant in the period of imperial expansion were stories of military action and brutality. Thus, in some eleventh-century Byzantine histories there are traces of frontier epics, which pick up on the training for a raiding style of cavalry warfare.[49] In the early twelfth century some of this epic material was written up more fully in the shape of the narrative of Digenes Akrites, a tale famous for its evocation of a world of Christian–Muslim conflict and coexistence, hypermasculinity and predatory bride-snatching.[50]

It has sometimes been suggested that the world reflected in Diogenes was far from that of the imperial court in Constantinople, and as much as anything represented a rejection of imperial values by those who lived in the rough and rugged world of the eastern frontier.[51] But even if that is the case, then we should not overlook the way in which imperial forces could create their own very powerful stories when campaigning on the frontiers or well beyond them. These were stories which were borne by the mutilated bodies of the conquered, including, in the reign of Basil, not just blinded Bulgarians (the incident for which as 'Bulgarslayer' Basil became infamous) but Christian Georgians and Arab Bedouin, who may have been Christians as well as those who were Muslims. This evidence is complex because just as the Byzantines were capable of extreme physical violence, they also sought quite actively to encourage conquered populations into arrangements in which local agents could be very closely involved in imperial administration. These were nuanced arrangements in which some did not run from imperial power but sought actively to engage with it.[52]

Nonetheless, while there was undoubted reciprocity about governance in areas where the Byzantines claimed imperial control, the role that violence,

---

[47] Samuel Hazzard Cross and Olgerd P. Sherbowitz-Wetzor (tr.), *The Russian Primary Chronicle: Laurentian Text* (Cambridge, MA, 1953), 110–11.

[48] Nadia Maria el Cheikh, *Byzantium Viewed by the Arabs* (Cambridge, MA, 2004), 142–62, for Harun ibn Yahya's observations of Constantinople as transmitted by the early tenth-century geographer Ibn Rusteh.

[49] Skylitzes, *Synopsis*, 291–4; tr. Wortley, *John Skylitzes*, 278–81.

[50] Elizabeth Jeffreys, *Digenis Akritis: The Grottaferrata and Escorial Versions* (Cambridge, 1998); Roderick Beaton, David Ricks and Peter Mackridge (eds.), *Digenes Akrites: New Approaches to Byzantine Heroic Poetry* (Aldershot, 1993).

[51] I. Sevcenko, 'Byzantium Viewed from the Eastern Provinces in the Middle Byzantine Period', *Harvard Ukrainian Studies*, 3–4 (1979–80), 732–5.

[52] Catherine Holmes, 'Basil II the Bulgar-Slayer and the Blinding of 15,000 Bulgarians in 1014: Mutilation and Prisoners-of-War in the Middle Ages', in *How Fighting Ends: A History of Surrender*, ed. Holger Afflerbach and Hew Strachan (Oxford, 2012), 86–93; for the evolution of Basil's reputation as 'Bulgarslayer' see Stephenson, *Bulgarslayer, passim*.

or at least the threat of violence, played should not be overlooked. That the Byzantines were fully aware of the power of stories about the impact of their armies is revealed by the letters of the emperor Constantine VII who exhorted his armies to military action, precisely so that those outside the empire would hear stories of the army's achievement: 'Let your heroic deeds be spoken of in foreign lands, let the foreign contingents accompanying you be amazed at your discipline, let them be messengers to their compatriots of your triumphs and symbols which bring victory, so that they may see the deeds you have performed.'[53] One example of the conveying of such information by external witnesses may come at the moment when Liudprand of Cremona, the Italian bishop and envoy of the German emperor Otto I, passed on the story that the new emperor Nikephoros Phokas was celebrated in Constantinopolitan ceremonial as the 'pallid death of the Saracens'.[54] One imagines that news about this sobriquet lent additional frisson to the message that Nikephoros wanted Liudprand to convey to Otto I: that if the German emperor continued to annoy the Byzantines in southern Italy, then he would be smashed like an earthenware pot.[55] Of course there is always the question of what was style and what was substance. A letter from John Tzimiskes to the Armenian princes datable to c. 975, claiming that he had raided not just as far as Damascus but all the way to Jerusalem, was clearly far-fetched.[56] But that the kinesis of Byzantine imperial forces was not all just empty imperial rhetoric is made clear by the fact that stories about the brutality of Byzantine raiding armies of the tenth century continued to circulate in the east when the crusaders arrived in the same region nearly a century later. The explicit imperial memorialisation of stories of brutality, or at least of the physicality of victory, was clearly actively cultivated by the Byzantines themselves. In his Balkan grand tour of 1018, Basil I stopped off to see the heap of bones near Thermopylae where a Byzantine army had won a huge and slightly unexpected victory against the Bulgarians more than twenty years earlier.[57] In this sense the Byzantines' military activity, both in practice and memorialisation, seems to constitute the 'dark matter' of kinetic empire (a term I take from Hämäläinen): that is, a sense of empire which was simultaneously intangible and yet residually powerful, and in the Byzantine case, a sense of empire strikingly far away from what we customarily regard as its epicentre in the imperial palace and the city of Constantinople.

If there is anything in the evidence for a strong kinetic dimension to the tenth- and eleventh-century Byzantine Empire, how far do we want to take this idea? Of course there are several possible answers, but I will focus on two. Both are connected to issues of control.

---

[53] McGeer, 'Two Orations', 131–2.

[54] Squatriti, *Liudprand of Cremona*, 244.

[55] *Ibid.*, 271.

[56] Paul E. Walker, 'The "Crusade" of John Tzimisces in the Light of New Arabic Evidence', *Byzantion*, 47 (1977), 301–27.

[57] Skylitzes, *Synopsis*, 364; tr. Wortley, *John Skylitzes*, 344.

First: could those who claimed imperial hegemony really control the kinetic elements which helped to create their power? Here, I would suggest that while the kinetic could be a potent force for extending the reputational reach of Byzantium, it was also something that was not always easy to control at the level of domestic politics. This is most visible when we think about the increasing frequency with which the Byzantine armed forces, those engaged in kinetic activity, became integral to politics in the imperial city of Constantinople and to authorising who it was that held imperial power. In other words, an increasing danger to the Byzantine body politic of the tenth and eleventh centuries was the powerful general who would turn a mobile field army to march on Constantinople.[58] Constantine VII, a mid-tenth-century armchair emperor who was brought to the throne with the support of those with military command, betrays a great deal of anxiety in the harangues that he sends to his troops about his own capacity to control their activities. His solution was to suggest that at some point he intended to join the army; in the meantime he intended to send dignitaries who would write down the deeds of those who deserved reward.[59] But one wonders whether a predominantly sedentary empire solution to a kinetic empire problem was ever likely to work. Thus, despite a great deal of legislation connected to the financing and organisation of the Byzantine army in the tenth century, it is clear from legal rulings concerned with the difficulties of retaining Armenian forces that it was actually quite difficult to control troops by bureaucratic means from the Constantinopolitan centre.[60] If command from the imperial centre did not always have much purchase on real-world conditions, an alternative option was for those running the empire to become more peripatetic themselves, the solution adopted by the emperor Basil II, who led his armies personally, as on occasion did Alexios Komnenos, famous as the emperor at the time of the first crusade. Of course, personal leadership of the kinetic was not the solution adopted by all emperors in the eleventh century, and we need to be wary of overstating this phenomenon. Kekaumenos, an astute later eleventh-century provincial observer of politics, noted that the emperor who holds power in Constantinople always wins, a maxim which has been regarded as foundational to the operation of political culture in Byzantium.[61] And, of course, it is striking that most coups were focused on seizing the administrative and ceremonial resources of the palace and the city. But even when focusing on the capital, it is possible that we need to think more about the kinetic. One of the most striking developments of the tenth century was the revival of the imperial triumph

---

[58] Holmes, *Basil II*, 461–8.

[59] McGeer, 'Two Orations', 119–20.

[60] E. McGeer, 'The Legal Decree of Nikephoros Phokas Concerning Armenian Stratiotai', in *Peace and War in Byzantium: Essays in Honor of George T. Dennis*, ed. Timothy S. Miller and John W. Nesbitt (Washington, DC, 1995), 123–37.

[61] Kekaumenos: G. Litavrin, ed. and Russian tr., *Cecaumeni Consilia et Narrationes* (Moscow, 1972), 268; English translation by Charlotte Roueché available online: https://ancientwisdoms.ac.uk/library/kekaumenos-consilia-et-narrationes. It is worth noting, however, that in the same work Kekaumenos also advises emperors on the wisdom of a mobile form of governance; leaving Constantinople was wise, so that the emperor had good knowledge of the state of the provinces.

through the streets of Constantinople.[62] Such occasions can perhaps be inter-preted as the means by which imperial authorities sought to celebrate and yet also to control the kinetic genie that inspired the expansion of the empire.

A second, and perhaps more significant, aspect of control of the kinetic, or indeed lack of control, was the fact that for much of the period I have been speaking about, Byzantium was just one of many political entities underwrit-ten by highly mobile power. Indeed one of the most striking aspects of Byzantine history in this period is just how similar many aspects of its military campaigns were to those of its neighbours; and just how many neighbours also engaged in raiding. Indeed, one could argue that this kinetic commonality between Byzantium and its neighbours is just as striking an aspect of Byzantine warfare in the tenth and eleventh centuries as are other dimensions of the empire's military culture which have traditionally been more central to scholarly enquiry.[63]

The most obvious point of kinetic comparison for this paper are the Fatimids, who differed from the Byzantines in that it took some time before they were able to find a stable political centre, with Cairo only coming to be such after other sites in North Africa had been tried and abandoned, including al-Mahdiya and al-Mansuria in modern-day Tunisia. But in other respects many of the Fatimids' politico-military practices seem rather similar to those of the Byzantines, namely the cultivation of an elaborate ceremonial culture in a fixed urban centre, coupled with a projection of power from that centre which involved long-distance raiding. Such Fatimid raids came as early as 935 for instance against the city of Genoa and the coast of southern France.[64] Also similar to the Byzantines' modus operandi was the Fatimids' threat of lending mobile military support, particularly maritime support, to their enemies' enemies. Thus in the early tenth century the Byzantines were terrified by the prospect of their principal Bulgarian rival being able to enlist Fatimid naval support.[65] The Fatimids' combination of elaborate ceremonial power and long-distance raiding activity undoubtedly had parallels elsewhere in the contemporary Islamic world, most obviously in the Umayyad caliphate of Cordoba in Spain, which engaged in very widely reported raids on sites in Christian Iberia, including at the shrine of Santiago de Compostella, as well

---

[62] Michael McCormick, *Eternal Victory: Triumphal Rulership in Late Antiquity, Byzantium, and the Early Medieval West* (Cambridge, 1986), 159–230; Stephenson, *Bulgarslayer*, 49–65; Pentcheva, *Icons and Power*, 31–5; see also McGeer, 'Two Orations', 128–9.

[63] Discussions of Byzantine military culture have focused very extensively on the significance of the revival of the late Roman military handbook tradition, especially in the tenth century. For a recent contribution to this literature see Georgios Chatzelis, *Byzantine Military Manuals as Literary Works and Practical Handbooks: The Case of the Tenth-Century Sylloge Tacticorum* (Abingdon, 2019). Examination of clear similarities in tactics and fighting personnel between Byzantium and its neighbours is less frequent, although this topic is touched upon in a thought-provoking discussion of Byzantine warfare with the Hamdanids, an aggressive mid-tenth-century emirate based in Aleppo and Mosul (McGeer, *Sowing the Dragon's Teeth*, 228–48).

[64] Yaacov Lev, 'A Mediterranean Encounter: The Fatimids and Europe, Tenth to Twelfth Centuries', in *Shipping, Trade and Crusade in the Medieval Mediterranean: Studies in Honour of John Pryor*, ed. Ruth Gertwagen and Elizabeth Jeffreys (2016).

[65] Skylitzes, *Synopsis*, 264–5; tr. Wortley, *John Skylitzes*, 253–4.

as in naval raids against Fatimid North Africa.[66] In many ways raiding had been typical of the operation of the ninth- and tenth-century Abbasid caliphate centred in Baghdad before its decline from the 920s onwards.[67] And further north the Byzantines were also accustomed to encountering those whose power was predicated on long-distance kinetic activity, whether in the shape of the nomad Magyars whose raids across central Europe and into Italy were a striking feature of the later ninth and tenth centuries, or even the revived western empire under the Ottonians of Saxony, whose power in Italy from the 950s onwards often took the form of dramatic and unexpected appearances in the peninsula, with Otto II's raid into southern Italy in 987 being one instance that was particularly resonant for Byzantine interests.[68] But of course these are just some of the most well-known examples of kinetic imperialists. There were others whose exploitation of mobility was also integral to their power: most obviously from a Byzantine perspective, steppe nomads such as the Pechenegs who operated north of the Black Sea and about whom the Byzantine client manual the *De Administrando Imperio* has much to say, and the Rus who by the tenth century were settling on the Dnieper river.[69] There are also those who are often dismissed merely as pirates or brigands, or controllers of 'enclaves', but who in this period are probably best regarded as incipient kinetic states, such as the Muslim-ruled enclaves at Fraxinetum, on the river Garigliano and on the island of Crete; the latter before its conquest by the Byzantines in 961 indeed struck its own coinage in an interesting example of the interplay between the kinetic, communication and power.[70]

One could go on cataloguing examples, but the more important question is what to make of the widespread incidence of the kinetic in this period, especially the importance of raiding to the operation and projection of power. I would suggest that the first implication is that any power such as Byzantium which tried to impress and express its might through kinetic means always had rivals who were doing the same thing, and who could prove to be more successful in enlisting the resources, including human capital, necessary for such activity. Thus in writing to his armies Constantine

---

[66] Hugh Kennedy, *Muslim Spain and Portugal: A Political History of Al-Andalus* (1996), 119–20; Brett, *Rise of the Fatimids*, 230–5.

[67] John Haldon and Hugh Kennedy, 'The Arab–Byzantine Frontier in the Eighth and Ninth Centuries: Military Organisation and Society in the Borderlands', *Zbornik Radova Vizantološkog Instituta*, 19 (1980), 79–116; Michael Bonner, *Aristocratic Violence and Holy War: Studies in the Jihad and the Arab-Byzantine Frontier* (New Haven, 1996).

[68] Nora Berend, Jozsef Laszlovszky and Bela Zsolt Szakacs, 'The Kingdom of Hungary', in *Christianization and the Rise of Christian Monarchy: Scandinavia, Central Europe and Rus' c. 900–1200*, ed. Nora Berend (Cambridge, 2007), 322–4; Liudprand of Cremona makes several references to tenth-century Magyar raids in the Balkans, Moravia, Germany and Italy (Squatriti, *Liudprand of Cremona*, 75–96, 111–14, 194, 266); G. A. Loud, 'Southern Italy and the Eastern and Western Empires, c. 900–1050', *Journal of Medieval History*, 38 (2012), 1–19, especially at 12.

[69] *De Administrando Imperio*, ed. G. Moravcsik and tr. R. J. H. Jenkins (Washington. DC, 1967), 56–63.

[70] Vassilios Christides, *The Conquest of Crete by the Arabs (ca.824): A Turning Point in the Struggle between Byzantium and Islam* (Athens, 1984); *idem*, 'The Raids of the Moslems of Crete in the Aegean Sea: Piracy and Conquest', *Byzantion*, 51 (1981), 76–111.

VII expresses some clear paranoia about the ways in which a new raiding emirate in the east, the Hamdanids of Mosul and Aleppo, was utilising the tricks of the kinetic trade in regional warfare, above all the spreading of rumours about the mass movement of resources, men as well as money.[71] The legislation of Emperor Nikephoros Phokas, the letter of John Tzimiskes to the Armenians and the dispatch of relics to potential allies demonstrate that Byzantine emperors, even in the military heyday of empire in the later tenth century, still needed to attract troops. Those who themselves had kinetic fighting skills would not necessarily come to serve Byzantium without inducements; those that did could easily be attracted away by others with more to offer.[72] Or, as the Byzantines discovered to their cost when they employed the Rus of Kyiv to invade and destabilise Bulgaria in 968, hired kinetic forces could become too successful: having destroyed Bulgaria, the Rus ruler Svyatoslav elected not to go back safely up the Dnieper but instead to establish a new position on the Bulgarian Black Sea coast at Pereiaslavets, a very perilous development for the Byzantines given the proximity of this site to Constantinople.[73] In a similar way, just as the Byzantines had rivals in the practice of building power through kinetic warfare, so too could they be victims of that kind of martial culture, especially in the sense of being taken prisoner of war and in some cases enslaved: a long narrative by John Kaminiates describing the sack of the Byzantine city of Thessaloniki in 904 by Leo of Tripoli was written so that its author could be ransomed.[74] Indeed Leo's own route to power as a naval commander operating loosely under the auspices of caliphal power started as a Byzantine taken captive in a raid who subsequently converted to Islam.[75]

This point about the multiplicity of those making power through kinetic means in the tenth- and eleventh-century Mediterranean also has potential implications for wider issues of periodisation. As I indicated at the beginning of this paper, if we think about power in the eastern Mediterranean in the tenth and eleventh centuries largely in terms of sedentary empires administered from fixed-point centres with civil and military infrastructures paid for from the taxes collected from an agrarian peasantry, then we can suggest that the final decades of the eleventh century represented a period of seismic

---

[71] McGeer, 'Two Orations', 130–1.

[72] For example, once in Egypt, the Fatimids also looked to employ Armenian troops. On the career of the Armenian commander Badr al Jamali in the later eleventh century, see Brett, *Fatimid Empire*, 199ff.; on the wider point of Armenians in the armies of Islamic powers, including the Fatimids, see John France, *Victory in the East: A Military History of the First Crusade* (Cambridge, 1994), 205–6. On mercenaries serving in Hamdanid armies, and the eagerness of the Hamdanid emirs to employ such forces for the purposes of raiding, see McGeer, *Sowing the Dragon's Teeth*, 232–42.

[73] Franklin and Shepard, *Emergence of Rus*, 139–51.

[74] John Kameniates, *The Capture of Thessaloniki*, ed., tr. and commentary D. Frendo and A. Fotiou (Perth, 2000); see Shaun Tougher, *The Reign of Leo VI (886–912): Politics and People* (Leiden, 1997), 181–9, for the campaign of 904, and for an interpretation of eastern Mediterranean Arab naval activity in the early tenth century as devastating raids rather than attempts to occupy territory.

[75] Tougher, *Leo VI*, 184–5.

change, as this region came under pressure from new and aggressive kinetic powers. These new powers included the Seljuk Turks, steppe nomads from the east who moved into Fatimid-controlled regions in Syria, as well as large swathes of Byzantine Anatolia, at the same time as the Byzantines faced other aggressive steppe nomad peoples beyond the Danube (Pechenegs and Cumans) and as a new type of itinerant fighter in search of liquid assets arrived in Italy: the Normans, some of whom later contributed to crusading forces. But if we think that there was a strongly kinetic dimension to the exercise of regional power *before* the arrival of these more obviously kinetic groups, what then?

One option is to argue for an incremental case, that the large-scale regional powers of Byzantium and Fatimid Egypt were at heart sedentary empires, but ones which for a while were able to absorb, channel, harness and even exploit the kinetic, as when in the 1040s some groups of Pecheneg steppe nomads were co-opted by the Byzantines to raid against their fellow Pechenegs.[76] In this sense we might also consider the Varangians from Rus and Scandinavia who were employed as mercenaries in the imperial guard, or even the crusaders who were funnelled across the Bosphorus to help Byzantium regain territory lost to the Turks in Anatolia. This modest and incremental account of the integration of the kinetic might fit well with a relatively conservative approach to the Byzantine military state taken recently by Anthony Kaldellis. He argues that while Byzantine emperors undoubtedly employed a modest number of extra-Byzantine troops, such forces were always in the minority, even during periods when the Byzantine army and the state apparatus which supported it saw substantial growth; it was only in the 1070s that mercenary troops from outside Byzantium became the martial majority.[77] If we adopt this stance, then what happened across the tenth and much of the eleventh century could be interpreted in terms of a gradualist shift in the balance of power, as what were initially controllable kinetic incomers gradually began to eat away at the fabric of the state which sustained them. These are processes in Byzantium which can appear to have striking parallels in polities elsewhere: thus, we could think of the gradual takeover of the Lombard principalities in Italy by the Normans, or the reorientation of the Fatimid polity in the 1070s by incomers such as the Armenian commander Badr al Jamali.[78]

However, there is a third possibility which is that the kinetic in the terms that I have described was an ever-present across the tenth- and eleventh-century eastern Mediterranean, a set of mobile practices which characterised the political–military culture of all polities, not just the big imperial complexes or those we have traditionally regarded as newcomers in the eleventh century; but instead a variety of indigenous polities of all sizes which were used to exercising and projecting power through raiding, with the purpose of those raids being about accessing and controlling (or defending and preserving) key routes

---

[76] Stephenson, *Byzantium's Balkan Frontier*, 89–91.

[77] Kaldellis, *Streams of Gold, Rivers of Blood*, 11–12, 275–6.

[78] Graham A. Loud, *The Age of Robert Guiscard: Southern Italy and the Norman Conquest* (Harlow, 2000); Brett, *Fatimid Empire*, 191ff.

of communication and entrepôts rather than extending control of territory and acquiring new tax revenues based on exploitation of an agrarian peasantry. If there is anything in this idea, then rather than seeing the eastern Mediterranean in terms of frontiers akin to lines on maps, or even in terms of deep borderland zones, we could instead think about a very jagged geography of interpenetration both on land and at sea, in which different polities' raiders were frequently criss-crossing one another over considerable distances. Such a geopolitical environment could help to make sense of some rather bewildering and contradictory chronologies of the eleventh century, especially in Byzantium, where at points in time when the empire was supposed to be very secure and had achieved substantial victories (for instance, the latter part of the reign of Basil II and the reigns of his immediate successors), Rus and Arab (perhaps Fatimid?) raiding vessels could still suddenly appear in the seas very close to Constantinople;[79] in contrast, in the middle of the eleventh century when the Seljuk Turks were raiding deep into central Asia Minor, and one might assume the Byzantines were very weak, we discover that they were still able to acquire new positions in eastern Armenia, far to the east of the Turks' raids in the central plateau regions.[80] Indeed the notion of a long-established complex weave of raiding activity from multiple players may help to explain why it is so difficult to track the arrival of genuine newcomers in the historical record – the first appearance of the Turks in the eastern reaches of Byzantium is famously difficult to date.[81] And if we did not have a wealth of Western sources plus the very *sui generis* Anna Comnena to tell us otherwise, then we might be tempted to view the arrival of the crusaders in northern Syria in the 1090s as simply the return of a new Byzantine field army. Certainly the rather delayed and initially relatively small-scale response from neighbouring Islamic powers may suggest that contemporaries also saw the crusaders in that traditional light.[82]

Interpreting the eastern Mediterranean world in the tenth and eleventh centuries in terms of a long-standing tradition of raiding polities may help to explain why the Normans, Turks and crusaders were able to make such rapid progress when they did arrive in bigger numbers. And what that may mean in terms of wider periodisation is that we should think less about distinct, chronologically circumscribed, phases in the history of political change in the eastern Mediterranean and more about very *longue durée* regional continuities, especially in the vast majority of land- and seascapes of this region, beyond the imperial capitals and their immediate hinterlands. And in these senses of raiding as a shared political and military culture across many polities,

---

[79] Skylitzes, *Synopsis*, 367–8, 373; tr. Wortley, *John Skylitzes*, 347, 352; for a raid on the island of Gymnopelagisia by Muslim Arabs in Basil II's reign, see also George Ostrogorsky, 'Une Ambassade serbe auprès de l'empereur Basile II', *Byzantion*, 19 (1949), 187–94; Holmes, *Basil II*, 406.

[80] For example, the principality of Kars was annexed as late as 1065, only six years before the Battle of Manzikert.

[81] Alexander Beihammer, *Byzantium and the Emergence of Muslim-Turkish Anatolia, ca. 1040-1130* (2017).

[82] There are hints of this argument in France, *Victory in the East*, 203.

I would suggest that the kinetic empire model proposed by Hämäläinen has considerable potential for forcing historians of the eastern Mediterranean to loosen their traditional capital-centric gaze and expand, as well as potentially contract, what they mean by empire in this period and in this region of the medieval world.

There is, however, of course a gigantic elephant in the room, in that while most of the polities that I have discussed in this paper may have been kinetic, their rulers were not nomads; and most of those they claimed to govern were not mobile pastoralists. Do those omissions mean that this approach of applying kinetic to other kinds of peoples, polities and hegemonies risks falling into a classic global history trap: of taking a concept and applying it so generally that it flattens and homogenises that which it is trying to explain; or perhaps worse, deflects attention back onto the usual imperial suspects while condemning to the sidelines precisely the kinds of hitherto 'marginal' groups which an approach like kinetic empire was supposed to 'centre'?

In concluding, I would accept the challenge but argue against the charge. In the eastern Mediterranean world of the period I have described in this paper, thinking about the kinetic dimensions to empire actually allows us to see just how fluid and contingent were *all* the polities of the tenth and eleventh centuries, despite intermittent attempts by those in long-standing centres of imperial power, such as Byzantium, to rebrand and reorder that fluidity in traditional administrative terms. The degree to which that reordering from imperial capitals was only ever a very partial feature of a much wider and more fluid landscape of power is, paradoxically, revealed by the ubiquity of the kinetic in the ways in which those empires projected and communicated their own claims to power and authority.

Acknowledgements. A version of this article was first presented as a Royal Historical Society lecture, read on 6 May 2021.

Cite this article: Holmes C (2022). The Making and Breaking of Kinetic Empire: Mobility, Communication and Political Change in the Eastern Mediterranean, *c.* 900–1100 CE. *Transactions of the Royal Historical Society* **32**, 25–45. https://doi.org/10.1017/S0080440122000093

Transactions of the RHS (2022), **32**, 47–72
doi:10.1017/S0080440122000081

ARTICLE

A (Dis)entangled History of Early Modern Cannibalism: Theory and Practice in Global History

Stuart M. McManus[1]* and Michael T. Tworek[2]

[1]Department of History, Fung King Hey Building, Chinese University of Hong Kong, Shatin, New Territories, Hong Kong, China and [2]Department of History, Harvard University, Cambridge, Massachusetts, USA
*Corresponding author. Email: smcmanus@cuhk.edu.hk

(Received 30 December 2021; accepted 2 May 2022)

Abstract

This article offers a new approach to early modern global history, dubbed *(dis)entangled history* as a way to combine the conventional focus on the history of connections with a necessary appreciation of the elements of disconnection and disintegration. To exemplify this approach, it offers a case study related to the history of cannibalism as both a disputed anthropophagic practice and a cultural reference point across the early modern world. Through a rich multilingual and multimedia source base, we trace how the idea of Indigenous Tapuya endo-cannibalism in Brazil travelled across the Atlantic through Europe and Africa to East Asia. The idea of Tapuya cannibalism crossed some linguistic borders, stopped at others and interacted unevenly with long-standing Ottoman, Polish, West African, Islamic and Chinese ideas about 'cannibal countries', of which it was just one more example. This trajectory challenges the historiographical consensus that early modern ideas about cannibalism were centred on the Atlantic world. By tracing how one particular discourse did and did not travel around the globe, this article offers not just a theoretical statement, but a 'fleshed out' and concrete approach to writing about intermittent connectedness during the period 1500–1800.

Keywords: global history; cannibalism; globalisation; colonialism; Atlantic history; Eastern Europe; Brazil; China; Africa; historiography

Global history is the subject of lively debates. For some, it remains stubbornly and disappointingly Eurocentric. For others, the incessant search for extra-European origins of locally contingent events, like the French Revolution, has dented our ability to explain causality, surely one of the primary tasks of historians. For some, the path forward involves collaboration, the study of more languages and the consultation of ever more disparate archives to find connections across time and space that have been obscured by generations of nationalist and area-studies historiography as well as the contingencies of archival formation. Others echo the famous 1943 remark of US congresswoman Clare Boothe Luce that we have fallen for 'globaloney' in obsessing about increased connectedness, even going as far as to parse this into teleological phases, like archaic globalisation and proto-globalisation, when the reality is that important elements of disconnection and decline are visible at every step.[1] Even the origins of global history are disputed. It is certainly true that it partly emerged from an intellectual milieu steeped in postcolonialism and 'history from below'. However, it is also clear that the inauguration of a new phase of globalisation in the 1990s, driven by geopolitical change, advances in technology and the evolution of global supply chains, provided the final push and the immediate context for the development of global history as practised today.[2]

Of course, 'global history' is not one thing, but a series of approaches that use, as Merry Wiesner-Hanks has put it, 'different terms to describe their studies of connections, exchanges, intersections, interactions, and movements'.[3] Of these, connected history and entangled history are undoubtedly the most prominent. The former rose to fame as a powerful tool to challenge the implicit exoticism, and at times even orientalism, among historians in both India and the West who consciously and unconsciously privileged the developmental trajectory of Europe when looking at early modern South Asia. For its most prominent practitioner, Sanjay Subrahmanyam, the societies of the premodern world prior to European imperial hegemony were equal participants in a nascent pluralist modernity that was in the process of arising organically and chaotically at a planetary level, rather than being engineered by European states.[4]

---

[1] 'American Air Rule Urged by Mrs. Luce; In First House Speech She Calls Wallace's Views of Sky "Freedom" Just "Globaloney"', New York Times, 10 Feb. 1943, 27.

[2] Bruce Mazlish and R. Buultjens (eds.), Conceptualizing Global History (Boulder, 1993); A. G. Hopkins, 'Is Globalisation Yesterday's News?' Itinerario, 41 (2017), 109–28; David Bell, 'Questioning the Global Turn: The Case of the French Revolution', French Historical Studies, 37 (2014), 1–24; Jeremy Adelman, 'Is Global History Still Possible, or Has It Had Its Moment?' Aeon, 2 March 2017, https://aeon.co/essays/is-global-history-still-possible-or-has-it-had-its-moment; Richard Drayton and David Motadel, 'Discussion: The Futures of Global History', Journal of Global History, 13 (2018), 1–16; Frederick Cooper, 'What Is the Concept of Globalization Good For? An African Historian's Perspective', African Affairs, 100 (2001), 189–213; Matthew Hilton and Rana Mitter (eds.), Transnationalism and Contemporary Global History (Past & Present Supplements, VIII) (New York, 2013); Catherine Holmes and Naomi Standen (eds.), The Global Middle Ages (Past & Present Supplements, XIII) (New York, 2018); John-Paul A. Ghobrial (ed.), Global History & Microhistory (Past & Present Supplements, XIV) (New York, 2019).

[3] Merry Wiesner-Hanks, 'Early Modern Gender and the Global Turn', in Mapping Gendered Routes and Spaces in the Early Modern World, ed. Merry Wiesner-Hanks (Burlington, 2015), 55–74.

[4] The locus classicus for connected history in Anglophone historiography is Sanjay Subrahmanyam, 'Connected Histories: Notes towards a Reconfiguration of Early Modern Eurasia', Modern Asian Studies, 31 (1997), 735–62, although it mirrors C. A. Bayly, The Birth of the Modern World, 1780–1914: Global Connections and Comparisons (Malden, 2004).

In a somewhat similar vein, the latter, entangled history (a calque of *histoire croisée*), challenges an overreliance on comparative history and a binary model of cultural transfer studies that has perpetuated singular Eurocentric comparisons of enclosed national and continental units.[5] Either consciously or unconsciously, many examples of these take the form of what Francesca Trivellato has called 'global microhistories', an approach that has been elegantly described by John-Paul Ghobrial in this way: '[one] first looks for the world in a grain of sand, [then] sifts through many beaches around the same ocean with a fine toothed comb.'[6] In the hands of its best practitioners, such global microhistories have uncovered unexpected interactions and movements that linked rural China, North Africa and Baghdad to the shores of Lake Texcoco, and, in the case of Dominic Sachsenmaier's recent history of a Chinese Christian from Ningbo 'who never travelled', highlighted the global entanglements that underpinned apparently stationary lives.[7]

Yet, as globalisation's political fortunes have fallen in the tumultuous decade and a half since the Great Recession of 2008, even the aforementioned masters of the art increasingly raise eyebrows. As Jeremy Adelman noted several years ago, 'we need narratives of global life that reckon with disintegration as well as integration, the costs and not just the bounty of interdependence.'[8] In the spirit of constructive debate, we therefore offer a subtly different approach to global history: *(dis)entangled history*. As the bidirectional adjective suggests, (dis)entangled history argues for the simultaneous importance of integration *and* disintegration in explaining transregional historical phenomena. Rather than simply focusing on globalisation or those who 'got left out' of it, (dis)entangled history tries to take an even-handed approach to connections and disconnections. This purposely leaves space for oblique, sometimes unrecognised contributions to global history that do not fall neatly into teleological narratives about the creation of our modern globalising, if not fully globalised, world. Furthermore, (dis)entangled history does not necessarily entail a focus

---

[5] Michael Werner and Bénédicte Zimmermann, 'Beyond Comparison: *Histoire croisée* and the Challenge of Reflexivity', *History and Theory*, 45 (2006), 30–50; Sebastian Conrad, 'Entangled Histories of Uneven Modernities: Civil Society, Caste Councils, and Legal Pluralism in Postcolonial India', in *Comparative and Transnational History: Central European Approaches and New Perspectives*, ed. Heinz-Gerhard Haupt and Jürgen Kocka (New York, 2009), 77–104. For an Iberian Atlanticist approach to entangled history, see Ralph Bauer and Marcy Norton, 'Introduction: Entangled Trajectories: Indigenous and European Histories', *Colonial Latin American Review*, 26 (2017), 1–17.

[6] Francesca Trivellato, 'Is There a Future for Italian Microhistory in the Age of Global History?', *California Italian Studies*, 2 (2011), http://www.escholarship.org/uc/item/0z94n9hq; John-Paul Ghobrial, 'Introduction: Seeing the World like a Microhistorian', *Past & Present*, 242 (2019), 1–22.

[7] For well-executed global microhistories in the conventional mode, see John-Paul A. Ghobrial, 'The Secret Life of Elias of Babylon and the Uses of Global Microhistory', *Past & Present*, 222 (2014), 51–94, and Clare Griffin, 'Disentangling Commodity Histories: Pauame and Sassafras in the Early Modern Global World', *Journal of Global History*, 15 (2020), 1–18. Sachsenmaier's position on global history also echoes in many ways the view articulated here. Dominic Sachsenmaier, *Global Entanglements of a Man Who Never Traveled: A Seventeenth-Century Chinese Christian and His Conflicted Worlds* (New York, 2018).

[8] Adelman, 'Is Global History Still Possible?'.

on the entire world, nor does it preclude it.[9] Even the term 'global' is not a necessity; it means different things to different people.

Although earlier scholars have practised many of the individual elements of the (dis)entangled approach, we combine them here to offset the focus on the centrality and inevitability of integration.[10] In particular, (dis)entangled history departs from mainstream approaches in two distinct ways. First, it actively and simultaneously seeks out both connections and disconnections, both rise and decline, as constituent parts of all historical phenomena. Second, it explicitly encourages historians to question inherited meta-geographies (i.e. the sets of spatial categories, labels and assumptions that organise our mental map of the world) and their applicability to particular cases. By foregrounding these two concerns, (dis)entangled history provides a framework for approaching early modern and other global histories.

Indeed, the emphasis on both connections and disconnections means that highly localised phenomena can be given their due. This could be applied to the transmission of indigenous medicinal knowledge within one family in the Americas or culturally specific ideas surrounding caste in South Asia, which would be just as much a part of a (dis)entangled history as widely traded commodities, Japanese slaves in Río de la Plata and highly globetrotting Muslim courtiers. In such contexts, (dis)entangled history is concerned with both the impermeability of cultures and the creation of new 'hybrid' cultural forms within and across borders. Though not opposed to them, (dis)entangled history therefore entails a healthy scepticism regarding recent scholarship on the formation of a 'world culture' and processes of 'world-making' emerging from the growth and imbrication of various networks of people, objects and institutions.[11] This is a trend that has led to a veritable avalanche of books and articles that include the phrase 'early modern world' and other similarly

---

[9] Caroline Douki and Philippe Minard, 'Histoire globale, histoires connectées: un changement d'échelle historiographique?', *Revue d'histoire moderne et contemporaine*, 54, no. 4 (2007), 7–21. On the distinction between global and world history, see Patrick Manning, *Navigating World History: Historians Create a Global Past* (New York, 2003); Bruce Mazlish, 'Comparing Global History to World History', *Journal of Interdisciplinary History*, 28 (1998), 385–95.

[10] We have been particularly influenced by Douki and Minard, 'Histoire globale, histoires connectées'; Sebastian Conrad, *What Is Global History?* (Princeton, 2016); Jean-Paul Zuniga, '"L'Histoire impériale à l'heure de l'histoire globale". Une perspective atlantique', *Revue d'histoire moderne et contemporaine*, 54, no. 4 (2007), 54–68; Jorge Cañizares-Esguerra (ed.), *Entangled Empires: The Anglo-Iberian Atlantic, 1500-1800* (Philadelphia, 2018); Sanjay Subrahmanyam, 'Holding the World in Balance: The Connected Histories of the Iberian Overseas Empires, 1500-1640', *American Historical Review*, 112 (2007), 1359–85; Zoltán Biedermann, *(Dis)connected Empires: Imperial Portugal, Sri Lankan Diplomacy, and the Making of a Habsburg Conquest in Asia* (Oxford, 2018).

[11] For an overview of this broader tendency in global studies, see Nathalie Karagiannis and Peter Wagner, 'Introduction: Globalization or World-Making?', in *Varieties of World-Making: Beyond Globalization*, ed. Nathalie Karagiannis and Peter Wagner (Liverpool, 2007), 1–16; Ayesha Ramachandran, *The Worldmakers: Global Imagining in Early Modern Europe* (Chicago, 2015).

expansive meta-geographical categories.[12] Though rich and varied, this body of work has had the cumulative effect of creating a teleological, almost Whiggish vision of the inevitability of globalisation in every interaction, encounter and development whether in the Americas, Asia, Europe or Africa (although Oceania and Antarctica are conspicuous by their absence). This now seems as problematic as now-defunct teleological narratives about the rise of the nation state.

Similarly, (dis)entangled history is alive to the limits of a vision of history that heavily emphasises the circulation of ideas, human actors and material objects.[13] This is because such an approach has decidedly mixed results. On the one hand, it has helped to decentralise elite and urban sites of production like academies and cities, problematised the notion of separate centres and peripheries, and even revealed instances of bidirectionality in flow.[14] On the other hand, as Stefanie Gänger has argued, such an approach relies on the assumption that people, information and material objects flowed evenly and continuously along networks and channels. Blockages and gaps are still of insufficient concern to the global historian.[15] At the same time, there is a tendency to study and locate 'networks' for their own sake without reflecting sufficiently on the significance and implications of their existence. Indeed, as a noted historian of science, Lissa Louise Roberts, has rightly pointed out, this craze for networks gives little attention to the importance of local exchange and even the creation of the networks themselves.[16] It is therefore essential to pay close attention to the genesis of particular networks and the specific points in time and space where people, goods and ideas met hurdles they could not clear; trajectories were not limitless.

Moreover, (dis)entangled history rejects any implicit geocentric bias, Eurocentric or otherwise. This is increasingly necessary as the 'early modern world' becomes the preferred focus for practitioners of what used to be called 'early modern European history'. In truth, much of recent early modern global history is essentially repackaged imperial or missionary history in a Whiggish globalising vein.[17] In parallel to this (and conscious of the upcoming case

---

[12] For instance, see Anne Gerritsen and Giorgio Riello (eds.), *The Global Lives of Things: The Material Culture of Connections in the Early Modern World* (2016); Nicholas Terpstra, *Religious Refugees in the Early Modern World: An Alternative History of the Reformation* (New York, 2015).

[13] Kapil Raj, *Relocating Modern Science: Circulation and the Construction of Knowledge in South Asia and Europe, 1650–1900* (New York, 2007).

[14] Fa-ti Fan, *British Naturalists in Qing China: Science, Empire, and Cultural Encounter* (Cambridge, MA, 2004); Antonella Romano and Stéphane Van Damme, 'Science and World Cities: Thinking Urban Knowledge and Science at Large (16th–18th century)', *Itinerario*, 33 (2009), 79–95.

[15] Stefanie Gänger, 'Circulation: Reflections on Circularity, Entity, and Liquidity in the Language of Global History', *Journal of Global History*, 12 (2017), 303–18. On the ebbs and flows in globalisation, see Heidi J. S. Tworek, 'Communicable Disease: Information, Health, and Globalization in the Interwar Period', *American Historical Review*, 124 (2019), 813–42.

[16] Lissa Roberts, 'Situating Science in Global History: Local Exchanges and Networks of Circulation', *Itinerario*, 33 (2009), 9–30; cf. Bruno Latour, *Reassembling the Social: An Introduction to Actor-Network-Theory* (Oxford, 2005).

[17] Luke Clossey, *Salvation and Globalization in the Early Jesuit Missions* (New York, 2008); Mark H. Danley and Patrick J. Speelman, *The Seven Years' War: Global Views* (Leiden, 2012); Bayly, *Birth*

study), we should also be wary of a growing and ultimately teleological Sino-Western-centrism.[18] The economic and geopolitical clash of the People's Republic of China with various nations has rightly lent contemporary relevance to long-standing debates about the divergence of 'China' and the 'West' during the early modern period, with interactions between Europe (as the geopolitical precursor to the United States and the European Union) and China taking centre stage.[19] However, we should not allow this 'proto-Chimerica' to become an object of fixation, just as a reified Europe was for previous generations.

To turn to the second major element of (dis)entangled history, it is important for historians periodically to revisit how they divide up the globe.[20] Building on the insights of Martin Lewis and Kären Wigen, (dis)entangled history invites challenges to established meta-geographies across all subfields. Indeed, at a time when we are seeing the decline of older concepts like the 'Atlantic', and the birth of new ones like the 'Indo-Pacific', it is particularly important to be alive to the shifting sands of meta-geography, on which we built our historiographical houses.[21] Practitioners of (dis)entangled history should also ask themselves: does the 'Iberian world' that has become so popular among historians of Spain, Portugal, Latin America and Iberian Asia hide as much as it reveals? We fear so. How global and cosmopolitan was the European 'Republic of Letters' really? What about the 'Sanskrit cosmopolis'? Did purported cultural and economic peripheries like Eastern Europe, Abyssinia and Japan really ignore global currents until the nineteenth century? Was 'territoriality' in the sense of political contestations for control of finite global space an invention of the seventeenth century?[22] Was there really an 'early modern world' as so many have presumed, and how did it differ from the 'modern world' in its worldliness?[23] Was there one Europe or one China, or many, active in this period? One-size-fits-all answers are unlikely to exist for many of these questions.

---

of the Modern World; Kimberly Lynn and Erin Kathleen Rowe, The Early Modern Hispanic World: Transnational and Interdisciplinary Approaches (New York, 2017); Liam Matthew Brockey (ed.), Portuguese Colonial Cities in the Early Modern World (Farnham, 2008).

[18] For a largely Sino-European approach, see David Porter (ed.), Comparative Early Modernities, 1100-1800 (New York, 2012).

[19] Kenneth Pomeranz, The Great Divergence: China, Europe, and the Making of the Modern World Economy (Princeton, 2000).

[20] Martin Lewis and Kären Wigen, The Myth of Continents: A Critique of Metageography (Berkeley, 1997); Victor B. Lieberman, Beyond Binary Histories: Re-imagining Eurasia to c.1830 (Ann Arbor, 1999).

[21] The 'Indo-Pacific' is a term which began life in marine biology but has since spread to international relations and is now making inroads into other fields, especially in India and Australia: David Scott, 'India and the Allure of the "Indo-Pacific"', International Studies, 49 (2012), 165–88; Hansong Li, 'The "Indo-Pacific": Intellectual Origins and International Visions in Global Contexts', Modern Intellectual History (2021): 1–27.

[22] Charles S. Maier, 'Transformations of Territoriality, 1600–2000', in Transnationale Geschichte: Themen, Tendenzen und Theorien, ed. Gunilla Budde et al. (Göttingen, 2006), 33–55.

[23] For a critical account, see Jerry Bentley, 'Early Modern Europe and the Early Modern World', in Between the Middle Ages and Modernity: Individual and Community in the Early Modern World, ed. Charles H. Parker and Jerry Bentley (New York, 2007), 13–31.

In the interests of simplifying these overlapping historiographical imperatives, the following metaphor might be useful for thinking about (dis)entangled history: imagine the history of the world in a particular moment as an intricate fabric, one so large and complex that it is almost impossible to parse the conglomerate of many materials, colours, thicknesses and lengths. Some threads are long and winding. Others are short and stumpy. Some clump at one corner. Others are distributed throughout the cloth. Historical objects, people, practices and ideas are like these threads. Some connect and circulate. Others do not. Each thread is spread across a certain space, but each knot and twist occupies its own particular place. It might be useful to divide the cloth into sections, but any division will inevitably do a disservice to the whole. When seeking to untangle the morass, the historian must begin by looking for loose threads, pulling on them to reveal their length and whether or not they pull on other parts of the wider fabric. This is the starting point for a (dis)entangled history.

One example of such a (dis)entangled history might focus on the uneven global circulation of reports of Tapuya anthropophagy from early modern Brazil. News of their alleged endo-cannibalism (eating relatives) travelled across the Atlantic through Europe and Africa to East Asia, crossing some linguistic borders, stopping at others, and interacting unevenly with pre-existing Ottoman, Polish, West African, Arabic and Chinese ideas about 'cannibal countries'. This trajectory challenges the historiographical consensus that places the expansion of Western European empires into the Atlantic at the centre of early modern discourses around cannibalism. In addition, these non-European reflections on Tapuya and other cannibalisms (including accusations that Europeans were guilty of it too) underline the fact that Iberian, British and French ideas were to a large degree unexceptional and could easily be integrated into non-European patterns of thought in parts of the world with polities and humanistic traditions that proved relatively resistant to incursions. In the interests of providing a concrete example, rather than just a theoretical statement on (dis)entangled history, we now pull on this particular historical loose thread that connected large, but far from all, parts of an early modern globe characterised by intermittent connectedness. In this way, we also seek to 'decolonise' the study of early modern cannibalism as both reality and discourse, i.e. overturn a long-standing Eurocentric framework to reveal hitherto obscured perspectives, especially with reference to underappreciated European and non-European language sources (including Polish, Chinese and Japanese).[24]

---

[24] Walter D. Mignolo, 'Delinking: The Rhetoric of Modernity, the Logic of Coloniality and the Grammar of De-coloniality', *Cultural Studies*, 21 (2007), 449–514; Dipesh Chakrabarty, *Provincializing Europe: Postcolonial Thought and Historical Difference*, 2nd edn (Princeton, 2009); 'Decolonizing the AHR', *American Historical Review*, 123 (2018), xiv–vii; Raymond F. Betts, 'Decolonization: A Brief History of the Word', in *Beyond Empire and Nation: The Decolonization of African and Asian Societies, 1930s–1970s*, ed. Bogaerts Els and Raben Remco (Leiden, 2012), 23–38; Amanda Behm et al., 'Decolonizing History: Enquiry and Practice', *History Workshop Journal*, 89 (2020), 169–91.

In an account of his sea voyage, a premodern traveller recorded that the inhabitants of a certain group of remote islands were known to 'eat people alive'. These cannibals, he continued, are 'black and have frizzy hair, hideous faces and eyes, and long feet ... and they are naked'. With a sense of relief, however, he noted that they had 'no boats, [for] if they did, they would eat anyone who passed by them'. Some ships had been forced to make 'slow passage' of the island due to unfavourable winds and lack of fresh water, and in doing so they took serious risks. Though 'the islanders often catch some of the crew,' the traveller noted that 'most of them get away' – fortunately.

If one had to guess the identity of the author, one might assume that he (and one would normally think of a he as there are vanishingly few travel accounts by women before the nineteenth century) was a European.[25] Indeed, one would likely venture that he was Spanish, Portuguese or perhaps English as these were the trader-raiders historians normally associate with the early modern Caribbean and West Africa, whose native inhabitants were frequently branded as 'cannibals', at least partly to justify European colonialism. However, the reality is somewhat different. In fact, the account treats the Andaman Islands in the Bay of Bengal, and was drafted in Arabic in the tenth century by an unknown writer from the Abbasid Empire and completed by a merchant from Siraf in the Persian Gulf named Abū Zayd al-Sīrāfī (893–979 CE).[26]

Of course, there are good reasons for the association of accusations of cannibalism with the Atlantic empires of Western Europe, in particular of Britain and Iberia. In searching for the imperial roots of the Euro-American West, scholars in various national traditions have long referred to the accounts of indigenous cannibalism by Hans Staden (1525–1576), Jean de Léry (1536–1613) and others. These echoed earlier reports by Columbus about the Caribs (the root of the word 'cannibal' in various languages) and popularised the idea of the Americas as a hotbed of man-eating.[27] Since the postcolonial turn, such accounts have been explored as representations and cultural projections of European power in the Atlantic world, with the origins of this stratagem going as far back as Herodotus who used such accusations as a way to create an ethnographic 'other'.[28] It was in the early modern period, however, that these and other reports became the frequent basis for both justifications of conquest and vociferous self-critique in the Atlantic world. For instance, people in the Americas and Africa enslaved according to the Mediterranean logic of 'rescue' (*rescate*, *resgate*) were considered better off as the slaves of their Christian 'rescuers' rather than the dinner of a cannibal. Slave-raiding and -trading were therefore

---

[25] One notable exception is Catalina de Erauso, *Lieutenant Nun: Memoir of a Basque Transvestite in the New World*, ed. Gabriel Stepto and Michele Stepto (Boston, MA, 1996).

[26] Tim Mackintosh-Smith and James E. Montgomery (eds.), *Two Arabic Travel Books: Accounts of China and India* (New York, 2014), 27.

[27] Frank Lestringant, *Jean De Léry, ou, l'invention du sauvage: essai sur l'histoire d'un voyage faict en la terre du Brésil* (Paris, 1999).

[28] E. M. Murphy and J. P. Mallory, 'Herodotus and the Cannibals', *Antiquity*, 74 (2000), 388–94; Jay Rubenstein, 'Cannibals and Crusaders', *French Historical Studies*, 31 (2008), 525–52.

defensible as acts of charity.[29] Conversely, Brazilian cannibalism famously inspired Montaigne's *Of Cannibals* and Shakespeare's *The Tempest*, which exposed the hypocrisies of religious warfare and colonialism. The discourse also inspired an artistic tradition centred on the 'noble savage', from engravings of reported cannibalistic rituals (Figure 1) to idealised paintings of one particular indigenous group, the Tapuya (Figure 2), that threw into relief European perceptions of their own savagery.[30] Even the modern anthropological study of human cannibalism, also known as anthropophagy (literally, 'man-eating'), was first taken up within the context of European settler-colonial societies, although many now question the veracity of the practice entirely in precolonial Australia and elsewhere.[31]

However, such, admittedly well-founded, critiques of an older imperial-nationalist impulse have had the unintended consequence of reifying the very Eurocentric narratives which they sought to overturn. Indeed, al-Sīrāfī's account of the Andaman Islands is just one example of non-European 'cannibal talk'.[32] Perhaps even more unexpectedly, Atlantic cannibalism had a history beyond the ocean with which it is normally associated, where it overlapped and interacted with these parallel traditions. Without doubt, the best example of this phenomenon centres on the Tapuya, a catch-all for various Amazonian peoples branded by other indigenous groups, such as the Tupinamba, as barbarians who ate human flesh.[33] Even the name *tapuya* given to them by the coastal-dwelling speakers of the *lingua geral* meant 'enemy'. When the Portuguese arrived on the coast and began to form alliances with certain Tupinamba factions, they inherited their allies' prejudices. This attitude was hardened in the 1630s when the Dutch joined forces with the Tapuya to

---

[29] David Brion Davis, *The Problem of Slavery in Western Culture* (New York, 1988), 19, 184, 348; Herman L. Bennett, *African Kings and Black Slaves: Sovereignty and Dispossession in the Early Modern Atlantic* (Philadelphia, 2019).

[30] Cătălin Avramescu, *An Intellectual History of Cannibalism* (Princeton, 2009); Frank Lestringant, *Cannibals: The Discovery and Representation of the Cannibal from Columbus to Jules Verne*, trans. Rosemary Morris (Berkeley, 1997). For the place of cannibals in European maps, see Frank Lestringant, *Mapping the Renaissance World: The Geographical Imagination in the Age of Discovery* (Berkeley, 1994).

[31] For cannibalism and its existence from an anthropological perspective, see William Arens, *The Man-Eating Myth: Anthropology and Anthropophagy* (New York, 1980); Shirley Lindenbaum, 'Thinking about Cannibalism', *Annual Review of Anthropology*, 33 (2004), 475–98; and Donald W. Forsyth, 'The Beginnings of Brazilian Anthropology: Jesuits and Tupinamba Cannibalism', *Journal of Anthropological Research*, 39 (1983), 147–78.

[32] This term was popularised in Gananath Obeyesekere, *Cannibal Talk: The Man-Eating Myth and Human Sacrifice in the South Seas* (Berkeley, 2005). While we follow the conventional usage of the word cannibalism here, we agree with Obeyesekere's point that the term 'cannibalism' might be better applied exclusively to examples of accusations of anthropophagy used to attack out-groups, while 'anthropophagy' should refer to the actual practice of eating human beings.

[33] John M. Monteiro, *Blacks of the Land: Indian Slavery, Settler Society, and the Portuguese Colonial Enterprise in South America*, trans. Barbara Weinstein and James Woodward (Cambridge, 2018), 9–10; Cristina Pompa, *Religião como Tradução: Missionários, Tupi e Tapuia no Brasil Colonial* (São Paulo, 2003); Pedro Puntoni, *A Guerra dos Bárbaros: Povos Indígenas e a Colonização do Sertão Nordeste do Brasil, 1650-1720* (São Paulo, 2002). On food culture and the colonisation of the Americas, see Rebecca Earle, '"If You Eat Their Food ...": Diets and Bodies in Early Colonial Spanish America', *American Historical Review*, 115 (2010), 688–713.

Figure 1. Theodor de Bry, *Dritte Buch Americae, darinn Brasilia … aus eigener erfahrun in Teutsch beschrieben* (Frankfurt, 1593). Image courtesy of the John Carter Brown Library. Reproduced under Creative Commons Licence.

Figure 2. Albert Eckhout, *Dance of the Tapuyas*, 1641, oil on canvas, 272 × 165 cm. Image courtesy of Nationalmuseet, Copenhagen. Reproduced under Creative Commons Licence.

counter the aggression of the Portuguese and the Tupinamba, although many likely had misgivings, especially those who saw Albert Eckhout's image of a Tapuya woman carrying severed limbs (Figure 3).[34]

Much less well known than Eckhout's painting is the fact that the Dutch brought the Tapuya into contact with a part of early modern Eurasia rarely associated with European expansion, Poland-Lithuania. For instance, an important figure in the Dutch conquest of Brazil was a Polish soldier in the service of the Dutch West India Company, Krzysztof Arciszewski (1592–1656).[35] Before being forced to return to Holland on charges of treason, Arciszewski had led a joint Dutch–Tapuya force to attack a Portuguese fort. He recorded these exploits in a now lost account reproduced in part by the Dutch humanist Gerardus Vossius (1577–1649), which describes how during the siege Arciszewski had the chance to observe a funeral feast of the Tapuya involving anthropophagic rituals. Sparing no gory detail, he described how the Tapuya prepared, roasted and consumed every part of their dead relatives in a highly dignified manner. Rather than allowing their loved ones to be consumed by maggots in the ground, the Tapuya preferred them to be buried within their

---

[34] Rebecca Parker Brienen, *Visions of Savage Paradise: Albert Eckhout, Court Painter in Colonial Dutch* (Amsterdam, 2006), 117–18; Yobenj Aucardo Chicangana-Bayona, 'Os Tupis e os Tapuias de Eckhout: o Declínio da Imagem Renascentista do Índio', *Varia História*, 24, no. 40 (2008), 591–612; Hal Langfur, 'Frontier/Fronteira: A Transnational Reframing of Brazil's Inland Colonization', *History Compass*, 12 (2018), 843–52; Pablo Ibáñez-Bonillo, 'Rethinking the Amazon Frontier in the Seventeenth Century: The Violent Deaths of the Missionaries Luis Figueira and Francisco Pires', *Ethnohistory*, 65 (2018), 575–95.

[35] For a relatively recent biography of Arciszewski, see Maria Paradowska, *Krzysztof Arciszewski: admirał wojsk holenderskich w Brazylii* (Wrocław, 2001).

Figure 3. Albert Eckhout, *Tapuya Woman*, 1641, oil on canvas, 264 × 159 cm. Image courtesy of Nationalmuseet, Copenhagen. Reproduced under Creative Commons Licence.

kin. Indeed, they considered themselves better than other tribes because they did not care for the meat of their enemies.[36] In stark contrast to the common view of the Tapuya propagated by both the Portuguese and other indigenous groups, Vossius agreed with the Tapuya's self-assessment, considering such practices, while far from Christian, to be natural and rational in the manner of ancient Mediterranean religions.[37]

Following this particular historical thread still further, we find that it tugs on the religious politics of Poland-Lithuania due to an unexpected confluence of events. In 1638, the Polish Sejm (or Parliament) ordered the closing of the school and printing press of the Polish Brethren in Raków, an Antitrinitarian group sometimes called the 'Socinians' after Fausto Sozzini (1539–1604).[38] Many prominent members found refuge in Amsterdam, and a well-connected ally in the person of Arciszewski who had invited a prominent Antitrinitarian, Andrzej Wissowatius the Elder (1608–1678), to sail with him into exile in Brazil. Indeed, Arciszewski thought, the Tapuya would not only leave the Brethren alone (unlike the religious and political authorities in Poland-Lithuania), but would also be more open to converting to their version of Christianity due to the pristine simplicity of their own religion. In addition, the Socinians were often called 'cannibals' by both their Catholic and Protestant adversaries. A lapsed Antitrinitarian himself, Arciszewski may have imagined a natural comradery between these two much-maligned groups.[39]

A large early modern polity without overseas colonies, Poland-Lithuania rarely appears in accounts of the transatlantic encounter. However, the multi-religious, multi-ethnic commonwealth belongs to one of the manifold 'Europes' that were at once connected to and isolated from other parts of the early modern world. Indeed, being 'European' did not necessarily entail being a globe-trotting imperialist; not being born into an imperial 'European' state did not automatically mean being remote from empire. The discourse of 'cannibalism' did not always serve as a justification for colonialism, or a tool of Western self-critique. For members of such Europes, this discourse could also open up new pathways for belonging, or even a means to salvation for a persecuted minority. In the end, however, these plans did not come to fruition. After

---

[36] As related in Gerardus Joannes Vossius, *De theologia gentili, et physiologia Christiana; sive de origine ac progressv idololatriae* (Amsterdam, 1668), 28–34. For an attempted reconstruction of the contents of Arciszewski's now lost journal, see Antoni Danysz, 'Pamiętnik Krzysztofa Arciszewskiego z pobytu w Brazylii', *Rocznik Towarzystwa Przyjaciol Nauk w Poznaniu*, 21 (1895), 421–32.

[37] These views can be found in contemporary accounts like Caspar Barlaeus, *Rerum per octennium in Brasilia et alibi gestarum* (Amsterdam, 1647).

[38] For an overview of the Polish Brethren and their broader influence, see Piotr Wilczek, *Polonia Reformata: Essays on the Polish Reformation(s)* (Göttingen, 2016).

[39] Stanisław Cynarski (ed.), *Raków - ognisko arianizm* (Cracow, 1968). References to this venture were made in Wissowatius's biography, *Anonymi Epistola, exhibens vitae ac mortis Andreae Wissowatii nec non ecclesiarum vnitariorum eius tempore breuem historiam*, which was published in a collection of Polish Brethren and Antitrinitarian writings: Christopher Sandius, *Bibliotheca antitrinitariorum* (Freistadt, 1684), 232.

Arciszewski, few early modern Poles found their way to Brazil. Connectivity could ebb and flow.

Another non-European 'Europe' where American (although not necessarily Tapayu) cannibalism was chewed over was the Ottoman metropolis of Istanbul. There, the great encyclopedist Kātib Çelebi (1609–1657) composed a monumental geographical work, entitled *Cihānnümā*, that combined the most up-to-date Islamic and Christian European knowledge of the day. The latter was made available to him by a mysterious French convert to Islam named Shaikh Meḥmed İḫlāṣī who produced translations of Mercator's *Atlas Minor* and Ortelius's *Theatrum orbis terrarum*, as well as works by Philippus Cluverius (1580–1622), Giovanni Lorenzo d'Anania (1545–1609), Giacomo Gastaldi (1500–1566) and Jodocus Hondius (1563–1612). Drawing on this broad source base, the *Cihānnümā* notes the presence of cannibals on the Caribbean islands of Dominica and Marie-Galante, as well as their extensive presence in the Indian Ocean and Malay Archipelago, including the Solomon Islands, where 'people are savages and cannibals. They do not interact with anyone. They paint their bodies in motley colours and have thick skins. They go around naked.' Many, but not all, of these accounts of cannibals are taken from 'Frankish' writers, since Islamic geographers had long recognised the existence of 'cannibal countries'. This included the island of Khālūs in the Indian Ocean where, Çelebi reported, 'people are supposedly naked cannibals and its soil is a silver mountain.'[40] While only partly geographically European, Ottoman scholars too adopted the practice of 'cannibal talk' about the peoples of the western hemisphere, which squared neatly with long-standing Islamic traditions of writing about the anthropophagic inhabitants of distant islands.

Other loose 'threads' around the Tapuya worth pulling also link alleged Brazilian cannibalism to other places and phenomena within the context of another meta-geographical category: the Iberian world. More than the sum total of the Spanish and Portuguese empires, the Iberian world is conventionally understood as the interrelated series of kingdoms, viceroyalties, alliances, entrepôts and missions that were united by global Catholicism, certain Iberian cultural practices and usually (but not always) allegiance to Iberian monarchs.[41] Purported cannibals in the Americas like the Tapuya engaged simultaneously as insiders and outsiders in this space, serving as occasional allies of both the Portuguese and the Dutch depending on where they saw their interests. Though Iberian colonisers might have viewed such 'cannibalistic' groups in the Americas as the ultimate outsiders, the reality of interactions and encounters proved more complicated. This kind of cooperation could even lead to the sort of West-to-East indigenous mobility that historians are only

---

[40] Kātib Çelebi, *An Ottoman Cosmography: Translation of Cihānnümā*, ed. Robert Dankoff and Gottfried Hagen (Leiden, 2021), 116 (Caribbean), 132 (Solomon Islands), 135 (Gilolo Island), 139 (Selebe), 140 (Ambon), 142 (Andaman), 144–5 (Sumatra), 152 (*Khālūs*), 179 (Ania).

[41] For redefinitions of the Iberian world, see Bartolomé Yun-Casalilla, *Iberian World Empires and the Globalization of Europe 1415-1668* (Basingstoke, 2019); Pedro Cardim, Tamar Herzog et al. (eds.), *Polycentric Monarchies: How Did Early Modern Spain and Portugal Achieve and Maintain a Global Hegemony?* (Eastbourne, 2012).

now beginning to reconstruct, as happened in 1641 when several hundred Tapuya warriors took part in the Dutch capture of Portuguese Luanda. This led to a seven-year Dutch occupation of this important slave-trading port, although it was decided not to recruit more indigenous Brazilian forces into Dutch forces since most of the 1641 group did not survive the round trip.[42]

Of course, from an African perspective the arrival of the Tapuya was not the first appearance of suspected cannibals on the African coast, for slave-trading Europeans had long been thought to be man-eaters as they had a voracious appetite for human beings.[43] Both European and African actors also accused certain African ethnic groups of cannibalism. The most feared of these were the mysterious Jaga, a poorly understood conglomeration of cannibalistic marauders in central Africa, divided by Joseph Miller into Jaga in the Kongo and Imbangala in Angola, although recent scholarship has questioned this distinction. What is undeniable, however, is that their strategy of guerrilla warfare centred on mobile military camps (*kilombo*) combined with eating, or threatening to eat, their enemies proved so effective that it was mimicked by other groups who wished to prevail in the chaotic decades of the early seventeenth century.[44] Such soldiers even appeared in the army of Queen Njinga of Ndongo (1583–1663), with whom the Dutch concluded a treaty following the capture of Luanda by the aforementioned Dutch–Tapuya force. As Capuchin missionaries seized during her invasion of Kongo following the departure of the Dutch in 1648 reported:

They were taken to a hut, or straw house. Entering it they saw a great fire, and some soldiers who were roasting and smoking the legs, arms and ribs of those killed in battle. Other soldiers were like butchers cutting the meat from the bodies to eat them. They left that spectacle stunned, half dead and shocked to see such horrible food; they left the house with tears and sighs, saying that under no circumstances would they settle into it, not among such an inhuman and cruel people. They then informed the Queen, who ordered them to be brought to her presence and told them: 'Fathers, I and my captains do not eat human meat, but the soldiers do. Do not be frightened; it is their custom'. She ordered them to be placed in lodgings in a barrack not far from hers, and then she sent

---

[42] Lodewijk Hulsman, 'Brazilian Indians in the Dutch Republic: The Remonstrances of Antonio Paraupaba to the States General in 1654 and 1656', *Itinerario*, 29 (2005), 51–78, at 63; Nancy E. Van Deusen, *Global Indios: The Indigenous Struggle for Justice in Sixteenth-Century Spain* (Durham, NC, 2015).

[43] William D. Piersen, 'White Cannibals, Black Martyrs: Fear, Depression, and Religious Faith as Causes of Suicide among New Slaves', *Journal of Negro History*, 62 (1977), 147–59; John K. Thornton, 'Cannibals, Witches, and Slave Traders in the Atlantic World', *William and Mary Quarterly*, 60 (2003), 273–94.

[44] Jared Staller, *Converging on Cannibals: Terrors of Slaving in Atlantic Africa, 1509-1670* (Athens, OH, 2019); Joseph C. Miller, 'The Imbangala and the Chronology of Early Central African History', *Journal of African History*, 13 (2009): 549–74; José Rivair Macedo, 'Jagas, Canibalismo e "Guerra Preta": os Mbangalas, entre o Mito Europeu e as Realidades Sociais da África Central do Século XVII', *História* (São Paulo), 32 (2013), 53–78.

them a little game with one of her maids so they could eat meat. The maid told them on behalf of the Queen, her lady, that she had sent them this gift, which was the meat she gave her own children so they could be sure that it was not human flesh, and every day at the requisite time she sent them such a dish with her own maid.[45]

While the missionaries were horrified at the mere sight of it, such real or imagined cannibalism was also not necessarily a barrier to cooperation if it served Christian purposes. Indeed, the Portuguese fleet entered into an alliance with a purportedly cannibalistic African group, the Zimba, when they took on the Ottomans near Mombasa in 1589 in an effort to disrupt the empire's influence in the Indian Ocean.[46] This was far from a one-off event. The governor of Angola, Luís Mendes de Vasconcelos (1542–1623), had already used Imbangala troops against the kingdom of Ndongo during the war of 1617 to 1621. During the fighting, tens of thousands of slaves would be captured, including importantly the score or so who were eventually transported to Virginia in 1619 where they became the first documented African slaves in British North America, an event that is rarely linked to cannibalism in the growing number of studies of this foundational moment in Anglo-American slavery.[47]

Following the thread of Tapuya cannibalism through the Iberian world ultimately takes us to East Asia, where Jesuit cartography brought European visions of Tapuya anthropophagy in Brazil to Chinese and Japanese literati – whether sympathetic to Christianity or not. For instance, the widely circulated world map of Matteo Ricci and his Chinese co-author Li Zhizao 李之藻 included an extensive excursus on Brazil which it described as a country

---

[45] Antonio de Teruel, *Descripción narrativa de la misión seráfica de los Padres Capuchinos y sus progresos en el Reino de Congo*, Biblioteca Nacional de España, ms 3533, 90: 'Llevaron los a una chosa, o casa de paja. Entrando en ella vieron un grande fuego, y algunos soldados que estaban asando y ahumando piernas, brazos y costillas de los muertos en aquella batalla, y otros que estaban como carniceros cortando la carne de los cuerpos para cenarse en ellos. Quedaron con aquel espectáculo atonitos, y como medio difuntos y lastimados de ver tan horrorosa comida, se salieron de la casa con lagrimas y suspiros, diciendo que por ningún caso avian de aposentarse en ella, ni entre gente tan inhumana y cruel. Dieron luego aviso de la Reyna, que los mando traer a su presencia y les dijo: Padres yo y mis capitanes no comemos carne humana, sino los soldados: no se espanten que estan acostumbrados a ella. Dio orden los alojassen en una barraca no lejos de la suya. Y ahora de comer carne les embió un poco carne de venado con una de sus donzellas, que de parte les dijo: que la Reyna, la señora embiava aquel regalo a sus hijos que comiesen con toda seguridad, de que no era carne humana y todos los días a sus horas les embió con la propia criada semejante plato.' Linda M. Heywood, *Njinga of Angola: Africa's Warrior Queen* (Cambridge, MA, 2017), 166–8.

[46] Giancarlo Casale, 'Global Politics in the 1580s: One Canal, Twenty Thousand Cannibals, and an Ottoman Plot to Rule the World', *Journal of World History*, 18 (2007), 267–96; Eric Allina, 'The Zimba, the Portuguese, and Other Cannibals in Late Sixteenth-Century Southeast Africa', *Journal of Southern African Studies*, 37 (2011), 211–27.

[47] John K. Thornton, 'The African Experience of the "20. and Odd Negroes" Arriving in Virginia in 1619', *William and Mary Quarterly*, 55 (1998), 421–34; Linda Heywood and John K. Thornton, 'In Search of the 1619 African Arrivals: Enslavement and Middle Passage', *Virginia Magazine of History and Biography*, 127 (2017), 200–11; Paul Musselwhite et al. (eds.), *Virginia 1619: Slavery and Freedom in the Making of English America* (Chapel Hill, 2019).

Figure 4. Matteo Ricci and Li Zhizao, *Map of the Ten Thousand Countries of the Earth* (坤輿萬國全圖, *kunyu wanguo quantu*), 1602. Reproduced by Wikimedia Commons from an original in Kano Collection, Tohoku University Library. Image in the Public Domain.

where they 'like to eat human flesh, but only of men not of women' (好食人肉，但食男不食女, *hao shi renrou, dan shi nan bushi nü*) (Figure 4). Frequent reprintings and borrowings meant that this cast a long shadow in Chinese accounts of the Americas, including the famous encyclopedia compiled in 1607 by Wang Qi and Wang Siyi, which described Brazil simply as 'eating-person country' (食人國, *shirenguo*) (Figure 5).[48] This characterisation of Brazil was later carried (via Korea) to the Mukden Palace in Later Jin

---

[48] Qiong Zhang, *Making the New World Their Own: Chinese Encounters with Jesuit Science in the Age of Discovery* (Leiden, 2015), 68, 280–4.

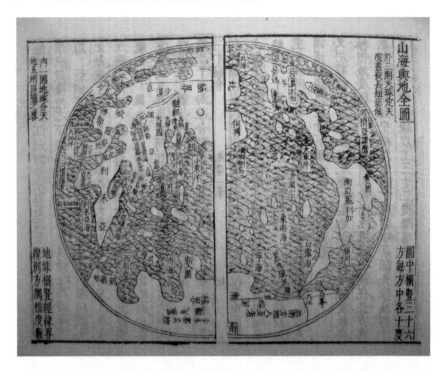

Figure 5. Wang Qi and Wang Siyi, *Collected Illustrations of the Three Realms* (三才圖會, *sancai tuhui*), 1609. Reproduced by Wikimedia Commons from an original in the Asian Library, University of British Columbia. Image in the Public Domain.

Khanate Manchuria, where bilingual court scholars read and annotated Ricci and Li's map in its draughty halls well before the 1644 conquest of Beijing. Here, however, the thread stops dead for practical reasons. Since the Manchu court was concerned primarily with the areas in its immediate imperial purview, their cartographic and ethnographic interest in the western hemisphere was limited to twice transliterating the name for South America from Chinese into Manchu. Early modern entanglement was far from limitless.[49]

Looking beyond continental East Asia, we find that Ricci's map (and related Jesuit sources) was also read and copied in Japan (Figure 6), where it later found its way into an important eighteenth-century encyclopedic work by the neo-Confucian geographer Nishikawa Joken 西川如見 (1648–1724), which featured an 'eating-person country' (Figure 7).[50] There is also evidence that

[49] Florin-Stefan Morar, 'Relocating the Qing in the Global History of Science: The Manchu Translation of the 1603 World Map by Li Yingshi and Matteo Ricci', *Isis*, 109 (2018), 673–94.

[50] Nishikawa Joken 西川如見, *Zoho Kai Tsushoko* 増補華夷通商考, 5 kan 巻 (Kyoto, 1708), 44–5: 好ンデ人ノ肉つ喰. It has recently been suggested that Nishikawa Joken borrowed more directly from the geographical works of Giulio Aleni, although the influence of Ricci's map cannot be excluded: Rômulo da Silva Ehalt, 'Gândavo na China, Índios no Japão. A leitura de um confucionista japonês sobre a colonização do Brasil (s. XVII e XVIII)', in *Diversos orientes*, ed. Andre Bueno (Rio de Janeiro), 91–102.

Figure 6. *Bankoku-sōzu*, 1671. Image courtesy of the Bayerische Staatsbibliothek München, (cod.jap. 4, Nagasaki, 1671). Image in the Public Domain.

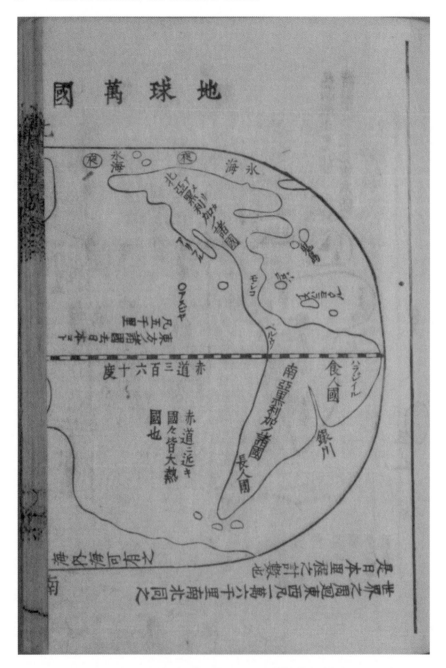

Figure 7. Nishikawa Joken 西川如見, *Zoho Kai Tsushoko* 増補華夷通商考, 3 kan 巻 (Kyoto: Kansetsudō, 1708), 3. Reproduced with the permission of Waseda University Library, Tokyo.

Figure 8. Arnold Florent an Langren, *Delineatio omnium orarum totius australis partis Americae.* Image courtesy of the Bibliothèque Nationale de France. Image in the Public Domain.

it circulated alongside the engravings of Arnold Florent an Langren (1580–1644) that accompanied Jan Huyghen van Linschoten's famous *Itinerario* (Figure 8).[51] These influenced an anonymous folding screen produced around the year 1600 by Christian Japanese artists trained by the Jesuit master Giovanni Niccolò (1560–1626). On one side of this is an image of the Battle of Lepanto modelled on a Renaissance engraving of the Battle of Zama in the Second Punic War. On the other side is a world map with ethnographic vignettes of the peoples of each region (Figure 9).[52] While most of these feature one man and one woman, the largest depicts eight dark-skinned and naked 'Brazilians' (ふらしるの人, *burajiru no hito*) of various ages who are dismembering, roasting and eating a lighter-skinned body in a forest. This was produced for display either in the home of a wealthy Japanese Christian, or in one of the seminaries that the Society of Jesus began constructing from the 1580s onwards. However, while the object survived into the modern period, the connections between southern Japan and the Iberian world would soon be violently severed. Following the final proscription of Christianity in 1614, most of the Christian artists fled Japan. In other words, the global fabric began to unravel.

---

[51] Helen Wallis, 'The Influence of Father Ricci on Far Eastern Cartography', *Imago Mundi*, 19 (1965), 38–45; Elke Papelitzky, 'A Description and Analysis of the Japanese World Map Bankoku Sōzu in Its Version of 1671 and Some Thoughts on the Sources of the Original Bankoku Sōzu', *Journal of Asian History*, 48 (2014), 15–59.

[52] Grace A. H. Vlam, 'Western-Style Secular Painting in Momoyama Japan' (Ph.D. thesis, University of Michigan, 1976), 28–31; Radu Leca, 'Brazilian Cannibals in Sixteenth-Century Europe and Seventeenth-Century Japan', *Comparative Critical Studies*, 11, Supp. (2014), 109–30; Stuart M. McManus, 'Imperial History without Provincial Loyalty? Reading Roman History in Renaissance Japan', *KNOW: A Journal on the Formation of Knowledge*, 3 (2019), 123–57.

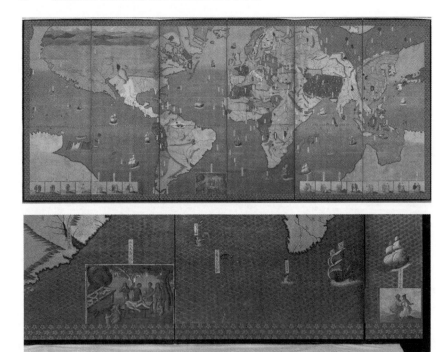

Figure 9. Reverse of folding screen *Battle of Lepanto and World Map* (upper) with image of Brazilian cannibals (lower). Courtesy of Kōsetsu Museum of Art, Kobe.

This petering-out of discussions of Tapuya endo-cannibalism on the edges of East Asia, however, was not caused by the alien nature of these reports. Indeed, there was an extensive pre-existing tradition of attributing cannibalistic tendencies to immoral peoples, both nearby and distant. Among Chinese literati, human-eating had long been a byword for the worst possible society, echoing the words of Mencius that:

> If the Ways of Yang and Mo do not cease, and the Way of Confucius is not made evident, then evil doctrines will dupe the people, and obstruct benevolence and righteousness. If benevolence and righteousness are obstructed, that leads animals to devour people. I am afraid that people will begin to devour one another (人將相食, *ren jiangxiang shi*)![53]

The Ways of Yang and Mo referred to here are the self-interest of Yang Zhu (denying the supremacy of the emperor) and the impartial universality (as opposed to filial piety) of Mozi, both of which Confucians branded as being as unnatural as eating human flesh.

---

[53] *Mengzi*, 3B9. L. I. Jinglin, 'Mencius' Refutation of Yang Zhu and Mozi and the Theoretical Implication of Confucian Benevolence and Love', *Frontiers of Philosophy in China*, 5 (2010), 155–78.

This is not to say that cannibalism was just a literary trope useful merely for ornamenting philosophical speculation. Chinese literary and historical sources provide wide-ranging examples of both survival anthropophagy and ritualistic endo-cannibalism, with the latter mirror of Tapuya practices arguably being an extreme form of orthodox Confucian filial piety.[54] Later, Qing authorities would also be greatly concerned about unnatural religious rituals that bordered on cannibalism.[55] Rumours of anthropophagy appear too in foreign accounts of premodern China. Already in the tenth century, Abū Zayd al-Sīrāfī noted the prevalence of cannibalism as a punishment among Chinese warlords of the Five Dynasties and Ten Kingdoms period:

> The warlords, acting neither with the king's blessing nor at his bidding, supported each other in their quest for further power: when a stronger one besieged a weaker, he would conquer his territory, annihilate everything in it, and eat all the defeated warlord's people, cannibalism being permissible for them according to their legal code, for they trade in human flesh in their markets.
>
> On top of all this, they extended the hand of injustice against merchants coming to their land. And, in addition to the harm done to the merchants, Arab captains and shipowners began to be subjected to injustices and transgressions. The Chinese placed undue impositions on merchants, seized their property by force, and sanctioned practices in which the custom of former times would in no way have allowed them to engage. Because of this, God – exalted be His name – withdrew His blessings altogether from the Chinese.[56]

This providential view of history that had God punish ungrateful cannibals mirrors European accounts of geopolitical struggles in the Atlantic. Like later Renaissance European writers, Abū Zayd al-Sīrāfī also marshals examples from Greco-Roman antiquity to describe the situation, including a comparison between China and Persia, which, he notes, began to collapse following the conquests of Alexander the Great. Following the threads of Brazilian anthropophagy, therefore, reveals degrees of convergence and divergence between the Atlantic world and Asia that the traditional historiographical division of labour has tended to conceal or ignore.

Furthermore, accusations of cannibalism were being levelled at the Portuguese in Macau just as they were spreading their ideas about man-eating groups in the Americas. For instance, the official history of the Ming dynasty (明史, *Mingshi*) compiled during the early Qing states quite clearly:

---

[54] The most extensive English-language summary of Chinese sources and scholarship on cannibalism is Key Ray Chong, *Cannibalism in China* (Wakefield, NH, 1990).

[55] Philip A. Kuhn, *Soulstealers: The Chinese Sorcery Scare of 1768* (Cambridge, MA, 1990), 91–2

[56] Tim Mackintosh-Smith and James E. Montgomery (eds.), *Two Arabic Travel Books: Accounts of China and India* (New York, 2014), 69–71.

Portugal is adjacent to Malacca. During the reign of Emperor Zhengde, Portugal occupied Malacca and expelled their King. In the thirteenth year of Zhengde (1518), they sent a diplomatic corps, including *jiabidanmo* [i.e. the Portuguese *capitão mor*], to pay tribute with gifts, and asked for a conferment of nobility. This is the reason why his name is known. After they paid their tribute, they were ordered to leave. However, they did not leave and stayed in China for a long time. They plundered, and even kidnapped children and ate them (至掠小兒為食, *zhilüe xiao'er wei shi*).[57]

Here, the *Mingshi* presumably relied on earlier accounts by local literati who maintained that the Portuguese were guilty of kidnapping, steaming and eating children, just like the anthrophagic people of the semi-mythical tributary states near Java that frequently appear in Chinese geographical works.[58] Indeed, this was an association that the Chinese shared with early Arabic trading accounts from the Indian Ocean, which also engaged in cannibal talk about Java and the nearby islands.[59] All writers agreed that such 'barbarians' should be avoided by all but the most avaricious merchants, a reminder that connectivity was a double-edged sword that thrust historical actors apart just as it beckoned them together. Accusations of cannibalism were one way to create this sort of distance.

In addition, interesting connections and comparisons do not negate the fact that many areas remained disconnected from the news of Tapuya cannibalism, from central Asia to Oceania, just as some areas like Japan were at one point integrated and at others much less so. These gaps and interruptions are important parts of the history too: it is hard to argue that the lack of direct connections eliminates a continent from the map. It also does not mean that these areas did not feature acts of cannibalism or the marshalling of a discourse of cannibalism. While anthropologists continue to debate whether anthropophagy was a long-standing and institutionalised practice in early modern Australia, there are certainly numerous accounts of it from the nineteenth century. These may or may not have been separate from the burial practices later observed in the Upper Mary River area of Queensland that involved dismembering, defleshing and then burying the dead, with the scraped bones being distributed among relatives. On the basis of the limited evidence, one leading anthropologist has concluded that anthropophagy likely took place, although only *in extremis*. Moreover, the claims by later aboriginal informants that they themselves did not practise it, but other groups did, was likely 'an unconscious but effective mechanism for maintaining self-identity, social superiority, and "humanness" at the cost of the identity, social status, and "humanness" of aliens'.[60] Such conclusions offer an important reminder

---

[57] 明史 *Mingshi* (Beijing, 1974–85), 8430.

[58] Jin Guo Ping and Wu Zhiliang, 'A (Des)canibalização dos Portugueses', *Revista de Cultura* (Macau), 16 (2005), 94–104.

[59] Mackintosh-Smith and Montgomery (eds.), *Two Arabic Travel Books*, 26–27.

[60] Michael Pickering, 'Consuming Doubts: What Some People Ate? What Some People Swallowed', in *The Anthropology of Cannibalism*, ed. Laurence Goldman (Westport, CT, 1999), 51–74, at 56.

to historians with global ambitions that one apparently common trait or practice might actually be masking another.

A final advantage of bringing disconnected contexts into the early modern story is to provide a fuller understanding of later connections, as the case of Australia shows. While conventional written evidence is non-existent before the mid-eighteenth century, there was an explosion of 'cannibal talk' in nineteenth- and twentieth-century Australia as British colonialism brought the Atlantic discourse to the continent. This was one of a number of justifications used for the unequal treatment of aboriginal people, another poignant reminder that globalisation has also produced both winners and losers.[61] Given this sorry history, there is an even greater need to understand both the larger history of cannibal talk and the parallel (although disconnected) development of precolonial Australia in order not to be taken in by later reports, which should be seasoned with more than a pinch of decolonial salt.

In sum, if we follow the thread of Tapuya cannibalism, we see that it had a history far beyond the transatlantic context with which it is normally associated. Indeed, the standard narrative omits the fact that the idea of Tapuya cannibalism crossed a number of linguistic borders, stopped at others and interacted unevenly with long-standing Ottoman, Polish, West African, Islamic and Chinese ideas about 'cannibal countries'. In almost all contexts, these accusations of consuming human flesh were used to highlight the alien nature of distant people whose transgressive dietary choices rendered them 'uncivilised' by the standards of various traditions. Indeed, Muslim merchants and Confucian scholars had long accused each other of being cannibals, the often-maligned Javanese appear as cannibals in texts in multiple languages and Europeans were also accused of anthropophagy in both South China and West Africa. The case of the Tapuya, therefore, reveals that cannibalism has a history that can be viewed from multiple perspectives, of which that offered by familiar European-produced images and European-language sources from the Atlantic world is just one, and in the light of other contemporary examples a rather predictable one at that. Of course, this is not a call to relativism. Cannibal talk was certainly misused in the Atlantic world. Rather, it is an attempt to underline that we have fallen prey to an implicit Eurocentrism in framing the question with this particular meta-geography.

As this case study shows, a (dis)entangled approach is particularly valuable when seeking the previously hidden threads that link Tapuya cannibalism to not only other parts of the Atlantic world as traditionally conceived, but also other less well-known contexts, and the ways these pull (or not) on other parts of the wider early modern fabric. While rightly underlining that news of the Tapuya circulated widely in the Ricci–Li map and other maps in East Asia influenced by Jesuit cartography, it also encourages us to contemplate why the thread stops dead at the gates of the Mukden Palace, where the map was annotated in Manchu. Similarly, while there is little evidence of how the involvement of Tapuya troops in the 1641 Dutch seizure of

---

[61] 'Cannibalism and Infanticide in Australia', *London Journal*, 7, 163, 1848 (1909), 74–5; Obeyesekere, *Cannibal Talk*, 193–222.

Luanda was received locally, a (dis)entangled history approach encourages us to extend our gaze inland where Queen Njinga (with whom the Dutch soon signed a treaty) also made use of allegedly cannibalistic Imbangala troops. Even entirely disconnected contexts like early modern Australia appear on the (dis)entangled map, providing important comparative context for later developments.

Finally, it is worth stressing that this short study of Tapuya cannibal talk is also just one example of what a (dis)entangled history might look like, and is perhaps not even the best possible example. But we hope this is a starting point. The methodology could just as easily have been applied to the reception of the Great Ming Code, South Asian ideas about caste, or the hot cross bun. While their subject, focus and meta-geographical ambitions are all flexible, (dis)entangled histories share an attention to both the extent and limits of historical connectedness and an inbuilt scepticism about how we should divide up the 'early modern world'. Connections waxed and waned, and some parts of the world were left seemingly untouched by larger trends. We should celebrate the fact that historians have generated important insights on some of the increasing connections across continents and oceans between 1500 and 1800. Yet, we should not write out those people and places, perhaps the majority of them, that also experienced divides, blockages and gaps. This is sometimes recognised in theory, but very rarely seen in practice. As net beneficiaries for the most part from more recent globalisation, historians can perhaps be forgiven for this, although they should not let their enthusiasm for a particular vision of humanity's future lead them to ignore important elements of humanity's past. Although devoid of the opportunities for cross-cultural communication and hybridity, disconnection is not a priori less desirable than connection. Furthermore, not every connection had universally positive results. Just ask aboriginal Australians. (Dis)entangled history, we hope, might offer a way to square this circle. It is possible to write global history without falling prey to 'globaloney'.

Acknowledgements. This is the David Berry Prize Essay awarded for Stuart M. McManus, 'Scots at the Council of Ferrara–Florence and the Background to the Scottish Renaissance', *Catholic Historical Review*, 106 (2020), 347–70. The essay itself has its origins in a conference, entitled '(Dis)entangling Global Early Modernities, 1300–1800', held at Harvard University in 2017. The authors would like to thank the following scholars for their participation and support at various stages of the writing process: Gregory Afinogenov, David Armitage, Bryan Averbuch, Alexander Bevilacqua, Ann Blair, Jorge Cañizares-Esguerra, Ananya Chakravarti, Roger Charier, Devin Fitzgerald, Anja-Silvia Goeing, Tamar Herzog, Darrin McMahon, Charles Maier, Eugenio Menegon, Laura Mitchell, Holly Shaffer, Nir Shafir, Carolien Stolte, Heidi Tworek, Anand Venkatkrishnan, Xin Wen and Kristen Windmuller-Luna.

Funding statement. The research for this article was partially supported by a grant from the Research Grants Council of the Hong Kong Special Administrative Region, China (grant number CUHK 24612619). The authors also want to thank their research assistants.

Cite this article: McManus SM, Tworek MT (2022). A (Dis)entangled History of Early Modern Cannibalism: Theory and Practice in Global History. *Transactions of the Royal Historical Society* 32, 47–72. https://doi.org/10.1017/S0080440122000081

Transactions of the RHS (2022), **32**, 73–91
doi:10.1017/S0080440122000019

ARTICLE

Popular Propaganda: John Heywood's Wedding Ballad and Mary I's Spanish Match

Jenni Hyde (iD)

Department of History, Lancaster University, Lancaster, UK
Email j.hyde2@lancaster.ac.uk

Abstract

The text of John Heywood's wedding ballad for Mary I and Philip of Spain, *A Balade spe-cifienge partly the maner,* has been underestimated for many years. It is criticised for the poor quality of its poetry and lambasted for its tortured imagery. Instead, this article re-evaluates the ballad as a highly effective popular song intended to spread propaganda defending the queen's Spanish match. It argues that the song performed an excellent job of addressing complex constitutional issues through a quintessentially popular genre, while at the same time successfully overcoming the problem of fitting new words to a pre-existing tune. Furthermore, it is proposed that the song was deliberately set to the melody from Henry VIII's ballad 'Pastyme with good companye' and, by drawing on the latest research into cultures of creativity and examining what resonances the tune would have had for its listeners, it suggests that the potential multivalency of the melody was crucially important for understanding the song and its reception.

Keywords: Mary I; ballads; John Heywood; Philip I of England; song

If ever there was a royal wedding which needed political spin, it was Mary Tudor's marriage to Philip of Spain in the summer of 1554. It brought an end to a tumultuous first year for England's pioneering queen regnant. Mary's accession to the throne the previous summer had been far from straightforward. She was challenged by a Protestant coup organised by the Duke of Northumberland that sought to place his daughter-in-law, Lady Jane Grey, on the throne. Support for Jane quickly melted away, but the rule of an unmarried queen raised practical constitutional questions that were only made more complex by Mary's determination to marry. The problem was compounded by her choice of husband: rather than a good Englishman, she chose Philip of Spain who was the son of Mary's first cousin, the Holy Roman Emperor, Charles V, and a member of the most powerful family in Europe, with an empire stretching halfway across the globe. Their wedding at Winchester Cathedral on 25 July 1554 took place in the face of fierce opposition. MPs and privy councillors had expressed their dismay that Mary had chosen to marry someone from outside her realm. Even her Lord Chancellor, the ever-loyal Stephen Gardiner, had voiced his concerns, preferring that Mary should marry one of her own countrymen. Sir Thomas Wyatt, meanwhile, had resorted to open rebellion.

Opponents of the Spanish match feared that, as a female, Mary would become subject to her husband the moment they were wed. The imperial ambassador, Simon Renard, reported the House of Commons' belief that, regardless of any restrictions placed on Philip, once he was married he would effectively be king, with all the powers that title brought with it. He could subjugate England to imperial authority with impunity, drawing the country into expensive wars and robbing it of its wealth. Any child of the marriage would be entitled to a place in the Spanish succession, while the queen herself might be spirited out of England by 'husbandly tyranny'.[1]

Up stepped John Heywood to help Mary win over her subjects to her cause. A gifted musician and wordsmith, his attachment to the old religion made him her devoted champion. To celebrate the wedding he penned and printed *A Balade specifienge partly the maner, partly the matter, in the most excellent meetyng and lyke mariage betwene our Soueraigne Lord, and our Soueraigne Lady, the Kynges and Queenes highnes.*[2] Once dismissed by critics as 'poor in poetry' and 'preposterous' in its imagery, it earns, for example, only one rather disdainful page in Robert Bolwell's *The Life and Works of John Heywood*.[3] While more recent judgements have been less scornful, even Greg Walker, who devotes a chapter of his recent biography of Heywood to the ballad, was ultimately unconvinced of its merits, declaring it to be 'not wholly successful'.[4] But such conclusions fail to recognise the work's true nature: it is a song and, as such, it was not intended for recitation but for singing.

Mary's loyal balladeer

John Heywood was a multi-talented playwright, poet, epigrammist, player of virginals, and singing man. Born around 1496–7, probably in Coventry, it is conceivable that as a child he had sung treble as a chorister in the chapel royal. The first positive link we have between Heywood and the royal court is from 1519, when he was paid a salary as a member of the royal household, and by the following autumn he was receiving payment as one of the king's singing men. Later, he was employed as a player of the virginals and by

---

[1] Simon Renard to the Emperor, 17 Nov. 1553, in *Calendar of State Papers, Spain, Volume 11, 1553*, ed. Royall Tyler (1916), pp. 363–74, via *British History Online*, www.british-history.ac.uk/cal-state-papers/spain/vol11/pp363-374, accessed 5 March 2021.

[2] John Heywood, *A Balade specifienge partly the maner, partly the matter, in the most excellent meetyng and lyke Mariage betwene our Soueraigne Lord and our Soueraigne Lady, the Kynges and Queenes Highnes* (1554), English Short Title Catalogue (ESTC) S3934, http://ebba.english.ucsb.edu/ballad/36295/album, accessed 26 February 2021.

[3] Robert Bolwell, *The Life and Works of John Heywood* (New York, 1921), 56.

[4] Greg Walker, *John Heywood: Comedy and Survival in Tudor England* (Oxford, 2020), 396.

1525 he was one of the grooms of the household. For reasons unknown, it appears that he lost his job as a court musician in 1528.[5] Indeed, at this point he may even have been transferred to Princess Mary's household.[6]

Heywood was certainly consistently loyal to Mary. In 1534, he composed the congratulatory poem 'Give place, ye ladies' to praise the princess on the occasion of her eighteenth birthday.[7] During this period, the king's daughter was ostracised from court. Since Mary was under significant pressure to acknowledge the legitimacy of Henry's marriage to Anne Boleyn and reject papal authority, Heywood's composition suggests a genuine allegiance to Mary's cause as much as an attempt to gain patronage and favour. It is only during the late 1530s, however, that we can securely link Heywood with Princess Mary's household. Although his formal role, if indeed he had one, remains obscure, he appears several times in the household accounts.[8] Heywood also wrote and published at least two other ballads, one a patriotic song on the failure of Thomas Stafford's attempted rebellion in April 1557, *A breefe balet touching the traytorous takynge of Scarborow Castell*, and the other a song of social commentary called *A ballad against slander and detraction*.[9] In addition to his songs, Heywood published an extended allegorical poem, *The Spider and the Flie*, in 1556, which celebrated the royal couple as well as providing a political commentary on the defeat of Northumberland's coup and Philip and Mary's controversial religious policy of executing Protestant heretics. He was also called upon to lend a hand in the pageants which had greeted Mary at her coronation in 1553.[10] Alongside his loyalty to the queen, he remained a lifelong Catholic. During Mary's reign he was involved with a network of religiously conservative musicians centred upon the parish of St Mary-at-Hill, London. Finally, in July 1564 he left England for religious exile on the Continent, most likely to avoid taking the Elizabethan oath of allegiance.[11]

Heywood's political allegiance to the new queen was never in question, yet it seems his relationship was personal too. As Walker has reminded us,

---

[5] For a comprehensive biography, see Walker, *Heywood*.

[6] Andrew Ashbee, 'Groomed for Service: Musicians in the Privy Chamber at the English Court, c.1495–1558', *Early Music*, 25 (1997), 185–96, at 193.

[7] Walker, *Heywood*, 198–9.

[8] *Ibid.*, 20–2.

[9] *A breefe balet touching the traytorous takynge of Scarborow Castell* (1557), ESTC S3943, http://ebba.english.ucsb.edu/ballad/36296/image, accessed 5 March 2021; *A ballad against slander and detraction* (1562), ESTC S118129, http://ebba.english.ucsb.edu/ballad/37039/image, accessed 5 March 2021. *A ballad against slander and detraction* can be found in British Library Additional Manuscript 15233, which contains songs which seem to have been in circulation for more than twenty years (Louise Rayment, 'A Note on the Date of London, British Library, Additional Manuscript 15233', *Notes and Queries*, 59 (2012), 32–4). Other songs in favour of the Marian regime were written by William Forrest and Thomas Watertoune, amongst others, although there is little indication of whether these songs had official backing (see Jenni Hyde, *Singing the News: Ballads in Mid-Tudor England* (Abingdon, 2018, ch. 7).

[10] John Heywood, *The Spider and the Flie* (1556), STC (2nd edn) / 13308; Walker, *Heywood*, 276–7, 287.

[11] Louise Rayment, 'A New Context for the Manuscript of "Wit and Science"', *Early Theatre*, 17 (2014), 49–73; Walker, *Heywood*, 365.

Heywood knew the queen's tastes and was confident that he could amuse her when others might have shied away. He was comfortable enough to engage the monarch in witty banter. While still technically Supreme Head of the English Church, Mary reimposed priestly celibacy, meaning that priests who had married during Edward VI's reign now had to resign their positions or put aside their wives. Being informed of this by the queen herself, Heywood 'merrily aunswered, Your Grace must allow them Lemmans [lovers] then, for the Cleargie can not live without sawce'. On another occasion,

> He being asked of the saide Queene Mary, what winde blew him to the Court, answered her, Two specially, the one to see your Maiestie, We thanke you for that, said Queene Mary; But I pray you, what is the other? That your Grace (saide he) might see me.[12]

That Heywood was a known wit, there is no doubt; but by teasing his sovereign in this way his punchline shamelessly breached protocol and in anyone else would have 'risked causing career-ruining offence'.[13] Heywood knew his audience and was clearly confident that his sovereign would enjoy the repartee. We can be sure that Heywood's wedding ballad was likewise carefully tailored in all respects to appeal to the queen.

The consummate ballad

Broadside ballads such as *A Balade specifienge partly the maner* were multimedia material objects which exploded in popularity during the sixteenth century.[14] While their affordability can sometimes be overplayed, the fact remains that their price, ranging from ½d to 1d, was within the reach of everyone but the poorest in society, at least occasionally. It is nevertheless difficult to pin down their intended market. On the face of it, printed broadside ballads appear to have targeted a literate audience. Recent scholarship, however, has noted that even very long texts were intended to be 'voiced', or read aloud in some way.[15] Broadside ballads were simple enough to be sung by everyone, so they became potentially accessible to a much wider audience than the literate minority.

Of all the varieties of print in the Tudor marketplace, broadside ballads were some of the cheapest and easiest to produce. This meant that they could be published quickly to capitalise on newsworthy events. Certainly, this was a period when the print trade was undergoing significant change. On one hand, Philip and Mary oversaw the incorporation of the Company of

---

[12] William Camden, *Remaines of a greater worke, concerning Britain ...* (1605), ESTC S107408, 234.

[13] Walker, *Heywood*, 280–1.

[14] Patricia Fumerton and Anita Guerrini, 'Introduction: Straws in the Wind', in *Ballads and Broadsides in Britain, 1500–1800*, ed. Patricia Fumerton, Anita Guerrini and Kris McAbee (Farnham, 2010), 1–9, at 1. See also Tessa Watt, *Cheap Print and Popular Piety* (Cambridge, 1993); Christopher Marsh, *Music and Society in Early Modern England* (Cambridge, 2012); and Patricia Fumerton, *The Broadside Ballad in Early Modern England: Moving Media, Tactical Publics* (Philadelphia, 2021).

[15] See, for example, Jennifer Richards, *Voices and Books in the English Renaissance* (Oxford, 2019).

Stationers, which received a royal charter in 1557. Under the charter's terms, only printers who were members of the Company or who had received a crown privilege were allowed to publish printed material. Although not without problems, this system helped to establish a printer's rights to a particular work.[16] On the other hand, Mary (and later, Philip) attempted to control the flow of printed material through a series of proclamations, the first of which outlawed printing any texts without the queen's 'speciall licence in wry-tinge'.[17] Interestingly, an earlier draft of this proclamation had allowed for this licence to be granted verbally by the queen (something that was impractical to enforce), yet it seems likely that her personal involvement with the licensing process was soon replaced by the use of deputies appointed by the bishops.[18]

Indeed, a second versified description of the wedding was printed in 1554 by royal privilege. Hadrianus Junius's pamphlet, *Philippeis, seu, In nuptias diui Philippi*, printed by Thomas Berthelet, was in Latin throughout, suggesting that it was aimed at an elite and possibly international audience.[19] Heywood's wedding ballad, conversely, was in English and aimed at a domestic audience. It was printed by Wyllyam Ryddell, who the following year would print another panegyric ballad on Mary's supposed pregnancy.[20] Ryddell's name appears in the 1558 Stationers' Registers as the printer of several commercial ballads including 'The panges of love', 'Be mery good Jone', 'Hold the ancer fast' and 'The robbery at Gaddes Hill'.[21] This indicates that Heywood's wedding ballad was aimed at an equally popular audience.

As a physical object, the single surviving copy of *A Balade specifienge partly the maner* is hardly the world's most alluring broadside. Like many of the broadside ballads before the late 1560s, it has none of the ornamental characteristics which became commonplace by the end of the century, such as illuminated initial letters, woodcut images and decorative borders. Although it is undeniable that few of the surviving ballads from the decade 1550–60 include these features, it is also true that the majority can be found in the same collection – a single book in the Society of Antiquaries' library in London. The Society of Antiquaries' broadsides appear to have been cropped, however, so any decorative elements could have been removed. Even one of the earliest broadside ballads we have, *An elegy on the death of Henry VII*, displays many decorative features despite the heavy damage which left it a fragment.[22]

[16] 'The Stationers' Company and the London Book Trade', *Stationers' Register Online*, https://stationersregister.online/about?g=stationersCompany#stationersCompany, accessed 12 July 2021.

[17] *By the Quene the Quenes Highnes Well Remembrynge ...* (1553), ESTC S3751.

[18] Peter W. M. Blayney, *The Stationers' Company and the Printers of London, 1501-1557* (2 vols., 2013), II, 826–8.

[19] Hadrianus Junius, *Philippeis, seu, In nuptias diui Philippi* (1554), ESTC S107903.

[20] A surviving copy of this song, which indicates that Ryddell was the printer, can be found in manuscript 'The Ballad of Ioy, upon the publication of Q. Mary, Wife of King Philip, her being with child', Cambridge, Cambridge University Library, Registry guard book CUR 8, fo. 7.

[21] *A Transcript of the Registers of the Company of Stationers of London, 1554-1640 A.D*, ed. Edward Arber (3 vols., 1875), I, 96.

[22] *An elegy on the death of Henry VII* [1509], ESTC S111375.

Ballad singing was a profoundly physical and emotional experience, and the residue on the printed page remains the merest sketch of what that performance might have been. Ballads could be sung solo, but at the heart of the ballad is sociability. Both words and tunes were passed on from person to person by word of mouth. In fact, like many mid-sixteenth-century ballads, Heywood's wedding ballad does not even specify the tune to which it was to be sung: instead, it relies on the oral transmission of this information. Oral transmission is hardly ever recorded in the archive, yet it is key to unlocking songs' importance in early modern society: you did not need to be able to read to enjoy singing and hearing a ballad. This made them the perfect means to share and relish exciting news and entertainment.

Heywood's wedding ballad is no exception, as will become clear. His song opens by announcing that the new king, Philip (represented by the symbol of the Habsburg monarchy, the eagle), had travelled to England to be with Mary, who is represented both as England's lion and a lamb. As 'the eagle's heir', Philip flew to the rose 'both red and whight' of England, alighting in 'the lions boure, to bilde his nest' in July. The song goes on to describe the solemnising of the wedding before 'suche notable nobilitie'. The ballad then finishes with a prayer that everyone should demonstrate their allegiance to the 'lamblyke lyon, and lamblike burde' and to their Catholic faith.[23]

Despite its title, there is more to A Balade specifienge partly the maner than the simple description of a royal wedding. Heywood was trying to help others come to terms with female rule and the concomitant problem of whom Mary should marry – or if she should marry at all. He was attempting to reassure the queen's subjects that she would not be dominated by her foreign husband. For Heywood, Mary combined the feminine characteristics of a lamb with the masculine qualities of a lion, and a lion of England too. It was difficult enough for a patriarchal society to accept that a woman might govern the country alone, yet a queen regnant's situation was even more complicated if she chose to marry. The fact that she was part lion, and therefore masculine, meant that she would not, as per the norm, be overcome by her marriage to Philip. Instead, she would be a 'queenelie queene', and he a 'kinglie king'. Heywood's use of allegedly 'preposterous' imagery therefore goes to the heart of the ballad, as he attempts to explain why Mary's marriage to Philip was not only appropriate but also advantageous. It rendered this quixotic marriage safe for the country.

The emphasis on the construction of a nest for the royal couple not only implies that the pair planned to raise children to secure the future of the dynasty, but also that Philip intended to stay in England for the long term. This is echoed by his decision to remain for 'rype right rest'. Heywood presumably intended to set English minds at ease, suggesting that they would not be subject to an absentee sovereign. He emphasised that, despite the opposition to the match, all those who witnessed the event, both Spanish and English, were able to get along without argument:

Nombre so greate, in place so small
Nacions so manie, so different

---

[23] For a full analysis of the text, see Walker, Heywood, 288–301.

So sodenlie met, so agreed all
Without offensyve word let fall.[24]

As Walker has noted, this flies in the face of the extant accounts of the wedding's context, which suggest that there was more than a little rivalry and conflict between the English and the Spanish, not only in the streets but even within the royal court itself.[25]

Heywood went on to make further associations between the 'lamblike' sovereigns and the Lamb of Lambs, suggesting that God had blessed the pair's union 'That it may lyke that lorde on hie / In healthe and welth to prosper theese'. Finally, he urged his audience to 'Them and their lawes, love and obay' in order to bring the country together in unity, hoping that in return, the union would be blessed with a child to inherit the throne:

And that between these twayne and one
The thre and one, one once to sende
In one to knit us everichone
And to that one, such mo at ende
Graunte this good god, adding thie grace
To make us meete tobtayne this case.[26]

Heywood's convoluted imagery was not a sign of lack of inspiration. It was partly the unavoidable result of trying to make sense of the monarchical gender-crossing that resulted from the marriage of a queen who sat on the throne in her own right. In Walker's words, it was indeed 'a bold attempt to redefine her relationship with her spouse'.[27] Yet it is crucial to note that there were also *genre*-related reasons which resulted from the need to adapt high-flown constitutional ideas to a ballad, a quintessentially popular art form.

Far from being an ungainly, and therefore unsuccessful, composition, Heywood's patriotic song is, in fact, the consummate ballad. Despite the seriousness of its content, it is brilliantly successful as a song for an unlettered audience because it skilfully incorporates techniques which help the listener to remember the words. It is purposely repetitive at both a macro- and a micro-level. First and foremost, the stanza form and prosody repeat throughout. This has obvious advantages in allowing the words to be set to strophic music where the tune repeats over and over again. This in turn reinforces the mnemonic effect. Rhyme is also a form of repetition, when sounds at the ends of lines are repeated. Heywood's chosen rhyme scheme of *ababbcc* opens with

[24] Heywood, *A Balade specifienge partly the maner.*

[25] Walker, *Heywood*, 300–1.

[26] Heywood, *A Balade specifienge partly the maner*; Hyde, *Singing the News*, 169–71, expanded on in Jenni Hyde, 'Gender, Authority and the Image of Queenship in English and Scottish Ballads, 1553–1603', *History*, 105 (2020), 758–61; Walker, *Heywood*, ch. 13; Matthew Tibble, *Nicolaus Mameranus: Poetry and Politics at the Court of Mary Tudor* (Leiden, 2020), 71. Walker's book had not been released before my article in *History* was prepared for publication – any similarities between the readings of this ballad are therefore coincidental.

[27] Walker, *Heywood*, 289.

the standard 'ballad' rhyme scheme of *abab* which would have been familiar to everyone hearing it:

> The egles byrde hath spred his wings
> And from far of, hathe taken flyght
> In whiche meane way by no leurings
> On bough or braunch this birde wold light

Of course, we have already seen that themes and images, such as the eagle and lamb, recur throughout the song, but individual words and phrases also recur:

> So meete a matche in parentage
> So meete a matche in dignite
> So meete a matche in patronage
> So meete matche in benignite
> So macht from all malignite

Another notable feature of the song is the use of alliteration, itself another form of repetition:

> What matche may match more mete then this ...

> For that they lamblike be concurde
> The lamb of lambs, the lorde of lordes
> Let us lyke lambs ...

Many of these repetitions are deliberately placed on the stressed syllables in the poetic lines and musical phrases in order to impress them on the audience.

Devices such as these were essential to sixteenth-century ballads and indicate that the songs were generally aimed at an audience with limited literacy who relied instead on memory. Another master of the genre, William Elderton, also used them extensively. He too was used to providing entertainment at the Tudor court as well as producing broadside ballads.[28] His song *The Lamentation of Follie* regretted that

> Flatterie is the Forte of Fame,
> and trueth is troden downe:
> The innocent do beare the blame,
> the wicked winne renowne[29]

---

[28] See Hyder E. Rollins, 'William Elderton: Elizabethan Actor and Ballad Writer', *Studies in Philology*, 17 (1920), 199–245; and Hyde, *Singing the News*, 35.

[29] William Elderton, *The Lamentation of Follie* (1588), ESTC S121788, http://ebba.english.ucsb.edu/ballad/32228/image, accessed 5 March 2021.

while his *Newes from Northumberland* repeated not only the refrain, but the phrase 'You bragge':

> You bragge not of the almighties name,
> you bragge not of your Princes fame,
> You bragge of never a faithfull knight ...

> You bragge to see your countrey spoylde,
> you bragge to see poore men begilde,
> You bragge to see your brothers blood[30]

Not dissimilar to Heywood's use of dynastic imagery, this ballad on the Northern Rebellion of 1571 also invoked extended heraldic metaphors to characterise the high-born rebels, Charles Neville, Earl of Westmorland, and Thomas Percy, Earl of Northumberland.

But what was the point of these repetitive patterns? As propaganda in support of a marriage which not only faced considerable opposition, but also raised unheard-of constitutional questions, it was essential that Heywood use every weapon in his armoury to get his message across quickly, effectively and memorably. His song allows us to access 'the 'complex relationships ... between popular and learned culture'.[31] Poetic techniques such as those used by Heywood 'create rhythm (meter, rhyme), emphases and connections (rhyme, anaphora, assonance), and invite comparisons and contrasts (parallelism, stanzas, alliteration)'.[32] They also provide 'a way of adding levels of information without adding words'.[33] Moreover, all types of repetition act as constraints, reducing the 'memory load' and helping the audience to recall what it has heard.[34] This is critically important for the success of orally transmitted songs.[35] Ballads, in particular, make 'abundant use of all the kinds of repetition that occur within literary works, not to mention the repetitive features of music'.[36] Although printed, Heywood's ballad remains at its core oral literature and 'repetition is a direct consequence of [its] oral

---

[30] William Elderton, *Newes from Northumberland* (1569–70), ESTC S91819, http://ebba.english.ucsb.edu/ballad/36306/image, accessed 5 March 2021.

[31] Fumerton and Guerrini, 'Introduction', 8.

[32] Anna Christina Ribeiro, 'Intending to Repeat: A Definition of Poetry', *Journal of Aesthetics and Art Criticism*, 65 (2007), 189–201, at 192. Ribeiro raises an interesting distinction between poetry and song lyrics based on the writer's intent (the poet intends to write poetry, whereas the songwriter intends to write a song, p. 196). Nevertheless, I believe the intent here was to write a song which drew on poetic techniques to make it memorable.

[33] *Ibid.*, 200

[34] David C. Rubin, *Memory in Oral Traditions: The Cognitive Psychology of Epic, Ballads, and Counting-out Rhymes* (Oxford, 1995), 271.

[35] Joseph C. Nunes, Andrea Ordanini and Francesca Valsesia, 'The Power of Repetition: Repetitive Lyrics in a Song Increase Processing Fluency and Drive Market Success', *Journal of Consumer Psychology*, 25 (2015), 187–99.

[36] Bennison Gray, 'Repetition in Oral Literature', *Journal of American Folklore*, 84 (1971), 289–303, at 297.

nature'.[37] Heywood had to choose his words carefully, not only to fit his chosen metre, but also to hit home quickly with strong images that his audience could easily assimilate, whether or not they could read and despite the important political messages he needed to get across. He employed familiar heraldic and biblical imagery, made heavy use of repetition and parcelled it up in an entertaining, multimedia experience which explained how and why Philip and Mary's wedding was a bright new beginning for England. His wedding ballad might not be good literature, but it was certainly effective orature.

Identifying a tune

Given Heywood's propensity to repeat ideas of all sorts in the song, it seems possible that the tune he had in mind might also be recycled. Perhaps we should have been alerted to this earlier, as the song has a rather unusual seven-line stanza and metre. It is likely Heywood, like many musicians at both elite and popular levels, drew on an existing melody when he wrote his song, fitting his words to a tune he already knew. Writing words to a pre-existing *tune* is precisely what explains why some have dismissed this ballad as unimpressive as *poetry*. We have misunderstood its genre. Although the text needed to express the appropriate ideas, as words it was their metrical value that was of paramount importance. The process of setting words to music is 'first and foremost a discipline in sound: the poet has to make words to a pattern and, in a strophic song with several verses, to go on repeating that pattern'.[38] The resulting poetry was therefore a compromise between textual expression and metrical suitability. Nonetheless, setting new words to an *existing* tune magnifies this process because 'words [were] straightjacketed into the metre of the music'.[39] The implication is that words were chosen because they fitted the existing rhythms. While it is true that Heywood, as a talented writer – and musician – was ultimately looking for unity between words and music, the fact that he was prepared to select his words according to the tune's metre – rather than adapting the melody to fit the words – suggests that the melody was itself a vital part of the song's message.

Although it was common for sixteenth-century printed ballads not to indicate the tune to which they were sung, it seems that Heywood's chosen melody also had something to say for itself. Only a relatively small number of melodies survive from this period, but the choice of tunes which fit Heywood's words is particularly limited. Very few extant tunes will fit a seven-line stanza and even fewer can confidently be dated to the mid-sixteenth century or before. William Chappell identified only thirty-three extant ballad tunes for the reigns of Henry VII to Mary I (1485–1558). Most of these fit stanzas of four, six or

---

[37] *Ibid.*, 290. 'Orature' is defined by the *Oxford English Dictionary* as 'A body of poetry, tales, etc., preserved through oral transmission as part of a particular culture, esp. a preliterate one'. 'Orature, n.' *OED Online*, Oxford University Press, December 2020, www.oed.com/view/Entry/246701, accessed 24 February 2021.

[38] John Stevens, *Music and Poetry in the Early Tudor Court* (Cambridge, 1979), 131.

[39] *Ibid.*, 37.

Figure 1. John Heywood, *A Balade specifienge partly the maner, partly the matter, in the most excellent meetyng and lyke mariage betwene our Soueraigne Lord, and our Soueraigne Lady, the Kynges and Queenes highnes* (London, 1554), set to 'Pastyme with good companye'.

eight lines. The eight-bar melody 'Donkin Dargeson', for example, suits stanzas of four lines with four stresses each such as 'A mery new ballet of the hathorne tre'. The popular ballad tune 'The shaking of the sheet' takes an eight-line stanza in which each has four stressed syllables.[40] Only a single extant tune, 'Pastyme with good companye', accommodates the more complex seven-line stanza (see Figure 1).[41]

The melody is a perfect fit. Often, tunes were substantially adapted in order to fit new sets of words or even to accommodate different numbers of syllables in different verses of the same song. In Heywood's wedding ballad, no compromise was necessary to make the words fit the music. Though at first we might think that a few lines require the musical rhythm to be adapted, if we read Heywood's words as they are written, and not as we might assume they were pronounced, there is an effortless match. In the fourth stanza's final couplet, we should trust Heywood that the final words are in fact the two-syllable expressions 'al-eurth' and 'as-seurth', rather than 'a-lu-reth' and 'as-su-reth'. Likewise, in stanza 8 line 2, it is easy to sing 'solempne' as one syllable, sounding, 'solm', especially as the adjective is repeated immediately as a four-syllable noun, 'solempnite'. Indeed, this has the additional advantage of enhancing the emphasis on 'solempnite' rather than losing the noun in a stream of rushed syllables. Conversely, in stanza 11 line 2, 'prayer' has two syllables, echoing its use in other ballads and poetry of the period.[42] In fact, the only rhythmic adaptation required to make the wedding ballad fit the melody for 'Pastyme' is the simple addition of an anacrusis (upbeat) at the beginning of the first and third lines of each verse – a common adaptation throughout balladry.

---

[40] William Chappell, *Popular Music of the Olden Time* (2 vols., 1859), I, 56–97 (see 65 and 85 in particular).

[41] *Ibid.*, 56; Hyde, 'Gender, Authority and the Image of Queenship', 751–72.

[42] See, for example, William Kethe, *A ballet declaringe the fal of the whore of babylone intytuled Tye thy mare tom boye* (1548), ESTC S107428, or *The[n]terlude of youth* (1557), ESTC S108291.

Although there do not appear to be any direct echoes of 'Pastyme"'s previous words in Heywood's wedding ballad, this was by no means unusual. Several sets of mid-Tudor words to the popular tune 'Downright squire' relate to the theme of men's attitudes to women, but there are few if any linguistic resonances.[43] Nevertheless, Heywood's song puts his chosen melody to good use. For instance, Heywood's repetition in stanza 6 of the phrase 'so meete a matche' highlights the important similarities between the two monarchs, which are emphasised at the end of the line on the decorated parts of the melody. This verbal repetition is echoed in the melody, which in some versions of the tune not only repeats the first and second phrase exactly but also remains on the same repeated note. In stanza 8, meanwhile, 'Suche honour with suche honeste' places the repetition of the two words which begin with the same syllable on equivalent notes in the repeated phrase. Even the pointing, where commas subdivide the lines, neatly matches the position of the musical phrasing. So while Heywood's verses might seem strained if we look at them as poetry, they are anything but strained when sung.

It is almost impossible to believe that Heywood would not have known 'Pastyme', as it was closely associated with Henry VIII's court. His familiarity with popular song melodies from Henry VIII's court can be seen from the presence of his song lyrics in British Library, Additional Manuscript 15233, which also includes a moralised version of 'The hunt is up', by John Thorne. This song is known to have been popular at the Henrician court and was attributed to 'one Gray', who grew into 'good estimation ... with the same king Henry, and afterward the Duke of Sommerset Protectour, for making certaine merry Ballades'.[44] The sort of music which was popular at Henry's court can also be found in the Henry VIII Manuscript, a collection of English and foreign part-songs, rounds, instrumental pieces and puzzle-canons.[45] One of those songs is a version of 'Pastyme'. Dating the manuscript has proved something of a puzzle. Two studies independently placed the manuscript after 1522, but their findings were challenged by David Fallows who is adamant that 'it would be hard to date anything [in the manuscript] much later than 1516'. He notes that 'Adew adew le company' is the only piece which can be confidently dated, referring as it does to the birth of Henry and Catherine's short-lived son, Prince Henry. This piece, therefore, dates from between the prince's birth on 1 January and his death on 22 February 1511, it being highly unlikely that such a celebratory piece would have been copied after the royal parents' bereavement.[46]

Two further versions of 'Pastyme' can be found in the Ritson Manuscript, a music collection compiled over a period of at least seventy years beginning around 1440:

---

[43] Hyde, *Singing the News*, 89–92.

[44] George Puttenham, *The arte of English poesie ...* (1589), ESTC S123166, 12.

[45] London, British Library, Add. MS 31922 (Henry VIII's Book aka The Henry VIII Manuscript); Stevens, *Music and Poetry*, 4. For a facsimile of the manuscript, see the *Digital Image Archive of Medieval Music* (DIAMM), https://www.diamm.ac.uk/sources/1238/#, accessed 12 February 2021.

[46] David Fallows, 'Introduction', in *The Henry VIII Book (British Library, Add. MS 31922)*, ed. David Fallows (2014), 1–85, at 25.

The first, on ff. 136v–137, is a mess: it has passages crossed out and replaced (in one case with entirely wrong material, though it is easy enough to see what was intended), has the middle voice labelled 'Contra Tenor' rather than Tenor, and has only a single stanza of text. The second, on ff. 141v–142, is a fair copy with the three voices correctly labelled 'Triplex', 'Tenor' and 'Bassus', all three stanzas underlaid directly below the music, and the annotation 'The Kynges Balade' at the end, which – if the 'kynge' concerned is Henry VIII rather than any earlier king – means that it was copied there after Henry's accession in April 1509.[47]

Fascinating discrepancies between the musical arrangements of 'Pastyme' in the Ritson and the Henry VIII Manuscripts suggest that the music circulated widely during the early sixteenth century, yet mainly through aural circulation rather than scribally.[48]

'Pastyme' certainly 'had resonance in courtly circles for the next several decades', but more widespread familiarity with the songs from Henry's court is demonstrated by the fact that each individual item in the Henry VIII Manuscript appears in a relatively high number of other music manuscripts.[49] Several pieces, including an instrumental version of 'Pastyme' for lute, are also included in Royal Appendix Manuscript 58, a commonplace book of solo songs, virginal pieces, lute songs and part songs, dating probably from after 1551.[50] So far from being outdated, the music in the Henry VIII Manuscript was still being copied out and imitated into the middle of the century. This suggests that it contained a collection of pieces that any musician who, like Heywood, was plying his trade at the royal court in the 1520s and 30s was required to know.[51] Various theories as to the Henry VIII Manuscript's purpose and ownership have been put forward, but one that seems plausible is that it was copied in royal circles and that it perhaps belonged to the king's Master of the Revels, Sir Henry Guildford.[52] John Stevens has even singled out Heywood as the 'obvious sort of person' to have owned such a manuscript.[53] All in all, it seems entirely reasonable to assume that Heywood would have been familiar with 'Pastyme'.

---

[47] British Library, Add. MS 5665 (Ritson Manuscript); Fallows, 'Introduction', 33. For a facsimile, see the *Digital Image Archive of Medieval Music* (*DIAMM*), https://www.diamm.ac.uk/sources/796/#, accessed 12 February 2021.

[48] Fallows, 'Introduction', 33.

[49] Raymond G. Siemens, 'Henry VIII as Writer and Lyricist', *Musical Quarterly*, 92 (2009), 136–66, at 141; Dietrich Helms, 'Henry VIII's Book: Teaching Music to Royal Children', *Musical Quarterly*, 92 (2009), 118–35, at 119–20.

[50] John Ward, 'The Lute Music of MS Royal Appendix 58', *Journal of the American Musicological Society*, 13 (1960), 117–25, at 117.

[51] Helms, 'Henry VIII's Book', 119–20.

[52] Raymond Siemens, 'The English Lyrics of the *Henry VIII Manuscript*' (Ph.D. thesis, University of British Columbia, 1997), 92–9, quoted in Fallows, 'Introduction', 24.

[53] Stevens, *Music and Poetry*, 129–31; London, British Library Royal Appendix MS 58.

Despite not being named as a tune on any later broadside ballads, 'Pastyme' clearly had a life well beyond Henry's immediate circle. In addition to appearing in these sixteenth-century manuscripts, it was mentioned during a sermon as early as 1521, and the song was still in circulation 100 years later, when it appeared in a Scottish songbook.[54] Although tradition has it that 'Pastyme' was Henry VIII's composition, David Fallows argues that 'on balance [we can] now conclude that the melody and the chordal basis already existed', meaning that Henry's contribution was the familiar text.[55] By the early 1530s 'Pastyme' was so firmly connected to Mary's father that it was known as 'The Kynges Ballade'.[56] Heywood could easily have seen its potential as a melody for his wedding ballad, especially given the associations that the tune would have brought to the song, and not least for Queen Mary herself.

Meanwhile, the influence of court culture on commercial music was visible from the earliest days of print. John Rastell's first extant use of his system of movable type was for a ballad known as 'Tyme to pass', from his interlude, *The Nature of the Four Elements* (1520). Interludes of this sort were commonly associated with aristocratic entertainments. What is notable is that Henry VIII's compositions were so well known that they could be implicitly referenced in commercial music printing. The musical setting for 'Tyme to pass' was a composition again attributed to Henry VIII, the song '*Adew madam et ma mastres*'. But while the tune was taken from one of Henry's *chansons*, the words were also modelled on one of the king's own ballads, none other than 'Pastyme with good companye'.[57]

Given 'Pastyme''s clear association with the royal court, it is important to note that no musical training is needed to sing its melody. David Fallows points out that the music in the Henry VIII Manuscript is suitable for 'enthusiastic amateurs' rather than representing the flowering of elaborate English music, such as that seen in the choral polyphony of the Eton Choirbook.[58] It has even been suggested that the manuscript might have been intended as an instructional tool for Henry's children Princess Mary and Henry Fitzroy.[59] Contemporary accounts do indeed note that the young Mary was a skilled musician. She was a proficient lutenist and, like Heywood, a keen player of the virginals.[60] She would have begun her musical education in about 1520 at the age of four, at a time when this music from her father's early court was still very much current, but Fallows notes that a 'fair proportion of pieces [in the Henry VIII Manuscript] should never serve as a model for anybody'.[61] Even if the manuscript was not compiled in order to teach music to Princess Mary, 'Pastyme' itself was clearly one of the songs in circulation at court at the

---

[54] Stevens, *Music and Poetry*, 143.

[55] Fallows, 'Introduction', 22.

[56] Ritson Manuscript, fo. 141^v–142.

[57] Matthew Lillo, 'John Rastell's Dramatic Ballad and the Early Tudor Court: Toward a Revised Understanding of Ballad History', *Studies in Philology*, 117 (2020), 681–716, at 683.

[58] Fallows, 'Introduction', 2.

[59] Helms, 'Henry VIII's Book', 118–35.

[60] Anna Whitelock, *Mary Tudor: England's First Queen* (2009), 27.

[61] Fallows, 'Introduction', 24.

time she began her musical studies, before her household was moved to the Welsh marches, away from her parents, in 1525. It seems virtually incontestable that Mary would have been familiar with the tune.

Musical associations

The identification of the melody for the wedding ballad as 'Pastyme with good companye' now seems inescapable. Christopher Marsh, Una McIlvenna and others have demonstrated how early-modern listeners were able to make associations between subsequent sets of lyrics to the same tune, and it may be that for Heywood this tune was too good an opportunity to miss.[62] The melody would certainly have been known to those in Mary's circle and was in all probability familiar outside the confines of the royal court. Indeed, the many and varied associations which those 'in the know' could make between the two songs serve to substantiate the suggestion that Heywood deliberately drew upon the past to create a resonant and multivalent song which was calculated to appeal to the queen, and quite likely to a much wider audience.

The first connection that the ballad's audience might be expected to make would be with the queen's father himself, Henry VIII. By using a melody which was so closely associated with the man whom many people saw as the towering figure of the Tudor line, Heywood implicitly reinforced Mary's dynastic right to the throne as her father's daughter and his legitimate heir. Likewise, it cast her new husband in the role of the popular and successful monarch by musically linking Philip with that most English of kings, Henry VIII. While it is arguable that connecting Philip to such a strong king might have alienated those who feared his power, it is also true that it would musically reinforce the message that Philip was a 'kinglie king' and that as his wife, Mary had become a 'queenelie queene', thus restoring the natural gender balance.

The early sixteenth-century date of the song outlined above can also lead us back to a connection with a previous Tudor wedding to a Spanish royal. As we have seen, three of the extant manuscript versions of the song can be securely dated to the early years of Henry VIII's rule and the time of his marriage to Catherine of Aragon. Catherine was first married to Henry's elder brother, Arthur, but the pair's life together proved fleeting: Arthur died on 2 April 1502, only months after the wedding, leaving Catherine a widow searching for a role in a foreign court while the young Prince Henry became heir to his father's throne. Henry VII died on 21 April 1509, and shortly after the funeral in early May the new king announced that he would marry his brother's widow. The couple were married on 11 June, and their coronation took place on 23 June at Westminster Abbey. They appeared to be deeply in love. Both the Ritson Manuscript and Henry VIII Manuscript place the creation of 'Pastyme' roughly contemporaneously with the 'honeymoon period' of

[62] Marsh, *Music and Society*, 300; Una McIlvenna, 'The Power of Music: The Significance of Contrafactum in Execution Ballads', *Past & Present*, 229 (2015), 47–89; Una McIlvenna, 'The Rich Merchant Man, or, What the Punishment of Greed Sounded Like in Early Modern English Ballads', *Huntington Library Quarterly*, 79 (2016), 279–99; Hyde, *Singing the News*.

Henry's relationship with his new wife, and it is difficult not to concur that Catherine 'must have heard it sung often'.[63]

All this is not to suggest that Henry's songs were necessarily written for Queen Catherine. Despite their composition during the early years of Henry VIII's reign, Raymond Siemens gives several reasons for not reading the lyrics in the Henry VIII Manuscript as 'little poems' written to Catherine of Aragon (or indeed any of Henry's later paramours). Firstly, they were composed in an environment in which 'courtly love' was a commonplace. Secondly, they were performed not by the king alone as a soloist, but often as part of a group of performers, undermining any personal connection between the singer and the subject of the songs. Finally, even when the songs were sung solo, they were not the private preserve of the singer and his lover, but instead were performed in a public environment, however small or courtly their audience.[64] Still, it seems that many of the 'small courtly songs were written for specific court festivals ... during the years of Henry's courtship of Katherine of Aragon'. Whether or not they were directly written for Henry's bride, they were certainly associated with this early, happy period of his rule.[65]

Rather than being a love song, 'Pastyme' is, of course, what Fallows refers to as a 'lifestyle song', one which describes or justifies the writer's preferred way of life.[66] Nevertheless, it is also true that the first two lines ('Pastyme with good companye / I love & shall untyll I dye') place love and courtship at the very centre of this existence. Likewise, Siemens acknowledges that the various songs ascribed to the king in the Henry VIII Manuscript are more intensely personal in feeling than the rest of the lyrics.[67] It is undeniable that the object of Henry's affections at this time was Catherine of Aragon. The performance of these songs in a public environment therefore serves to bolster the suggestion that 'Pastyme' became associated not only with Henry as 'The Kynges Ballade', but also with the queen because it was heard by many people in the context of a court which celebrated the idealisation of love at a time when the king was infatuated with his new wife. By reusing this melody, Heywood may have intended to reiterate the validity of Catherine's marriage to Henry, thereby reinforcing Mary's dynastic right which had been undermined when Henry had cast off his first wife and Mary had been declared a bastard. Mary never stopped believing that her mother was Henry's lawful wife despite her father's actions in putting Catherine aside. Heywood's decision to use 'Pastyme' as the melody for the wedding ballad would have been personally pleasing to the newly married queen. Moreover, the tune would have reminded Mary, and those in the know, of the unity between England and Spain which had existed

---

[63] Giles Tremlett, *Catherine of Aragon: Henry's Spanish Queen* (2010), 162.

[64] Siemens, 'Henry VIII as Writer and Lyricist', 140–2. Any association between *Pastyme* and Henry's infatuation with Anne Boleyn has been shown to be spurious; see also Raymond Siemens, 'Revisiting the Text of the Henry VIII Manuscript (BL Add Ms 31,922): An Extended Note', *Early Modern Literary Studies*, 14, 1–36 (2009).

[65] Helms, 'Henry VIII's Book', 120.

[66] Fallows, 'Introduction', 22.

[67] Siemens, 'Henry VIII as Writer and Lyricist', 139.

before the break with Rome and which the marriage to Philip was meant to restore.

Nevertheless, those close to the queen might also have noted some further family associations based on the pre-existing English words to the melody. The third line in 'Pastyme', 'gruch who lust but none denye' (meaning 'let grudge whosover will, none shall refuse [it to me]'), was a reference to Margaret of Austria's motto, '*groigne qui groigne et vive Burgoigne*'.[68] This reference indicates the close political and personal alignment between Henry and the duchess, as well as playing on Philip's own claim to be a future head of the House of Burgundy. Margaret was married in 1497 (albeit briefly) to Catherine of Aragon's brother, Juan, and was later appointed as regent of the Habsburg Netherlands and guardian of the future Holy Roman Emperor, Charles V, Philip's father. She was instrumental in uniting England, Spain and the Holy Roman Empire in an alliance against France in 1513, a period which has been seen 'to represent the ascendance of the culture of revelry that characterised Henry's kingship'.[69] During the siege of Tournai that autumn, Henry and Margaret were frequent visitors, with the duchess's court being famous as a 'centre of courtly love'.[70]

Bearing this in mind, it seems fair to say that 'Pastyme', that most widely circulated of all early Tudor ballads, 'had a strong chance of cueing its audience's cultural knowledge of the king's thoughts about disport'.[71] While contemporary evidence for Henry VIII's court being modelled on the chivalric 'court of love' remains mainly circumstantial, the May games and masques that Edward Hall describes in his Chronicle are strongly redolent of a courtly game of love performed in a social setting and similar to those of Margaret's court. Indeed, they present a rosy picture of these early years of Henry's reign, with the palace hosting chivalric tournament romances or being suddenly overrun by royal mummers, while courtiers often took part in 'disguisings' with singing and dancing. Hall describes how, for example, in the summer of 1510, the king and queen went on a progress where Henry was to be seen 'exercisyng hym self daily in shotyng, singing, dauncing, wrasteling, casting of the barre, plaiying at the recorders, flute, virginals, and in setting of songes, makyng of balettes'.[72] Given the dates around which the Ritson and Henry VIII Manuscripts must have been created, it is easily possible, if not more than likely, that one of these ballads might have been 'Pastyme with good companye'. Heywood's choice of tune, then, had plenty of messages of its own, especially for those with knowledge of Henry VIII's court. It demonstrated Mary's lineage as a daughter of England, and the queen's intimate and auspicious links with Spain which set her up as a major player on the European stage.

---

[68] *Ibid.*, 140, 148; Stevens, *Music and Poetry*, 45.

[69] David R. Carlson, 'Skelton, Garnesche, and Henry VIII: Revels and Erudition at Court', *Review of English Studies*, N.S., 66 (2015), 240–57, at 247.

[70] Steven Gunn, *Charles Brandon, Duke of Suffolk c.1484-1545* (Oxford, 1988), 29.

[71] Lillo, 'John Rastell's Dramatic Ballad', 689, 697, 698. See also John Milsom, 'Songs and Society in Early Tudor London', *Early Music History*, 16 (1997), 235–93.

[72] Edward Hall, *Hall's chronicle; containing the history of England ...*, ed. Henry Ellis[?] (1809), 513–16.

Conclusion

The evidence overwhelmingly suggests that the intended tune for Mary's wedding ballad was 'Pastyme with good companye'. Considering the prominence given to heraldry in the ballad, it seems possible that the piece was composed for one of the five pageants which the Court of Aldermen organised for the newly-weds' entry into the City of London a few days after their wedding at Winchester Cathedral. Heywood had been called upon to lend a hand in planning these pageants, and although it seems that he was not directly involved in their production, he could have contributed a song for the festivities.[73] Perhaps *A balade specifienge partly the maner* was part of the 'fourth and most excellent pageant of al' at Cheapside, which focused on the two monarchs' genealogy and apparently was 'throughlye vewed and much comm[en]ded of their maiesties'.[74] It is certainly tempting to think that the song was written for public performance of this sort. If so, it would suggest that the song was heard not just by the newly wed royals but also, presumably, by large crowds at the London pageants. Heywood after all accentuated the fact that Mary and Philip were a 'meete ... matche in parentage' and, by the time of the wedding, 'matcheth feyre / Croune unto croune'. This, however, also indicates that the ballad was written after the nuptials, as it was not known until the eve of the wedding that Charles V would raise his son to be king of Naples in order that their marriage would be one of equals.[75] So even if the pageant was not the song's intended context, its publication as a broadside either for sale or distribution indicates that a wide audience was anticipated. As such, the song was intended to work on many levels. For all those in the know, the melody played on resonances from a pre-Reformation past. Given Heywood's familiar relationship with Mary, his careful choice of music amplified his textual message in numerous ways. At a personal level, he would have expected his chosen melody to please the queen, since 'Pastyme with good companye' was closely associated with Henry VIII's court at the happiest point in his marriage to Catherine of Aragon.

Yet there was also a strong element of propaganda. For the wider public, the song was a patriotic ballad which attempted to reconcile the difficulties faced by a queen regnant who chose to marry outside the realm, as well as to persuade the civic community to accept Mary, her new husband and their Catholic faith. It was unnecessary for the public to understand every nuance of melodic association in order to enjoy the song, but with its simple tune, repetitive words, and entertainment value, the ballad's powerful central message would be memorable and could be accessed even by those unable to read. By using a melody that was intimately linked to her father, the song had the added bonus of reinforcing Mary's dynastic heritage. At a time of increased tension, using this well-known tune reminded Mary and others of an idyllic period before the upheavals of the Reformation had both soured the relationship between England and Spain, and divided the English along confessional

---

[73] Walker, *Heywood*, 276–7, 287.

[74] John Elder, *The Copie of a Letter Sent in to Scotland ...* (1555), ESTC S126215, Ci[v] & Ciii.

[75] Hyde, *Singing the News*, 171; Walker, *Heywood*, 289.

lines. It was an integral part of Heywood's attempt to bring the country together, united behind Mary and her new Spanish king.

Supplementary material. The supplementary material for this article can be found at https://doi.org/10.1017/S0080440122000019.

Cite this article: Hyde J (2022). Popular Propaganda: John Heywood's Wedding Ballad and Mary I's Spanish Match. *Transactions of the Royal Historical Society* **32**, 73–91. https://doi.org/10.1017/S0080440122000019

Transactions of the RHS (2022), **32**, 93–112
doi:10.1017/S0080440122000068

ARTICLE

The Roads Not Taken: Liberty, Sovereignty and the Idea of the Republic in Poland-Lithuania and the British Isles, 1550–1660

Robert Frost 🆔

Department of History, University of Aberdeen, Aberdeen, UK
Email: robert.frost@abdn.ac.uk

(Received 31 March 2022; accepted 12 April 2022)

Abstract

In the mid-sixteenth century, there were many parallels between the political cultures of Poland-Lithuania and the kingdoms of the British Isles, as thinkers inspired by the ideals of Renaissance civic humanism challenged traditional currents of thought. Across the British Isles and Poland-Lithuania there were strong native traditions asserting the liberties of communities of the realm and the need to check unbridled royal authority through parliamentary assemblies. As the Reformation swept across the British Isles and Poland-Lithuania, traditional claims concerning the right to resist tyrannical authority were bolstered. Finally, in 1603, Scotland and England formed a loose political union as Poland and Lithuania had formed a loose political union in 1386, although it was not until 1707 that England and Scotland followed the example of the 1569 Lublin Union, when Poland and Lithuania established the first parliamentary union in European history. Despite these parallels, the fates of these composite polities were very different, and their political cultures diverged substantially. This article considers the idea of the Renaissance republic in Poland-Lithuania and the British Isles. It suggests why their roads diverged, and asks what made all the difference.

Keywords: civic humanism; Renaissance republicanism; history of Poland-Lithuania; early modern British and Irish history

It is a strange feeling, having studied history all your adult life, when you realise that you don't understand the history of your own country. I took courses on British and Irish history at St Andrews with Norman Gash, and Scottish history with Bruce Lenman, and taught Tudors and Stuarts at A-level for three years, but my research career has focused on the Polish-Lithuanian union. By 2004, when I returned to Scotland, I felt that I had a reasonable understanding of Polish-Lithuanian political culture, and that it might be interesting to investigate the political culture of the British Isles, whose kingdoms formed the other great parliamentary union of the early modern period.

I recall the moment when I realised that I understood nothing at all. I was reading the *Ius regium* of Sir George Mackenzie of Rosehaugh, the great Scottish lawyer of the late seventeenth century: Lord Advocate, opponent of witch trials, persecutor of Covenanters, and founder of the Faculty of Advocates Library, celebrated in a memorial window in the National Library of Scotland to this day. I was jerked awake by the following passage:

> What Nations under Heaven were so happy as we, under the Reign of King Charles the First?[1]

Now would that be the same King Charles I who managed to start at least two wars in each of his three kingdoms, who was sold to his English subjects by his Scottish subjects for the knockdown price of £400,000 sterling, and who ended up on the scaffold on account of his magnificent intransigence and refusal to compromise his exalted view of monarchy? Or was Sir George referring to another Charles I, living in one of Stephen Hawking's parallel universes, in which a benign and shrewd monarch governed peacefully and happily with the consent of his parliaments, cropped no ears, and kept his head on his shoulders?

What followed was even more perplexing:

> Whatever proves Monarchy to be an excellent Government, does by the same Reason prove absolute Monarchy to be the best Government; for if Monarchy be to be commended because it prevents Divisions, then a limited Monarchy, which allows the People a share, is not to be commended, because it occasions them. I cannot but exceedingly commend our Predecessors, for making this reasonable choice of an absolute Monarchy; for a Monarch that is subject to the impetuous caprices of the Multitude when giddy, or to the incorrigible Factiousness of Nobility when interested, is in effect no Government at all ...[2]

I was intrigued by Mackenzie's assertion that his predecessors had *chosen* absolute monarchy, and by his trenchant attack on the classic Aristotelian and Polybian *forma mixta*, the mixed form of government, that combined monarchy with aristocracy and popular government and underpinned the idea of the Renaissance *res publica*. I had read enough to know that before 1660 most British political theorists, far from endorsing absolute monarchy, spoke a language that I, as a historian of Poland-Lithuania, largely understood. In the British Isles, as in Poland-Lithuania, political theorists read the same classical authors: Aristotle, Polybius, Cicero, Seneca, Sallust, Tacitus and their ilk, although

---

[1] George Mackenzie of Rosehaugh, *Ius regium* (1684), 2.

[2] *Ibid.*, 42.

Tacitus was not as popular on the Vistula as he was on the Thames. They wrestled with the same age-old problems: What is the essence of good government? How can tyranny be prevented? In what circumstances can and should royal authority be resisted? And they drew on the wisdom of the ancients to answer them.

The answers given by sixteenth-century writers in the British Isles seemed broadly familiar to me. The world of Sir Thomas Smith, of Philip Sidney – who remarked that Poland was a 'well-balanced aristocracy'[3] – or of George Buchanan – to whose *De iure regni apud Scotos* Mackenzie's *Ius regium* was a counterblast – did not seem far removed from that of Polish-Lithuanian writers, such as Andrzej Frycz Modrzewski, Andrzej Wolan or Wawrzyniec Goślicki (Laurentius Goslicius) whose 1568 treatise *De optimo senatore* was translated several times into English.[4]

What road led the Scotland that had deposed Mary Stewart in 1567; the Scotland of George Buchanan and the 1638 National Covenant, to Mackenzie's vision of absolutist Arcadia? What road led the England of Coke, Pym and Hampden; the England that executed its king and abolished monarchy in 1649, from the 1628 Petition of Rights and the 1641 Grand Remonstrance to the bleak dystopianism of Hobbes's *Leviathan* and the 1684 resolution of the Convocation of Oxford University, which welcomed Mackenzie's *Ius regium*, and praised its author for 'the Service done to His Majesty'.[5] Of course then, as now, the Convocation of Oxford University did not speak for all of Oxford, let alone all of England, while Mackenzie's views were by no means accepted by all his compatriots. Nevertheless, although Poland-Lithuania had its supporters of strong monarchy, such as Krzysztof Warszewicki or the Jesuit firebrand Piotr Skarga, it chose a very different road in this period, and I believe that I am safe in claiming that even Poland-Lithuania's most ardent regalists stopped well short of expressing sentiments remotely akin to those of Sir George Mackenzie.

The question of why the paths of political cultures that drank deeply at the wells of classical and Renaissance political thought should diverge so markedly in the seventeenth century is a serious and, I hope, an interesting one. The cynic might suggest that the reason many Scots and the Convocation of Oxford University were beguiled by Sir George can be encapsulated in two words, 'Oliver' and 'Cromwell', but the problem, I would suggest, is rather more complex. I hope that considering it comparatively might shed light on current debates in Polish-Lithuanian and British Isles history.

---

[3] Markku Peltonen, *Classical Humanism and Republicanism in English Political Thought, 1570–1640* (Cambridge, 1995), 47.

[4] Laurentius Goslicius, *De optimo senatore libri duo* (Venice, 1568). There were two separate manuscript translations by 1584, and there were three further editions: in 1598, 1607, when part of the 1598 translation was issued under a different title; in 1660, when much of the 1598 translation was included in a regalist pamphlet; and finally, in the best translation published under the author's correct name, in 1733. For the definitive account of the English translations see Teresa Bałuk-Ulewiczowa, *Goslicius' Ideal Senator and Its Cultural Impact over the Centuries: Shakespearian Reflections* (Cracow, 2009).

[5] Clare Jackson, 'Sir George Mackenzie of Rosehaugh', *Oxford Dictionary of National Biography*, https://www.oxforddnb.com/view/10.1093/ref:odnb/9780198614128.001.0001/odnb-9780198614128-e-17579 (accessed 20 May 2021).

Let me begin with a question that is central to what follows: what do we mean when we talk of early modern republicanism? On the banks of the Thames, where I am more or less sitting this evening, this is not an easy question to answer. This difficulty stems, I would suggest, from too little caution in reading back into this period more modern understandings not just of the term 'republic', but also of the term 'state'. Here, I believe the example of Poland-Lithuania helps to complicate the general picture of the idea of the republic in early modern Europe.

For this teleological temptation, as in so much, Machiavelli bears much of the responsibility, on account of the famous first sentence of his *Prince*: 'All the states and all the dominions under whose authority people have lived in the past and live now have been and are either republics or principalities.'[6] Machiavelli's stark binary division between monarchical and republican forms of the state has encouraged scholars to stress a distinction that, I would suggest, took time to embed itself. Nevertheless, Quentin Skinner and Martin van Gelderen argue that 'whatever else it may have meant to be a republican in early-modern Europe, it meant repudiating the age-old belief that monarchy is necessarily the best form of government,' adding that 'many republicans took it as obvious that a republican constitution should eschew all traces of monarchical authority.'[7]

That Machiavelli's distinction gained traction in this period is undeniable, encouraged as it was by the 1581 repudiation of Philip II of Spain by the United Provinces and by the Rump Parliament's abolition of monarchy shortly after Charles's execution. These acts indeed helped cement our modern understanding of republicanism, but as Skinner and van Gelderen admit, there were republicans who thought differently.[8] Certainly, in Poland-Lithuania, the *res publica*, or *Rzeczpospolita* as it was known, was not understood to imply any repudiation of monarchy, although most Poles and Lithuanians would have agreed that pure monarchy was not the best form of government. Deep into the eighteenth century, they remained profoundly attached to the *forma mixta*, and saw their republic as its modern incarnation. I use the term republic deliberately. For although 'commonwealth', the early modern English translation of *res publica*, is generally applied to the *Rzeczpospolita Obojga Narodów*, the Commonwealth of the Two Nations, as Poland-Lithuania termed itself after 1569, Poles and Lithuanians did not doubt that their polity was a republic of which the king was an essential component.

I use the term 'polity' rather than 'state' because this is another problem that bedevils study of the impact of civic humanism. Machiavelli's usage of *stato* indicates that already in the early sixteenth century something akin to our understanding of the term 'state' was emerging. By 1600, encouraged by

---

[6] Niccolò Machiavelli, *The Prince*, tr. George Bull (Harmondsworth, 1976), 33.

[7] 'Introduction', in *Republicanism: A Shared European Heritage*, ed. Martin van Gelderen and Quentin Skinner (2 vols., Cambridge, 2002), I, 1, 3.

[8] Including Machiavelli: in chapter two of the *Discourses on the First Ten Books of Livy*, he approvingly presented the republican form of government in terms of the classic Aristotelian forms of government, and recommended the mixed form of government, of which monarchy was a constituent part.

Giovanni Botero's concept of reason of state, the idea of the abstract state as a juridical construct with a legal personality distinct from the person of its ruler or rulers was becoming increasingly influential and was to become ever more so in the age of Richelieu and Hobbes. The Aristotelian *polis*, however, was conceived as a community of citizens, and to represent it as the same beast as the abstract juridical construct of the state formed in sixteenth- and seventeenth-century Europe is to confuse two rather different animals.

Long before 1550 Poles and Lithuanians grasped this fundamental distinction, as is demonstrated by the crucial clause in the 1569 Union of Lublin:

> That the Kingdom of Poland and the Grand Duchy of Lithuania already form one indivisible and uniform body and are not distinct, but compose one common Republic, which has been constituted and formed into one people out of two states and two nations.[9]

The distinction drawn here between the republic – the *polis*, the community of citizens – and the two states that formed it, for which the text uses the modern Polish word for state, *państwo*, was essential to the transformation of the union between the kingdom of Poland and the grand duchy of Lithuania, first established in 1386, into a stable partnership of legal equals, and a union of peoples that forged one republic, conceived as a community of citizens, not subjects of a sovereign monarch. The 1569 Lublin treaty ended a long argument that dated back to 1386 over the relationship between Lithuania and Poland. Lithuanians rejected the incorporationist Polish interpretation of the union, claiming that the grand duchy was an equal partner to the kingdom of Poland. Civic humanism was crucial to the settling of this squabble. With its vision of a self-governing citizen republic, in which communal liberties were protected, it provided the intellectual framework within which Poles and Lithuanians could unite. As the values of civic humanism spread among the Polish and Lithuanian elites after 1500, the road opened up to the triumph of the Lithuanian concept of union in 1569. Thereafter, the two states were legally distinct, with separate governments and armies, but a common parliament, the Sejm, and one monarch, elected jointly by the republic's citizens.[10]

Civic humanism also provided the intellectual underpinnings for the constitutional revolution that followed the death in July 1572 of Sigismund August, the last of the Lithuanian Jagiellon dynasty in the male line. The central vision of civic humanism, of a community of virtuous citizens defending their republic through the mechanisms of the mixed form of government, complemented and completed an older, Polish tradition with deep medieval roots. Poland established itself as an independent kingdom in the eleventh century, but fell apart in the twelfth. It was partly reconstituted by Władysław the Short in 1320, but his son, Casimir III, failed to produce an heir. Casimir agreed to

---

[9] *Akty Unji Polski z Litwą 1385–1791*, ed. Stanisław Kutrzeba and Władysław Semkowicz (Cracow, 1932), no. 149, 358. My translation.

[10] Robert Frost, *The Oxford History of Poland-Lithuania*, I, The *Making of the Polish-Lithuanian Union, 1385–1569* (Oxford, 2015), 492–4.

the succession of his nephew Louis of Anjou, King of Hungary, on his death, but he met resistance in 1370 when, as he lay dying, he sought to carve out a duchy for his legitimised grandson, Kaźko of Stolp. The rejection of this last fling of patrimonial monarchy established the principle that kings could not alienate any territory of the kingdom without the consent of the community of the realm, the *corona regni Poloniae*: the Crown of the Polish Kingdom. This distinction between the *regnum* as a state, and the *corona regni* as an Aristotelian *polis*, a community of citizens, was reflected in the 1413 Horodło union, in which the term *res publica* appears.

The authority of the community of the realm was entrenched when Louis of Anjou, who failed to produce a male heir, sought to ensure the succession of one of his two daughters to the Polish throne. The price was the 1374 Privileges of Koszyce, the first of the great grants of privileges to the Polish *szlachta*, the nobility. On Louis's death in 1382, however, the community of the Polish realm rejected Mary, the daughter Louis intended to succeed him in Poland, in favour of the ten-year-old Jadwiga, who did not succeed her father until she was elected queen regnant two years later. Elective monarchy was consolidated by the Krewo Act in August 1385, in which Jogaila, the forty-four-year-old pagan grand duke of Lithuania, agreed to convert to Catholicism as the price of his marriage to Jadwiga and his election to the Polish throne, which followed in February 1386, initiating the Polish-Lithuanian union.

The elective principle was crucial for the protection of the expanding liberties of the Polish *szlachta*. Władysław Jagiełło, as Jogaila is known in Polish, fought to establish his hereditary right to the Polish throne in 1399 on Jadwiga's death and in the 1420s, when – to everyone's surprise – he produced two male heirs in his mid-seventies with his fourth wife. He secured a promise that one of them would be elected to succeed him, at the price of agreeing the 1433 Privileges of Jedlnia. After 1386 Polish liberties were gradually extended to Lithuanian and Ruthenian nobles. Crucially, the elective principle was granted to the grand duchy in 1413. Jagiełło had installed his cousin Vytautas as grand duke in 1401 to govern Lithuania on his behalf, retaining the hereditary title of supreme duke. The 1413 Horodło union granted the Lithuanians the right to elect a successor to Vytautas.

Other privileges followed, notably at Nieszawa in 1454, which laid the foundations of the Polish-Lithuanian parliamentary system by establishing that the king could not call out the noble levy without the consent of the local sejmiks, the dietines. The establishment of the rights of the sejmiks thus predated the definitive establishment of the Sejm, the central diet, which emerged as a bicameral body between the 1460s and the 1490s, and whose powers were definitively established in 1505 with the statute of *Nihil Novi*, which decreed that no new positive law could be enacted without Sejm consent.

This system embodied the Roman Law principle of *quod omnes tangit ab omnibus tractari et aprobari debet* (that which touches all should be discussed and approved by all). The Polish instututions embodying this principle – the sejmiks and the locally elected courts – were extended to Lithuania by the Second Lithuanian Statute in 1566. From the 1530s, statutes were printed in

Polish, enabling politically active citizens to acquire what was often a deep knowledge of the law.

Renaissance republicanism fitted this tradition well, and inspired the constitutional revolution following the death of Sigismund August on 7 July 1572. Many historians have presented the two interregna during which it took place in a negative light. It took nineteen months to elect and crown Henry of Valois, and his escape back to France in June 1574, four months after his coronation, is often taken to indicate the impossibility of governing Poland-Lithuania. Henry's successor, Stefan Batory, was only elected after a largely senatorial faction had declared Emperor Maximilian II king. The Lithuanians did not participate, and Batory was crowned nearly two years after Henry's flight, despite furious Lithuanian protests at this breach of Lublin. The 1587 election sparked a brief civil war before Sigismund III Vasa was confirmed as king. In 1592, when Sigismund succeeded to the Swedish throne, it seemed as if he too was intending to flee and cede his throne to the Habsburgs. Sigismund did stay after the humiliating 1592 Inquisition Sejm, at which his conduct was robustly criticised. In 1606 his modest reform proposals provoked a full-blown revolt, a *rokosz* as it was known. This was a rebellion undertaken in defence of the law, which claimed to be constitutional. At its height, on 24 June 1607, in a camp at Jeziorna, Sigismund's deposition was declared, following the invocation of the principle of *de non praestanda oboedientia*, the formal right to withdraw obedience from a monarch who had broken his coronation oath, which had been included in the Henrician Articles, prepared for Henry of Valois, and sworn to by Batory and all subsequent monarchs at their coronations.

Hindsight, as Mackenzie's rosy view of the reign of Charles I demonstrates, can be profoundly distorting. What is impressive about the four years between 1572 and 1576, during which the union had a monarch for a mere four months, is the integrative force of the republican idea, and the capacity of the republic's institutions to cope with the absence of a king. There was no descent into anarchy. In a religiously divided age, during which France experienced eight civil wars over three decades, the republic reached agreement remarkably quickly over how to manage the election, and then how to deal with Henry's flight. In 1572–3, despite no precedents, and considerable opposition from some quarters, it was agreed that the Catholic primate, the Archbishop of Gniezno, should act as interrex. A Convocation Sejm, summoned to establish the form of the election, took the momentous decision to institute the principle that kings should be elected *viritim*, with every citizen having the right to participate; some 40,000 did so in 1573. Despite concern that the law was silent in the absence of a king, local sejmiks established special courts to judge the most urgent criminal cases. After Henry scarpered, he was given a deadline for his return; when he failed to appear, he was deposed with little fuss.

That framework embodied the mixed form of government. In the bicameral Sejm, the chamber of envoys, elected by the sejmiks, represented the popular element of the Aristotelian constitution. Its members, envoys not representatives, conveyed the wishes of the *populus* as expressed in the sejmiks and set down in the instructions with which they were furnished. These provided the basis for negotiation to reach the consensus necessary to agree legislation under the principle of unanimity which regulated Sejm decisions, a principle that was steadily debased after 1660, but which down to 1648 functioned tolerably enough. The upper chamber, the Senate, comprising Catholic bishops, government ministers and the most important provincial office-holders, doubled as the Senate Council, whose dual function involved giving counsel to the king, while acting as guardians of the king and the law – *custodes regis ac legis* – to ensure that the monarch, in governing, did not breach the laws that constrained his actions according to the Thomist principle of *Lex est Rex*: the law is king.[11]

Attachment to the system was profound. Poles and Lithuanians were confident that the *bonum commune*, the common good, would be protected so long as its principles were upheld by virtuous citizens. This vision of Renaissance republicanism was taken to be fully in accord with constitutional tradition, the Ancient Constitution, to use the contemporary English term. The king was a constitutive part of the republic, but it could, if necessary, function without him. There was no need for the mystic malarkey of the King's Two Bodies. As Piotr Zborowski, palatine of Sandomierz, put it when conveying the news of Sigismund August's death to the Sandomierz *szlachta*: 'It was no novelty for our ancestors that kings die, and must die; they understood that their republic was and must be eternal.'[12] From the interregnum following the death of Louis of Anjou in 1382, the *szlachta* had developed the institution of confederation, in which citizens bonded formally together and swore oaths to provide a legal basis for their political actions. The summoning of sejms and sejmiks was formally the prerogative of the king, but in the absence of a king, sejmiks confederated themselves to ensure that their decisions had a legal basis. As was stated by the general sejmik of the Ruthenian palatinate: 'although the king dies, authority does not perish.'[13] Thus was the principle of Renaissance self-government institutionalised.

Civic humanism in the British Isles travelled down different roads. J. G. A. Pocock claims, indeed, that it had minimal influence in England until June 1642, when Charles I's reply to the Nineteen Propositions presented by the Long Parliament constituted, according to Pocock, 'one of the keys that opened the door to Machiavellian analysis'.[14] Charles, on the

---

[11] Igor Kąkolewski, *Melancholia władzy. Problem tyranii w europejskiej kulturze politycznej XVI stulecia* (Warsaw, 2007), 18.

[12] Proclamation of Piotr Zborowski, palatine of Sandomierz, to the nobility of the palatinate concerning the king's death, 11 July 1572. *Henri de Valois et la Pologne en 1572*, ed. Marquis de Noailles (3 vols., Paris, 1872), III, 82.

[13] *Chociaż król umrze, władza nie umiera.* Instructions of the knightly estate of the palatinate of Ruthenia, Wiśnia, 13 December 1572, in *Kronika za Zygmunta Augusta w Knyszynie, i inne dokumenty polityczne z czasów pierwszego bezkrólewia, I, Od lipca 1572 do marca 1573*, ed. Krzysztof Koehler (Cracow, 2016), no. 36, 293.

[14] J. G. A. Pocock, *The Machiavellian Moment: Florentine Political Thought and the Atlantic Republican Tradition* (Princeton, 1975), 361. Pocock's view was based on that of Corinne Comstock Weston, 'English Constitutional Doctrine from the Fifteenth Century to the Seventeenth: II The Theory of

advice of two moderate royalists, Viscount Falkland and Sir John Culpepper, presented the English political system in terms of the classic *forma mixta*, in a gambit that Pocock considered to be 'constitutionally incorrect and a disastrous tactical error'. Hitherto, Pocock argued, English interest in civic humanism was limited to the idea of the humanist as 'counsellor to his prince'. He concluded that 'the community of counsel does not become a republic in the acephelous sense ... it remains a corpus of which the prince is head, a hierarchy of degree in which counsel is given by every man sitting in his place.'[15]

If Pocock is right, then in England – in contrast to Poland-Lithuania – civic humanism was impossible to accommodate within the Ancient Constitution, the medieval tradition of limited monarchy that was appealed to in the Nineteen Propositions, a tradition founded on Magna Carta, the common law and Sir John Fortescue's notion of *dominium politicum ac regale*, which drew on medieval ideas of lordship rather than humanism.[16] Why should this be so? Was it also the case in Scotland, where George Buchanan, the great Scottish humanist and advocate of limited monarchy, showed little interest in the *forma mixta*, despite his belief that civic virtue was the key to political life, as Roger Mason observes?[17]

In considering this problem, I would suggest, we need to guard against privileging texts and opinions that seem to us to reflect a more modern mode of thinking over older patterns of thought. The desire of scholars for precision of thought can often hinder an appreciation of the messy reality of what the Annalistes termed collective *mentalités*. Lucien Febvre warns us about 'our overriding need for logic, coherence and unity: this or that, not this and that at the same time'.[18] It seems to me that in confronting the question I have put before you today we need to restrain our scholarly desire for conceptual precision: thinkers and politicians in such a turbulent age were not necessarily entirely coherent as they struggled to reconcile the political traditions and modes of thought inherited from their medieval forebears with the more recent principles of civic humanism, whether imbibed directly from Aristotle, Livy and Cicero, or mediated through Machiavelli, Guicciardini or Botero.

Pocock's characteristically trenchant contention has been challenged. Markku Peltonen has provided us with much evidence of the reception of civic humanism in the England of Elizabeth and James I, although he is sufficiently influenced by Pocock to suggest that what he calls 'classical republicanism' had a 'limited but undoubted impact' on English political thought, and agrees with Blair Worden and Kevin Sharpe that 'an unmixed republic

---

Mixed Monarchy under Charles I and After', *English Historical Review*, 75 (1960), 426–43. For the Nineteen Propositions see John Kenyon, *The Stuart Constitution*, 2nd edn (Cambridge, 1986), no. 68, 222–6.

[15] Pocock, *Machiavellian Moment*, 361, 338–9.

[16] Weston, 'English Constitutional Doctrine II', 426.

[17] Roger Mason, Introduction, in George Buchanan, *A Dialogue on the Law of Kingship among the Scots. A Critical Edition and Translation of George Buchanan's De Iure Regni apud Scotos Dialogus*, ed. Roger A. Mason and Martin L. Smith (2017), li.

[18] Lucien Febvre, *The Problem of Unbelief in the Sixteenth Century: The Religion of Rabelais* (Cambridge, MA, 1985), 100.

was hardly a practical option in England before the Civil War.'[19] Peltonen does not, however, define what he means by 'classical republicanism', and does not consider whether a mixed republic might have been a practical option, despite suggesting, in the context of the vexed question of the succession to the childless Elizabeth as she aged, that a 'dominant section of the political nation' could conceive of England – under highly exceptional circumstances – as a 'Polish-style' republic or as a 'mixed polity'. He almost immediately retreats from this position, however, observing that 'it is perhaps even more astonishing to find that the English displayed a particular reticence about the mixed constitution' and had very little relevant to say about it, before again qualifying his position by stating that there was a greater interest in the mixed constitution under James I without asking why that might be.[20]

Peltonen finds this lack of appreciation for the *forma mixta* surprising. He is, however, struggling with a definition of republicanism based on the Machiavellian distinction between different forms of the state, and the modern definition of a republic as a system without a king, which forces him to conclude – as the title of his second chapter indicates – that classical republicanism existed only in the margins of Elizabethan politics.[21] This struggle is also evident in the influential challenge mounted by Pat Collinson to Pocock – on which Peltonen draws extensively – with his concept of the English monarchical republic. Collinson's critique centres on Pocock's blunt assertions that 'in no way was Tudor England a polis, or its inhabitants citizens'; and that the concept of a republic of equal citizens was 'something not to be found in England and as yet scarcely to be imagined there'.[22]

Collinson challenged Pocock on two fronts. He claimed, firstly, that the idea of the *polis* had considerable appeal at the local level, especially in the towns and cities of Tudor and Jacobean England, a suggestion warmly endorsed by Mark Goldie, who stresses its attraction to office-holders, and my former colleague in Aberdeen, Phil Withington.[23] Secondly, Collinson pointed out that in 1585 Sir William Cecil confronted the succession problem by drafting a parliamentary bill authorising temporary government by a great council in the event of Elizabeth's death and establishing arrangements for designating or choosing a successor. In January 1585, indeed, Cecil sounded rather Polish when he declared that 'the government of the realme shall contynew in all respects' in the event of Elizabeth's death.[24]

---

[19] Peltonen, *Classical Humanism*, 11–12.

[20] *Ibid.*, 49–50.

[21] *Ibid.*, 54–118.

[22] Pocock, 'England', in *National Consciousness, History and Political Culture in Early Modern Europe*, ed. Orest Ranum (Baltimore, 1975), 113; idem, *Machiavellian Moment*, 354.

[23] Patrick Collinson, 'The Monarchical Republic of Queen Elizabeth I', in Collinson, *Elizabethan Essays* (1994), 31–58, at 32–4; Mark Goldie, 'The Unacknowledged Republic: Officeholding in Early Modern England', in *The Politics of the Excluded, c. 1500-1850*, ed. Tim Harris (London, 2001), 153–94; Phil Withington, *The Politics of Commonwealth: Citizens and Freemen in Early Modern England* (Cambridge, 2005).

[24] Collinson, 'Monarchical Republic', 48–56.

As Paulina Kewes has shown, calls for the exclusion of Mary Stewart from the succession, and consideration of the possibility of Parliament electing a successor to Elizabeth were more widespread than was traditionally recognised, despite censorship and Elizabeth's willingness to use the law to suppress them.[25] Andrew Hadfield has argued that Shakespeare's plays, written as Elizabeth aged, 'emerged out of a culture that was saturated with republican images and arguments', even if he follows Collinson and Peltonen by suggesting that these were 'never clearly defined or properly articulated'. Nevertheless, Hadfield argues that republicanism was 'one of the key problems that defined [Shakespeare's] working career'.[26]

I have not the time today, nor indeed, the expertise, to enter the lists in this entertaining English joust. From the outside, it seems to me self-evident that classic civic humanism had a considerable influence across the British Isles. Writers from a variety of political and religious positions invoked the concept, including John Aylmer, John Ponet, the Puritan Thomas Cartwright and the Jesuit Robert Parsons.[27] Aylmer presented England as a classic example of the *forma mixta*, while Sir Thomas Smith, who devotes chapter six of his *De republica Anglorum* to it, concludes 'that so seldome or never shall you finde common wealthes or governement which is absolutely and sincerely made' of any of the Polybian forms of government, which Smith refers to frequently, arguing that commonwealths are 'always mixed with an other, and hath the name of that which is more, and overruleth the other always or for the most part'.[28] That qualification is significant, and I shall return to it.

Despite this evidence for the influence of civic humanism, Collinson and those influenced by him are peculiarly tentative, essentially because they implicitly accept Pocock's definition of republicanism. Collinson presents his monarchical republic as a paradox – Elizabethan England 'was a republic that happened to be a monarchy, or vice versa' – and is almost apologetic about advancing it.[29] There is talk of 'republican elements' in the English system of government, and terms such as 'quasi-' or 'semi-'republican abound in the literature. Yet if we adopt Machiavelli's distinction, such formulations are dubious. Collinson talks of 'citizens concealed within subjects', as if in claiming to be citizens, Elizabethans had to be secretive, and implies that the categories of citizen and subject were, or are, incompatible. He also invokes an 'anti-monarchical virus' that he sees as 'part of the legacy of sixteenth-century humanism', a revealing formulation.[30]

---

[25] Paulina Kewes, 'Parliament and the Principle of Elective Succession in Elizabethan England', in *Writing the History of Parliament in Tudor and Early Stuart England*, ed. Paul Cavill and Alexandra Gajda (Manchester, 2018), 106–32.

[26] Andrew Hadfield, *Shakespeare and Republicanism* (Cambridge, 2005), 1.

[27] Weston, 'English Constitutional Doctrine II', 427.

[28] Sir Thomas Smith, *De republica Anglorum: A Discourse on the Commonwealth of England*, ed. L. Aston (Cambridge, 1906), 14.

[29] Collinson, 'Monarchical Republic', 43.

[30] Patrick Collinson, 'The State as Monarchical Commonwealth: "Tudor" England', *Journal of Historical Sociology*, 15 (2002), 89–95, at 94; 'Monarchical Republic', 44.

Here we see the yearning for the 'either/or' precision criticised by Febvre. If we consider the Polish-Lithuanian republic, the problem disappears. For Poland-Lithuania was not a modern republic; it was a Renaissance republic, and a Renaissance republican saw no paradox in a republic that possessed a monarch; indeed the monarchical element was essential to a well-balanced, mixed republican system, as Machiavelli himself argued in his *Discorsi*. Dorota Pietrzyk-Reeves, in her splendid account of sixteenth-century Polish republican discourse, which has just been translated, uses the term 'republican tradition' for this discourse, to distinguish it from republicanism in the acephalous Pockockian sense.[31] Here, since I am considering both the republican discourse and its embodiment in Poland-Lithuania, I prefer Renaissance republicanism.

In Poland-Lithuania, the king was an official of the republic, as Stanisław Zaborowski argued as early as 1507.[32] His functions were to govern, to appoint to office, and above all to execute the law. There was considerable support among the ordinary *szlachta* for a monarchy with substantial powers, to be used to uphold the law and protect the *populus*, the lesser nobility, from oppression by wealthy magnates who had traditionally dominated politics. From the 1530s the Polish Execution Movement urged the monarchy to execute the 1504 statute outlawing the alienation of royal land, which had benefited powerful magnates. The movement reached its height in the 1560s, when considerable amounts of alienated land were recovered for the royal treasury.

For Poles and Lithuanians the *polis* and the state were distinct conceptual entities, and we should therefore not assume that the terms *Rzeczpospolita* and state can be used interchangeably, as they frequently are by historians of Poland-Lithuania. Polish and Lithuanian nobles saw themselves *both* as citizens of a common republic *and* as subjects of their elected monarch, the king of Poland and the grand duke of Lithuania respectively. There was no conflict, and citizens were not concealed in subjects; they did not need to be. As members of a mixed *polis* they collectively determined the limitations placed upon royal power and, through the Senate council, regulated its exercise.

I would suggest that before 1642 it was perfectly possible for the political elites of the British Isles to think, up to a point, in similar terms. Civic humanism did not suddenly arrive as Falkland and Culpepper scrabbled around to produce a defence against the Nineteen Propositions. That Falkland and Culpepper clearly saw the appeal to the *forma mixta* as a tactically useful response to the Long Parliament shows that it was well known and potentially effective, whatever Pocock asserts. Portraying the monarchy as an integral part of a well-balanced commonwealth involved no paradox. Yet I would nevertheless agree with Pocock and Worden that the 1640s proved transformative.

[31] Dorota Pietrzyk-Reeves, *Polish Republican Discourse in the Sixteenth Century* (Cambridge, 2020), 6.

[32] Stanisław Zaborowski, *Tractatus quadrifidus de natura iurium et bonorum regis et de reformatione regni ac eius reipublicae regimine incipit feliciter* (Cracow, 1507). Zaborowski uses various terms to express this concept, including *administrator, tutor, conservator, rector, mediator* and *praepositus*: Henryk Litwin, Introduction to Stanisław Zaborowski, *Traktat o naturze praw i dóbr królewskich* (Cracow, 2005), xlv.

Charles's response to the Nineteen Propositions represented a last hurrah rather than a new beginning for Renaissance republicanism in England. There had always been problems reconciling the mixed form of government with the various political traditions of the British Isles. To understand why, it is necessary to return to Poland-Lithuania, where the sociopolitical context was more favourable. The Polish-Lithuanian *szlachta* was very different to the landed elites of the British Isles. Thanks to the systems of partible inheritance enshrined in customary law, the *szlachta* was not just a privileged class, it was a numerous one. All children of nobles were noble by birth, which is why the frequent translation of *szlachta* as gentry is misguided: an English squire might be a gentleman, but he was a commoner at law; a Polish *szlachcic* was not, however poor he might be. And many were poor. Perhaps 6–8 per cent of the population were noble – nearly a million by the late eighteenth century – with concentrations of poorer nobles in certain provinces, such as Samogitia in Lithuania, and Mazovia in Poland; in the latter nearly a quarter of the population claimed noble status.

The political implications were considerable. Poland and Lithuania never developed the hierarchical relationships of mutual obligation seen across western Europe in the medieval period, although many poorer nobles, especially in the eastern lands, became economically dependent on magnates. The constant division and subdivision of the family property over the generations, however, meant that families, or individual branches of families, could decline rapidly in status and wealth.

This harsh reality had two major consequences, which help explain the appeal of Renaissance republicanism. Firstly, partible inheritance fostered *szlachta* egalitarianism. There were no titles of nobility to provide a hierarchy of status; the law, indeed, banned them, and the principle was enshrined in the Union of Lublin, which limited use of the title of prince (*książę* or *kniaź*) to descendants of the royal dynasties of Lithuania and Rus': the Gedimins and the Rurikids. Sustained by the numerous middling nobles who formed the crucial office-holding class at local level, and from among whom envoys to the Sejm were elected, the principle of noble equality was tenaciously defended.

Status was provided by office-holding. Since the power to appoint to the major offices of state and provincial office was a royal prerogative – which meant that the king determined the composition of the Senate and his council, the aristocratic part of the constitution – the monarchy retained considerable influence. Thus the ideals of civic humanism, which stressed the service of virtuous citizens to the republic and proclaimed the equality of citizens, confirmed and strengthened principles already embedded in the Polish system, and proved attractive to nobles in Lithuania, where magnate power was greater than in Poland.

In England and Scotland, primogeniture and entail established a very different system for the inheritance of property and status among the landed elites, and limited the appeal of an egalitarian model of citizenship. It was much harder to enter the House of Lords in England than it was to become a senator in Poland-Lithuania, where monarchs consistently sought to check the power of wealthy magnates by appointing ambitious new men from families without a previous history of senatorial status, who constituted one-third and more of appointments. Thus Pocock is probably right to stress the 'obstinate adherence to the vision of England as a hierarchy of degree' as an important factor that reduced civic humanism's appeal.[33] While office provided a hierarchy of status in Poland-Lithuania, and wealthy magnates did lord it over poorer nobles, attachment to the principle of equality remained strong, encapsulated by the popular proverb which asserted that a simple nobleman on his manor was the equal of a palatine (*szlachcic na zagrodzie równy wojewodzie*). It was no empty phrase.

There was another problem. I again agree with Pocock when he speaks of England's 'highly wrought theory of kingship and authority'.[34] If there is one word that encapsulates the difference between the debates in England and Poland-Lithuania, it is 'sovereignty'. Historians of Poland-Lithuania, seduced by the Machiavellian notion that the republic is simply a form of the state, have long debated where sovereignty lay in Poland-Lithuania's mixed form of government, but this is to miss the point. There was no need to talk of sovereignty in a system predicated on the notion of balance between the three forms of government. There were, it is true, some opponents of the king who claimed that supreme authority lay with the *populus*, such as one pamphlet published in 1607 during the Sandomierz *rokosz*:

> The third estate, the *szlachta*, which enjoys the prerogative and preeminence in this Republic, is the leading estate. In accordance with this privilege supreme authority in this kingdom lies with it, for as this privilege states, the nobility is the most powerful part of the kingdom ...[35]

Yet such assertions were relatively rare, and the immediate qualification of the claim that supreme authority lay with the wider *szlachta* by the statement that it formed 'the most powerful, part' of the kingdom indicates that the grip of the *forma mixta* was still strong, and that sovereignty was not seen as indivisible. Bodin's assertion that it was, and that sovereignty should lie with the king, was highly unpopular in Poland-Lithuania. Bodin's loathing for the *forma mixta* owed much to his detailed knowledge of the Polish system, as relayed to him by Jan Zamoyski, a member of the embassy that arrived in France to inform Henry of Valois of his election in 1573. Bodin's frequent sour references to Poland-Lithuania meant that he did not top the bestseller lists on the Vistula.

Although discontented magnates, like Mikołaj Zebrzydowski, palatine of Cracow and a leader of the 1606 *rokosz*, or Polish Grand Marshal Jerzy Sebastian Lubomirski, who launched another *rokosz* in 1665, could raise the spectre of absolute monarchy and appeal to the principle of *de non praestanda oboedientia*, it proved impossible in practice to secure enough support to depose

---

[33] Pocock, *Machiavellian Moment*, 348.

[34] *Ibid.*

[35] 'Libera respublica, quae sit?', *Acta zjazdu stężyckiego*, in *Pisma polityczne do rokoszu Zebrzydowskiego*, ed. Jan Czubek (3 vols., Cracow, 1916–18), II, 404.

the king. Radical firebrands declared Sigismund III deposed in June 1607, but it was easier to claim that the citizen body had a right to depose the king than it was to agree on its implementation. There was minimal support for dethronement: only 400 signed the document of deposition, compared with over 10,000 who had signed the articles of confederation a year earlier.[36] The sejmiks overwhelmingly preferred to reach accommodation through the Sejm. Sigismund won the only battle fought during this short civil war, and although his reform proposals failed, he secured Sejm agreement in 1609 that obedience could only be withdrawn at a Sejm under the primate's authority. That rendered deposition even less likely, since bishops were predominantly regalist in sentiment.

In England, however, the idea of the imperial, sovereign monarchy proved a fundamental obstacle to the integration of the *forma mixta* and the Ancient Constitution, especially after the Henrician Reformation, which installed the monarch as head of the Anglican Church. The tension is evident in Smith's *De republica Anglorum*. Although the abstract term 'sovereignty' does not appear, the term sovereign certainly does.[37] Richard Knolles's translation of Bodin did not appear until 1606, but already Smith echoes Bodin in his very first chapter:

> To rule, is understoode to have the highest and supreme authoritie of commaundement. That part or member of the common wealth is saide to rule which doth controwle, correct, and direct all other members of the common wealth.[38]

This is not a mixed system at all, as Smith makes clear:

> I do not understand that our nation hath used any other generall authoritie in this realme neither Aristocratical, nor Democraticall, but onely the royall and kingly majestie.[39]

Smith's formulation makes clear that although the concepts of Renaissance republicanism were very familiar to English political thinkers, and although he had not yet reached the position of either/or, he was struggling to reconcile the idea of the *forma mixta* with post-Reformation ideas of imperial monarchy as the basis of the English state.

What, then, of Scotland, which might seem to provide more fertile ground for Renaissance republicanism? North of the border, the Reformation was institutionalised from below, not above, Presbyterian ecclesiology mirrored the institutions of the secular republic, and Calvin himself had lauded the *forma mixta* in his writings. In Buchanan, Scotland had a sophisticated, well-connected and influential European intellectual who was convinced that legitimacy was conferred on monarchs through election: 'unless we have a king

---

[36] Henryk Wisner, *Najjaśniejsza Rzeczpospolita. Szkice z czasów Zygmunta III i Władysława IV Wazy* (Warsaw, 2001), 94.

[37] L. Alston, 'Introduction', in Smith, *De republica Anglorum*, xxii.

[38] Smith, *De republica Anglorum*, 9.

[39] *Ibid.*, 19.

chosen by election, I am afraid we are not going to have any legitimate ruler at all.'[40] He sought to demonstrate the elective and contractual nature of Scottish kingship by enumerating the many kings of Scots who had been deposed, assassinated, or killed in battles by their own subjects. Far from limiting the right of resistance to inferior magistrates as Calvinist resistance theorists proposed, Buchanan endorsed the assassination of a tyrant by any citizen.[41]

Buchanan's contention that kingship was elective was taken up by others. In 1639 Alexander Henderson declared that 'the people maketh the Magistrate, but the Magistrate maketh not the people,' while in 1644 another prominent Covenanter, Samuel Rutherford, invoked the *forma mixta* in claiming that 'royalists cannot deny but a people ruled by aristocratic magistrates may elect a king, and a king so elected is formally made a lawful king by the people's election.'[42] Rutherford believed that the covenant between the king and the people entered into at the time of his election was conditional, and that the people could withdraw their allegiance if the king upheld false religion.[43] These arguments sound very familiar to a historian of Poland-Lithuania; they reflected a long Scottish political tradition: as in Poland, Scots had asserted in the 1320 Declaration of Arbroath that the king had no right to alienate the kingdom or any part of it without the consent of the community of the realm.

And Scots were prepared to defy their king. The National Covenant, drafted in Greyfriars Kirkyard in Edinburgh in February 1638 and sent round the parishes to garner tens of thousands of signatures, was the foundation document of what is termed the Scottish Revolution. It appealed to the covenant between God and his people, citing a long list of Acts of the Scottish Parliament establishing the 'true Kirk of God' in Charles's northern realm. It explicitly referred to the oath he had sworn at his 1633 coronation to uphold that religion.

To a historian used to the robust exchanges of Polish-Lithuanian politics, however, the Covenant is a peculiarly half-hearted document. There is no explicit warning to Charles of the consequences of breaking his oath, and no claim of any right to withdraw obedience; indeed the signatories solemnly promised 'that we shall to the utmost of our power, with our means and lives, stand to the defence of our dread Sovereign the King's Majesty, his person and authority, in the defence and preservation of the aforesaid true religion'.[44]

That word 'sovereign' again. In reading Buchanan, one can sense a Scot looking down the road travelled by Poles and Lithuanians as far as he could, yet he is held back by his attachment to the ancient Scottish monarchy. This problem, as in England, is reflected more widely in Scottish political thought. Allan Macinnes, another former colleague in Aberdeen, has stressed

---

[40] Buchanan, *Dialogue*, 18.

[41] *Ibid.*, 6–7.

[42] Anon. [Alexander Henderson], *Some Special Arguments for the Scottish Subjects lawfull defence of their Religion and Liberty ...* (Amsterdam, 1642), 5; Samuel Rutherford, *Lex, Rex, or the Law and the Prince; a dispute for the Just Prerogative of King and People* (Edinburgh, 1893), 9.

[43] *Ibid.*, 54–68.

[44] The National Covenant (1638), https://www.fpchurch.org.uk/about-us/important-documents/the-national-covenant-1638 (accessed 29 Mar. 2022).

the growth of federative senses of commonwealth in a Scotland struggling to adjust to absentee monarchy after 1603, and drawn attention to the parallels between the institutions of covenanting and the practice of confederation in Poland-Lithuania.[45] Covenanters claimed that they were not seeking to impose government on Scotland, but were seeking to restore Scotland's ancient mixed constitution.[46] And yet the text of the National Covenant, and the writings of prominent Covenanters, including Archibald Johnston of Warriston and Alexander Henderson, who drafted it, draw predominantly on religious, not secular, principles to justify resistance to Charles.

In contrast, the most remarkable feature of the constitutional revolution in Poland-Lithuania was its entirely secular nature. It took place against a background of intense religious division, between Catholics and Orthodox – a division that long predated the Reformation – and between Catholics and Protestants. By 1569 around half the Senate were non-Catholics, most of them Protestant, predominantly Calvinists. Yet religion intruded remarkably little upon the constitutional revolution. The 1573 Warsaw Confederation stipulated that those that differed in religion – *dissidentes in religione* – would not perpetrate violence or bring legal cases against each other on religious grounds. Protestants accepted the Catholic primate as interrex, and while Catholic bishops were only too happy to cause trouble, the strongly secular basis of civic humanism and the *forma mixta* united citizens who differed in religion round the secular concept of the republic. Only in Poland-Lithuania was it conceivable that a confirmed antitrinitarian, Mikołaj Sienicki, could be elected on ten occasions as speaker of the chamber of envoys, which was far more Catholic than the Senate.

Buchanan's great works are similarly secular in nature, and he draws on Scottish history and civic humanism to justify his radical vision of politics, despite his lack of interest in the *forma mixta*. The Covenanters, however, justified their resistance largely in religious terms. The Covenant defined the nation's political and historic identity in a religious and monarchic framework, with little or no reference to the ideals of citizenship propounded by Buchanan and the civic humanists. Laura Stewart observes that in contrast to what Goldie and Withington found for England, the language of citizenship 'was not commonplace in early modern Scotland', even in the burghs; she suggests that traditional vertical ties of lordship meant that Collinson's monarchical republic 'was not easy to translate into practice north of the border'.[47]

In political terms, this absence of discourses of citizenship north of the border has much to do with the fact that since Buchanan had published his great works, the union of the crowns had transformed the context for Scottish politics. Charles's religious policy may have alienated a majority of his Scottish

---

[45] Allan Macinnes, 'The Hidden Commonwealth: Poland-Lithuania and Scottish Political Discourse in the Seventeenth Century', in *Citizenship and Identity in a Multinational Commonwealth: Poland-Lithuania in Context, 1550-1772*, ed. Karin Friedrich and Barbara Pendzich (Leiden, 2009), 233–60.

[46] Laura Stewart, *Rethinking the Scottish Revolution: Covenanted Scotland, 1638-1651* (Oxford, 2016), 124.

[47] *Ibid.*, 7.

subjects, but as the text of the Covenant reveals, monarchy was central to the Scottish sense of identity. James VI's succession to the English throne had ended the need for the long, stubborn Scottish resistance to the claims of lordship advanced over the centuries by English kings, but it provided no constitutional framework in which Scots could assert the equality of the kingdom of Scotland within the union, as Lublin provided for Lithuania. Claims for the antiquity of the Scottish monarchy advanced by Hector Boece, first principal of my university, and Buchanan himself, therefore became central to attempts by Scots to assert their status within the union. The superior antiquity of their monarchy was the one area – apart, of course, from their superior understanding of God's word – in which Scots could demonstrate their manifest superiority to their English neighbours. After 1603, Buchanan's vision of elective kingship gradually lost its appeal. Sir Thomas Craig of Riccarton, an advocate of union, asserted that God preferred hereditary monarchy: 'As everyone knows,' he wrote, 'the will of the people can no more call a prince to the throne than it can eject him from it.'[48]

Thus Renaissance republicanism did not gain sufficient traction in Scotland to underpin a secular revolution. The confederative institutions established to defy Charles I embodied the principles of self-government, but they were justified in religious, not secular terms – they were confessional confederations, as Macinnes observes – and the centrality of monarchy to Scottish identity was encapsulated in the Scottish refusal to have anything to do with Charles's trial, and the rapid declaration of Charles II's succession following his father's execution. The incorporation of Scotland into the English republic by Cromwell without so much as a by-your-leave ensured that, when the Restoration came, support for monarchy in Scotland was all but universal.

So I no longer find the views of Sir George Mackenzie quite so surprising. Long before 1684, the attractions of civic humanism in Scotland had faded. On the other side of the Irish Sea, Ireland's colonial situation and its deep religious divisions rendered civic humanism of mere academic interest; here the instrument of confederation was used in the 1640s not to defy but to support a monarchy that seemed to provide the only hope of protection for native and Old English Catholics, for whom the ideal of virtuous citizenship seemed distant indeed in a system in which the subordination of a Protestant-dominated Irish Parliament to the English Parliament rendered the *forma mixta* irrelevant. Even in England, where Charles's execution abruptly removed the monarchical element of the constitution, civic humanism could offer little to a polity in which the army had reduced Parliament to an impotent rump. Yet older modes of thought persisted. After all, Cromwell was offered the throne. He refused, although as Lord Protector he effectively restored the monarchical element in the constitution, which his son was to inherit on his death, since nobody could think of what else to do. It seems that a republic without a king was rather harder to imagine than is sometimes suggested.

The contrast with 1572 in Poland-Lithuania is striking. After 1566, both states of the union possessed a political framework in which the ideals of Renaissance

---

[48] Thomas Craig, *De unione regnorum Britanniae tractatus* (1607), 228, 270.

republicanism could be realised. In this process, Sigismund August played a central role. Early in his reign, he had, like his predecessors, largely ruled through his ministers and senate council. His lack of an heir, however, led him to fret about the continuation of the union after his death. In 1564 he took the remarkable step of resigning his hereditary rights as supreme duke of Lithuania in favour of the community of the Polish realm – the citizen body – much to the chagrin of his three sisters, opening the way to a fully elective monarchy. Finally, in the testament prepared shortly before his death, he endorsed the republican vision laid out in the Lublin Union in the language of civic humanism:

> ... I beseech, remind, and urge all ... ecclesiastical and lay senators, the equestrian order, all nobles and towns ... being inhabitants, whether of the kingdom of Poland or of the grand duchy of Lithuania, that they should maintain their unity in one eternal, indivisible body, forming one people, one nation, one unitary republic as constituted and formed by oath two years ago at the Lublin assembly; and that they should continue in sincere and true fraternal affection, just as if their heads and limbs formed one people, one republic.[49]

A republican king? There are more things in heaven and earth, Professor Pocock, than are dreamt of in your philosophy.

There was one more major barrier to the *forma mixta* in the British Isles. To understand what it was, we need to consider another aspect of the Polish-Lithuanian constitution. The *forma mixta* worked in Poland-Lithuania on account of a feature of the system that attracted considerable criticism from contemporary commentators: the fact that the popular and aristocratic elements of the constitution were drawn from the same social class. From 1572 the major cities effectively withdrew from the system; they were content to form their own self-governing republics on the basis of German law – mainly Magdeburg Law – which was extended to royal burghs and private towns alike. In the *szlachta* republic, therefore, the *populus*, the popular element in the polity, did not pose any wider social challenge. Debates raged about where the balance between the three elements of the system should lie, but even if some among the *szlachta* felt that the preponderance lay with the *populus*, that claim constituted no threat to the social order.

Not so in the British Isles. Historians are often eager to detect support for popular sovereignty in the political thought of the age, and it is not hard to find statements that authority ultimately, or at least originally, lay with the community of the realm. Nevertheless, while political philosophers could talk in general terms of ancient contracts, fundamental laws and the bestowal of authority on monarchs by the people, their earnest treatises were based on speculation and the sort of mythical history peddled by Boece and Buchanan in Scotland, or Geoffrey of Monmouth and Raphael Holinshed in England. There were no documents corroborating their speculations. England might have its Magna

---

[49] *Testament Zygmunta Augusta*, ed. Antoni Franaszek, Olga Łaszczyńska and Stanisław Edward Nahlik (Cracow, 1975), 7.

Carta, and Scotland its Declaration of Arbroath, but there was nothing to match the detailed republican constitutional documents that regulated political life in Poland-Lithuania and specified the nature of the contract with the monarch.

In the British Isles the 1640s demonstrated that ordinary people from almost all social classes were eminently capable of political agency. In both Scotland and England, there was, as Stewart notes, a 'sudden expansion of "the public" as a regular descriptor for an organized and coherent body politic, "a community" encompassing "the whole nation"'.[50] Nevertheless, while political rhetoric frequently invoked such a community, the political activism of the lower orders, once unleashed, proved unsettling. The Edinburgh crowds who turned out in raucous numbers during the prayer book controversy were one thing; Levellers, Diggers and army radicals in England quite another. In Ireland, a broad conceptualisation of the body politic was impossible for the governing elite in a country in which Catholics comprised a large majority of the people. The spectre of popular radicalism stalked the land; for many among the elites of the British Isles 'the impetuous caprices of the Multitude when giddy', in Mackenzie's words, proved terrifying.

Thus neither England nor Scotland nor Ireland possessed the institutional or social structure that might have made the *forma mixta* more than a scholarly chimera. The execution of Charles I was cathartic. Across the British archipelago, thinkers and politicians had long struggled to reconcile the ideal of the Aristotelian *polis* with traditions of imperial monarchy, now bolstered by the Bodinian concept of indivisible sovereignty. The *forma mixta*, which was suited to the Aristotelian *polis*, the community of citizens, but not the juridical, abstract state, was no longer fit for purpose, although the fact that Algernon Sidney was still appealing to it in the 1690s suggests that we should be properly cautious of reports of its demise. After 1660, different means of controlling the dread sovereign monarch needed to be found; ultimately the peculiarly British fiction of the indivisible sovereignty of the King in Parliament was devised to solve the problems posed by Charles II and his Catholic brother. It was a solution which neatly kept Mackenzie's absolutism at bay while avoiding the perilous consequences of assigning sovereignty to that vague concept, the people. Poland-Lithuania, however, by creating a Renaissance republic through the institutionalisation of the *forma mixta*, took the road less travelled in a Europe in which, after 1648, the concept of the sovereign state gradually emerged as the foundation of the international states system. That decision had consequences, because the Aristotelian and Polybian conceptualisation of the *forma mixta* said much about how power was to be shared and tempered, but offered little guidance as to how it was to be exercised. That, however, is another story for another day.

Acknowledgements. A version of this article was first presented as the Royal Historical Society's 2021 Prothero Lecture, read on 2 July 2021.

---

[50] Stewart, *Rethinking the Scottish Revolution*, 222.

Cite this article: Frost R (2022). The Roads Not Taken: Liberty, Sovereignty and the Idea of the Republic in Poland-Lithuania and the British Isles, 1550–1660. *Transactions of the Royal Historical Society* 32, 93–112. https://doi.org/10.1017/S0080440122000068

Transactions of the RHS (2022), **32**, 113–133
doi:10.1017/S0080440122000020

ARTICLE

Four Axes of Mission: Conversion and the Purposes of Mission in Protestant History

Alec Ryrie[1] and D. J. B. Trim[2]*

[1]Department of Theology and Religion, University of Durham, Durham, UK and [2]General Conference of Seventh Day Adventists, Office of Archives Statistics and Research, Silver Spring, Maryland, USA
*Corresponding author. Email alec.ryrie@durham.ac.uk; davidtrim@icloud.com

(Received 21 January 2022; accepted 28 January 2022)

Abstract

This article offers a framework for historical analysis of the goals of Protestant missionary projects. 'Conversion' in Protestantism is not clearly defined, is liable to be falsified and may (in some missionary views) require preparatory work of various kinds before it can be attempted. For these reasons, Protestant missionaries have adopted a variety of intermediate and proxy goals for their work, goals which it is argued can be organised onto four axes: orthodoxy, zeal, civilisation and morality. Together these form a matrix which missionaries, their would-be converts and their sponsors have tried to negotiate. In different historical contexts, missionaries have chosen different combinations of priorities, and have adapted these in the face of experience. The article suggests how various historical missionary projects can be analysed using this matrix and concludes by suggesting some problems and issues in the history of Protestant missions which such analysis can illuminate.

Keywords: missions; Church history; imperial history; Protestantism

Protestant missionaries, almost by definition, set out to foster 'conversion' of some kind. This article sets out a scheme for analysing that aim historically, by attending to how missionaries have conceived it and measured their own success or failure. We do so against the background of a generation of scholarship on the problem of conversion which has enriched the field by directing our attention beyond the missionaries themselves. Since the groundbreaking work of Jean and John Comaroff in the 1990s, historians and other scholars of missions have come to appreciate that conversion is a game for multiple players, and one which necessarily includes political, cultural, economic and anthropological dimensions as well as (indeed, sometimes almost to the exclusion of) explicitly 'religious' ones. The Comaroffs' foundational notion of conversion as 'conversation', a dialectic between missionaries and 'indigenous' people, now seems almost a truism, and some more recent scholars have argued that even their enhanced understanding gives insufficient weight to the ways in which indigenous people can participate in and, to some degree, control the nature of their own conversions. Christian missiologists long treated indigenous people as essentially passive or indeed resistant actors in the drama of conversion, but the work of the psychologist of religion Lewis Rambo, with his emphasis on conversion as 'turning' or movement, has unavoidably turned the focus onto the converts themselves. It is now possible, as David Kling has masterfully demonstrated, to write a comprehensive history of Christian conversion in which converts – not missionary agents – take centre stage.[1] Christian theological commentators on the globalisation of Christianity, such as Lamin Sanneh and Philip Jenkins, have come to emphasise Christianity's protean nature, and to describe conversion as a process of 'translation' in which, in Jenkins's terms, 'foreign cultural trappings' were 'purge[d] away' by indigenous converts. David Lindenfeld's recent history of the globalisation of Christianity aims to tell that story primarily through the eyes of indigenous people, developing a complex taxonomy of how they were snared on Christianity's manifold 'cultural hooks', with responses ranging from selective incorporation of Christian practices and ideas; through 'dual religious participation', in which distinct traditions are retained in separate cultural spaces; to various processes of 'translation' in which Christian practices and ideas are given new cultural expressions.[2] Some of these processes amount to 'cultural imperialism', but by no means all. Some historians of mission have even begun to talk of mutual conversion, in which missionaries and those who send them undergo transformations as profound as any they are trying to bring about in their flocks.[3]

Given this direction of scholarly travel, to turn our attention back to the missionaries and their intentions – as this article does – may seem perverse. Our suggestion, however, is that missions are indeed a game for multiple players; while our understanding of the parts played by indigenous peoples has been greatly enriched, the other side of the story has not quite kept up. In particular, since the conversionary encounter is typically initiated by missionary agents, this is a game in which missionaries have a first-mover

---

[1] Jean Comaroff and John Comaroff, *Of Revelation and Revolution*, 2 vols., i, *Christianity, Colonialism and Consciousness in South Africa*, ii, *The Dialectics of Modernity on a South African Frontier* (Chicago, 1991, 1997); Lewis Rambo, *Understanding Religious Conversion* (New Haven, 1993), esp. 3; David W. Kling, *A History of Christian Conversion* (Oxford, 2020).

[2] Lamin Sanneh, *Translating the Message: The Missionary Impact on Culture* (Maryknoll, NY, 2009); Philip Jenkins, *The Next Christendom: The Coming of Global Christianity* (Oxford, 2002), esp. 43–50, at 45; David Lindenfeld, *World Christianity and Indigenous Experience: A Global History 1500–2000* (Cambridge, 2021), esp. 9–30.

[3] For an example of the phenomenon of the 'conversion' of missionaries, eased in this case by Vatican II's avowed openness to learning from 'what is good and holy' in non-Christian religions, see Laura Rademaker, 'Going Native: Converting Narratives in Tiwi Histories of Twentieth-Century Missions', *Journal of Ecclesiastical History*, 70 (2019), 98–118, esp. 113. This is distinct from the wider notion that missionary ventures could be transformative, even 'conversionary', for the societies which sent them: see David A. Hollinger, *Protestants Abroad: How Missionaries Tried to Change the World but Changed America* (Princeton and Woodstock, Oxon., 2017).

advantage. If we are to understand how the game plays out, it is important not only to understand the motives and responses of indigenous peoples, but also to understand what missionaries have thought they were trying to achieve, and why they set about their work as they did.

If this question has been neglected, it is partly because the answer is too simple and obvious to be interesting. Missionaries were (and are) trying to convert peoples from different cultures to Christianity, in some of the many senses in which that is possible. They may use a wide range of means to pursue very varied kinds of conversion, and they may (of course) meet with little or no success. They will also have a variety of other motives, from personal ambition to patriotic support for imperial enterprises.[4] But insofar as conversion in some sense is no longer their aim, then they are no longer really Christian missionaries. If a good deal of scholarly attention has focused on those 'mixed', secular motives,[5] it is partly because the baseline of conversionary intent goes without saying.

Yet if conversion is a tangled, negotiated and contested problem, missionaries are necessarily drawn into those tangles, negotiations and contests. What counts – in missionaries' eyes, or the eyes of those who send and support them – as a sufficient, authentic or valid conversion? This is a 'persistent and controversial issue within the history of Christian conversion'.[6] The problem is a particularly acute one for the Protestant missionaries who are the focus of this article. In the Catholic tradition, the fundamental purpose of mission is less the securing of individual conversions than the establishment of the Church in new lands.[7] Moreover, when individuals do convert, the process is framed by reasonably clear-cut external and sacramental markers. For Catholics, unlike for most Protestants, baptism is understood to be an *ex opere operato* means of grace, which incorporates even an infant or uncomprehending candidate into the Church: such people's conversion is hardly complete, but they can meaningfully be described as Catholic.

In Protestantism, the emphasis on the exclusive importance of faith and the move away from sacramental or ecclesiastical elements in salvation has made the problem of missionary goals a much more vexed one. With salvation understood as above all an inward event, individual conversion came to be enduringly important for many varieties of Protestants, with many traditions valuing conversion narratives or testimonies of faith as markers of full

---

[4] Comaroff and Comaroff, *Of Revelation and Revolution*, i, 7, 10–11; and see next note.

[5] Norman Etherington, 'Introduction' to *Missions and Empire*, ed. Norman Etherington (Oxford, 2005), 2, 4, reviews literature depicting missionary motivations as tainted by commercial and imperial imperatives, which Etherington sees as of the past; but cf. John Barker, 'Where the Missionary Frontier Ran ahead of Empire', *ibid.*, 86–106, esp. the conclusion at p. 105; and Mark Thomas Edwards, *Faith and Foreign Affairs in the American Century* (Lanham and London, 2019), 19–23, 52–5. The tendency in the social sciences to see missionaries' motivations predominantly in negative terms is effectively problematised by Robert J. Priest, 'Missionary Positions: Christian, Modernist, Postmodernist', *Current Anthropology*, 42 (2001), 29–68.

[6] Kling, *A History of Christian Conversion*, 662–3 and cf. 18–19, 261–2.

[7] David Bosch, *Witness to the World: The Christian Mission in Theological Perspective* (Louisville, 1980; Eugene, 2006), 117–18.

membership.[8] Even in more traditionally structured Protestant churches, it was axiomatic to missionary theorists, practitioners and promoters from the beginning that *conversio* had to precede *plantatio*. 'Wee have not learnt as yet,' wrote the publicists for one of the first Protestant missions in the 1640s, 'the art of coyning Christians, or putting Christs name and Image upon copper mettle': nor, indeed, did they have any wish to imitate such corrupt and superficial mass production, which they associated with Catholicism and with Spain. A church had to be built from individuals.[9]

But in the absence of unambiguous ritual or legal markers, what constitutes an authentic individual conversion? How can anyone be sure of the authenticity of someone else's conversion, or indeed of their own? This is a recurrent problem of Protestant theology and pastoral practice in a great many contexts, including in evangelistic work in missionary homelands. However, it is perhaps at its most acute in the missionary encounter, where the lack of a shared set of cultural languages and practices makes it unusually difficult to 'read' other people with any confidence.

In this essay, we suggest a framework for analysing the different ways in which Protestant missionaries have tried to tackle this problem.

In the absence of windows into the soul, Protestant missionaries have from the earliest times felt obliged both to apply a series of presumptions about what conversion means, and to use various proxies to measure it, and its sufficiency or authenticity. This grew from the belief that certain individual and communal patterns of behaviour were outward manifestations of the inward, invisible transformation that was Protestant missionaries' underlying aim. And so missionaries have adopted those patterns as proxies or surrogates for conversion. These proxies tended, by elision, to become the actual goals of the missionary enterprise. At the simplest level, certain types of behaviour were taken to be signifiers of inner change, so much so that the signifier became the signified.

Nor did proxies need to signify profound inner transformation to be significant. Missionary work is very often attended with meagre success.[10] Under such circumstances, it is common for missionaries to modulate their goals, and to pursue patterns of communal behaviour which might not represent complete and 'authentic' conversion, but which might be steps towards it: the early nineteenth century British missionary John Philip referred to this

---

[8] Cf. Kling, *A History of Christian Conversion*, 663.

[9] *The Day-Breaking, if not the sun-rising of the Gospell with the Indians in New-England* (Wing S3110. London, 1647), 15; Jan Jongeneel, 'The Missiology of Gisbertus Voetius', *Calvin Theological Journal*, 26 (1991), 47–79, at 64–5.

[10] For some compelling recent case studies that illustrate this truism, see Travis Glasson, *Mastering Christianity: Missionary Anglicanism and Slavery in the Atlantic World* (Oxford, 2012); D. L. Noorlander, *Heaven's Wrath: The Protestant Reformation and the Dutch West India Company in the Atlantic World* (Ithaca, 2019); James Van Horn Melton, 'Conversion and Its Discontents on the Southern Colonial Frontier: The Pietist Encounter with Non-Christians in Colonial Georgia', in *Protestant Empires: Globalizing the Reformation*, ed. Ulinka Rublack (Cambridge, 2020), 228–53. In the nineteenth century, famously, David Livingstone won only a single African convert.

as the '"indirect" or "reflected influence" of the gospel'.[11] Soon enough, missionaries might see these patterns as legitimate proxies for, and thus metrics of, missional 'success', and even claim them as a mission's purpose. Preparatory projects, such as teaching indigenous people to speak and read European languages, could blur into the conversionary task itself.[12] So could charitable or medical work by missionaries which did not have an explicitly conversionary aspect.

Going down such paths has been particularly tempting when conversion in the conventional sense has seemed out of reach: when it has appeared that inner change is not being effected, or not sufficiently so. Under those circumstances, there could be considerable pressure (whether internal, from the missionaries themselves, or external, from their sponsors or funders) to redefine success as something that was both achievable and measurable, such as attendance at schools, changes to patterns of communal behaviour, or even the construction of buildings. In this way, goals conceived of as proxies for conversion might come to substitute for it, as that unmeasurable and, apparently, barely attainable aim receded over the horizon.

What makes this process of historical interest is that it was rare for any one of these proxies to be seen as adequate on its own. Our argument, therefore, is that historic Protestant missions can be profitably analysed in terms of the range of proxies they used to measure and direct their activities, and in terms of how those proxies were understood to relate to each other in terms of sequencing, attainability, interdependence and importance. In what follows, we propose a simple matrix for analysing these proxies; offer some historical examples of how they have interacted in practice; and suggest ways that this matrix can be used to interrogate some of the persistent problems of the history of Protestant missions.

Four axes of conversion

We propose a conceptual matrix in which the proxy measures of conversion used and sought by Protestant missionaries may be plotted along four axes. The historical question then becomes which axes were prioritised over others, to what extent, why and with what consequences. The four axes are:

1. *Orthodoxy.* Does a convert openly profess doctrines which the missionary regards as correct, for example by affirming a confession of faith or other creedal statement, or by demonstrating a satisfactory understanding of key doctrinal issues?
2. *Zeal.* Is a convert earnest, persistent and committed in their practice of Christianity, rather than formal, intermittent and indifferent? How confident can the missionary be of their sincerity?

---

[11] Comaroff and Comaroff, *Of Revelation and Revolution*, ii, 77.
[12] See Clifford Putney, 'Introduction' to *The Role of the American Board in the World: Bicentennial Reflections on the Organization's Missionary Work, 1810–1920*, ed. Clifford Putney and Paul T. Burlin (Eugene, 2012), xx.

3. *Civilisation*. Does a convert live in a mode which the missionary regards as civilised and fully human (typically including functional literacy), or in a mode perceived as primitive, wild or animalistic ('heathen')?

4. *Morality*. Does a convert live in accordance with the ethical priorities the missionary teaches (regardless of any formal religious basis for their ethics)?

These axes are here phrased in individual terms, but even the most individualistic of Protestant missionaries have always understood that conversions are made possible (or prevented) by a social context, and have social consequences.[13] All four axes can be applied to societies as well as to individuals, albeit to different extents. The first two are more inherently individualistic in nature; the latter two more collective. This is one of the factors governing which axes are prioritised in particular circumstances.

None of the axes represent stark dichotomies, although they can be expressed as such. Each has its opposing poles (zeal vs apathy, morality vs depravity), but each axis represents a spectrum. They were potentially liable in missionary eyes not only to deficiency, but to excess or at least perversion: civilisation could become decadence, and zeal, enthusiasm or fanaticism – faults that many missionaries knew all too well from their home countries. Even orthodoxy and morality could be corrupted into dry book-learning and legalistic self-righteousness. Such flaws were usually the result of the four axes becoming unbalanced: enthusiasm, for example, was zeal without sufficient orthodoxy, and decadence, civilisation without morality.

It is rare to find this matrix being articulated in full in the sources, but some witnesses come close. In 1649, for example, England's governing Rump Parliament established the Society for the Propagation of the Gospel in New England, one of the first Protestant missionary corporations.[14] The legislation celebrates the conversions that had been reported amongst Native Americans in Massachusetts, but immediately asks: how can anyone be sure these conversions are authentic? The answer is keyed to all four of our axes. They are 'not only of Barbarous become Civil' (*civility*); they have also proved the authenticity of their conversions by

> their diligent attending of the Word so preached unto them [*orthodoxy*], with tears lamenting their mis-spent lives [*zeal*], teaching their Children what they are instructed in themselves, being careful to place their said Children in godly English Families, and to put them to English Schools [*orthodoxy* and *civility*], betaking themselves to one wife, putting away the rest [*morality*], and by their constant prayers to Almighty God morning

---

[13] Ira Katznelson and Miri Rubin (eds.), 'Introduction' to *Religious Conversion: History, Experience and Meaning* (Aldershot, 2014), 1; Kling, *A History of Christian Conversion*, 661–2.

[14] Not to be confused with the better-known Society for the Propagation of the Gospel in Foreign Parts (SPG), established in 1701.

and evening in their families, expressed (in all appearance) with much Devotion and Zeal of heart' [*zeal*] ...[15]

Even if such a comprehensive and explicit appeal to all four axes is unusual, all four are pervasively evident in Protestant missional thought and practice. While the pattern originates in the early modern period, it also persists, in somewhat changed form, to the post-imperial age. As the English legislators of 1649 suggest, most Protestant missionaries' *ideals* would include 'conversion' in all four senses – to bring people, ultimately, to the point of being orthodox, zealous, civilised and moral. Yet missionaries, as well as bringing their own distinctive preconceptions to the problem, have always had to recognise that the peoples they are attempting to reach begin from different points in the matrix. They therefore need to decide which measures they see as most ultimately important, which as the most immediately urgent, and which as practically attainable. They may believe, for example, that it is futile to teach doctrine before morals have been reformed – or the reverse. This decides what map through the matrix to the hoped-for destination they may attempt to chart. Missionaries might prioritise the teaching of doctrine, the fostering of personal commitment, the reformation of modes of living, or the inculcation of ethical norms – and in each case meaningfully regard themselves not only as pursuing conversion, but as doing so by the most urgent means in the particular circumstance they faced.

The matrix in practice

When the Protestant missionary endeavour was first taking shape, in the years around 1700, the conventional maps plotted through the matrix would have varied dramatically in different geographical and cultural settings of missionary activity. A typical Euro-American Protestant of that era might rank the native peoples of the Americas as having neither orthodoxy (if they had notions of deity, they were distant from Christian ones) nor civility. Yet the same peoples might be ranked highly for zeal, and perhaps for morals, with any perceived depravity often being blamed on the traders, soldiers and settlers who were corrupting them. However, the general consensus of the age was that civility was a prerequisite for true conversion. It was commonplace to argue that until Native Americans came to adopt settled agricultural lifestyles, any talk of Christianity was futile, and to blame missionary failure on their stubborn attachment to their traditional way of life. The early eighteenth-century Anglican catechist Elias Neau, justly renowned as a sympathetic missionary to enslaved Africans, took a much dimmer view of Native Americans: 'people, who have nothing but the Figure of Men'. After two decades' American experience, he wrote, 'I never see any of them that were true Converts ... but must needs say that if the Purity of manners be not joined with that of doctrine I have no good opinion of such Professors of Christianity'.

---

[15] *An act for the promoting and propagating the Gospel of Jesus Christ in New England. Die Veneris, 27 Julii, 1649. Ordered by the Commons assembled in Parliament* (Wing E2505A. London, 1649), 407–8.

Barbarism was tied to immorality: Neau saw it as futile 'to run in the woods after miserable Creatures who breath nothing but Blood and Slaughter'. And he was clear as to why superficial conversions were meaningless: although 'it is good to propose the Truth to the Mind', nevertheless 'the most difficult part is not to instruct Mens minds but to carry the affections of the Heart to the Love and Obedience of the Supream Good'.[16] Or, in our terms: until they had attained civilisation and morality, training in orthodoxy alone could not be crowned with the zeal which he saw as the final desideratum of his mission. As such, efforts to induce or even compel them to change that way of life, even though devoid of any apparently religious content, might be understood as missionary endeavours.[17] Later in the eighteenth century, missionary opponents of the slave trade would advance a similar argument: until slaves were enabled by freedom to enter into some semblance of civilised life, rather than being brutalised by servitude, they would be unable to embrace Christianity.

The priority on civilisation was not universally shared in the seventeenth and eighteenth centuries, however, with some Protestants even suggesting that European notions of civility in fact amounted to decadence and served to hinder rather than to further the propagation of the faith.[18] Differing views on this meant that if Native Americans professed Christianity, a missionary might – or might not – prioritise zeal and ethical norms (such as marriage) over civilisational norms such as diet and dress. By contrast, the same missionary might rank the 'carnal Protestant' of England as civilised and orthodox, but as apathetic and formal in faith, and depraved in morals – even using the virtues of the pagans to reproach nominal Christians back home.[19] The 'wild Irish', by contrast, our missionary would regard as partially orthodox – they were baptised and professing Christians even if they were papists – and as zealous, but as so lacking in either civility or morality, and indeed in knowledge of their supposed faith, that they might be counted as effectively pagan.[20]

Our hypothetical Protestant missionary in 1700 would, however, have regarded many non-Christian peoples as civilised. The 'Turks' were also typically seen as zealous, with their piety and especially their iconophobia putting Christians' lax orthodoxy to shame; their morals were a mixed picture, their charity being admired and their polygamy deplored. Protestant visitors to the Ottoman Empire often thought the Turks compared favourably to Orthodox Christians, who were seen as lamentably lacking in zeal, morality

---

[16] Elias Neau to John Chamberlayne, 3 Oct. 1705, Rhodes House Library, Oxford, SPG Letterbooks A2/125 p. 3.

[17] R.G., *Virginia's cure, or, An advisive narrative concerning Virginia discovering the true ground of that churches unhappiness, and the only true remedy* (Wing G1624. London, 1662); W. Stitt Robinson Jr, 'Indian Education and Missions in Colonial Virginia', *Journal of Southern History*, 18 (1952), 152–68, esp. 160.

[18] Gerald J. Goodwin, 'Christianity, Civilization and the Savage: The Anglican Mission to the American Indian', *Historical Magazine of the Protestant Episcopal Church*, 42 (1973), 93–110.

[19] *The Day-Breaking, if not the sun-rising*, 5.

[20] Jenny Shaw, *Everyday Life in the Early English Caribbean: Irish, Africans and the Construction of Difference* (Athens, GA, 2013), esp. 30.

and civilisation compared to their Turkish neighbours – deficits which were easy to blame on those Christians' doctrinal shortcomings.[21] The Chinese, by contrast, were usually classed as pagans, and so sunk deeper in theological error than the monotheistic Turks, but to a Protestant admirer such as Gottfried Wilhelm Leibniz, China's civility matched or even exceeded Europe's: it was that very civility which offered him hope that China might be brought to embrace the one thing it lacked, namely Christianity.[22]

Missiological solutions to these different challenges varied depending on the theological assumptions which were brought to the task. Lutheran Orthodoxy generally prioritised orthodoxy over zeal, to the extent that the seventeenth-century Lutheran establishment was hostile to any notion of cross-cultural mission.[23] Likewise, a Dutch Calvinist might place a premium on doctrinal education, to the extent that a minister in seventeenth-century Ceylon might measure his success by the fact that his converts 'could refute the Popish Errors concerning Purgatory, the Mass, Indulgences, Auricular Confession, &c.'.[24] A Pietist might value zeal over civility, accepting, for example, the legitimacy of working in indigenous languages such as Sámi or Tamil.[25] Anglo-American Calvinists, and indeed Huguenots such as Elias Neau, might emphasise the need for civility. English Latitudinarians might prioritise morals.

By the nineteenth and twentieth centuries, Protestant missionaries were populating the matrix differently, but the basic framework remains. While many missionaries of this later era plainly desired to effect deep spiritual transformations, their priorities frequently slipped from orthodoxy and zeal towards civilisation and morality, through an often unwitting elision of Christian beliefs with the cultural practices and technologies of western Christendom. Robert Moffat wrote about his mission to the Tswana in the 1830s that:

> The same Gospel which had taught them that they were spiritually miserable, blind, and naked, discovered to them also that they needed reform externally, and thus prepared their minds to adopt those modes of comfort, cleanliness, and convenience which they had been accustomed to view only as the peculiarities of a strange people.[26]

[21] Cf. Mark Mazower, *The Balkans: A Short History*, The Modern Library edn (New York, 2002), xxxii–xxiii, 25, [38]–39, 56–9.

[22] Gottfried Wilhelm Leibniz, *Writings on China*, ed. and trans. Daniel J. Cook and Henry Rosemont, Jr (Chicago, 1994), 45–7, 51.

[23] Dennis C. Landis, 'Lutherans Meet the Indians: A Seventeenth-Century Conversion Debate', in *The Spiritual Conversion of the Americas*, ed. James Muldoon (Gainesville, 2004), 99–117.

[24] Philip Baldaeus, 'A True and Exact Description of the Most Celebrated East-India Coasts of Malabar and Coromandel, as also of the Isle of Ceylon', in *A Collection of Voyages and Travels*, 4 vols. (ESTC T097848. London, 1704), III, 802.

[25] Dikka Storm, 'The Church, the Pietist Mission and the Sámi: An Account of a Northern Norwegian Mission District in the Early Eighteenth Century', *Norwegian Journal of Missiology*, 3 (2017), 59–75; Robert Eric Frykenberg, *Christianity in India: From Beginnings to the Present* (Oxford, 2008), 147–67.

[26] Robert Moffat, *Missionary Labours and Scenes in Southern Africa* (1842), p. 505.

If success could reorientate missions in this direction, so could failure.[27] In the Islamic world, long experience told Christian missionaries that individual conversions were particularly difficult to obtain or even to pursue. Under such circumstances, social programmes could become a surrogate for conversion. Education and public health work were seen by many Christian missionaries as emulating Christ's ministry; even hostile regimes might permit missionaries to undertake such work, and it was usually possible to demonstrate some tangible success. Well before the end of the nineteenth century, the American Board of Commissioners for Foreign Mission's work in the Ottoman Empire had become so given up to schools and clinics, with success measured in numbers of graduates and patients, that explicit interest in individual conversion is hard to find.[28] Civilisation, to be achieved through the medium of Western-style education, had become the most important aim, with morality (since schools taught pupils ethical conduct) a distant second. Christian orthodoxy was at best implicit in this education, and zeal was quite out of reach. Missionaries settled for using the more societal axes as proxies for individual transformation.

One time-honoured way round the difficulties of Protestant mission in the Islamic world and elsewhere was to target indigenous Christian churches: Assyrians, Copts, Maronites, and the Mar Thoma Christians of India, among others. The question of whether such missionary efforts were legitimate became urgent in the late nineteenth century and after, with declining interdenominational conflict and incipient ecumenism: the Protestant establishment gathered at the World Missionary Conference in 1910, for example, took the view that South America was *not* a mission field, because Protestant mission to Catholics was unnecessary.[29] Whether this was accepted or rejected depended on the view taken of our matrix. For those who prioritised orthodoxy, the conversion of so-called Christians sunk in ancient error was essential; the urge to 'civilise' such Christians could be almost as powerful. The advocates of morality or zeal were more sympathetic to their separated brethren.[30]

---

[27] Indeed, Comaroff and Comaroff, *Of Revelation and Revolution*, ii, 118, conclude that, due to the 'disappointingly low' number of converts, missionaries to the Tswana gradually but overwhelmingly came to prioritise 'the civilising mission' over 'salvation' – as if the two were alternatives.

[28] See e.g. Yvette Talhamy, 'American Protestant Missionary Activity among the Nusayris (Alawis) in Syria in the Nineteenth Century', *Middle Eastern Studies*, 47 (2011), 215–36; I. Okkenhaug, 'Christian Missions in the Middle East and the Ottoman Balkans: Education, Reform, and Failed Conversions, 1819–1967', *International Journal of Middle East Studies*, 47 (2015), 593–604; J. H. Proctor, 'Scottish Medical Missionaries in South Arabia, 1886–1979', *Middle Eastern Studies*, 42 (2006), 103–21; Dorothy Birge Keller and Robert S. Keller, 'American Board Schools in Turkey' and Virginia A. Metaxas, 'Dr. Ruth A. Parmelee and the Changing Role of Near East Missionaries in Early Twentieth-Century Turkey', in *The Role of the American Board*, ed. Putney and Burlin, chs. 4–5.

[29] See Brian Stanley, *The World Missionary Conference, Edinburgh 1910* (Grand Rapids, MI, and Cambridge, 2009), 54–8, 64–6, 72, 297, 306.

[30] See Gareth Atkins, 'Missions on the Fringes of Europe: British Protestants and the Orthodox Churches, c. 1800–1850', in *British Protestant Missions and the Conversion of Europe, 1600–1900*, ed. Simone Maghenzani and Stefano Villani (New York, 2021), 215–34.

Similar issues confronted missionaries from the state and 'mainline' Protestant churches of Europe and North America as they decided how to relate to the Pentecostal and Holiness denominations and other minority or sectarian movements – movements that were undeniably Protestant, but of dubious orthodoxy; with a zeal that had become excessive or perverted; alarmingly uncivilised; and (it was often alleged) suspect in morals. Those new denominations, by contrast, viewed the old establishments as fatally lacking in zeal, lax in their morals, somewhat erroneous in their doctrines and hypocritically decadent in their priority on civilisation – so much so that, in some cases, they targeted missionary efforts not only at Catholics in Latin America (the World Missionary Conference notwithstanding) but also at mainline Protestants in Europe.[31]

If the 'civilisation' axis appears less dominant in the modern era than in earlier centuries, this is in part because it shifted its form. The medical and educational missions that spread across the world in the modern era may not have insisted on the adoption of European modes of living as peremptorily as their predecessors, but their conviction that it was in the best interests of indigenous people for them to embrace certain material and behavioural norms of Western civilisation (such as hygiene and sanitation) was no weaker. Yet this was never unchallenged. Among the evangelicals there was a suspicion that medical and educational missions were a manifestation of the 'social gospel' which they rejected in their home countries.[32] By the 1930s, missionaries who established schools and taught modern agricultural methods might also be affirming indigenous patterns of dress and obstructing colonial authorities.[33] Even medical missionaries did not necessarily privilege civilisation over the other axes. One Swiss missionary nurse wrote in the early 1940s: 'Human beings in the Belgian Congo, as in all other countries, are less in need of civilization and of schools than of the gospel of Jesus Christ, a gospel which delivers from the old life and renews the heart, which preaches love of one's neighbor.'[34] One missiological strand thus came to see civilisation, not merely as less important than morality or zeal, but as potentially *antithetical* to inward transformation.

---

[31] See e.g. Philip Wingeier-Rayo, 'The Impact of the World Missionary Conference on Mexico: The Cincinnati Plan', in *The Reshaping of Mission in Latin America*, ed. Miguel Alvarez (Oxford, 2015), 36–46, 731–3, 736–7; Kling, *A History of Christian Conversion*, 414–15, 420–2; Fernando Santos-Granero, *Slavery and Utopia: The Wars and Dreams of an Amazonian World Transformer* (Austin, 2018), 21–2, 139–64, 167–9, 173–7; Richard W. Schwarz and Floyd Greenleaf, *Light Bearers: A History of the Seventh-Day Adventist Church*, rev. edn (Nampa, ID, 1995), 276–8, 283–6; G. Alexander Kish, *The Origins of the Baptist Movement among the Hungarians* (Leiden, 2012); Peter Ackers, 'West End Chapel, Back Street Bethel: Labour and Capital in the Wigan Churches of Christ c.1845–1945', *Journal of Ecclesiastical History*, 47 (1996), 298–329; and, for more recent history, Hans Krabbendam, *Saving the Overlooked Continent: American Protestant Missions in Western Europe 1940–1975* (Leuven, 2020).

[32] Comaroff and Comaroff, *Of Revelation and Revolution*, II, 67.

[33] See e.g. Norma Youngberg, *Under Sealed Orders* (Mountain View, CA, 1970).

[34] Maria Haseneder, *A White Nurse in Africa* (Mountain View, CA, 1951), 120.

Another reason for a decreasing stress on the civilisation axis was the increasing emphasis from major missionary societies in Africa, China and elsewhere on using local converts in evangelisation. Protestants had recognised this principle since the seventeenth century, but now began to pursue it in earnest. Such people were often eloquent and capable missionaries, who thought they were 'participating in a shared missionary endeavour that operated above racial and ethnic distinctions' even while experiencing 'the inequalities of power', and who complicated notions of agency and exploitation.[35] These indigenous believers were, in the missionaries' explicit categorisation, more 'civilised' than those around them, but generally not much more. Yet they were entrusted with missionising: partly because there were few Western missionary boots on the ground; partly because they had shown themselves to be zealous, sufficiently orthodox, and morally upright; and partly because their very 'barbarism' was recognised as an advantage, making them able to be heard by their own kin. Indeed, wildly inflated hopes were sometimes attached to such people, who were consequently liable to be blamed when they inevitably fell short.

Yet as the centrality of Western-style education and biomedicine in the modern missionary enterprise demonstrates, 'civilisation' has remained a decisively important marker of Christianisation. The agonised twentieth-century debates over the treatment of polygamy are a case in point: willingness to abandon existing polygamous norms was seen as a critical test both of civility and morality, even in the face of burgeoning arguments that a rigid line on this matter was both a stumbling block to conversion and potentially cruel to individuals.[36]

The point of this *tour d'horizon* of changing Protestant attitudes to the missionary task is to indicate that, even as a wide range of Protestants pursued highly varied missionary projects with very diverse methods and presuppositions, our matrix of four cross-cutting axes – orthodoxy, zeal, civilisation and ethics – can be used to place, compare and interpret them. Our suggestion, therefore, is that this persistent underlying framework for analysing missionary intentionality can be a valuable tool for historical analysis of a wide variety of Protestant missionary enterprises. To understand the purpose, and thus the consequences (intended and unintended), of any mission, we need to understand what kinds of 'conversion' were being pursued, how, and in what order; that is, we need to understand which of these axes missionaries regarded as most urgent, how they proposed to move their people along them, and how they proposed to test whether they had done so.

---

[35] See Emma Wild-Wood, *Apolo Kivebulaya: Religious Change in the African Great Lakes c.1870–1935* (Woodbridge, Suffolk, 2020), quotation at p. 33; Peggy Brock, 'New Christians as Evangelists', in *Missions and Empire*, ed. Etherington, 132–52; Jehu Hanciles, *Euthanasia of a Mission: African Church Autonomy in a Colonial Context* (Westport, 2002); and, for early commitment to the same principle, Edward E. Andrews, *Native Apostles: Black and Indian Missionaries in the British Atlantic World* (Cambridge, MA, 2013).

[36] Timothy Willem Jones, 'The Missionaries' Position: Polygamy and Divorce in the Anglican Communion, 1888–1988', *Journal of Religious History*, 35 (2011), 393–408,

Applying the model

Examining the history of Protestant missions with the aid of this model can help to bring certain issues more clearly into focus: some have received insufficient historical attention, others are the subject of historical controversy.

We have already noted how the matrix can be used to analyse decisions about which missionary projects were seen to deserve priority: decisions that mixed bluntly practical questions of accessibility and expected receptiveness with theological and apocalyptic views of who ought or ought not to be missionised, and when. Likewise, it can be worthwhile to examine the distinctive language and metaphors of missionary projects ('planting the church', 'bringing to Christ', 'taking the Gospel') through the lens of our matrix. It can help us to understand missions' distinctive time frames: missionary tasks measured in generations and centuries imply a civilisation- and morality-focused project based around education in which those who have already reached adulthood might be given up as unreachable.[37] Whereas, if there is a last desperate chance to save souls, it makes sense to proclaim orthodoxy and whip up zeal to snatch whoever can be saved from the impending fire.[38]

What links each of these and other issues to the proxies for conversion which our four axes measure is the knotty question of authenticity. A Protestant 'conversion' is virtually impossible to evidence conclusively, even allowing for the wide range of definitions of what true 'conversion' might be. This problem has bedevilled Protestant missionary enterprises from the beginning – whether in the shape of straightforward dissimulation, perhaps in a ploy to secure material benefits from a colonial power (what was sometimes called 'rice-Christianity'[39]); of calculated adjustment to official persecution (what in the sixteenth century was known as Nicodemism[40]); or, more insidiously, of 'converts' who believed that they were truly Christian but

---

[37] This was typical of eighteenth-century projects in both the Dutch and British empires: see for example the Congregationalist missionary to the Native Americans, John Sergeant, who in 1743 concluded, after five years in the field, that there was no alternative but to 'take such a *Method* in the Education of our *Indian Children*, as shall in the most effectual Manner change their whole Habit of thinking and acting; and raise them, as far as possible, into the Condition of a civil industrious and polish'd People ... to *root out* their vicious Habits, and to change their whole Way of Living': most of the adults were beyond hope. Samuel Hopkins, *Historical memoirs, relating to the Housatunnuk Indians* (ESTC W14473. Boston, MA, 1753), 97–8. For a similar, more systematic approach in the Dutch empire, see Jurrien van Goor, *Jan Kompenie as Schoolmaster: Dutch Education in Ceylon 1690–1795* (Groningen, 1978).

[38] This was typical of late-eighteenth- and nineteenth-century evangelical Anglicans, and of the rather different evangelicals of twentieth-century North America: Grayson Carter, *Anglican Evangelicals* [2001] (Eugene, 2015), ch. 1; Richard Turnbull, *Shaftesbury: The Great Reformer* (Oxford, 2010), 28–34, 51–7; Matthew Avery Sutton, *American Apocalypse: A History of American Evangelicalism* (Cambridge, MA, 2014), 2–5, 326–31; Kling, *A History of Christian Conversion*, 401–5.

[39] This term apparently originated in the early seventeenth-century Dutch East Indies: Johannes Keuning, 'Ambonese, Portuguese and Dutchmen: The History of Ambon to the End of the Seventeenth Century', in *Dutch Authors on Asian History*, ed. M. A. P. Meilink-Roelofsz, M. E. van Opstall and G. J. Schutte (Dordrecht, 1988), 362–97, at 383.

[40] Carlos M. N. Eire, 'Calvin and Nicodemism: A Reappraisal', *Sixteenth Century Journal*, 10 (1979), 44–69; Andrew Pettegree, 'Nicodemism and the English Reformation', in his *Marian Protestantism: Six*

whose conversion might not measure up to the missionaries' exacting standards. The proxies we have described might have been the best solutions available to this problem, but they were very inadequate: for all of them are falsifiable, and the more priority is placed on any one of them, the more incentives are created to falsify it. Missionaries have consequently often lurched between excessive credulity and a systematic fear of hypocrisy which can almost amount to asserting the inevitability of their own failure.[41] Protestantism's classic insistence on 'faith alone' and on conversion as an inward event made assessing the authenticity of conversions difficult enough in their 'home' cultural contexts – a difficulty which helped shape, for example, classical Puritan casuistry, the culture of revivalism, and Pentecostalism's tellingly named doctrine of 'initial evidence'. In alien cultural contexts, with all the accompanying incomprehension and suspicion, those looking to assess conversion were inevitably compelled to measure its outward manifestations, whether prescribed (conformity to doctrinal, civil or moral norms, or even to outward shows of zeal, which might be laid down as shibboleths in particular circumstances) or more spontaneous – for with painful irony, it was the *unexpected* manifestation of apparently spontaneous life-changes, which might be displayed on any of our axes, that missionaries most eagerly sought. Such spontaneous displays could even redraw the paths through our matrix that missionaries had plotted. A long-serving Canadian missionary in Korea in 1907 admitted that he had long assumed that 'the Korean would never have a religious experience such as the West has' – until, that is, the outpouring of what he was compelled to recognise as zeal in that year's revival changed his mind.[42]

As this indicates, although our matrix is about missionaries and their intentions, it can also shed light on the dialectic between missionaries and the missionised which has informed so much recent scholarship. Missionaries' abstract intentions may have determined their entry-point into our matrix, but the path they actually took was determined by their interaction with indigenous peoples. For they themselves often traced their own paths through the matrix, reflecting their own convictions and priorities. Some converts might value clear-cut norms of ethics or orthodoxy – abstention from alcohol, monogamy, correct recitation of a confession of faith – as unambiguous markers of Christian legitimacy, as well as being of intrinsic value. Others might exploit missionaries' concern for civilisation and orthodoxy to secure benefits which they valued primarily for worldly reasons: the appeal of education, and literacy in particular, to enslaved people and many others dealing with conquest or occupation is a well-known lubricant of the missionary process.

Studies (Aldershot, 1996), 86–117; Peter Marshall, *Heretics and Believers: A History of the English Reformation* (New Haven, 2017), 382–5, 464–5.

[41] As in, archetypally, the debacle of Karl Gützlaff's 'Chinese Union' and the resulting long hangover of scepticism: Jessie G. Lutz and R. Ray Lutz, 'Karl Gützlaff's Approach to Indigenisation: The Chinese Union', in *Christianity in China from the Eighteenth Century to the Present*, ed. Daniel H. Bays (Stanford, 1996), 269–91.

[42] Eunsik Cho, 'The Great Revival of 1907 in Korea: Its Cause and Effect', *Missiology*, 26 (1998), 289–300, at 296.

This could reach a point at which missionaries and missionised collaborated in maintaining a mutually agreeable fiction: missionary schoolmasters pretended to convert their students, and students pretended to be converted. Missionaries might hope that those who came seeking education with secular motives might be infused with the Gospel regardless. Or, wary of indigenous people attempting to exploit them, they might try to prevent civilisation from crowding out orthodoxy, and orthodoxy from crowding out zeal.

In other situations, indigenous people might prioritise inward, subjective definitions centred on zeal, whose subjectivity ensured that greater agency fell to the converts. Surprised or sceptical missionaries might not be able to gainsay the spiritual authority of displays of zeal, especially if such displays aligned to a missionary's own religious culture or to a distinctive doctrine in such a way as to sweep aside any nagging suspicions of hypocrisy. In the right context, the right practice could be self-authenticating. Tears of repentance had a particular weight. In an early encounter with Native Americans in New England, sceptical missionaries could not but be impressed that one of their hearers 'powred out many teares and shewed much affliction', especially because he did so 'without affectation of being seene, desiring rather to conceale his griefe which (as was gathered from his carriage) the Lord forced from him': this fitted like a glove their preconceived understanding of how repentance was manifested.[43] Nearly two centuries later and half a world away, Moffat vividly described Tswana converts weeping for their sins: 'eyes now wept, which never before shed the tear of hallowed sorrow.' Moffat was sceptical enough of the motivations of some apparent converts that he 'found it necessary to exercise great caution in receiving members into the little church'. Yet the weeping converts fitted his conception of a true Protestant conversion experience so well that he could not but see this as a 'manifest outpouring of the Spirit from on high'.[44] Likewise, for Pentecostal missionaries of the following century, the gift of tongues put an end to doubts: where converts manifested it, the Holy Spirit had undeniably endorsed the reality of their conversion. Other denominations found different shibboleths centred on different axes. For Seventh-Day Adventists, observing the seventh-day Sabbath was so central, culturally as well as doctrinally, that it served synecdochically as a signifier of true conversion: both a desired public outcome in its own right and irrefutable proof of inward transformation. Almost as important for Adventists was renunciation of pork, tobacco and alcohol.[45] For the many other Protestant denominations that preached 'temperance', abstinence from spirits or from all alcohol could likewise serve as convincing moral evidence of 'genuine' conversion.[46]

---

[43] *The Day-Breaking, if not the sun-rising*, 9; Alec Ryrie, *Being Protestant in Reformation Britain* (Oxford, 2013), 187–95.

[44] Moffat, *Missionary Labours*, pp. 496, 508.

[45] Malcolm Bull and Keith Lockhart. *Seeking a Sanctuary: Seventh-Day Adventists and the American Dream*, 2nd edn (Bloomington, 2006).

[46] David Bebbington, *The Nonconformist Conscience* (1982), 46–51; Norman Etherington, 'Outward and Visible Signs of Conversion in Nineteenth-Century Kwazulu-Natal', *Journal of Religion in Africa*, 32 (2002), 432; Jennifer Fish Kashay, '"We will banish the polluted thing from our houses":

What makes this significant is that these criteria were never wholly under missionaries' control. Converts themselves could have a considerable degree of agency, in particular for balancing civilisation and morality – that is, for deciding what aspects of an indigenous culture were matters of indifference that were compatible with Christianity (or indeed supported it), and which were damaging or contrary to it. 'Conversion' changes some aspects of a convert's life and leaves others relatively unaltered: quite where the line should fall will always be a matter for negotiation.[47] Whatever course those iterative negotiations took, missionaries never exactly got the 'conversions' they sought. Nor, indeed, could they quite desire to do so. If they had – if converts had simply conformed, and shown no initiative of their own – that would in itself have demonstrated that their conversions were 'inauthentic'. Considering missionary communities through the four-axis perspective underscores a key point: some loss of control is a necessary condition for missionary 'success'. This was by no means always acknowledged by the communities that sent and sustained missionaries; many others that might accept it in theory balked at its implications. Yet even highly centralised denominations sought inward authenticity, and evidence for this had to be *both* conformist *and* individual.

One result of this is that missionaries as individuals, their institutions, and the churches and wider societies which sent them, were changed by the missionary process, both in the simple sense that their theoretical ideas about conversion were often revised following contact with the reality of a different culture, and in the more complex sense that a large part of a missionary's task is to learn from and about that culture. This was foregrounded in many missionaries' minds because the Christian tradition gives spiritual weight to concepts such as *pilgrimage* and *exile*, but in any case long-distance travel involved dislocation to a new, cross-cultural setting. It is no coincidence that the most translated Protestant missionary text aside from the Bible itself is that textbook of self-dislocating zeal, *Pilgrim's Progress*. In particular, this presses on the tension between individualism and community. The missionary is a dislocated individual or part of a small, tight-knit group: the same is often true of early converts. Yet the ultimate aim is not to detach converts from their families and social context (even though that is often in fact the outcome).[48] Instead, the ideal is ultimately to bring their whole communities with them – even if that sometimes means that Bunyan's brand of zeal must be downplayed in favour of the more communal axes.

Moreover, missionaries' paths through the matrix had to be negotiated not only between missionaries and their would-be converts, but also with the churches, agencies, donors and support networks who made missionary work possible. If Protestants never quite endured a catastrophe like the Catholic Church's Chinese Rites controversy, episodes like the Bishop Colenso

---

Missionaries, Drinking, and Temperance in the Sandwich Islands', in *The Role of the American Board*, ed. Putney and Burlin, 287–311.

[47] Kling, *A History of Christian Conversion*, 13–14.

[48] Cf. Hebrews 11:13–15; Avihu Zakai, *Exile and Kingdom: History and Apocalypse in the Puritan Migration to America* (Cambridge, 1992); Comaroff and Comaroff, *Of Revelation and Revolution*, I, 172–5

crisis in Natal show that similar tensions were at work.[49] The priorities or theories of theologians and armchair missionaries were distinctive and often unrealistic or impractical; donors had pet projects they insisted missionaries pursue; churches had rules they insisted be adhered to regardless of context; colonial governments had their own priorities which typically pushed missionaries towards agendas of civilisation and morality. All of these forces had to be managed. If missionaries attempted actively to oppose one of them, they usually required other groups of supporters. For example, in the eighteenth-century Caribbean, much of the planter and local church elite opposed attempts to Christianise enslaved people by teaching them to read. The missionaries of England's Society for the Propagation of the Gospel in Foreign Parts (SPG) were divided on the subject, and some recommended working within this constraint; it was argued that appropriate zeal and morality could be nurtured without the need to pursue too much orthodoxy or civility.[50] Although the Society's London establishment generally supported literacy efforts, this clash between local and metropolitan forces left missionaries with limited room for manoeuvre.[51] The promising missionary projects in Dutch Brazil in the 1640s were, their most recent historian has concluded, stymied by the determination of the church authorities in Amsterdam to micromanage a situation which they only dimly understood, by placing a near-absolute priority on a certain precise definition of orthodoxy.[52] In the modern era, this tension has often been triggered by ecumenical projects; uniting bodies such as the Church of Christ in China or the Church of South India appeared self-evidently necessary to many missionaries on the ground, whereas denominational conservatives in the West regarded them as unacceptably compromising orthodoxy.

Historiographical implications

Our suggestion, then, is that our four-axis framework can provide a useful matrix, not merely for understanding missionary motivations themselves, but for thinking about the wider history of Protestant missions and their cultural, political, social and economic impacts around the world (both in 'sending' and 'receiving' societies). In what follows we offer some outline suggestions of the questions which our framework might be used to ask and to indicate ways in which it may be of value even to historians whose primary fields of interest do not include mission.

1. Colonisation and coercion

Most (but not all) historic Protestant mission has taken place within imperial contexts in which it was deeply implicated on multiple levels. However, it is

---

[49] D. E. Mungello (ed.), *The Chinese Rites Controversy: Its History and Meaning*, Monumenta Serica 33 (Nettetal, 1994); Peter Hinchliff, 'Colenso, John William', *Oxford Dictionary of National Biography*.

[50] See e.g. Oxford, Bodleian Library, USPG Papers 2: Committee Minutes, vii.134–7.

[51] Glasson, *Mastering Christianity*.

[52] Noorlander, *Heaven's Wrath*, esp. 174–83.

increasingly recognised that the relationship between missionary and imperial projects was as awkward as it was intimate.[53] Historians' role is of course neither to defend nor to condemn missionary projects, but to disentangle how these relationships worked. A rigorous understanding of missionary intentions is a necessary part of this work. Imperial power structures were often either hostile to missionary projects, or 'cooperative' in ways that forced them, sometimes reluctantly, in specific directions. Like mating spiders, missionaries and empires needed, exploited and manipulated each other. Their purposes might sometimes be aligned but were rarely *very* similar. And some missionaries – for example, non-European missionaries working across the circles of empire, those from dissenting or marginalised denominations, or those from such European countries as Norway and Switzerland (or indeed the United States up to the 1890s) with little or no direct imperial presence – were largely excluded from and often at odds with imperial power structures, even if some of them could also exploit the cultural context of colonialism. The resulting differences can meaningfully be plotted and interpreted using our matrix, for imperial authorities had their own views on these proxies: often valuing civilisation, but not in cases where it might lead to colonised (or enslaved) peoples making unwelcome assertions of status; broadly favouring (Christian) morality insofar as it fostered industrious and loyal subjects, yet wary of it insofar as it might foster social conflict or undermine trade in alcohol or opium; often indifferent to orthodoxy as such, except insofar as it might encourage helpful or unhelpful political affiliations; frequently suspicious of zeal. In other cases, even the most nakedly coercive instruments of imperial power could actively understand themselves as having a missionary purpose, as in, for example, the British navy's nineteenth-century campaigns against the slave trade – purposes which would, inevitably, be shared far more by some individuals within those institutions than others. This naturally led to those institutions pursuing 'conversions' of the kind that they might be able to deliver, as hammers look for nails – targeting the enemies of civilisation and morality with their own particular brand of zeal. Whatever routes through the matrix secular rulers favoured, missionaries who chose to follow in their footsteps would find their paths made straight for them. Those with their own priorities would not.

2. Missionary martyrdom and suffering

Missionary work is often profoundly costly for the individuals involved, and sometimes extremely dangerous. This fact is so central to missionary hagiography that historians are justly uneasy about emphasising it. The analysis of missionary priorities and motivations provides a useful perspective on this. The active seeking of martyrdom is a 'problem' more often found in

---

[53] E.g. Brian Stanley, *The Bible and the Flag: Protestant Missions and British Imperialism in the Nineteenth and Twentieth Centuries* (Leicester, 1990); Brian Stanley (ed.), *Missions, Nationalism, and the End of Empire* (Grand Rapids, 2003); Andrew Porter, *Religion versus Empire? British Protestant Missionaries and Overseas Expansion, 1700-1914* (Manchester, 2004); Etherington, *Missions and Empire*; Hilary M. Carey, *God's Empire: Religion and Colonialism in the British World, c.1801-1908* (Cambridge, 2011).

Catholic missions, but it has its Protestant equivalent in the tendency to validate mission work through suffering and labour, and to use suffering to build support networks. There have certainly been Protestant martyrs: David Livingstone's death was described in these terms; the deaths of John Williams in the New Hebrides (today's Vanuatu) in 1839 and John Patteson in the Solomon Islands in 1871 elevated each man's posthumous reputation even while helping to generate donations.[54] Even though martyrdom is on one level a mark of missionary failure, as a demonstrative act it was understood to model Christian orthodoxy and morals to indigenous people – even if that understanding in fact existed largely in the minds of martyrs' metropolitan supporters. It might also, especially when associated with a 'barbaric' practice such as cannibalism, shift missionary priorities in a particular situation towards civility. General Charles Gordon was a much more effective missionary to the Sudan as a 'martyr', his self-sacrifice repeatedly invoked by Protestant publicists to inspire emulation, than he had been in life.[55] And when all else was done, it was possible to use virtue ethics to turn an account of a martyrdom away from failure to a celebration of the missionary's duty and spiritual quest, however apparently fruitless. This may mean that martyrdom could become a receptacle for failure, in which self-endangerment and even seeking out violent confrontation become ways forward for thwarted missionaries, and in which martyrdom becomes a measure of success. In this sense, the pursuit of suffering can almost become a fifth axis, an exceptionally unsatisfactory proxy for real conversionary work, but also a passive-aggressive dynamic in which missionaries become accelerants of violence.

3. Language and translation

How missionaries have dealt with language barriers has been one of the most persistent and revealing problems of the Protestant missionary enterprise. Approaches which prioritise civilisation might prefer to educate indigenous people in a European language, believing that pagan tongues could not adequately convey Christian doctrine; those that favour zeal might prefer indigenous languages, while not prioritising translation of the entire Bible as aggressively as those who favour orthodoxy. Early Pentecostal missionaries attempted to use their commitment to zeal to bypass the question altogether, via the gift of tongues. Regardless of whether and how translation is prioritised, it is itself a fraught and dialectic process of 'conversion' through which Christianity is by necessity decanted into a pre-existing set of containers of meaning and association.[56] How missionaries tackle these dilemmas is largely a function of their preferred route through our matrix. Here we

---

[54] See e.g. Sujit Sivasundram, *Nature and the Godly Empire: Science and Evangelical Mission in the Pacific, 1795–1850* (New York, 2011), 127–31; Etherington, 'Introduction', 7.

[55] Cynthia F. Behrman, 'The After-Life of General Gordon', *Albion*, 3 (1971), 50–2, 55.

[56] Lindenfeld, *World Christianity and Indigenous Experience*, pp. 21–4. And see Andrew Walls, 'The Translation Principle in Christian History', in his *The Missionary Movement in Christian History: Studies in the Transmission of Faith* (Maryknoll, NY, 1996), 26–42.

might note in particular that the specifically Protestant ambition to translate and to distribute Bibles, biblical materials, and devotional material by Protestant authors, and the recurrent confidence that those materials will prove to have intrinsic power, unavoidably gives agency to 'converts' to form orthodoxies and moralities of their own, often with unexpected results which missionaries struggle to contain.[57]

4. Medical and educational missions

Just as missionary organisations can lose control of the missionising process when they adapt to local languages, so schools, colleges, clinics and hospitals can take on a life of their own: healthcare and education have their own internal dynamics. We are accustomed to seeing such projects, which either do not focus on conversion at all or do so only indirectly, in a missionary context, but our matrix reminds us that they deserve closer analysis.[58] Are they intended as supporting the conversionary enterprise? If so in what sense – by laying the educational groundwork seen as necessary for embracing Christian orthodoxy (literacy, for example), by inculcating moral norms, by modelling the missionaries' zealous personal commitment to serving the needy, by demonstrating the superiority of missionaries' civilisation? Or are these projects seen as ends in themselves? (If so, in what sense? Is the claim to disinterested altruism in fact a conversionary attempt to demonstrate Christian morality?) How might these motives interact with the shifting ethical codes of medical or educational professionalism – an interaction happening both within institutions and within individuals?[59] How do the different missionary discourses interact? A school or clinic might be described as taking very different paths through, or around, the matrix by denominational fundraising reports, by professional bodies and by individual staff members' correspondence. To say nothing of the views of their pupils and patients, whose demand for (or resistance to) such institutions was coloured by their own sense of missionary priorities as well as by more immediate and practical concerns. The responses of these 'clients', of course, also feed back into the paths chosen through the matrix. In particular, medical or educational missions often arose when more explicitly conversionary efforts had failed or been blocked, and another route had to be chosen: both because institutional pressures pushed missionaries towards paths on which measurable success was possible, and because the mission experience forced missionaries themselves to rethink their ways through the matrix.

---

[57] On perhaps the most spectacular and certainly the bloodiest example of this process of indigenisation, see Carl S. Kilcourse, 'Instructing the Heavenly King: Joseph Edkins's Mission to Correct the Theology of Hong Xiuquan', *Journal of Ecclesiastical History*, 71 (2020), 116–34.

[58] For a pioneering overview of the terrain, see Andrew F. Walls, 'The Domestic Importance of the Nineteenth-Century Medical Missionary', in his *Missionary Movement*, 211–20.

[59] *Ibid.*, 217–19; Hilary Ingram, 'A Little Learning is a Dangerous Thing: British Overseas Medical Missions and the Politics of Professionalisation, c.1880–1910', in *Complaints, Controversies and Grievances in Medicine: Historical and Social Science Perspectives*, ed. Jonathan Reinarz and Rebecca Wynter (New York, 2015), 75–90.

Conclusion

These are only a sample of the knot of questions raised by this perspective. A final recurrent theme is worth underlining, however: the importance of seeing missionary history through the lens of failure. Winning non-Christian converts to Protestantism has, in most historical contexts, been slow, difficult and sometimes impossible. It has almost always been harder than simplistic readings of the Acts of the Apostles and of stirring missionary narratives apparently implied, or than naive enthusiasm for the intrinsic power of Scripture or of the preached Word assumed. The history of Protestant missions is therefore largely a history of how missions and missionaries (and convert minorities) have responded to difficulty, danger and disappointment. There is a recurrent cycle of responses, in which initial intentions are frustrated, leading to reflection, reassessment and (sometimes) renewed or redirected efforts. Sometimes failure is denied; sometimes it becomes so dominant that even successes are not recognised. This cycle of frustration can be gradual, or can be punctuated by periodic lurches: in particular, war or other moments of political crisis can be decisive in moving the cycle onwards.

It is largely because of this cycle that the matrix of approaches to conversion we are suggesting is not static but dynamic. It is driven by unexpected failure – and, more rarely, by unexpected success. The first English settlers in North America were genuinely surprised that Native Americans appeared uninterested in their religion, and concluded that civility had to be prioritised; a century of disappointment later, missionaries of David Brainerd's generation rejected that in favour of a priority on orthodoxy and morality. American missionaries in late nineteenth-century Korea became suspicious of the conversions produced by their emphasis on orthodoxy and morality; they began instead to long for zeal, and were eventually rewarded with the revivals of 1907.

Which is to say: a primary lesson of our focus on missionary intentions is that missionary history is largely a story of unintended consequences. If missions' longed-for results rarely materialised, their consequences were nevertheless often profound, on many levels – including the 'feedback' consequences on metropolitan churches sparked by their involvement with missionary enterprises. And unintended consequences are still consequences; the intention remains essential if we are to understand them. This requires a means of analysing what the missionaries were attempting, and why; and of probing deeper into their own understanding of what they were attempting. We offer this model as an aid in that task.

Cite this article: Ryrie A, Trim DJB (2022). Four Axes of Mission: Conversion and the Purposes of Mission in Protestant History. *Transactions of the Royal Historical Society* **32**, 113–133. https://doi.org/10.1017/S0080440122000020

Transactions of the RHS (2022), **32**, 135–158
doi:10.1017/S0080440122000056

ARTICLE

Alternate Attendance Parades in the Japanese Domain of Satsuma, Seventeenth to Eighteenth Centuries: Pottery, Power and Foreign Spectacle

Rebekah Clements

Catalan Institution for Research and Advanced Studies (ICREA), and Department of Translation, Interpreting, and East Asian Studies, Autonomous University of Barcelona, Building K, 08193, Bellaterra (Barcelona), Spain
Email: rebekah.clements@icrea.cat

(Received 28 July 2021; accepted 29 March 2022)

Abstract

This study examines the practice of 'alternate attendance' (*sankin kōtai*), in which the daimyo lords of Tokugawa Japan (1600–1868) marched with their retainers between their home territories and the shogunal capital of Edo, roughly once a year. Research on alternate attendance has focused on the meaning of daimyo processions outside their domains (*han*), along Japan's highways and in the city of Edo. Here I argue that, even as daimyo embarked upon a journey to pay obeisance to the shogun, the ambiguous nature of sovereignty in early modern Japan meant that alternate attendance could also be used for a local agenda, ritually stamping the daimyo's territory with signs of his dominance, much like what has been highlighted in the study of royal processions in world history. I focus on the seventeenth to eighteenth centuries, providing a case study of visits made by the Shimazu family, lords of Satsuma domain, to a village of Korean potters within their territory, whose antecedents had been brought as captives during the Imjin War of 1592–8. During daimyo visits, a relationship of mutual benefit and fealty between the Shimazu and the villagers was articulated through gift-giving, banqueting, dance and displays of local wares. This in turn was used to consolidate Shimazu power in their region.

Keywords: Japan; Korea; early modern; Imjin War; alternate attendance

Introduction

Royal progresses have been observed in various forms throughout world history, from journeys made by Assyrian kings, to the progresses of England's Elizabeth I.[1] This study uses the concept of the royal progress to

---

[1] Jaume Llop and Daisuke Shibata, 'The Royal Journey in the Middle Assyrian Period', *Journal of Cuneiform Studies*, 68 (2016), 67–98; Mary Hill Cole, *The Portable Queen: Elizabeth I and the Politics of*

re-examine a related phenomenon: that of alternate attendance (*sankin kōtai*) performed by the elite warriors of Japan's Tokugawa period (1600–1868). Approximately once a year, for two and a half centuries, daimyo lords, their samurai retainers and servants paraded along Japan's highways between their castle towns and the city of Edo in order to attend upon the shogun.[2] Daimyo wives and heirs lived permanently in Edo as hostages. Alternate attendance has been likened to Louis XIV's court at Versailles in the late seventeenth and early eighteenth centuries, and to the medieval German practice of *Hoffahrt*.[3] Here, I argue that the ambiguous nature of sovereignty in Tokugawa Japan, with effective rule divided between the shogun and the daimyo, also allows us to consider alternate attendance as a form of 'royal' progress in so far as concerns the leg of the journey that took place within the daimyo's own territory (his domain, or *han*). This approach reveals the localised semiotics of daimyo power, as daimyo lords spent time in villages within their territory, holding audiences, giving out favours and receiving signs of submission from locals, before leaving their domain and embarking on the journey to Edo.

The focus of this article is a case study for which there exists a cache of local history materials detailing the visits made by the lords of Satsuma domain to a village of Korean potters and their descendants, en route to Edo during the seventeenth and early eighteenth centuries. Satsuma was located on the southern Japanese island of Kyushu, its hereditary daimyo rulers belonged to a family called the Shimazu, and the Korean potters in question had settled in the village of Naeshirogawa in Satsuma after being taken there by the Shimazu armies during the Japanese invasions of Korea, which took place between 1592 and 1598 (the Imjin War).[4] Thanks to records kept by the villagers, fifteen eyewitness accounts of daimyo visits to Naeshirogawa between 1677 and 1714 are extant, including the ceremonies and entertainments that were performed on these occasions; in addition, the Naeshirogawa records depict, albeit in lesser detail, the growing relationship between the daimyo and the village in the first half of the seventeenth century.[5] Largely unused by historians, the extant manuscripts of these records were compiled in the nineteenth century, from older, as yet unknown, documents kept in the archives of families from Naeshirogawa. However, despite the late compilation period of the extant, nineteenth-century documents, a comparison with the dates of daimyo travel contained in official Satsuma sources reveals that the Naeshirogawa

Ceremony (Amherst, 1999); Zillah Dovey, *An Elizabethan Progress: The Queen's Journey into East Anglia, 1578* (Stroud, 1996).

[2] Constantine Nomikos Vaporis, *Tour of Duty: Samurai, Military Service in Edo, and the Culture of Early Modern Japan* (Honolulu, 2008).

[3] *Ibid.*, 2; Kasaya Kasuhiko, 'Sankin kōtai no bunkashiteki igi', in *Bunmei to shite no Tokugawa Nihon*, ed. Haga Tōru (Tokyo 1993), 137–56, at 138. Jeroen Duindam, *Dynasties: A Global History of Power, 1300–1800* (Cambridge 2015), 206–10.

[4] Naitō Shunpo, *Bunroku keichō eki ni okeru hironin no kenkyū* (Tokyo, 1976), 210–98.

[5] Fukaminato Kyōko, 'Satsumayaki o meguru Naeshirogawa kankei monjō ni tsuite', *Reimeikan chōsa kenkyū hōkoku*, 13 (2000), 101–33

records are highly accurate when it comes to the seventeenth- and eighteenth-century daimyo visits.[6]

Such details would otherwise have been lost to history, since Satsuma officials did not consider this information worthy of inclusion in the domain's official histories, although they did keep a record of the routes taken by the daimyo each year, as well as the protocols for what were considered more important stations along the way. A paucity of similar local historical materials discovered to date for other domains means that we know much more about the better-documented aspects of alternate attendance in the urban gaze, for example in the merchant city of Osaka or the shogunal capital of Edo, for an external audience of the non-domain public, the shogunate and other daimyo. Further reasons for focusing upon a village in Satsuma include the fact that this domain boasted the oldest ruling warrior family in Tokugawa Japan, operated with a high degree of agency in international affairs thanks to its annexation of the Ryukyuan kingdom (modern-day Okinawa) in 1609, and was instrumental in toppling the shogunate in the nineteenth century, thus making for a particularly intriguing case study when it comes to Tokugawa sovereignty and the dynamics of local power.

I contend that, even after being confirmed as daimyo of Satsuma by the new Tokugawa regime in the early seventeenth century, the Shimazu – who had much older links to their territory – simultaneously maintained their own local narratives of legitimacy, and that the Naeshirogawa encounters show how alternate attendance could be used for this internal, domain agenda. This agenda is not unlike that which has been highlighted in the study of royal processions in world history, which the anthropologist Clifford Geertz described as a kind of scent-marking that 'stamp[s] ... a territory with ritual signs of dominance'.[7]

Furthermore, the role of Naeshirogawans in Satsuma alternate attendance practices has echoes of what scholars have already noted concerning the periodic presence of representatives from the Ryukyuan kingdom in the retinue that the Satsuma lords took with them to Edo. It is well known that displays of foreign culture emphasised Satsuma's conquest of Ryukyu and were used to leverage Shimazu power vis-à-vis the shogunate.[8] Here I argue that the involvement of foreign culture in Satsuma's alternate attendance parades was also a factor in the internal domain significance of the processions, and that the symbolism of subdued foreign subjects from Naeshirogawa and their descendants paying homage to the Shimazu family was intended to

---

[6] Rebekah Clements, 'Daimyō Processions and Satsuma's Korean Village: A Note on the Reliability of Local History Materials', *Japan Review*, 35 (2021), 219–30. The records are written in the *sōrōbun* style of Japanese, which was used for letter writing and administrative documents. Although the villagers were encouraged to maintain their Korean language skills, they also adapted to the local linguistic environment.

[7] Clifford Geertz, *Local Knowledge: Further Essays in Interpretive Anthropology* (New York, 1983), 125.

[8] Miyagi Eishō, *Ryūkyū shisha no Edo nobori* (Tokyo, 1982); Kido Hironari, 'Shimazushi no sankin ni taisuru Ōsaka funa arake', *Ōsaka Rekishi Hakubutsukan kenkyū kiyō*, 13 (2015), 19–48; Travis Seifman, 'Performing "Lūchū": Identity Performance and Foreign Relations in Early Modern Japan' (Ph.D. thesis, University of California, Santa Barbara, 2019).

legitimise Shimazu's power in their local region. This in turn contributes to a growing body of scholarship which re-evaluates the symbolic importance of foreigners for early modern Japanese rulership.[9]

Royal origins of alternate attendance parades

From the eighth until the fourteenth century, royal progresses (*gyokō* or *miyuki*) in Japan were occasional rites that functioned as sites for the display of the emperor (*tennō*) and his or her entourage, and for the presentation of the ruler's munificence.[10] These elaborate public excursions were originally the purview of the sovereign, but over time were adopted by the warrior class, as effective rule shifted out of the hands of the court and into the jurisdiction of successive shogunates and local warlords, with the emperor coming to occupy a largely ceremonial role. During the fourteenth century, with the waning of the economic power of the court and the instability brought about by war, Japan's emperors curtailed their visits to locations far from the Kyoto Imperial Palace, and remained within their neighbourhood.[11] The tradition of the procession was instead adopted by the Ashikaga shoguns (1336–1573), who visited powerful temple complexes, performing ritual gift exchanges in order to demonstrate that the shogun stood at the peak of the temple power hierarchy, 'in essence holding kingly authority'.[12]

In the mid-seventeenth century, the newly established Tokugawa shogunate (1603–1868) further restrained emperors from travelling beyond the Kyoto Imperial Palace, and with very few exceptions only retired emperors were permitted to travel.[13] There were, however, numerous other types of parades during the seventeenth to nineteenth centuries, such that historians have described Tokugawa Japan as an 'age of parades'.[14] There were shogunal excursions, including pilgrimages to the shrine of the Tokugawa house, located in

---

[9] E.g. Ronald. P. Toby, 'Carnival of the Aliens: Korean Embassies in Edo-Period Art and Popular Culture', *Monumenta Nipponica*, 41 (1986), 415–56; Jiang Wu, 'The Taikun's Zen Master from China: Yinyuan, the Tokugawa Bakufu, and the Founding of Manpukuji in 1661', *East Asian History*, 38 (2014), 75–96; Rebekah Clements, 'Speaking in Tongues? Daimyo, Zen Monks, and Spoken Chinese in Japan, 1661–1711', *Journal of Asian Studies*, 76 (2017), 603–26; Seifman, 'Performing "Lūchū"'.

[10] Brian O. Ruppert, 'Royal Progresses to Shrines: Cloistered Sovereign, "Tennō", and the Sacred Sites of Early Medieval Japan', *Cahiers d'Extrême-Asie*, 16 (2006–7), 183–202.

[11] Okada Sōji, 'Jinja gyokō no seiritsu', *Ōkurayama ronshū*, 31 (1991), 29–58; Ōmura Takuo, 'Chūsei zenki no gyokō: Jinja gyokō o chūshin ni', *Nenpō chūseishi kenkyū*, 19 (1994), 154–77; Satō Kazuyuki, 'The Emperor's Gyoko and Funeral in Early Modern Japan', *Osaka Univ.-Harvard Univ. Joint Workshop for Young Scholars in Japanese Culture* (Osaka, 2020), 1, https://www.let.osaka-u.ac.jp/ja/research/file/sato-kazuki.

[12] Kaneko Hiraku, 'Unexpected Paths: Gift Giving and the Nara Excursions of the Muromachi Shoguns', trans. Lee Butler, in *Mediated by Gifts: Politics and Society in Japan, 1350-1850*, ed. Martha Chaiklin (Leiden, 2017), 24–47, at 43.

[13] Takano Toshihiko, 'Edo bakufu no chōtei shihai', *Nihonshi kenkyū*, 319 (1989), 48–77; Satō, 'The Emperor's Gyoko and Funeral'.

[14] Kokuritsu Rekishi Minzoku Hakubutsukan, ed., *Gyōretsu ni miru kinsei: Bushi to ikoku to sairei to* (Tokyo, 2012), i.

Nikkō to the north of Edo, and there were periodic embassies sent by Chosŏn-dynasty Korea and the Ryukyuan kingdom, which involved large processions and public spectacle.[15] In addition, there were regular street parades for local festivals celebrated across the archipelago. However, the overwhelming bulk of elaborate public processions each year was performed by Japan's daimyo as part of the alternate attendance system.

In the absence of imperial progressions, alternate attendance parades filled a gap left by the court, publicly displaying power on the streets. Unlike imperial progresses, however, these daimyo spectacles drew largely on the format of the military parade, and footmen carried weapons including lances, bows and firearms. The weapons used were highly decorated and primarily designed for display, and were usually carried only at important performance points in the journey such as the departure from the castle town, the arrival at the main camps en route and the arrival in Edo.[16] The parades thus provided an opportunity to symbolically assert warrior dominance during the 'Pax Tokugawa', roughly two and a half centuries of peace during which there were few opportunities to make an actual show of military force in battle.

As well as being a public spectacle in Japan's 'age of parades', alternate attendance was a military institution based on the centuries-old warrior practice of the lord requiring the periodic attendance of his retainers by his side.[17] It was one of the types of service that the daimyo lords owed to the Tokugawa shogunate by virtue of their vassalage, in return for which they received land grants and the right to rule their domains. The system was founded during the first half of the seventeenth century following the battle of Sekigahara in 1600, which established Tokugawa dominance. Many of the daimyo who had fought against the victor, Tokugawa Ieyasu (1543–1616), offered close family members to Ieyasu as hostages, following precedents dating back to the Warring States (1467–1568) period of Japanese history.[18] The Shimazu from Satsuma, who are the subject of this article, had fought against Ieyasu at Sekigahara, and were among the first to offer him family members as hostages, such that some historians of Satsuma suggest the alternate attendance system was institutionalised for the Tokugawa by the actions of the Shimazu.[19] In subsequent decades, the hostage arrangements were regularised. All daimyo were required to leave their family in Edo, and to divide their time between their home domain and the capital.[20] The system changed over the course of the seventeenth to nineteenth centuries with regard to the timing and frequency of the daimyo visits to the capital, but in practice they usually made an annual journey, travelling to Edo one year and returning to their domains the next.

---

[15] Toby, 'Carnival of the Aliens'.

[16] Kokuritsu Rekishi Minzoku Hakubutsukan, *Gyōretsu ni miru kinsei*, 64.

[17] Vaporis, *Tour of Duty*, 11–15.

[18] Maruyama Yasunari, *Sankin kōtai* (Tokyo, 2007), 6–53.

[19] Robert Sakai, 'The Consolidation of Power in Satsuma Han', in *Studies in the Institutional History of Early Modern Japan*, ed. John Whitney Hall and Marius B. Jansen (Princeton, 1968), 131–40, at 132; Vaporis, *Tour of Duty*, 12.

[20] Maruyama, *Sankin kōtai* (2007); Yamamoto Hirofumi, *Sankin kōtai* (Tokyo, 1998).

This study contributes to scholarly debates about the extent to which alternate attendance was compulsory, and the extent to which it served daimyo or shogunate interests. The vast outlay of resources required to maintain two residences, one in the daimyo's castle town in his domain and one in Edo, as well as the travel expenses associated with regularly moving retinues consisting of hundreds or thousands of people across the country, was a heavy burden.[21] Until recently, the main school of thought held that the requirement to divide their time between their domains and Edo was forced upon the daimyo by the shogunate, and that it served to reduce the threat of rebellion by keeping the daimyo in a state of permanent financial distress – a theory which dates back at least as far as the Confucian scholar Ogyū Sorai (1666–1728).[22] Recent research, however, has shown that the system changed over time, and from the mid-eighteenth century onwards the shogunate was unable to enforce set times for attendance, with daimyo choosing to attend when it suited them. Scholars have begun to investigate the mutual benefits of the system for both the daimyo and the shogunate.[23] In the case of Satsuma, the period during which alternate attendance and the visits to Naeshirogawa were established coincided with what Robert Sakai has dubbed the 'consolidation of power' in the domain, which followed several decades of regional instability resulting from late sixteenth-century power struggles in Kyushu, Satsuma's involvement in the Imjin War and the Shimazu defeat at Sekigahara. As we will see, the Shimazu found value in the alternate attendance system due to the opportunity it allowed them to be publicly visible as they travelled through their domain and to regularly assert their sovereignty in their local region.

Sovereignty

The delicate balance of power between the Tokugawa shogunate and the daimyo foregrounds this discussion. Despite being more powerful than any of Japan's rulers since the height of the imperial state in the eighth century, the shoguns who ruled during the first century of the Tokugawa period did not have direct control over commoners who resided outside of Tokugawa landholdings. Instead, the Tokugawa asserted authority over daimyo, requiring them to pay tax, perform public acts of loyalty like alternate attendance, and defer to the shogunate on matters of international diplomacy, trade, coastal defence and limiting contacts with foreigners.[24] The daimyo, in turn, directly ruled the warriors and commoners of their own domains. Daimyo might thus be considered, in Mark Ravina's words, 'sovereigns who were subordinate to a superior sovereign'.[25] Ravina uses the term 'compound state' to describe the

[21] Vaporis, *Tour of Duty*, 27–32; Yamamoto, *Sankinkōtai*, 156–76.

[22] Fujimoto Hitofumi, 'Sankin kōtai no henshitsu', *Rakuhoku shigaku*, 14 (2012), 74–98, at 74–5.

[23] Fujimoto, 'Sankin kōtai no henshitsu'.

[24] Philip C. Brown, 'The Mismeasure of Land: Land Surveying in the Tokugawa Period', *Monumenta Nipponica*, 42 (1987), 115–55. Robert Hellyer, *Defining Engagements Defining Engagement: Japan and Global Contexts, 1640-1868* (Cambridge, MA, 2009).

[25] Mark Ravina, 'Performing the Great Peace: Political Space and Open Secrets in Tokugawa Japan by Luke S. Roberts (Review)', *Monumenta Nipponica*, 71 (2016), 158–61, at 158.

overlapping sovereignties of Tokugawa Japan, a translation of the term *fukugō kokka*, coined by Japanese legal historian Mizubayashi Takeshi, who was in turn adapting the European idea of 'composite monarchies' as popularised by J. H Elliott.[26] This approach is not without its controversies in the Japanese case. The alternative position was summarised by Ronald Toby, who points out that daimyo control 'even in the minds of their most ardent local supporters – remained conditional and was not "sovereign" in any substantive sense', arguing that identification with the political space of a Japanese proto-nation was never effaced by domain loyalties.[27]

While a definitive answer about the precise nature of sovereignty in early modern Japan remains elusive – particularly when using structural concepts derived from European history – what is clear is that there existed overlapping regimes of power. And these regimes were expressed using parallel linguistic and semiotic registers. By employing the Tokugawa period political concepts of *omote* (exterior) and *naibun* (interior), Luke Roberts shows how power was discussed in two parallel vocabularies, depending on whether the context was 'external' shogunal business or 'internal' domain business. Warrior officials for example, used the term 'state' (*kokka*) when describing their domain for a local audience, but would recognise the superiority of the shogun when addressing documents to Edo.[28] In practice, such dualities meant that one official event or practice, like an alternate attendance parade, could have polyvalent meanings tailored to fit both 'internal' and 'external' audiences.

The polyvalent meaning of parades has been noted in relation to the ritual activities of the Ryukyuan embassies that were despatched to Edo, travelling either with the Satsuma alternate attendance retinue or escorted by Satsuma retainers. Travis Seifman argues that these embassies served to enact on the Tokugawa stage Ryukyu's position as a sovereign kingdom and loyal tributary of the Ming and Qing imperial courts, while at the same time asserting for a Japanese audience that the kingdom was under the banners of the Shimazu family.[29] Kido Hironari has further shown how this duality was expressed in two parallel terms describing Ryukyu's status: one as a vassal state (*fuyō*) of the Shimazu, and the other as a foreign state (*ikoku*) subservient to the Tokugawa. The Shimazu were able to deftly use these two statuses of

---

[26] Mark Ravina, *Land and Lordship in Early Modern Japan* (Stanford, 1999); Mizubayashi Takeshi, *Hokensei no saihen to Nihonteki shakai no kakuritsu* (Tokyo, 1987), 279–80; J. H. Elliott, 'A Europe of Composite Monarchies', *Past & Present*, 137 (1992), 48–71.

[27] Ronald P. Toby, 'Rescuing the Nation from History: The State of the State in Early Modern Japan', *Monumenta Nipponica*, 56 (2001), 197–237, at 200.

[28] Luke S. Roberts, *Performing the Great Peace: Political Space and Open Secrets in Tokugawa Japan* (Honolulu, 2012). The terms with which the structure of the Japanese polity and the practice of foreign relations were discussed began to change in the late eighteenth century, after the period covered in the present article. See Michael Facius, 'Terms of Government: Early Modern Japanese Concepts of Rulership and Political Geography in Translation', *Journal of the History of Ideas*, 83 (2021), 521–37.

[29] Seifman, 'Performing "Lūchū"'.

fuyō and *ikoku* for different strategies when describing Ryukyu to third parties, and this facilitated the dual meanings that the Ryukyuan processions held.[30]

Such dualities underpin the approach in this article. As noted, alternate attendance has been understood primarily through an external or Edo-centric lens. One of the leading authorities on alternate attendance, Constantine Vaporis, astutely notes that Tokugawa Japan was 'almost a mirror image' of countries elsewhere in the world in which the monarch was in motion and his or her lords were stationary points to be visited during royal progresses; in Japan 'the lords, and not the hegemon, were rendered portable.'[31] This is undoubtedly true for the external, Edo-facing aspects of alternate attendance which served to reiterate the shogun's position at the top of the Tokugawa warrior hierarchy. Adding to this picture, I argue here that alternate attendance, like many political phenomena in Tokugawa Japan, could also be symbolically used for an 'internal', local purpose, with the daimyo behaving like portable sovereigns within their own territories. Even as a daimyo embarked upon a journey to offer obeisance to the shogun, the rituals and spectacle of his procession could simultaneously be used to assert his own power and claims to rulership within his domain. Such was the case with Satsuma.

Alternate attendance in Satsuma

At the southernmost tip of the island of Kyushu, Satsuma was the furthest domain from the shogun's city of Edo. Thus, of all the daimyo, the Shimazu had the longest journey and one of the heaviest financial burdens involved in maintaining the practice of alternate attendance. The trip was approximately 1,400 km one way and took two months, travelling over rough terrain, by land and by sea.[32] The route to Edo and back again was regulated by the shogunate for the part of the journey between Edo and the merchant city of Osaka. However, between their castle town of Kagoshima and the edge of their territory, the Shimazu were in control. Based on the roads in their domain, they had several options, one of which took them through the village of Naeshirogawa that is the subject of this article (route A in Figure 1). Until the middle of the Tokugawa period, the Shimazu usually took either the Izumi Highway (Izumi suji, route A), or the Ōkuchi Highway (Ōkuchi suji, route B).[33] Ostensibly, their choice was dictated by the time of year they were required to travel, and the direction and strength of the prevailing

---

[30] Kido Hironari, 'Ryūkyū shisetsu no seiritsu: Baku han Ryūkyū kankeishi no shiza kara', *Shirin*, 99 (2016), 525–57.

[31] Vaporis, *Tour of Duty*, 63.

[32] The times and dates of Shimazu travel, as well as the routes taken, are recorded in official *han* documents reprinted in *Kyūki zatsuroku tsuiroku*, ed. Kagoshima-ken Ishin Shiryō Hensanjo (8 vols., Kagoshima-ken, 1971–8). See also Ueno Takafumi, *Satsuma han no sankin kōtai: Edo made nan'nichi kakatta ka* (Kagoshima, 2019).

[33] Hatano Tominobu, 'Satsuma han no shoki sankin to sankin kōtaiji', *Komazawa Daigaku shigaku ronshū*, 7 (1977), 46–56, at 54–5.

Figure 1. Three routes taken through Kyushu to Edo by Satsuma daimyo. (*Source:* Clements, 'Daimyō Processions and Satsuma's Korean Village', 227.)

winds at sea.[34] However, as we will see, the opportunity to visit Naeshirogawa, to observe the ceramic industry there, and to receive displays of loyalty from its 'foreign' inhabitants, may also have been a factor in which highways they chose to take within their domain.

The official records of Satsuma contain details of the elaborate preparations that were made for the beginning and end of their momentous journeys.[35] Strict protocols were followed as to the manner in which the lord, hidden within his palanquin, was to be transported, including how the castle should be decked out with particular folding screens for his arrival and departure, and precisely what refreshments were to await him. Before leaving for the capital, the Satsuma lord would conduct a ceremony known as *yakkō kenbun* (an inspection of his troops), and would visit a shrine.[36] According to Satsuma domain records from 1783, on the day of the daimyo's departure for Edo the streets of Kagoshima were to be swept clean, and proper decorum observed:

---

[34] Kido Hironari, 'Shimazushi no sankin ni taisuru Ōsaka "funaarake"', *Ōsaka Rekishi Hakubutsukan Kenkyū kiyō*, 13 (2015), 19–48, at 22–3.

[35] *Hanpōshū 8, Kagoshimahan shita*, ed. Hanpō Kenkyūkai (Tokyo, 1981), 90–7.

[36] Yamamoto, *Sankin kōtai*, 90.

... people outside their homes are to go inside ... As the procession passes they are to show proper respect, kneeling with their heads on the floor ... Most importantly, when the lord is going to and from the capital, people should not disperse in a vulgar manner until the part of his entourage containing his senior officials has passed by.[37]

The Satsuma procession ranged from as few as 500 men to as many as 3,100, including porters and other hired labourers.[38] All sections of the entourage did not necessarily travel together for the entire journey, and as the instructions above indicate, the greatest respect was reserved for the daimyo and his senior officials.

Similar rituals have been recorded for other domains and were designed to inspire awe and command obedience among the daimyo's subjects.[39] We do not have direct evidence of the extent to which the rules on decorum were followed by the citizens of Kagoshima. Research suggests that in other parts of Japan the enforcement was patchy.[40] However, at the very least, the rules prescribed here show an intent to remind the daimyo's subjects of his power in his home town. The example of Naeshirogawa shows how this power was ritually asserted in a village within the daimyo's domain.

The village of Naeshirogawa

Naeshirogawa (now incorporated with another village, and known as Miyama) is located approximately 22 kilometres north-west of Kagoshima, one day's journey for the Shimazu's lords in their palanquins.[41] The activities that took place during daimyo visits showcased the ceramic industry that flourished there, and the foreign culture of its inhabitants. Naeshirogawa's kilns were among the many that had been founded in Kyushu by Korean potters brought to Japan during the Imjin War.[42] Most of the Korean potters and their family members (seventy individuals in total) whom the Shimazu armies brought to Satsuma moved to Naeshirogawa early in the Tokugawa period, or were relocated there over the course of the seventeenth century, such that Naeshirogawa became the main site of Korean ceramics in the domain.[43] The kilns produced the distinctive 'black Satsuma' (kurosatsuma) and 'white Satsuma' (shirosatsuma) wares for which the area is still famous.[44]

---

[37] Hanpōshū 8, Kagoshimahan shita, ed. Hanpō, 100.

[38] Seifman, 'Performing "Lūchū"', 59–60.

[39] Murata Eitarō, Kinsei Nihon kōtsūshi: Denba seido to sankin kōtai (Tokyo, 1935), 308–87.

[40] Vaporis, Tour of Duty, 64–8.

[41] Ueno, Satsuma han no sankin kōtai, 85.

[42] Naitō, Bunroku keichō eki ni okeru hironin no kenkyū; Louise Cort, 'Korean Influences in Japanese Ceramics: The Impact of the Teabowl Wars of 1592–1598', Ceramics and Civilization, 2 (1986), 331–62; Andres Maske, Potters and Patrons in Edo Period Japan: Takatori Ware and the Kuroda Domain (Farnham, 2011).

[43] Kurushima Hiroshi, 'Kinsei no Naeshirogawa', in Satsuma Chōsen tōkōmura no yonhyaku nen, ed. Kurushima Hiroshi et al. (Tokyo, 2014), 3–57.

[44] Tazawa Kingo and Oyama Fujio, Satsumayaki no kenkyū (Tokyo, 1941).

Although the exact size of Naeshirogawa's contribution to the Satsuma economy is unknown, its ceramic industry was prolific, and this in part accounts for the attention they received from the Shimazu. Initially, the Naeshirogawa kilns produced large everyday domestic items such as storage vessels and mortars. In the latter half of the Tokugawa period, teapots were fired in large numbers and sold not only within the domain but to other parts of Japan, providing a source of income for Satsuma.[45] Sherds from Naeshirogawa teapots have been excavated at sites across mainland Japan and in Okinawa (formerly Ryukyu). The squat, black teapots exported by Satsuma and produced mainly in Naeshirogawa were so ubiquitous throughout Japan that this particular type came to be known as a 'Satsuma teapot' (*Satsuma dobin*) no matter where it had been produced.[46]

The Shimazu recognised the importance of the Naeshirogawa ceramics industry, and put measures in place to protect the village community. The Naeshirogawa documents record gifts of land rights in the seventeenth and eighteenth centuries, including cultivation lands and the right to cut wood from local forests for their kilns.[47] After tensions between locals and the potters over access to firewood led to an outbreak of fighting in 1666, the then daimyo, Shimazu Mitsuhisa, issued a decree that no one was to harm the 'Koreans' and that offenders and their families would be punished.[48] The domain also periodically built wells and constructed houses as the population of Naeshirogawa increased, and provided financial aid in times of difficulty.[49]

In addition, the domain promulgated regulations designed to protect the villagers' Korean identity, as the original war captives died out over the course of the seventeenth century.[50] In 1676 it was forbidden for the people from Naeshirogawa to marry outside the village and move away, although people from other villages were permitted to marry into the Naeshirogawa community. In 1695, the villagers were prohibited from using Japanese names, and any who had a Japanese name were ordered to change it to one from their country of origin.[51] The prohibition of marriage outside the village may be understood as being designed to prevent the loss of specialised knowledge of ceramic production, and was a regulation seen in other Satsuma villages

[45] Watanabe Yoshirō, 'Kamaato kara wakaru koto: Kinsei Satsumayaki no shōsei gijutsu', in *Yakimonozukuri no kōkōgaku*, ed. Kagoshima Daigaku Sōgō Kenkyū Hakubutsu Kan (Kagoshima, 2011), 18–37, at 19.

[46] Watanabe Yoshirō, 'Kinsei Satsuma dobin no hangai ryūtsū ni tsuite no nooto', *Kara kara*, 29 (2015), 13–21.

[47] E.g. 200 *koku* of land in 1669, and forestry rights in 1685. See *Sennen Chōsen yori meshiwatasare tomechō* (1872), reprinted in Fukaminato, 'Satsumayaki o meguru Naeshirogawa kankei monjō ni tsuite', at 113 and 117.

[48] *Ibid.*, 113.

[49] The term 'Korean' is used as a convenient shorthand in this article, for the modern nation state did not exist at this time. In the Japanese sources used in this article, the most common adjective used to describe the origins of the villagers and their identity is '*Chōsen*' (i.e. Chosŏn, the name of the dynasty that ruled the peninsula from 1392 until 1897).

[50] Watanabe Yoshirō, 'Naze Satsumahan wa Naeshirogawa ni Chōsen fūzoku o nokoshita no ka', *Kadai shigaku*, 52 (2005), 9–18; Naito, *Bunroku keichōeki ni okeru hirōnin no kenkū*, 224–55.

[51] *Sennen Chōsen yori meshiwatasare tomechō*, 119.

with a specialised occupation, such as mining or fishing.[52] The order to preserve Korean names may also be seen in this light, but it is likely that a desire to preserve the 'Korean-ness' of the village was also at work. Like the representatives of Ryukyu, the villagers were required to present themselves in foreign dress at the daimyo's castle in Kagoshima to offer New Year's greetings, together with Japanese vassals of the Shimazu.[53] Furthermore, Naeshirogawa provided Korean language interpreters for Satsuma throughout the Tokugawa period, in order to deal with Korean ships that arrived in Satsuma ports or were washed up on the coastline.[54] The foreign cultural capital and the perceived Korean otherness that the Naeshirogawans possessed was thus clearly valued by the Shimazu family. In the encounters discussed below, the display of Korean culture through dress, dance and displays of writing, as well as their ceramic products, was a key feature of the rituals and entertainments that took place.

Daimyo visits to Naeshirogawa

The earliest recorded daimyo encounters with the Naeshirogawa villagers occurred in the second decade of the seventeenth century. The Naeshirogawa village document, *Sennen Chōsen yori meshiwatasare tomechō* ('A record of how we were brought from Chosŏn [Korea] in years gone by'), and its variant manuscripts describe how the daimyo (referred to on this occasion as 'the counsellor' or *chūnagon*) would hold an audience with representatives from Naeshirogawa when he passed through on his travels, in order to receive updates on the production of white stoneware in the village.[55] Although this entry is undated, other documents from Naeshirogawa note that it was in 1614.[56] This indicates that the visitor was Shimazu Iehisa (1576–1638), who was daimyo of Satsuma between 1601 and 1638 and who held the honorary court rank of counsellor. Keen to improve the economy of his domain, Iehisa had ordered that a search be made for clay suitable for producing pottery, and had been delighted with the results achieved by the potters in Naeshirogawa.[57]

The village records then describe how Iehisa began to stay regularly at the district headquarters (*kariya* or *kaiya*) in nearby Ichiki on his journeys to and from Edo. On such occasions, he would summon the villagers to perform a type of religious dance, known in the Satsuma pronunciation as *kanme* ('sacred dance').[58] The *kanme* dances of Naeshirogawa were performed by priests from

[52] Haraguchi Torao and Robert Sakai, *The Status System and Social Organization of Satsuma: A Translation of the Shūmon tefuda aratame jōmoku* (Tokyo, 1975), 22–7.

[53] Watanabe, 'Satsuma han wa Naeshirogawa ni Chōsen fūzoku o nokoshita no ka', 15.

[54] Tokunaga Kazunobu, 'Satsumahan no Chōsen tsūji ni tsuite', *Reimeikan chōsa kenkyū hōkoku*, 8 (1994), 18–33; Naito, *Bunroku keichōeki ni okeru hirōnin no kenkū* (1976), 255–60.

[55] *Sennen Chōsen yori meshiwatasare tomechō*, 111.

[56] *Ibid.*, 125.

[57] *Ibid.*, 111.

[58] Chŏng Kwang, *Satsuma Naeshirogawa no Chōsen kayō* (privately published, 1990), 95–128. *Kanme* is usually pronounced '*kanmai*' in standard modern Japanese.

the village shrine, which was dedicated to Tan'gun, the mythical progenitor of the Korean people.[59] These dances were performed according to Korean rites and with Korean costumes and were a visible manifestation of the foreignness of Naeshirogawa's inhabitants displayed before their lord. The pride with which they were held by the domain is further indicated by the fact that the dancers, together with Naeshirogawa's kilns, were later depicted in *Sappan shōkei hyakuzu* ('A hundred superlative views of Satsuma'), a coloured, hand-illustrated guide promoting the domain, which was commissioned by the daimyo of Satsuma in 1815 and presented to the shogun.[60]

Not long after Iehisa began interacting with the Naoshirogawa villagers, an official rest house (*chaya*, lit. tea house) was built in Naeshirogawa near the kilns.[61] The early records of the rest-house encounters offer the first glimpse of the nature of the hospitality arrangements between the village and the daimyo entourage: rice was brought out from the official storehouse, there would be displays of dancing and the villagers would receive gifts of silver from the daimyo.[62] We see an expansion of the detail in which each of these visits was recorded in the Naeshirogawa documents from 1677 onwards, providing more information with which to interpret the meaning of such interactions (see Table 1). The district headquarters, where the daimyo stayed overnight when travelling through his domain, was moved to Naeshirogawa in 1675, and the records report fifteen overnight visits by the daimyo to Naeshirogawa between 1677 and 1714.[63]

As the following extract from 1679 serves to illustrate, visits usually revolved around displays of dancing, a ceramic market displaying the villagers' wares, and gift exchange ceremonies between the villagers and the daimyo:

In the seventh year of the same era, Kan'yōin (Shimazu Mitsuhisa) was going up to the capital. On the nineteenth day of the fourth month he arrived at Naeshirogawa. On the twentieth day he viewed the [ceramic] market and the dancing. On the twenty-first day of the same month, he commanded further dancing. The Keeper of the District Headquarters (*kariyamori*) and the Village Headman (*shōya*) offered up the usual gifts of one jar of distilled liquor and one basket of sweets. [The potter named] Sankan offered up one bowl with lilies and grasses on it. Seven people, including Taikan and Kinkan, offered up two jars of distilled liquor. On the twenty-second day of the same month ... the Keeper of the District Headquarters and the Village Headman were each given 100 *hiki* [3.75 kg] of bronze coins. Sankan and the previously mentioned seven people were given 12 *monme* [45 g] of silver coins. The young

[59] Chŏng, *Satsuma Naeshirogawa no Chōsen kayō*, 102.

[60] Watanabe Miki, '*Sappan shōke hyakuzu* ni yoru Minami Kyūshū seikatsu ebiki', in *Nihon kinsei seikatsu ebiki, Minami Kyūshū hen*, ed. Nihon Kinsei Seikatsu Ebiki Minamikyūshūhen Hensan Kyōdō Kenkūhan (Kanagawa, 2018), 149–56.

[61] *Sennen Chōsen yori meshiwatasare tomechō*, 112.

[62] *Ibid.*, 112.

[63] *Ibid.*

Table 1. Examples of gifts exchanged between Naeshirogawa villagers and the Satsuma, 1677–1714

Year	Gifts from Naeshirogawa	Gifts from Daimyo
1677	Dancing, ceramic market Two jars of distilled liquor from nine people who received the gift of a family name	The nine people: surnames, 130 *ryō* of silver coins, hanging scrolls written in the daimyo's own hand
1678	Dancing, ceramic market	The *kariyamori* (keeper of the district headquarters), the *shōya* (village headman) and Sankan (a potter): 100 *hiki* of bronze coins each Thirteen young women: five silver coins
1679	Dancing, ceramic market *Kariyamori* and the *shōya*: one jar of distilled liquor, and one basket of sweets Sankan (potter): one bowl with lilies and grasses Taikan, Kinkan and seven of their compatriots (potters): two jars of distilled liquor	*Kariyamori* and the *shōya*: 100 *hiki* of bronze coins each Sankan and the seven compatriots: 12 *monme* of silver coins Young women: three silver coins
1680	Dancing, ceramic market *Bugyō* (steward in charge of district), *kariyamori* and *shōya*: one jar (or one cup) of distilled liquor each	*Bugyō*, *kariyamori*, *shōya* and twelve young women: 12 *monme* of silver coins The village: tax exemption on land for three years, pine plantations to use as firewood for kilns
1681	Dancing, ceramic market *Bugyō*, *kariyamori*, *shōya* and Sankan: distilled liquor and goods in baskets, etc. Kinkan, Taikan, Junkan, Shōken and Chinkun performed Korean music before the daimyo	*Bugyō* and Sankan: 100 *hiki* of bronze coins each *Kariyamori*, *shōya* and five others: 12 *monme* of silver coins each Young women: 10 *monme* of silver coins each Kinkan, Taikan, Junkan, Shōken and Chinkun: received a few words from the daimyo
1684	Dancing, ceramic market *Kariyamori* and *shōya*: gifts according to the usual precedents	*Kariyamori* and *shōya*: 100 *hiki* of bronze coins each Thirteen of the young women: 500 *hiki* of bronze coins *Bugyō* (named as Nomura Umanosuke): three watermelons At that time thirteen houses in Atobaba were marked out in rope to be given to the second and third sons for their

(Continued)

Table I. (*Continued.*)

Year	Gifts from Naeshirogawa	Gifts from Daimyo
		homes (*yashiki*)
		People of Naeshirokawa: lands in Ichiki
		Dancers: distilled liquor
1688	Dancing, ceramic market *Jitō* (steward), the officials and the *kariyamori*: offerings according to the usual precedents	The three officials: 100 *hiki* of bronze coins each The young women: 500 hiki of coins to the young women Sake to the male dancers
1703	Dancing, ceramic market *Jitō* (named as Nagase Hyakuami), the officials and *kariyamori*: two types of gifts, according to the usual precedent	*Jitō* (Nagase Hyakuami): 100 *hiki* of bronze coins Shuzan, *kariyamori* and the officials: 100 *hiki* of bronze coins each
1714	Dancing, ceramic market *Jitō* (Nagase Hyakuami), the officials, and *kariyamori*: two types of gifts, according to the usual precedent	*Jitō* (Nagase Hyakuami), *kariyamori* and the officials: 100 *hiki* of bronze coins 300 *hiki* of bronze coins to be shared among the young women

Source: *Sennen Chōsen yori meshiwatasare tomechō*, and its variant manuscripts reprinted in Fukaminato, 'Satsumayaki o meguru Naeshirogawa kankei monjō ni tsuite'.

women were given three silver coins. The lord departed at the hour of the sheep [approx. 2 p.m.] that same day.[64]

As Table 1 shows, the gifts offered by the villagers usually took the form of jars of distilled liquor and baskets of sweets. The gifts most commonly given by the daimyo to the villagers were currency, followed closely by the bestowal of honours such as the right to a family name and a sword, which signified a rise in status for the recipient from commoner (*hyakushō*) to the warrior (*shi*) class. On occasion, there were unusual gifts such as the ceramic bowl with an illustrated design given by one of the senior potters as a symbol of the industry

---

[64] 'Bronze' and 'silver coins' were usually alloys. Japanese money, measures and weights were not standardised during the seventeenth century, and varied between domains. Due to the destruction of official documents in the nineteenth century, little is known of Satsuma's currency history. Here I offer approximate measures based on what is known of currency in other parts of Japan:

1 *kan* (= 1 *kanmon* = 1 *kanme*) = 1,000 *mon* (or *monme*) = 3.75 kg
1 *mon*(*me*) = 1 *sen* = 3.75 g
1 *kin* = 0.16 *kan* = 160 *mon*(*me*) = 16 *ryō* = 600 g
1 *hiki* = 10 *mon*(*me*)

Hitomi Tonomura, *Community and Commerce in Late Medieval Japan: The Corporate Villages of Tokuchin-ho* (Stanford, 1992), xiii.

they had founded, or the three watermelons given by the daimyo to the magistrate (*bugyō*, i.e. the vassal responsible for the outer castle district to which Naeshirogawa belonged), Nomura Umanosuke, in 1684, which were elite gifts popular at the time and a fitting reinforcement of Umanosuke's status.[65]

The meaning of gifts

For reasons of space, a detailed, anthropological study of the gifts exchanged between the Naeshirogawans and the daimyo will have to await another occasion. Instead, this article will examine the meaning of the most commonly exchanged gifts, as they relate to the role of alternate attendance in the domain. Gift exchange was fundamental to the workings of medieval and early modern Japanese society and remains so today, to the extent that Japan has been described as having a gift economy.[66] This has been explored through the theory of gifts founded by Marcel Mauss, who, although working on primitive societies, identified two main facets of gift-giving that proved to be particularly relevant to later studies of the Japanese case. Where gift-giving is part of the rituals of a society, Mauss argued, the appearance of a gift freely offered often belies the fact that at heart there is some obligation or economic interest at stake.[67] Japanese warrior society has been shown to be underpinned by principles of reciprocity between lord and retainer, as well as between lord and commoner.[68] Exchanges of goods, allegiances and patronage within this system were often couched in terms of gifts despite being transactional in nature.[69]

In the encounters between Naeshirogawa villagers and the Satsuma daimyo, the regular gifts of money from the daimyo may be understood as a kind of payment clothed in the form of a gift so as to make a public display of the lord's generosity. Although we do not have direct evidence of how the money was used in the Naeshirogawa case, earlier and contemporary precedents suggest that this currency was intended to cover at least some of the costs of hosting the daimyo and his entourage.[70] This money, together with less tangible gifts from the daimyo, such as the honour of his presence, or

---

[65] Fujimoto Masahiro, *Nihon chūsei no zōto to futan* (Tokyo, 1997), 90–122. Umanosuke held the highest-ranking domain office responsible for Naeshirogawa at this time, which was also referred to as the steward (*jitō*), a rank within Satsuma's outer castle system (Fukaminato, 'Satsumayaki o meguru Naeshirogawa kankei monjō ni tsuite', 124). *Bugyō*, usually translated as 'magistrates', were middle-ranking administrators during the Tokugawa period. However, as with many administrative offices in Satsuma associated with the outer castle system, their role was slightly different despite having the same name as that which was used elsewhere in Japan. On stewards and the outer castle system, see discussion below.

[66] Martha Chaiklin, 'Introduction', in Chailkin, *Mediated by Gifts*, 1–23, at 6; Katherine Rupp, *Gift-Giving in Japan: Cash, Connections, Cosmologies* (Stanford, 2003).

[67] Marcel Mauss, 'Essai sur le don. Forme et raison de l'échange dans les sociétés archaïques', *L'Année Sociologique* 1923–4 (1), 30–186, at 33.

[68] *Futan to zōto*, ed. Yamaguchi Keiji *et al.* (Tokyo, 1986); Fujimoto, *Nihon chūsei no zōto to futan*; Chaiklin, 'Introduction'.

[69] Oda Yūzō, 'Kodai chūsei no suiko', in *Futan to zōto*, ed. Yamaguchi, 93–116.

[70] Fujimoto, *Nihon chūsei no zōto to futan*, 15.

the right to bear a surname, furthermore went towards supporting the people responsible for the ceramic industry in Naeshirogawa, which in return provided an important source of income for the domain. The transactional 'gift' of a surname was also awarded to residents of other communities in Satsuma with special skills, such as the gold miners of Yamagano and tin miners of Taniyama.[71]

Mauss also argued that gift-giving strengthens the bonds of a society. During daimyo visits, a relationship of mutual benefit and fealty between the Shimazu and the villagers was thus articulated through elaborate ceremonies of gift-giving, banqueting, dance and displays of local wares. These exchanges symbolised the relationship of dependency that the Naeshirogawa village had with the Shimazu lords, as well as the importance of Naeshirogawa to the domain and the patronage to which they were entitled as a result. The villagers' offerings of symbolic gifts with low monetary value, such as wine and sweets, together with displays of their ceramic wares and foreign culture, were outward expressions of their dependency, 'offered up' (*shinjō*) to their lord for his enjoyment. This in turn placed an obligation on the daimyo to offer the villagers his protection and support. The gift exchanges, furthermore, reinforced social hierarchies, with district officials such as the steward, Umanosuke, receiving high-status gifts, officials from the village receiving the largest amounts of money, and so on, down to those who are listed last in the sources – usually the young women, whose role is unidentified, but were probably serving as wait staff during the festivities, and who usually received a few coins.

We have little information on the ritual exchanges that took place in other villages within Shimazu territory as they passed through on their way to Edo. This is particularly true of the early period that the Naeshirogawa records describe. However, there are later clues, which suggest that similar festivities were held elsewhere, although not with the same duration and regularity as in Naeshirogawa. A Satsuma protocol document from 1751, for example, includes a brief list of reception ceremonies that were to be conducted at rest stops in Satsuma – including Naeshirogawa – upon the occasion of the daimyo entering his domain for the first time.[72] In this document, one village is required to perform a dance, and for the other reception points, including Naeshirogawa, the requirement is to present 'offerings according to the usual precedents' (*shinjōbutsu, senrei no tōri*).[73] The wording of this latter requirement is identical to that which appears in the Naeshirogawa records in relation to the presentation of sweets and alcohol, suggesting that the presentation of these or similar items was standard practice in the domain. Further clues are to be found in nineteenth-century diaries of retainers who travelled in the Shimazu entourage. Yamada Tamemasa, a retainer of Shimazu Nariakira (1809–1858), recorded in 1854 that the daimyo viewed displays of fishing on the river in

---

[71] Haraguchi and Sakai, *The Status System and Social Organization of Satsuma*, 28.

[72] Daimyo heirs were hostages raised in Edo, and did not officially travel to their domains until they inherited them.

[73] *Hanpōshū* 8, *Kagoshimahan shita*, ed. Hanpō, 93.

Mukoda, and received a visit from Satsuma's representative in Nagasaki, who offered him sweets.[74] These patterns, including displays of local industries or entertainments and the offering of sweets, suggest that the broad framework for the Naeshirogawa ceremonies was couched in semiotic terms that would have been readily understood in Satsuma as conveying the relationship of daimyo and subject.

However, it should be noted that Naeshirogawa seems to have received particular attention, and more of the daimyo's time, than other villages. The daimyo sojourns in Naeshirogawa usually lasted at least two, sometimes three days, whereas retainer diaries show that less time was spent in other villages.[75] Furthermore, the Naeshirogawans were subject to the special regulations and appearances at the Shimazu's castle in Kagoshima discussed above, which they undertook together with senior Shimazu retainers and the Ryukyuan representatives living in Kagoshima. The Naeshirogawa village receptions thus occupied a special role in the Shimazu alternate attendance system, the reasons for which are discussed below.

Foreigners and the consolidation of power in Satsuma

The material and symbolic benefits of alternate attendance visits for the village of Naeshirogawa are clear. But why did benefits accrue to the domain from this particular village's displays of loyalty and submission? An explanation may be found in the localised power dynamics of Satsuma and its regional economy. The ritual activities of the Naeshirogawa visits were designed to publicly shore up the Shimazu's local claims to power, which rested not only on their investiture as daimyo by the Tokugawa, but on their long history of rulership in Kyushu, their ability to command obedience from foreigners in their region and to bring foreign resources, goods and trade into Satsuma for the benefit of the local economy.

Although invested by the Tokugawa with the right to rule their domain, the Shimazu continued to draw upon local claims to power that predated that investiture by over 400 years. Of all the families who ruled Japan's approximately 300 domains, the Shimazu had the longest continuous history of daimyo status, claiming to trace their origins to Koremune Tadahisa (1179–1227), who was supposedly the son of Minamoto no Yoritomo (1147–1199), the founder of Japan's first shogunate.[76] In 1197 Tadahisa's putative father made him governor (*shugo*) of Satsuma and Ōsumi provinces. Hyūga province was later added, and Tadahisa's descendants ruled in the region for the next 700 years, until they played a deciding role in the Meiji revolution of 1868, which overthrew the Tokugawa shogunate and established Japan's

---

[74] Yamada Tamemasa, *Ansei gannen Shimazu Nariakira sanpu otomo nikki* (1854), in *Kagoshima Kenshi Nariakira-kō shiryō* 4, ed. Kagoshimaken Ishinshiryō Hensanjo (Kagoshima, 1984), 902.

[75] Ueno Takafumi, *Satsuma han no sankin kōtai: Edo made nan'nichi kakatta ka* (Kagoshima, 2019).

[76] Modern research suggests that Tadahisa was in fact the son of a retainer in the Konoe family of regents, one Koremune Hirokoto (dates unknown). See Hayashi Tadasu, 'Shimazuke yuisho to Satsumahan kirokusho: Kan'ei kara shōtoku ki o chūshin ni', *Reimeikan chōsa kenkyū hōkoku*, 25 (2013), 1–40, at 1.

modern constitutional monarchy.[77] Powerful governors like Tadahisa became daimyo lords, exercising military and economic power in their provinces under the often nominal overarching power of the shogun. The precise nature of the daimyo–shogunate relationship evolved between the twelfth and the sixteenth centuries, from the twelfth-century '*shugo* daimyo' like Tadahisa, through the largely autonomous daimyo of the civil war period ('*sengoku* daimyo'), to the daimyo of the Tokugawa period ('*kinsei* daimyo'), who ruled their domains but with stricter requirements of vassalage to the shogun.[78] The Shimazu were the only daimyo family of the Tokugawa period to rule continuously throughout the development of the daimyo institution from its origins in the twelfth century.[79] The size and geographical spread of their holdings fluctuated as the family's political fortunes rose and fell; however, the Shimazu retained constant control over Satsuma province, and by the period covered by this article, once again controlled all three provinces, Satsuma, Ōsumi and Hyūga (collectively known as Satsuma domain or Kagoshima domain at the time).

Moreover, although the Shimazu were on the losing side at the epoch-making battle of Sekigahara in 1600, they retained control of their territory afterwards. In the post-Sekigahara period, Tokugawa Ieyasu stripped many daimyo of their lands entirely or moved them to new territories. The practice of regularly moving daimyo around in order to break ties with their traditional power bases, reduce the size of their agricultural incomes or surround the shogunal lands with friendly allies continued throughout the Tokugawa period. It was so common that the term 'potted plant daimyo' (*hachiue daimyō*) was coined to describe the situation.[80] However, the Shimazu retained their historical territories in Kyushu and were not moved throughout the entirety of the Tokugawa period.

The Shimazu used their long lineage as a source of local legitimacy in tandem with their confirmation as rulers by the Tokugawa shogunate. In 1641, in response to a request from the shogunate that all daimyo submit copies of their family trees, the Satsuma Office of Records compiled a family tree for the Shimazu, which claimed their ancestry could be traced to Tadahisa, and submitted this to the shogunate together with a list of the honours bestowed upon them by successive Tokugawa shoguns, from Ieyasu onwards.[81] Together, these two documents effectively laid out two sources of Shimazu legitimacy: their history of rulership, and the contemporary favour of the Tokugawa shoguns. These parallel sources of legitimacy are reflected in the parallel semiotics of Satsuma's alternate attendance parades: on the one hand, as previous

---

[77] Marius B. Jansen, *The Making of Modern Japan* (Cambridge, MA, 2000), 294–370.

[78] John Whitney Hall, 'Foundations of the Modern Japanese Daimyo', in *Studies in the Institutional History of Early Modern Japan* (1968), 65–78.

[79] Haraguchi Torao, 'Satsumahan tojō seido no seiritsu to genna no ikkoku ijichōrei 1', *Hōseishi kenkyū*, 36 (1986), 77–142, at 78.

[80] Jurgis Elisonias, 'Christianity and the Daimyo', in *The Cambridge History of Japan*, IV: *Early Modern Japan*, ed. John Witney Hall and James L Macain (Cambridge, 1991), 301–72, at 359; and John Witney Hall, 'The *bakuhan* System', *ibid.*, 121–82, at 150–1.

[81] Hayashi, 'Shimazuke yuisho to Satsumahan kirokusho', 3–5.

scholars have noted, the journeys were undertaken in order to show obedience to the shogun and to cement the Shimazu's external position in Japan's warrior hierarchy, while on the other, as I argue, within the domain they were used to assert Shimazu's own localised claims to sovereignty.

Such public assertions of power were necessary since, despite their long history of rulership and their investiture by the Tokugawa, Shimazu power in their region was not absolute, nor was it unchallenged. They were particularly vulnerable to local challenges to their authority due to Satsuma's system of 'outer castles' (tojō), an institution unique to the domain, that shored up their regime but also necessitated the careful management of local perceptions of Shimazu authority to counteract rebellion. In the late sixteenth century, the hegemon Toyotomi Hideyoshi had begun the process of disarming the peasantry and moving samurai off the land into castle towns where they were more easily controlled through being dependent on a stipend from their lord.[82] This process was consolidated by Tokugawa Ieyasu, who issued an edict in 1615 commanding 'one domain, one castle' (ikkoku ichijō), under which, as the name suggests, all domains were permitted to maintain only one castle, where the samurai were required to reside, and the other fortifications had to be destroyed.[83] Satsuma, however, was the exception to this rule. The domain was permitted to have 113 district seats, literally 'outside castles' (tojō, known as gō or 'villages' from 1784), in which rural samurai lived and which had a fortified dwelling (though not a castle after 1615) at their centre.[84] When tallies were taken in the nineteenth century, the ratio of samurai to commoner in Satsuma in 1871 was one to three, whereas in other areas of Japan the average ratio for the year 1873 was one to seventeen.[85] The outer castle system also meant that, rather than being concentrated in the castle town and thus more easily monitored as was the case in other domains, all the samurai in Satsuma except for around 5,000 who were clustered in the castle town of Kagoshima were dispersed across even the remotest parts of Satsuma.

The Shimazu undertook various strategies to mitigate the risk posed by having so many armed warriors dispersed throughout their territory, and the Naeshirogawa visits may be understood in this context. Like Japan's daimyo, who were required to divide their time between their domains and Edo, where their families resided under the watch of the shogunate, the stewards (jitō) of Satsuma's outer castle districts were required to reside with their families in the Satsuma castle town of Kagoshima and to visit their district seats periodically, while rural samurai and village elders administered the districts on their behalf. Like daimyo, who were moved between domains, the Satsuma stewards were moved between districts by the Satsuma

[82] Wakita Osamu, 'The Emergence of the State in Sixteenth-Century Japan: From Oda to Tokugawa', Journal of Japanese Studies, 8 (1982), 343–67, at 352–4.

[83] Hall, 'The bakuhan System', 159.

[84] Haraguchi, 'Satsumahan tojō seido no seiritsu to genna no ikkoku ijichōrei', 137.

[85] Robert K. Sakai, 'Feudal Society and Modern Leadership in Satsuma-han', Journal of Asian Studies, 16 (1957), 365–76, at 366.

administration, a tactic used to reduce threats to Shimazu authority by severing old local military ties between stewards and their traditional power bases.[86] The stewards responsible for the district in which Naeshirogawa was located, such as Umanosuke, the recipient of the watermelons noted above, were required to be present in the village when the daimyo visited, and to offer signs of submission in the form of gifts, which reinforced the steward's local authority, but also his vassalage under the ruling branch of the Shimazu family.

The late sixteenth and early seventeenth century, when the Naeshirogawa visits were established, was a particularly critical point for the Shimazu's hold on power. The period followed a series of events that had weakened the Shimazu regime financially and politically: a resounding military defeat at the hands of Toyotomi Hideyoshi and his allies in 1586–7, curtailing Shimazu territorial expansion in Kyushu; involvement and eventual defeat in the devastating Imjin War campaign against Chosŏn Korea between 1592 and 1598; and defeat at the battle of Sekigahara in 1600, during which the Shimazu had opposed the victor, Tokugawa Ieyasu, who went on to found the Tokugawa shogunate. The period during which alternate attendance visits to Naeshirogawa were established thus coincides with what Robert Sakai has dubbed the 'consolidation of power' in Satsuma domain between 1602 and 1638, during Shimazu Iehisa's tenure as daimyo.[87] Sakai showed how Iehisa exerted greater control over his territory through land surveys, reduction of debts within the domain finances, greater administrative control over the populace and the removal of threats to the Shimazu's reputation as wise and benevolent rulers. The public ritual activities that took place during Naeshirogawa visits may be understood as part of this process of consolidating Shimazu rule by stamping their territory with signs of dominance.

The foreign origins of Naeshirogawa's inhabitants and the successful importation of economically profitable industry that their ceramic production represented made the village particularly suitable for such articulations of authority. This was because, despite being one of the largest domains in Tokugawa Japan, Satsuma was agriculturally poor. The magnitude of domains during the Tokugawa period was calculated by reference to their official putative rice yield (*omotedaka*), which was measured using the unit of the *koku* (roughly equivalent to 5 bushels or 180 litres). With a value of 729,563 *koku* in 1634, Satsuma was the second largest domain. However, unlike other domains, the official rice yield of Satsuma lands was calculated in unhulled rather than hulled rice, meaning that the actual rice yield (*jitsudaka*) of Satsuma was comparatively low, reducing to about one-half of the official putative rice yield.[88] The reason for this low productivity was that the domain's territory was located within a pyroclastic plateau underlain by agglomerates, tephra and volcanic ashes that made the soil less productive than that of

[86] Haraguchi, 'Satsumahan tojō seido no seiritsu to genna no ikkoku ijichōrei', 139.
[87] Sakai, 'The Consolidation of Power in Satsuma Han'.
[88] Sakihara Mitsugu, 'The Significance of Ryukyu in Satsuma Finances during the Tokugawa Period' (Ph.D. thesis, University of Hawaii, 1971), 216.

other parts of Japan. The region was also subject to typhoons, and was highly mountainous, both of which made it less agriculturally productive.[89] This meant the domain authorities had to maintain other sources of income, from piracy, trade, mining, fishing, and manual industries like Naeshirogawa ceramics, in order to ensure the prosperity of their territory and their security as rulers.

Over the centuries, the Shimazu had established trade and piratical networks within their local region, receiving cargo ships from China, Korea, the Ryukyu Islands, and further afield in Southeast Asia, functioning, in Tokunaga Kazunobu's words, as a 'maritime nation' (*kaiyō kokka*).[90] In addition, as Robert Hellyer has argued, Satsuma was one of two domains of Tokugawa Japan that were officially allowed significant leeway to conduct relations with foreign nations, in its case via control of the Ryukyuan kingdom (the other such domain, Tsushima, was responsible for trade with Korea), so that Satsuma could be described as an 'independent partner' of the Tokugawa when it came to international affairs.[91] This ability to command foreign peoples and to bring wealth into the domain from overseas was arguably one means by which the Shimazu family demonstrated locally its fitness to rule, and alternate attendance processions provided an opportunity to demonstrate this for the public gaze within their domain. In the first decade of the seventeenth century the domain was faced with financial losses caused by the Tokugawa crackdown on piracy in the Kyushu region, and in 1609 it annexed the Ryukyuan kingdom in order to regain an income from the Ryukyuan trade, which had links with China and Southeast Asia.[92] After pledging allegiance to the Shimazu, the defeated Ryukyuan monarch was permitted to return to Ryukyu in 1611, but from then on all Ryukyuan kings were required to leave high-ranking hostages, usually imperial princes, behind in a newly built facility in the Kagoshima castle town, the *Ryūkyū kariya* (Ryukyuan administrative headquarters), later known as the *Ryūkyū kan* (Ryukyuan compound), and to send representatives to Edo under Shimazu escort.[93] The Naeshirogawa potters provided another, albeit smaller, source of revenue and prestige, likewise drawn from Shimazu military exploits in their region, having been captured during the Imjin War, and on one occasion even travelled to Edo in the Satsuma alternate attendance entourage.[94] This enabled the Shimazu to extract value from what had actually been a military defeat in Korea, and is consistent with the fact that, during the mid-seventeenth

[89] Haraguchi Torao, *Kagoshimaken no rekishi* (Tokyo, 1973), 2–4.

[90] Tokunaga Kazunobu, *Kaiyō kokka Satsuma* (Kagoshima, 2011).

[91] Hellyer, *Defining Engagements*, 25–48.

[92] Maria Grazia Petrucci, 'Caught between Piracy and Trade: The Shimazu of Southern Japan at the Outset of the New Tokugawa Regime, 1599–1630', in *Beyond the Silk Roads: New Discourses on China's Role in East Asian Maritime History*, ed. Robert J. Antony and Angela Schottenhammer (Wiesbaden, 2018), 99–114.

[93] Gregory Smits, *Visions of Ryukyu: Identity and Ideology in Early-Modern Thought and Politics* (Honolulu, 2017), 15–49; Satō Hiroyuki, 'Satsuma no naka no "ikoku": Enshutsusareta "Ryūkyūkan"', *Chizu jōhō*, 38, no. 2 (2018), 20–4.

[94] Clements, 'Daimyō Processions and Satsuma's Korean Village', 225.

century, the Shimazu's military defeat in the Imjin campaign was recast as a series of bold exploits, in war memoirs of surviving soldiers that had been commissioned by Satsuma domain authorities.[95] Thus, both the Ryukyuans and the Naeshirogawans were incorporated into Satsuma's domestic rituals, including alternate attendance, as a sign of their submission and Shimazu power in their region.

Concluding remarks

Alternate attendance, as practised within Satsuma domain, shares many characteristics with royal progresses elsewhere in world history. In the same manner that Geertz noted for the processions of Elizabeth I, Javanese sovereigns and Moroccan kings, alternate attendance travel in Satsuma clearly 'located society's center' in the daimyo 'by stamping a territory with ritual signs of dominance'.[96] Moreover, as has been shown in studies of the progresses of Elizabeth I, and the royal entries by the monarchs of Valois France, alternate attendance visits not only functioned as a way to express daimyo authority, but also provided moments of negotiation and exchange between the daimyo and Naeshirogawa elites: the ceremonies of gift-giving, banqueting, dance and displays of local wares that took place during the visits made manifest Satsuma's reliance on the Naeshirogawa pottery industry, and the honours, financial and status-based, that were due to the village officials, and the village, as a result. Other points of comparison with royal progresses are deserving of further investigation.[97] The role of religion and cosmology in the Satsuma processions, for example, seems to have been a factor in the shrine visits on the first day of travel in Satsuma, as well as in the sacred Korean dances performed for the daimyo; however, in the absence of more detailed source material, it is difficult to ascertain if religion occupied as central a role in the ritual statements made by the Satsuma processions as it did in the more classic cases of royal progress in world history.

Nevertheless, understanding how daimyo acted as rulers with power akin to sovereigns in their own territories when it came to alternate attendance allows us to examine the ways in which – in the case of Satsuma, at least – they laid claim to local legitimacy, not through having been invested as rulers by the shogun, but by virtue of other claims to power that lay with themselves. The daimyo journeys add further evidence to the complicated picture of sovereignty in early modern Japan, in which a delicate balance of power between the shogun and his daimyo was expressed in dual regimes of meaning that operated interchangeably, depending on whether the context was external or internal matters. Just as the alternate attendance parades could function as markers of domain status in the eyes of observers outside the domain en

---

[95] Murai Shōsuke, 'Post-war Domain Source Material on Hideyoshi's Invasion of Korea: The Wartime Memoirs of Shimazu Soldiers', in *The East Asian War, 1592-1598* (2015), 109–19.

[96] Geertz, *Local Knowledge*, 125.

[97] Cole, *The Portable Queen*, 78–84; Neil Murphy, *Ceremonial Entries, Municipal Liberties and the Negotiation of Power in Valois France, 1328-1589* (Leiden, 2016), 218.

route and in Edo, so too, as the processions passed through the domain of Satsuma, they were a visible reminder of local Shimazu claims to power, and were orchestrated to inspire awe, exert control and display the Shimazu ability to command 'foreign' captives and resources. Thus, although by the mid-seventeenth century most of the Naeshirogawa potters had been born in Japan, they were required to perform Korean-ness (or 'Chosōn-ness') and to show their loyalty to the descendants of those who had taken their parents and grandparents to the domain during the Imjin War.

Acknowledgements. I would like to thank the anonymous *Transactions* reviewers for their comments.

Financial support / Funding statement. This project has received funding from the European Research Council (ERC) under the European Union's Horizon 2020 research and innovation programme (grant agreement No. 758347).

Competing interests. None.

Author biography. Rebekah Clements is an ICREA research professor at the Department of Translation, Interpreting, and East Asian Studies at the Autonomous University of Barcelona. Her previous publications include *A Cultural History of Translation in Early Modern Japan* (Cambridge University Press, 2015); 'Brush Talk as the "Lingua Franca" of East Asian Diplomacy in Japanese–Korean Encounters, c.1600–1868', *Historical Journal*, vol. 62, issue 2, June 2019, pp. 289–309; and 'Speaking in Tongues? Daimyo, Zen Monks, and Spoken Chinese in Japan, 1661–1711', *Journal of Asian Studies*, vol. 76, issue 3, August 2017, pp. 603–26.

Cite this article: Clements R (2022). Alternate Attendance Parades in the Japanese Domain of Satsuma, Seventeenth to Eighteenth Centuries: Pottery, Power and Foreign Spectacle. *Transactions of the Royal Historical Society* **32**, 135–158. https://doi.org/10.1017/S0080440122000056

Transactions of the RHS (2022), **32**, 159–175
doi:10.1017/S008044012200007X

ARTICLE

Portraiture, Biography and Public Histories

Ludmilla Jordanova

Department of History, Durham University, Durham, UK
Email: ludmilla.jordanova@durham.ac.uk

(Received 20 January 2022; accepted 13 April 2022)

Abstract

Portraits and biographies play a central role in engaging non-specialists with the past, and hence invite careful scrutiny. Major enterprises, such as the National Portrait Gallery in London and the *Dictionary of National Biography*, in both its original and Oxford versions, provide rich examples for reflecting on public history and on the relationships between types of writing about past times. These issues relate to literature as well as to history, given the prominence of biographies of literary figures, and the role of literary scholars as authors of biographies. Using materials concerning the artist John Collier (1850–1934), the publisher George Smith (1824–1901) and the surgeon James Paget (1814–1899), this article examines the relationships between portraits and biographies and the types of insight they afford. Colin Matthew's innovation of including portraits in the *Oxford Dictionary*, together with his own scholarship on William Gladstone (1809–1898), including his portraits, provide the basis for suggestions about the role of work when representing lives, including those of historians. Public history can only benefit from research practices being discussed in an accessible manner, as attempted here.

Keywords: portrait; biography; John Collier; George Smith; James Paget; Colin Matthew; *Dictionary of National Biography*; public history; National Portrait Gallery; William Gladstone

On 6 June 1894, contributors to the *Dictionary of National Biography* (*DNB*) gave a dinner to honour George Smith (1824–1901), the publisher behind this complex, ambitious and costly venture. Drawing on newspaper reports, a pamphlet recounted the occasion in some detail. One copy found its way into the archives of London's National Portrait Gallery (NPG) in the folder, or 'registered packet', associated with a portrait of Smith 'presented by a group of the sitter's friends' to the gallery in 1911.[1] Smith died seven years after the

---

[1] The pamphlet was simply entitled 'Dinner to Mr. George Smith'. The wording is from the NPG website: https://www.npg.org.uk/collections/search/portrait/mw05841/George-Smith?LinkID=mp04146 &role=sit&rNo=0 (last accessed 8 Mar. 2022).

dinner; his likeness was painted posthumously by John Collier (1850–1934), a well-connected artist to whom many prominent figures sat from Charles Darwin and Thomas Henry Huxley in the 1880s to Rudyard Kipling in 1891 and 1900 and George Bernard Shaw in the 1920s.[2] It is not clear precisely how Collier went about making the image of Smith, although his sitters' book indicates that he undertook a number of posthumous works and so presumably had developed effective techniques for doing so.[3] In any case it seems highly likely that Smith and Collier knew one another. Towards the end of his life Smith dictated an autobiography to Dr Fitchett, substantial portions of which were published in a volume written by Collier's brother-in-law, Leonard Huxley (1860–1933).[4] The registered packet for NPG 1620 also contains letters from Smith's widow Elizabeth about the portrait.[5]

'Portrait' is an evocative idea, hence it is plausible to think of the pamphlet, with its verbatim reports of speeches, as portraying a special occasion associated with a great biographical venture. The painting of George Smith entered a prominent national institution dedicated to displaying representations of significant figures from the past. In Elizabeth's understanding it was his 'work for literature' that was being honoured: George was a successful publisher and businessman, a generous nurturer of writers and played a prominent role in the literary world of the British Empire.[6] Publishing was not Smith's only

---

[2] Information on many of Collier's portraits may be gleaned from the Art UK website: https://artuk.org/discover/artworks/view_as/grid/search/makers:john-collier-18501934 (last accessed 13 Jan. 2022). See also note 3 below. For the artist's views on portraiture see *The Art of Portrait Painting* (1905). His values were close to those of his father-in-law, Thomas Henry Huxley, and are set out in *The Religion of an Artist* (1926). Collier was skilled in finding suitable visual idioms for his subjects, including his controversial father-in-law. On portraiture in general see Richard Brilliant, *Portraiture* (1991); Joanna Woodall (ed.), *Portraiture: Facing the Subject* (Manchester, 1997); and Andreas Beyer, *Portraits: A History* (New York, 2003). On portrait prints, see Antony Griffiths, *The Print before Photography: An Introduction to European Printmaking 1550–1820* (2016), 396–400.

[3] A photocopy of John Collier's sitters' book may be consulted in the Heinz Archive of the National Portrait Gallery, London. It indicates that Collier made drawings for Thackeray in 1879 and that the originals were in the possession of George Smith, 5–6. Smith had hired Thackeray in 1860 to edit the *Cornhill Magazine*. See also notes 4 and 9 below.

[4] Leonard Huxley, *The House of Smith Elder* (1923). Huxley had worked for the firm. John Collier married Marian Huxley in 1879; two years after her death in 1887 he married her sister Ethel in Norway, since marriage to a deceased wife's sister remained illegal in England until 1907. He painted many members of the Huxley family and his own family. Smith's 'Recollections of a Long and Busy Life' is a two-volume typescript in the National Library of Scotland MS239191-2. Volume ii, chs. 18 and 19 concern artists he knew. Considerably more space is given to authors and his broader contacts in London society. Throughout, Smith is precise about the financial side of his businesses. Sidney Lee drew on it and many other sources for his 'Memoir' of Smith, first published in 1901, Sidney Lee (ed.), *Dictionary of National Biography* (1909), vol. xxii (Supplement), xi–xlix. See xlvi for the 1894 dinner and other honours Smith received.

[5] All items in the primary collection have a unique reference number, starting with NPG 1 (the Chandos portrait of Shakespeare), the first formal accession, and a registered packet in the Heinz Archive, which also contains administrative records and comparative materials on sitters and artists. Collier's portrait of Darwin is NPG1024, presented by one of his sons in 1896; his portrait of Huxley is NPG 3168, donated in 1943, also by a son.

[6] In addition to Leonard Huxley's book cited above, see Jenifer Glynn, *Prince of Publishers: A Biography of George Smith* (1986). Smith owned the *Cornhill Magazine* and the evening newspaper

business, as Sidney Lee's account of his life made clear; he was shrewd, hard-working and generous.[7] As a result he became wealthy, with his munificence to writers and artists whose company he enjoyed a manifestation of his success. Noting how the elements of a life such as his can be given expression is a historical-cum-literary task. Smith portrayed himself in his speech at the 1894 dinner, which was a deft blend of patriotic sentiment and becoming modesty about a unique and arduous achievement: 'Well gentlemen, the "Dictionary of National Biography" was my idea. (Loud cheers.)'[8] The agency of this particular publisher is historically significant, all the more so since credit for initiating the *DNB* is often given to Leslie Stephen. Smith's richly detailed memoir enabled Leonard Huxley, who knew him well, to record not only the history of a publishing business, but an individual's contributions to public life. Portraits and biographies intermingled then as they do now, enabling us to form a lively sense of the worlds of Thackeray and Darwin, Gladstone and Charlotte Brontë.[9]

Similar connections and resonances are alive in the present day. They are singularly apt when honouring Colin Matthew (1941–1999), a distinguished historian, editor and biographer, and the founding editor of the *Oxford Dictionary of National Biography*, the successor to George Smith's venture, from 1992 until his death. He also collected and wrote about portraits. Colin valued clear exposition and was deeply committed to sharing historical knowledge as widely as possible. He was indeed a public historian.

The story of George Smith, his dinner and the posthumous portrait is public history. The sources mentioned so far are in the public domain, they are not arcane but touch on areas of wide interest. Thus they can be put to work in accounts that are suitable for non-specialists. Such rich materials from Victorian and Edwardian Britain, a time when biography and portraiture were, as today, prominent genres, reveal the potential of two major cultural forms to speak to both academic and broader audiences. These genres enjoy

---

the *Pall Mall Gazette*, as well as trading extensively with India. Claire Harman, in *Charlotte Brontë: A Life* (2015), discusses Brontë's dealings with Smith, Elder and with George Smith. Both Leonard Huxley and Jenifer Glynn emphasise, as does Smith himself in 'Recollections', Smith's centrality in literary life.

[7] Sidney Lee initially assisted Leslie Stephen in editing the *DNB*, and then became sole editor. See note 4 above.

[8] 'Dinner', 7, where he also made claims about uniqueness; and on 8 emphasised his work as 'a private individual without any of that aid which is given by the State to the production of such national works on the Continent'.

[9] George Smith was closely associated with both Thackeray and Brontë. He published volumes by Darwin, who was painted by Collier (NPG 1024), and was on friendly terms with James Paget and Leslie Stephen, the first editor of the *DNB*. Gladstone consulted Paget for medical advice, and attended an oration he gave in 1877, discussed below. Leslie Stephen had worked with George Smith on the *Cornhill Magazine*, edited by Thackeray before Stephen did so; his first wife was Thackeray's daughter. Gladstone was familiar with works by Brontë, Darwin, Stephen and Thackeray: H. G. C. Matthew (comp.), *The Gladstone Diaries with Cabinet Minutes and Prime-Ministerial Correspondence*, XIV: *Index* (Oxford, 1994), 316, 352, 567, 576. John Collier's father Robert, politician, judge and amateur artist, also featured in Gladstone's life, 55.

a long-established place in hearts and minds and invite the attention of historians. Like 'portrait', 'biography' is an evocative and versatile notion with a life
history of its own, encompassing many types of text from brief dictionary
entries to popular books on familiar figures and learned multi-volume
works.[10] Biographical forms – including documentaries and biopics, websites
and blogs – make a major contribution to public history. While currently
some biographies at least are both profitable and popular, this category of
writing occupies a more complex position in the academy, especially among
historians.[11]

As a practice and as an object of study, biography does not sit neatly within
a single discipline. Its closest kinship is with literary studies – the background
of many biographers whether they work outside or inside the academy – but
biography is everywhere. Biographers come from many backgrounds and disciplines where the craft of writing is given less attention. In university depart-
ments of history, for instance, little emphasis is placed on close reading in the
service of analysing writing as such and on honing students' literary skills,
although historians too are writers. Writing in the spare way expected in biographical dictionaries presents its own distinctive challenges. Since biographers and biographees are necessarily historically located, life-writing in all
its forms is certainly a proper study for historians. Portraiture raises different
questions for the discipline of history. Few writers, no matter what their discipline, are likely to have the artistic skills to capture a likeness, while there
are distinct disciplines, such as art history, museology and visual culture studies, where the study of portraiture finds a home. As a practice and object of
study, then, portraiture is more distant from historical practice than biography, yet it occupies a prominent place in public history as is evident from
the popularity of portrait galleries, especially in the English-speaking world,
and from the ubiquity of portraits in publications, websites, film and televi-
sion. Taking our cue from Colin Matthew, historians do well to consider the
relationships between portraits and biographies, alongside public history and
routine historical activities. We can work at untangling the changing fortunes

---

[10] On the history of biography, in addition to works cited elsewhere, see Harold Nicolson, *The
Development of English Biography* (1927); A. O. J. Cockshut, *Truth to Life: The Art of Biography in the
Nineteenth Century* (1974); David Ellis (ed.), *Imitating Art: Essays in Biography* (1993); and Juliette
Atkinson, *Victorian Biography Reconsidered: A Study of Nineteenth-Century 'Hidden' Lives* (Oxford,
2010) – ch. 7 of which concerns the *DNB*.

[11] Introductions to 'biography' include Hermione Lee, *Biography: A Very Short Introduction* (Oxford,
2009), and Nigel Hamilton, *Biography: A Brief History* (Cambridge, MA, 2007). See also Barbara Caine,
Biography and History, 2nd edn (Basingstoke, 2018); Eric Homberger and John Charmley (eds.), *The
Troubled Face of Biography* (New York,1988); Paula Backscheider, *Reflections on Biography* (Oxford,
1999); and Peter France and William St Clair (eds.), *Mapping Lives: The Uses of Biography* (2004).
Any ambivalence historians may feel about a genre so closely associated with literature is seemingly allayed when the subject is politically powerful or intellectually majestic. Blanning and
Cannadine reveal something of historians' ambivalence: 'Few historians today trouble themselves
with large-scale, full-dress biographies. Even fewer biographers write anything that is recognisable
as serious history.' T. C. W. Blanning and David Cannadine (eds.), *History and Biography: Essays in
Honour of Derek Beales* (Cambridge, 1996), 1. These sentiments are repeated in the book's blurb:
'biography is too important to be left to the amateurs.'

of biography and portraiture and the genres' position within general culture, academic settings and distinct areas of scholarship. In any case, the fact remains that scholars are wordsmiths, and thus are less at home working with visual materials, such as paintings, prints, drawings and sculptures of specific people. Portraits are a fertile source for historians, but they still have to be elucidated verbally. When reflecting on visual culture we rely on words and their skilled deployment.

Historical practices are changing all the time. Approaches, subject matter and value systems shift; teachers, whether in schools or higher education, adapt accordingly, as do publishers and the media. It is an integral part of being historians that we note, reflect on and critique such trends. The rise of public history since the Second World War exemplifies the point. In so far as 'public history' refers to a field dedicated to charting and evaluating the innumerable ways in which versions of the past reach wide audiences, then it does indeed reveal significant alterations in historical practice over recent decades, with university courses and publications proliferating at a remarkable rate. 'Public history' has a second meaning, however, since it also refers to historical products – plays, merchandise, novels, documentaries, magazines, websites and much more – through which non-specialist audiences engage with the past.[12] Technological innovation notwithstanding, these broad phenomena are not new at all, and might be deemed coeval with history itself. The task of assessing the historical forms that reach wide audiences need not be confined to practitioners of a relatively new subfield called 'public history', it can be performed by historians no matter what their specialism, since it leads to the re-evaluation of methods, sources, consumers, audiences and co-creators, their interests and concerns.

Certain genres, portraiture and biography above all, have played a prominent role in bringing notable figures to diverse publics over many centuries. Statues with inscriptions in streets and squares, there for anyone to view, provide an excellent example, illustrating not only how likenesses together with key pieces of (verbal) information occupied public spaces, but also how the individuals they recognise, along with their deeds, were of general interest and of concern to a polity. Portraits and biographies are ancient, related, even co-dependent types of artefact through which the present is recorded, celebrated, represented and disseminated for the sake of the future, when they come to evoke a past. These genres continue to function in such ways, working together in the public realm to recognise a select few; hence they invite the attention of historians.[13] To explore such phenomena this article uses materials linked with the National Portrait Gallery in London, the *Dictionary of National Biography* and its successor the *Oxford Dictionary of*

---

[12] Works that indicate the range of public history include Roy Rosenzweig, *Clio Wired: The Future of the Past in the Digital Age* (New York, 2011); Hilda Kean and Paul Martin (eds.), *The Public History Reader* (2015); Alix Green, *History, Policy and Public Purpose: Historians and Historical Thinking in Government* (2016); James Gardner and Paula Hamilton (eds.), *The Oxford Handbook of Public History* (New York, 2017); and Ludmilla Jordanova, *History in Practice*, 3rd edn (2019), esp. ch. 7.

[13] I take 'the public realm' to include publications and websites.

National Biography. The goal is to examine lives and likenesses, the relations between them, and the insights these phenomena afford, insights that are, especially in a digital world, of wide significance. Historical activities, no matter who undertakes them, draw upon ubiquitous skills, habits and forms of curiosity.

In their different modes, portraits and biographies represent lives; so much is obvious. Precisely how they do so is less clear, given the diverse ways in which they work and the range of responses they elicit. 'Bringing the past to life' is a familiar claim, and people have been inclined not only to accept that portraits above all may do so but more generally to see the boundaries between living beings and images as distinctly fragile. Attributing animation to artworks has been common practice in Western art traditions. Finding life in a portrait is hardly far-fetched.[14] Visual representations of human beings, especially those depicting nameable persons, can provoke strong reactions in viewers.[15] It is thus no surprise to find that both Leslie Stephen and his successor at the *DNB*, Sidney Lee (1859–1926), reflected on the writing of biography in terms of portraiture and the ways in which it could animate figures from the past.[16] In any case, portraits can hardly exist apart from words, whether spoken or written. Records of commissions, conversations about likenesses, texts that evoke a life and images that accompany biographies show visual and verbal elements intermingling, illuminating and modifying each other. Take, for example, the use of signatures under portrait prints, which exemplifies the kinship of visual and verbal, and present in a book about the life of an eminent Victorian surgeon. The *Memoirs and Letters of Sir James Paget* (1814–99), edited by his son Stephen (1855–1926), was published in three editions between 1901 and 1903, and adorned with portraits of the prominent medical man. The frontispiece to the first edition includes his signature – 'Ever yours James Paget' – based on a work by George Richmond (1809–1896) from 1867 (see Figure 1).

Writing one's name with one's own hand may be construed as an act of portrayal, one that enhances viewers' sense of the person depicted and in a historically precise way. 'The signature, put under Mr. Richmond's portrait of him, was written in 1891, when he was 77 years old.'[17] Further, Paget's signature had an aural dimension: 'we knew the moment when he signed a letter, and the etching sound of his pen changed to a swishing sound as he wrote his name.' Richmond's original work, in the collections of London's Portrait Gallery (NPG 1635), is a chalk drawing on buff paper. It shows Paget's head

---

[14] Caroline van Eck et al. (eds.), *The Secret Lives of Art Works: Exploring the Boundaries between Art and Life* (Leiden, 2014), esp. the introduction.

[15] The names of sitters can be lost, but other evidence may indicate that the image is a 'portrait', a visual representation of a specific, *nameable* person, designed to indicate their appearance. There are many ways of defining 'portrait'.

[16] Key texts include Leslie Stephen, *Studies of a Biographer*, i (1898), 1–36, and *Men, Books and Mountains* (1956), 7–15; Sidney Lee, *Principles of Biography* (Cambridge, 1911).

[17] Stephen Paget (ed.), *Memoirs and Letters of Sir James Paget with Portraits and Other Illustrations* (1901), 256. The pagination and illustrations vary slightly over three editions; the second was published in 1902, the third in 1903, where all the previous impressions are listed.

Figure 1 Frontispiece to *Memoirs and Letters of Sir James Paget edited by Stephen Paget One of His Sons with Portraits and Other Illustrations,* London, New York and Bombay, 1901. Plate 11 × 15 cm, page 14 × 21.8 cm. Engraved by Walter L. Colls.

and shoulders, giving no indications of his surgical activities, and was made for an elite club to which he belonged. Members exchanged engraved versions of the drawings.[18] Richmond's artwork can be viewed on the NPG website, where the standard details of the size, medium, date and manner of acquisition are provided, alongside other depictions of Paget made from 1849 onwards.[19] The latter include prints after paintings by Richmond and Millais and a

---

[18] Paget was a member of Grillion's. See note 33 below.
[19] https://www.npg.org.uk/collections/search/portrait/mw04828/Sir-James-Paget-1st-Bt?LinkID=mp03420&search=sas&sText=James+Paget&OConly=true&role=sit&rNo=0 (last accessed 8 Apr. 2022).

Vanity Fair cartoon from 1876. Stephen Paget sold the drawing to the gallery in 1911 to raise funds for the children of a brother who had recently died.[20]

Such conjunctions of life and likeness were commonplace by the nineteenth century. Arguably their roots go back to the beginnings of European print culture and the common practice of placing portraits of authors as frontispieces, although in such cases the portrait was likely to be more prominent than any biographical material, which was frequently minimal or absent.[21] A tighter relationship is envisioned when the two forms are explicitly treated as complementary to one another, as if each on its own would somehow be incomplete. A notable example is the eighteenth-century work by Thomas Birch (1705–1766), *The Heads of Illustrious Persons of Great Britain*, where portraits and biographies sit side by side on facing pages. The 'illustrious persons' appear chronologically so that history unfolds before the reader's eyes. Birch was the author of other historical works; his selection of heads emphasises monarchs and those prominent in politics and military affairs. Isaac Newton and William Harvey, for example, figure, in acknowledgement of their exceptional intellectual attainments.[22] The elaborate, high-quality engravings by leading figures indicate the value placed on the portraits. It is noteworthy that the plates generally mentioned the owner of the original artwork from which the print was derived, so that patterns of collecting are woven into the engagement with lives and likenesses, encouraging wide-ranging associations to be made.[23]

The complementarity between biographies and portraits can also be discerned in extra-illustrated volumes, sometimes described as 'grangerised', after the Rev. James Granger (1723–1776), whose *A Biographical History of England from Egbert the Great to the Revolution: Consisting of Characters Disposed in Different Classes, and adapted to a methodical catalogue of engraved British heads* went through several editions from 1769 onwards, with a portrait of Granger as the frontispiece.[24] His *Biographical History* lists known portraits of individuals, generally accompanied by fairly brief biographical comments, and arranged first by reign and then by 'class' starting with the highest

---

[20] https://www.npg.org.uk/collections/search/person/mp03420/sir-james-paget-1st-bt (last accessed 14 Jan. 2022). Registered packet for NPG 1635, letter from Stephen Paget, dated 25 Oct. 1911. NPG Ax39071 is a 1916 photograph of Stephen. The importance of providing the basic details of artworks is articulated in Florence Grant and Ludmilla Jordanova (eds.), *Writing Visual Histories* (2020), e.g. 157–8, 164. Regrettably it is not standard practice in biographies illustrated by portraits.

[21] Griffiths, *The Print before Photography*, 185–6, is illuminating on frontispieces. Cf. Richard Wendorf, *The Elements of Life: Biography and Portrait-Painting in Stuart and Georgian England* (Oxford, 1990).

[22] Several copies of these prints are in the NPG collections, e.g. NPG D27271 (Harvey) and NPG D 19601 (Newton).

[23] *The Heads of Illustrious Persons of Great Britain, Engraved by Mr Houbraken and Mr. Vertue with Their Lives and Characters by Thomas Birch* (1743). Cf. his *The History of the Royal Society of London* (1756–7) and *The Life of Henry Prince of Wales* (1760). On Birch see A. E. Gunther, *An Introduction to the Life of the Rev. Thomas Birch* (Halesworth, 1984); 50–1 is about *Heads*, which had a complex publishing history and titles vary. I have used the copy in the library of New College, Oxford (NB.120.20. X3). The 1747 edition is available on Google Books.

[24] I have used the fourth edition, James Granger, *A Biographical History of England* ... (4 vols., 1804).

rank – working through the royal family, great officers of state, peers and so on, ending with class XII, 'Persons of both Sexes … remarkable from only one Circumstance of their Lives; namely such as lived to a great Age, deformed Persons, Convicts, &c.'[25] The practice whereby a book is disassembled, and prints, often but not always portraits, inserted into a blank sheet placed to face the relevant text, and then rebound, frequently in folio volumes, reveals much about the relationships between likenesses and lives. This labour-intensive and highly skilled activity continued into the twentieth century.[26] The resources and deliberation that extra-illustration demands invite us to follow past mindsets about the relationships between portraits and biographies. The set of seventy-three extra-illustrated volumes of the *Dictionary of National Biography* in the Heinz Archive was compiled by the twentieth-century print collector J. H. MacDonnell and includes some 7,000 portraits.[27] There is no additional commentary by the compiler, as is sometimes present. Somewhat like Birch's *Heads*, biography and portrait sit side by side complementing one another. Thanks to Colin Matthew, this is also the case for many lives in the *Oxford Dictionary of National Biography*, published in 2004 and continuously updated online since then.[28] The innovation arose from his own interest in portraits and the advent of digital technologies.[29] In its nineteenth-century form many entries noted the subject's physical appearance together with portraits of them – an indication of attentiveness to visual characteristics.

If Colin Matthew's commitment to public history found its fullest expression in the *Oxford Dictionary*, it is evident in his earlier research, including when it took the most rigorous scholarly forms, as in his work on William Gladstone (1809–1898). One of Matthew's crowning achievements is the index to the multi-volume edition of Gladstone's diaries, cabinet minutes and prime-

---

[25] On Granger, portraits and extra-illustration see Marcia Pointon, *Hanging the Head: Portraiture and Social Formation in Eighteenth-Century England* (New Haven, 1993), esp. 53–78; all Granger's classes are listed on 56. See also Lucy Peltz, *Facing the Text: Extra-illustration, Print Culture and Society in Britain: 1769-1840* (San Marino, CA, 2017).

[26] Extra-illustrated versions of Wheatley's *London Past and Present*, 1891, and of the DNB are in the Heinz Archive, NPG; for a twentieth-century extra-illustrated version of a nineteenth-century biographical compilation by William Munk, held in the Royal College of Physicians, London, see Ludmilla Jordanova, *Physicians and Their Images* (2018), 96–103; the compilers' explanatory preface is reproduced in full on 98.

[27] In some cases several prints accompany a single biographical entry. There is no additional commentary by the compiler, which is sometimes present, as in the version of Munk's *Roll* discussed in Jordanova, *Physicians*.

[28] On the ODNB see Robin Myers et al. (eds.), *Lives in Print: Biography and the Book Trade from the Middle Ages to the 21st Century* (New Castle, DE, 2002), 171–92; H. C. G. Matthew and Brian Harrison (eds.), *Oxford Dictionary of National Biography*, I (Oxford, 2004), Introduction, also issued as a separate pamphlet; and Keith Thomas, *Changing Conceptions of National Biography: The* Oxford DNB *in Historical Perspective* (Cambridge, 2005).

[29] Colin Matthew set up a partnership with the NPG in order to include portraits with entries and have a clear policy for doing so: Arianne Burnette, 'A Report on the Oxford Dictionary of National Biography Picture Research Project 1996–2003' (2003). Special thanks to ODNB staff for supplying a copy of the report. Colin Matthew collected portraits, especially of Gladstone, and was a trustee of NPG 1998-9.

ministerial correspondence. In fact his 1994 tome contains three indexes: a dramatis personae, Gladstone's lifetime reading and a subject index. As Dennis Duncan put it in *Index, A History of the*, its 'job is to mediate between author and audience ... The ordering of an index is reader-orientated ...'[30] Volume XIV allows those with no special knowledge of Gladstone's life and work to glimpse and grasp elements of them and explore them further. Formidable historical complexities are rendered accessible. It is possible to consider portraits of Gladstone, those by John Everett Millais (1829–1896) and George Richmond, for example, in the context of the sitter's biography through this publication.[31] As a result, the artists, their worlds and those of their sitters can be brought to life and given flesh so to speak. Thus we learn that Gladstone's relationship with Richmond included their shared religious interests, while many of those he knew, Thomas Henry Huxley (1825–1895), for example, held quite different views in key areas.[32]

Gladstone had consulted James Paget on medical matters in 1873; both were depicted by Millais, while George Richmond, who had drawn the politician in 1843, was a mutual friend.[33] A significant encounter occurred in 1877; thanks to Colin Matthew's labours, it is possible to marry Gladstone's and Paget's accounts and to appreciate something of the portrait–biography nexus in action.[34] Gladstone recorded that on Tuesday 13 February he heard Paget deliver the Hunterian Oration at the College of Surgeons between 3 and 4 in afternoon.[35]

---

[30] Dennis Duncan, *Index, A History of the* (2021), 2, 7.

[31] *Gladstone Diaries ... Index*, 177 and 762 (Millais), 215 (Richmond) and 792–3 for references to all Gladstone's portraits. See also H. C. G Matthew, 'Portraits of Men: Millais and Victorian Public Life', in *Millais Portraits*, ed. Peter Funnell et al. (1999), 139–61. John Collier commented on Gladstone and Millais in *Art of Portrait Painting*, 62–3, and was a great admirer of Millais, who in turn worked, and was close friends with, George Smith according to Sidney Lee's 'Memoir', xxv.

[32] For their shared religious interests see M. R. D. Foot and H. C. G. Matthew (eds.), *The Gladstone Diaries*, III: *1840-1847* (Oxford, 1974), 89 and 90. On Richmond's religiosity see Raymond Lister, *George Richmond: A Critical Biography* (1981). For Huxley, see 133 in *Gladstone Diaries ... Index*, and 431 for the works by Huxley that Gladstone read. Huxley was explicit about his disagreements with Gladstone when writing to his friend and associate Michael Foster; see W. F. Bynum and Caroline Overy (eds.), *Michael Foster and Thomas Henry Huxley, Correspondence, 1865-1895* (2009), e.g. letters 309–11 and 318.

[33] Millais's 1872 portrait of Paget is in St Bartholomew's Hospital, London, and is reproduced in Paget, *Memoirs*, 1901, facing 252. Gladstone, Richmond and Paget's membership of Grillion's club suggests further dimensions of these relationships. On Grillion's see Paget, *Memoirs*, 265, 287, 360, 362, 406: he joined in 1873 and encountered Gladstone there. Numerous references to the club appear in Matthew, *Gladstone Diaries ... Index*, 652. P.G.E., *Grillion's Club from its Origins in 1812 to its Fiftieth Anniversary* (1880), includes a portrait frontispiece of Thomas Dyke Acland with his signature, and specimen signatures of fifty-five members as an appendix; Richmond's is no. 36. *Grillion's Club: A Chronicle 1812-1913* compiled by the Secretaries (Oxford, 1914) lists all members, 35–92, where the biographical component consists of a list of offices and honours; 99–109 concerns club portraits (a collection of prints made after drawings, hung on the walls where dinners took place and circulated among members). Many of them were by Richmond, who is described as 'artist to the club', 79.

[34] For Gladstone's contacts with Paget see *Gladstone Diaries ... Index*, 195; see Paget's *Memoirs*, 155, 284, 362, 406, 416 for his references to Gladstone.

[35] H. C. G. Matthew (ed.), *The Gladstone Diaries with Cabinet Minutes and Prime-Ministerial Correspondence*, IX: *1875-1880* (Oxford, 1986), 193.

The Oration was named after John Hunter (1728–1793), whose collections form the centrepiece of the College, with him as venerated forebear. Gladstone then proposed Paget's health at the dinner, which took place in the 'Museum', that is, among items acquired by John Hunter and displayed by those who considered themselves his heirs. Stephen Paget observes that his father spoke 'under Reynolds's magnificent portrait of Hunter' and quotes passages from the oration. James was a renowned public speaker, who memorised his text, delivering it with apparent ease. He drew attention to Reynolds's canvas and its significance: 'In that masterpiece of portraiture, which teaches like a chapter of biography, Hunter ... is at rest and looking out, ... as one who is looking far beyond and from things visible into a world of truth and law which can only be intellectually discerned.' [36] It is not hard to see why Paget was drawn to Reynolds's version of Hunter, as a man who, although he was known to lack social graces, possessed intellectual prowess, a 'scientific mind', discernible to the artist, who was on visiting terms with John and his wife Anne. Through Reynolds, Hunter became both vividly present to and a strategic asset for later surgeons aspiring to combine commitment to 'the highest scientific culture' with the status of gentleman. As James Paget put it, 'Yes: Hunter did more than anyone to make us gentlemen'[37] – with the artist playing a vital mediating role. It is striking that this portrait spawned more than twenty derivative prints.[38] John Hunter and later commentators worked hard, in and through the portrait, which becomes a portal to concerns about science, social status, masculinity, collecting human remains – shown in the portrait – and more.[39]

Reynolds's 1786 depiction remains central to the College's identity; it features in later group portraits of the institution's leading figures and until recently was usually hung in the Council Room, its organisational heart.[40] When the work was first exhibited, anatomy and dissection remained controversial practices.[41] If portraits and biography are manifestly entwined in this example, so they are in the entry for John Hunter in the *Dictionary of*

---

[36] Paget, *Memoirs*, 284–5. A copy of Reynolds's portrait is in the NPG (NPG 77); the original, in the Royal College of Surgeons, is available on the Art UK website: https://artuk.org/discover/artworks/john-hunter-17281793-146023 (last accessed 14 Jan. 2022).

[37] Paget, *Memoirs*, 286

[38] Derivative prints may be found in the National Portrait Gallery, the Wellcome Collection and the British Museum, for example.

[39] On Paget's contexts see W. F. Bynum, *Science and the Practice of Medicine in the Nineteenth Century* (Cambridge, 1994), esp. 142–4, 218–19, and M. Jeanne Peterson, *Family, Love, and Work in the Lives of Victorian Gentlewomen* (Bloomington, 1989), which uses much material relating to the Paget family. It is possible that the long legs shown on the right-hand side of the canvas belonged to Charles Byrne (1761–1783), who had tried to prevent his corpse being dissected.

[40] At the time of writing, there is building work being undertaken so there will no longer be a 'Council Room'. Reynolds's portrait will hang in the museum. See also Keren Hammerschlag, 'The Gentleman Artist-Surgeon in Late Victorian Group Portraiture', *Visual Culture in Britain*, 14 (2013), 154–78. On 156 there is a painting of the Council 1884–5, including Paget, in the company of Reynolds's portrait of Hunter.

[41] David Mannings, *Sir Joshua Reynolds: A Complete Catalogue of his Paintings* (2 vols., New Haven, 2000), text volume, 271–2, is an authoritative, 'plain' account; the portrait was exhibited in 1786, 1813, 1846 and 1873 before the twentieth century. James Paget spoke in Oxford in 1886 when a

National Biography, written by George Thomas Bettany (1850–1891), who also penned articles on John's older brother William, Anne Hunter and John's nemesis Jesse Foot amongst his 206 contributions.[42] In Bettany's account both appearance and depiction were noteworthy:

> In person Hunter was of middle height, vigorous, and robust, with high shoulders and rather short neck. His features were strongly marked, with prominent eyebrows, pyramidal forehead, and eyes of light blue or grey. His hair in youth was a reddish yellow, in later years white. The fine portrait by Sir Joshua Reynolds ... in the possession of the Royal College of Surgeons was a happy and sudden inspiration, due to Hunter's falling into a reverie.[43]

Reynolds's 'chapter of biography', to use Paget's words, does not deny Hunter's surgical and anatomical interests, but it does elevate them, by visual means, to higher social and intellectual status.

Every figure mentioned so far, with the exception of Bettany, figures in the *DNB* and/or the *ODNB*.[44] In each case it was necessary for the editors to be clear about why individuals are worthy of inclusion, and if so how long an entry each merited. Such criteria are sensitive to historical change, including shifting languages for describing work, status, attainment and attributes. Leslie Stephen's writings make clear that these issues could generate considerable frustration, conflict and anger for those involved. He was also attentive to contributors' writing style, which he insisted should be spare and to the point given the pressures on space, a valuable reminder of the textual diversity of 'biography'. Conveying a subject's distinctive features was also effected by a 'tag' that follows name and date of birth. This practice may be found in Birch's *Heads*, and is also followed by the NPG on labels and the website.

---

statue of Hunter was unveiled in the University Museum, *Memoir*, 359–60. Although Hunter is shown standing, his head on hand and faraway look echo Reynolds's depiction.

[42] Gillian Fenwick, *The Contributors' Index to the Dictionary of National Biography 1885–1901* (Winchester and Detroit, 1989), xvi, 28–30. Jesse Foot, *The Life of John Hunter* (1794), is a relentlessly hostile account; there is an extra-illustrated version in the Wellcome Collection, London. Hunter's alleged coarseness was held up for ridicule in both versions.

[43] GTB, 'John Hunter', in *Dictionary of National Biography*, x, ed. Sidney Lee (1908), 287–93, at 290. The NPG version of Reynolds's painting is an 1813 copy by John Jackson; another copy is in Oriel College, Oxford. According to Bettany, 'Sharp's engraving from it (1788) is one of his best works.' See also Ludmilla Jordanova, 'Medical Men 1780–1820', in *Portraiture*, ed. Woodall, 101–15; 112 reproduces a watercolour from the grangerised version of Foot's biography that depicts John Hunter as a wheelwright or a carpenter before his brother William brought him to London – issues around manual and intellectual labour are central to surgical identity.

[44] Colin Matthew decided that everyone included the first time round would receive an entry in the *ODNB*. Candidates in both cases had to be dead; currently the interval between date of death and appearance online is four years. Bettany wrote popular science books, including ones with a historical slant – *Life of Charles Darwin* (1887); *Eminent Doctors: Their Lives and Their Work* (1885) – as well as more obviously 'historical' volumes, such as *A Popular History of the Reformation and Modern Protestantism* (1895).

Thomas Birch was simply 'historian' for the NPG, 'compiler of histories and biographer' for *ODNB*. James Granger is 'biographer and collector' on the gallery's website. Birch and Granger were both ordained and are shown with clerical bands in their portraits. John Hunter is 'surgeon and anatomist'.[45] Charles Byrne, one of the 'Irish giants' and dissected by John Hunter, is simply given the tag 'giant' in the *ODNB*; he would fit neatly into Granger's class XII. Such terms have their histories, including the organisational settings in which they arise and are deployed and broad linguistic shifts.

Ways of assessing past figures are further complicated by the presence of 'national', whether this pertains to an institution or a publishing project. Judging an individual's national significance takes place in contexts shaped by familiar, long-standing and well-worn debates, which have generally focused more on politics than on culture broadly defined. It seems *relatively* straightforward to judge the importance of the politically prominent, those who hold significant amounts of power whether by virtue of birth, election or wealth, and leaders within the domains that most closely align with the national interest, such as military commanders and judges. In reactions to these figures what Sidney Lee called the 'commemorative instinct' is deeply embedded and reinforced by institutional practices, although these have come under increasingly critical scrutiny in the twenty-first century.[46]

It is much less obvious, yet absolutely essential for understanding the interlacing of biography and portraiture, how historians might think afresh about 'work' – here simply a catch-all for diverse activities, whether directly remunerated or not, whether professional or amateur, whether a vocation, a craft or a form of art. Lives and likenesses can furnish invaluable 'occupational' insights.[47] The manner in which James Paget drew upon Hunter and specifically upon Reynolds's depiction of him reveals much about the occupational culture of surgeons, as Stephen Paget was certainly aware. A medically trained 'biographer and essayist', he emphasised the 'professional' status of medical men.[48] The distinguished audience present at the Hunterian Oration ensured that assertions about the intellectual and social refinement of surgeons reached influential ears, giving specific resonances to 'surgeon' that expressed collective aspirations. Close biographical inspection further allows Paget's full range of activities and the contexts in which he carried them out to be better appreciated. They include making watercolour depictions of specimens and cataloguing medical collections as well as his associations with prominent contemporaries such as Gladstone and Darwin. There is an analytical point here as well as an empirical one. In addition, an opportunity presents itself to bring

---

[45] Hunter's tag on both NPG website and *ODNB*; the terms are reversed in *DNB*.

[46] Lee, *Principles*, 7.

[47] Hermione Lee's biographies of writers, for example: *Virginia Woolf* (1996) and *Edith Wharton* (2007); see also her *Body Parts: Essays on Life Writing* (2005). Cf. Frances Spalding, *Virginia Woolf: Art, Life and Vision* (2014), where portraits are integral.

[48] M. Jeanne Peterson, *The Medical Profession in Mid-Victorian London* (Berkeley, Los Angeles and London, 1978); Anne Digby, *Making a Medical Living: Doctors and Their Patients in the English Market for Medicine* (Cambridge, 1994). The description of Stephen Paget comes from the NPG website; in the *ODNB* he is described as 'writer and pro-vivisection campaigner'.

aspects of medicine's past to general audiences in such a way that familiar tropes around 'blood and guts', with their proven popular appeal, are supplemented by an emphasis on friendship networks, collecting and the generation of artworks, also engaging topics.[49] Biography as a route into contexts is now a well-established conceptual device, which is all the more effective when the full range of the subject's activities and concerns are taken seriously.[50] Even in the more compact format of a biographical dictionary, it is possible to give a rounded sense of a life, indicating the settings and historical patterns within which it is best placed in an accessible manner. Portraits are integral to this approach: an understanding of portraiture can complement and extend the insights biographies afford and vice versa.

In practice, portraits often serve as illustrations to biographies accompanied by little that would enable readers to grasp their interconnections. For this to change, it is necessary not only to explore the changing relationships between these genres but to look afresh at the design of publications and websites, that is, to see portraits not as mere embellishments to a text, but as layered sources inviting considered attention.[51] In their efforts to make collections more widely accessible, most museums and galleries have constructed websites that enable users to appreciate the layered nature of artefacts. London's Portrait Gallery is no exception. Every item in the primary collection may be viewed, together with basic information such as date and manner of acquisition.[52] It is easy to find other representations of the same sitter and further works by the artists. Brief biographical information is commonly made available. In some cases, considerably more is provided.[53] Take, for example, Charles Darwin (1809–1882) – 'naturalist, geologist and originator of the theory of evolution' – of whom the NPG possesses thirty-five portraits, including the well-known painting by John Collier. Painted in 1883, NPG 1024 is an exact copy of a work he had undertaken for the Linnaean Society two years earlier. The website draws attention to the connections between Darwin and Thomas Henry Huxley, to Collier's status as the latter's son-in-law and quotes the

---

[49] I take the phrase 'blood and guts' from one of Roy Porter's many lively books that brought the history of medicine to wide audiences: *Blood and Guts: A Short History of Medicine* (2002).

[50] In the history of science, biographies of Darwin and Newton have done just this: e.g. Adrian Desmond and James Moore, *Darwin* (1991), and Rob Iliffe, *Priest of Nature: The Religious Worlds of Isaac Newton* (New York, 2017). See also Michael Shortland and Richard Yeo (eds.), *Telling Lives in Science: Essays on Scientific Biography* (New York and Cambridge, 1996); their preface and introduction are particularly useful and ch. 8 is on Darwin. See also Janet Browne, 'Making Darwin: Biography and the Changing Representations of Charles Darwin', *Journal of Interdisciplinary History*, 40 (2010), 347–73.

[51] Peter Burke, *Eyewitnessing: The Uses of Images as Historical Evidence* (2001), esp. 25–30, and Ludmilla Jordanova, *The Look of the Past: Visual and Material Evidence in Historical Practice* (Cambridge, 2012) esp. 188–206. Critical attention also needs to be paid to the reproduction of images and any accompanying text in historical publications.

[52] In a few cases, generally contemporary portraits, an image cannot be provided for copyright reasons.

[53] For NPG 1635 (Richmond's portrait of Paget), there is an extended entry, which forms part of the Later Victorians Portrait Catalogue: https://www.npg.org.uk/collections/search/personExtended/mp03420/sir-james-paget-1st-bt (last accessed 12 Jan. 2022).

former's eldest son, who presented the canvas to the gallery. Another son's account of this depiction of his father is also cited. A single canvas thus provides a jumping-off point for intellectual, personal and familial phenomena with rich biographical potential, whilst offering links to further materials. It is not just that the site is freely available and easy to use; it also indicates something of the research processes undertaken when placing an iconic image in context – public history indeed. With a light touch, then, it also sheds light on historians' work. Webs of association – Darwin–Huxley–Collier, for example – are present in the entry for NPG 1024. Collier's interpretations of his sitters also indicate ways in which historians can trace connections between people. Such palpable links enhance historical understanding.

One possible next step is to consider the NPG itself as an object of historical analysis; many accounts of its foundation in 1856 and its early years exist.[54] Its contemporary profile is illuminating for history and public history.[55] Given the popularity of portraiture, the gallery receives considerable media attention, for example, when (some) new works arrive, whether by purchase, gift or bequest.[56] Acquisitions are history in the making and they bear on biography and national history in their most generous senses. Economic and administrative processes are an integral part of the picture. Portraits become available in unpredictable ways and at varying costs, thus multiple contingencies bear on the composition of the collection. In this respect the *Oxford Dictionary of National Biography* could not be more different, since the staff are free to include a high-quality biography of anyone who meets the entry criteria. It does not depend on complex art markets or the wishes of donors and preferences of trustees, nor on the success of fundraising, to acquire highly prized items. Economic and administrative processes remain vital for an understanding of the *DNB* and of Colin Matthew's role at the *ODNB*. George Smith's 'Recollections' makes clear the meticulous approach he took to publishing in general and to the *DNB* in particular, enabling us to see not only the kinds of work involved but the business decisions he took. While he did not seek to make the *DNB* commercially viable, he nonetheless needed to keep an eye on his losses. The *ODNB* has been supported by the publisher, with some input from public funds; the online version is behind a paywall, although more than half the UK's public libraries subscribe and through them it is

---

[54] E.g. Pointon, *Hanging the Head*, 227–44; Paul Barlow, 'Facing the Past and Present: The National Portrait Gallery and the Search for "Authentic" Portraiture', in *Portraiture*, ed. Woodall, 219–38; Charles Saumarez Smith, *The National Portrait Gallery* (1997); Paul Barlow and Colin Trodd (eds.), *Governing Cultures: Art Institutions in Victorian London* (Aldershot, 2000), ch. 9; Lara Perry, *History's Beauties: Women and the National Portrait Gallery 1856–1900* (Aldershot, 2006); David Cannadine, *National Portrait Gallery: A Brief History* (2007).

[55] Like other public bodies that receive government funding, the NPG website includes, for example, annual reports and minutes of the Board of Trustees; it also contains research materials, details of events, publications and so on. On its governance issues, see Ludmilla Jordanova, 'Historians, Accountability and Judgement', *Historical Research*, 96 (2021), 849–68.

[56] Many recent acquisitions concern celebrities with a high profile in popular culture, a vital object of analysis for public historians, e.g. Jerome de Groot, *Consuming History: Historians and Heritage in Contemporary Popular Culture* (London and New York, 2009).

possible to use it at one's leisure. Details of access, costs if any to consumers and sources of funding need to be assessed when reflecting on vehicles for public history, just as governance and ethos are. While George Smith was not answerable to a board, he did employ staff to read and comment on manuscripts, and Leslie Stephen published lists of potential biographees, inviting comments. The *ODNB* staff consult widely and work with external advisers; the project is part of Oxford University Press, the largest such press in the world with its own governance structures. Producing and disseminating biographies, acquiring and displaying portraits are economic and administrative phenomena as well as literary, aesthetic, national, political and cultural ones. It is possible to move seamlessly from the life and visual representations of George Smith, for instance, into broader historical questions: from tags, through work and administrative processes to business history and commemoration, professional and social status, public personae, national recognition, state-funded institutions and cultural trends.

Portraits and biographies walk hand in hand; they go well, even naturally, together and have done for centuries. This was Colin Matthew's position. There is a huge amount of evidence that an 'authentic' portrait, one depicting a named sitter and demonstrably taken from life, exercises an especially powerful allure, while even those of doubtful origin can meet a deep need, experienced by individuals, families and institutions alike, to know what someone in the past (allegedly) looked like. Authenticity may be in the eye of the beholder. Whether portraits really can achieve such truthfulness is another matter; rather it is the thirst for a likeness, whatever the medium, that is remarkable. These points are only reinforced by frequent uses of 'portrait' to mean a faithful rendition of a phenomenon, whether that be a city, an area, a river, a period or a person. 'Portrait' is a compelling idea, evident in its use by Leslie Stephen and Sidney Lee. Its potency is further borne out by the notion's appeal to writers of fiction, including Nathaniel Hawthorne in the mid-nineteenth and Iain Pears in the early twenty-first centuries. The relevance of fiction for historical practice is considerable.[57]

The examples presented in this article suggest that it is useful to think in terms of a portrait–biography nexus, both in general terms, and in specific cases where it is possible to trace the relationships between these two means of grasping a life, which are a familiar part of everyday existence, now as in the past. They reveal the ways in which people, such as artists and those they depict, are connected, the routes through which collections are formed and publications assembled. They are well suited to public history

---

[57] Nathaniel Hawthorne, 'The Prophetic Pictures', first published 1837; Iain Pears, *The Portrait* (2005). Other fictional works about portraits include Edgar Allan Poe's short story 'The Oval Portrait', first published in 1842; Charles Atkins, *The Portrait* (New York, 2008); Willem Jan Otten, *The Portrait* (Melbourne, 2009); Antoine Laurain, *The Portrait* (2017). See ch. 3 of Ross McKibbin's *Democracy and Political Culture: Studies in Modern British History* (Oxford, 2019) for a recent example of a historian's engagement with fiction.

as well as to analysing the deployment of portraits and biography in historical practices of many kinds.

Colin Matthew's own entry in the *ODNB* exemplifies my key themes – 'historian and founding editor of the Oxford Dictionary of National Biography'.[58] Written by the eminent historian Ross McKibbin (1942–), a colleague and friend, the same generation as his subject, the entry follows an unfolding life starting with his family of origin, while also assessing the significance of specific aspects of it. The tone is frank yet affectionate, full of personal detail, but also soberly measured about Colin's contributions to scholarship. One finishes reading it with a genuine sense of a person, their achievements and legacy. It is an admirably rounded account. The portrait photograph that accompanies it shows a man at work, looking up for just a moment, we may suppose. The image maintains an emphasis on the sitter's occupation, which decontextualised head-and-shoulder representations cannot do unless a uniform of some kind is involved.[59] In addition to the narrative element of the *ODNB* entry, there are routine sections of further information at the end, which include the size of the estate, as well as sources and likenesses. As a result, it is indeed possible to imagine both the research processes behind the memoir and those that might be prompted by it, as the NPG website also permits. These points suggest the special value of forms of public history that hint at research processes and make historical toil transparent. All historians can share their labours, indicating why they matter, with the public, exploring in the process how portraits and biographies keep those we value alive. Thus Colin Matthew lives, not just in the hearts of his family, friends and colleagues, but in the fruits of his working life. He approved of the idea that historians should share their endeavours as fully as possible, that exploring portraits and biographies can have public benefit and that clear, well-crafted prose is a professional ideal. It is fitting that his portrait – available to all – shows him mid-flow, still present.

Acknowledgements. A version of this article was first presented as the Royal Historical Society's 2021 Colin Matthew Memorial Lecture for the Public Understanding of History, read on 2 November 2021.

I am deeply grateful to Sue Matthew for illuminating and inspiring conversations about Colin, to Philip Carter, Elizabeth Cowling, Mark Curthoys, Robert Faber, Jack Hepworth, Dawn Kemp, Margaret Pelling, Howard Nelson and staff at the *Oxford Dictionary of National Biography* for their help and insights and to the Warden, Senior Common Room members and the staff of the library of New College, Oxford, for their stimulating company and generous help while I was working on the lecture and article. The assistance of staff at the Heinz Archive, National Portrait Gallery, London, is, as ever, greatly appreciated.

Author biography. Ludmilla Jordanova is Emeritus Professor of History and Visual Culture at Durham University.

---

[58] On the NPG website, he is simply 'historian and editor'.
[59] NPG x132537 is the same image, taken in 1993 by Judith Aronson.

Cite this article: Jordanova L (2022). Portraiture, Biography and Public Histories. *Transactions of the Royal Historical Society* **32**, 159–175. https://doi.org/10.1017/S008044012200007X

Transactions of the RHS (2022), **32**, 177–197
doi:10.1017/S0080440122000044

ARTICLE

Accumulations and Cascades: Burmese Elephants and the Ecological Impact of British Imperialism

Jonathan Saha

Department of History, University of Durham, Durham, UK
Email: Jonathan.Saha@durham.ac.uk

(Received 11 January 2022; accepted 28 February 2022)

Abstract

What effect did British imperialism in Myanmar have on frogs? And, given that the lives of these small amphibian creatures were rarely ever recorded or preserved in archival collections, how might we find out? Sceptical readers may also wish to take a step back and ask, why should historians even care about their lives? These are unusual questions for a historian to confront, but they are occasioned by the deepening conversation between ecology and history. This paper delves into the ecological impact of colonial rule in Myanmar through the lives of Burmese elephants and the creatures that they lived alongside. In it I argue that the concepts of 'accumulation' and 'cascade' are useful for enabling historians to apprehend the full extent of the impact of imperialism on the lives of animals.

Keywords: Myanmar; ecology; imperialism; environment; elephants

The moist tracks left by elephants migrating through the monsoon forests of Myanmar make ideal homes for frogs. Although shallow for a human, when they fill with rain the divots and miniature dykes formed through the force of these giants' footprints are deep enough to provide protection for small amphibians to breed. If these passing herds happen to deposit substantial piles of dung, then frogs have even more inviting sites in which they could take up residence.[1] These are opportunities for frogs to flourish that would have been dramatically affected by the advent of British imperialism in Myanmar. Elephants in their thousands were conscripted into the timber

---

[1] Ahimsa Campos-Arceiz, 'Shit Happens (to Be Useful)! Use of Elephant Dung as Habitat by Amphibians', *Biotropica*, 41 (2009), 406–7; Steven G. Platt et al., 'Water-Filled Asian Elephant Tracks Serve as Breeding Sites for Anurans in Myanmar', *Mammalia*, 83 (2019), 287–9.

industry. Their ranges were encroached upon by human cultivation. The accidental amphibian-friendly architecture left in their wake would have been less expansive. Frogs would have had less security from predators and had fewer opportunities to reproduce. They were unseen collateral damage; one of the unrecorded victims of colonial rule. This abrupt disruption to their world was but a small episode in the history of the ecological impact of imperialism that played out on a planetary scale.[2]

Historians have long been interrogating this relationship between British imperialism and ecologies. This has usually taken one of four forms. Early studies sought to assess the impact of imperial policies in precipitating the degradation of colonial environments.[3] Concurrent with these studies, but with a focus on culture, imperial understandings of the natural world have been subject to critical textual analysis, exposing the place of nature within essentialising and othering colonial writings.[4] Drawing on both of these approaches, some landmark studies have examined the interplay of imperial (and, although to a lesser extent, indigenous) knowledge and practices as colonial states came to learn about the ecologies over which they nominally governed. This research emphasised the emergence of imperial regimes for protecting the environment alongside acknowledgement of the deleterious effects of the colonial exploitation of natural resources.[5] More recently still, historians have unsettled some of the premises of these earlier studies by exploring ecological factors as having a role in constituting empires. In these studies, imperialism has itself been shaped by plants, animals and germs in the colonies as much as it had an impact upon colonised ecologies.[6] Overall, the field has become more alert to the ambiguities of the impact of imperialism on ecologies and has given more space for appreciating the impact that ecologies had on imperialism.[7]

---

[2] Jason W. Moore, 'The Capitalocene, Part I: On the Nature and Origins of Our Ecological Crisis', *Journal of Peasant Studies*, 44 (2017), 594–630.

[3] Madhav Gadgil and Ramachandra Guha, *This Fissured Land: An Ecological History of India* (Berkeley, 1993); Mahesh Rangarajan, 'The Raj and the Natural World: The War against "Dangerous Beasts" in Colonial India', *Studies in History*, 14 (1998), 265–99.

[4] Harriet Ritvo, *Animal Estate: The English & Other Creatures in the Victorian Age* (Cambridge, MA, 1987); David Arnold, *The Problem of Nature: Environment, Culture and European Expansion* (Oxford, 1996); Peder Anker, *Imperial Ecology: Environmental Order in the British Empire, 1895-1945* (Cambridge, MA, 2001).

[5] John M. Mackenzie, *The Empire of Nature: Hunting, Conservation and British Imperialism* (Manchester, 1988); Richard Grove, *Green Imperialism: Colonial Expansion, Tropical Island Edens and the Origins of Environmentalism, 1600-1800* (Cambridge, 1995); Richard Harry Drayton, *Nature's Government: Science, Imperial Britain, and the 'Improvement' of the World* (New Haven, 2000).

[6] Fa-Ti Fan, 'Plants, Germs, and Animals: They Want to Be in History, Too!', *Cross-Currents: East Asian History and Culture Review*, 3 (2014), 231–44; James Beattie, Edward Melillo and Emily O'Gorman, 'Rethinking the British Empire through Eco-Cultural Networks: Materialist-Cultural Environmental History, Relational Connections and Agency', *Environment and History*, 20 (2014), 561–75; Rohan Deb Roy, 'Nonhuman Empires', *Comparative Studies of South Asia, Africa and the Middle East*, 35 (2015), 66–75.

[7] William Beinart and Lotte Hughes, *Environment and Empire* (Oxford, 2010); Corey Ross, *Ecology and Power in the Age of Empire: Europe and the Transformation of the Tropical World* (Oxford, 2017), 1–26.

A problem that runs across these varying approaches is that of the inherent instability of the historical subjects under study, both empires and ecologies. Neither stays still. Tracing the influence and effects of one on the other is, as a result, a delicate process that often rests on the use of necessary heuristic devices that can obscure as much as they reveal, such as: treating the colonial state as a stable, singular actor; framing Empire as a unified system clearly divided between metropole and periphery; or reifying a division between nature and culture.[8] The more recent framing of empires and ecologies as 'co-constituting' and 'becoming with' one another provides a more conceptually sound basis for examining the relationship, but it also makes causation nearly impossible to trace.[9] An avenue to mitigate against these problems of unstable subjects and obscure explanatory narratives, I wish to argue, is to frame empires and ecologies not so much as singular *entities* but as constituted by interactive *processes*. Put another way, rather than conceptualising the relationship between imperialism and ecology as one between two identifiable and discrete things, even if they are conceived of as historically fluid and entangled entities, historians might rethink them as two processes unfolding over time with discernible interactive dynamics. As it is, the fields of both imperial history, and ecology have ready-made concepts that can be used to facilitate such a shift in framing: 'accumulation' and 'cascade'.[10]

Of the two concepts, accumulation will likely be the more familiar to historians. Imperial history, in particular, has long used the concept to understand the economic drivers for European colonial expansion, especially the role of financial capital from the mid-nineteenth century.[11] More than simply accretion or gathering, accumulation is usually deployed to refer to the ongoing and

---

[8] For some critiques of these particular devices, see John L. Comaroff, 'Reflections on the Colonial State, in South Africa and Elsewhere: Factions, Fragments, Facts and Fictions', *Social Identities*, 4 (1998), 321–61; Frederick Cooper and Ann Laura Stoler, 'Between Metropole and Colony: Rethinking a Research Agenda', in *Tensions of Empire: Colonial Cultures in a Bourgeois World*, ed. Frederick Cooper and Ann Laura Stoler (Berkeley, 1997), 1–56; Joanna Latimer and Mara Miele, 'Naturecultures? Science, Affect and the Non-Human', *Theory, Culture & Society*, 30, no. 7–8 (2013), 5–31.

[9] Donna Haraway, *The Companion Species Manifesto: Dogs, People, and Significant Otherness* (Chicago, 2003); Donna Haraway, *Staying with the Trouble: Making Kin in the Chthulucene* (Durham, NC, 2016).

[10] A fantastic example of a study that takes such a dynamic approach already, and is particularly attentive to accumulatory dynamics, is Debjani Bhattacharyya, *Empire and Ecology in the Bengal Delta: The Making of Calcutta* (Cambridge, 2018). Accumulation has also recently been considered as a core process in environmental degradation. See Jason W. Moore, 'The Capitalocene Part II: Accumulation by Appropriation and the Centrality of Unpaid Work/Energy', *Journal of Peasant Studies*, 45 (2018), 237–79.

[11] J. A. Hobson, *Imperialism: A Study*, 3rd entirely rev. and reset edn (1968); Vladimir Il'ich Lenin, *Imperialism, the Highest Stage of Capitalism: A Popular Outline*, 13th edn (Moscow, 1966); Eric Williams, *Capitalism and Slavery* (1964); Rosa Luxemburg, 'The Accumulation of Capital', in *The Complete Works of Rosa Luxemburg*, vol. ii: *Economic Writings 2*, ed. Peter Hudis and Paul Le Blanc, trans. Nicholas Gray and George Shriver (London and New York, 2015), 7–331; Andre Gunder Frank, *Dependent Accumulation* (New York, 1979); Patrick Wolfe, 'History and Imperialism: A Century of Theory, from Marx to Postcolonialism', *American Historical Review*, 102 (1997), 388–420; Andrew B. Liu, 'Production, Circulation, and Accumulation: The Historiographies of Capitalism in China and South Asia', *Journal of Asian Studies*, 78 (2019), 767–88.

expanding reproduction of something, most often – although not exclusively – capital.[12] Crucially, at least in a Marxian formulation, accumulation is framed as a self-perpetuating drive and an end in itself.[13] However, it is a concept whose star has declined and in recent scholarship most imperial historians have not engaged with it as a central concept within their methodological toolkit. Regardless of this decline, in wider social theory it is a concept that has been freed from some of the economism of earlier works and has been used to account for the expanded reproduction of social hierarchies, cultural artefacts, and power relations more generally.[14] Even when studies have remained focused on capital in its money-form, recent scholarship has taken a broader view of the processes behind accumulation, acknowledging its gendered, racialised and environmental foundations and formations.[15] As a result, although it is a dated concept within imperial historiography, one that has largely fallen out of favour, it is overdue some renewed engagement given its continued theoretical relevance in aligned fields.

Cascade, on the other hand, is possibly a less well-known concept to historians. However, it has been in circulation since the 1960s and is a well-established and much-discussed concept in ecology. Its original and most common usage is more specifically focused on elaborations of what are called 'trophic cascades'. These are, in their most basic formulation, the indirect knock-on effects of predator species down the food chain in an ecosystem. For example, the study of a trophic cascade might entail examining how the size of a tiger population impacts upon the population and behaviour of deer, that then has a bearing on the spread and diversity of the plant life that the deer graze upon. The concept has been defined more loosely since its earliest uses, capturing 'trickle-up' and horizontal effects, and it has moved beyond a focus on the role of predators alone.[16] This has been to the frustration of some ecologists, but is perhaps to the benefit of historians who, as a result, have a more portable concept with which to conceptualise

---

[12] Jessica Ratcliff, 'Hand-in-Hand with the Survey: Surveying and the Accumulation of Knowledge Capital at India House during the Napoleonic Wars', *Notes and Records: The Royal Society Journal of the History of Science*, 73 (2019), 149–66; Steven Lee Rubenstein, 'Circulation, Accumulation, and the Power of Shuar Shrunken Heads', *Cultural Anthropology*, 22 (2007), 357–99.

[13] Karl Marx, *Capital*, trans. Ben Fowkes (3 vols., New York, 1977), ɪ; Jonathan Nitzan, 'Differential Accumulation: Towards a New Political Economy of Capital', *Review of International Political Economy*, 5 (1998), 169–216.

[14] Henri Lefebvre, *The Critique of Everyday Life*, trans. John Moore (2014); Pierre Bourdieu, 'The Forms of Capital', in *Handbook of Theory and Research for the Sociology of Education*, ed. J Richardson, trans. Richard Nice (New York, 1986), 241–58; Jonathan Nitzan and Shimshon Bichler, 'Capital Accumulation: Breaking the Dualism of "Economics" and "Politics"', in *Global Political Economy: Contemporary Theories*, ed. Ronen Palan (2000), 67–88.

[15] Nancy Fraser, 'Behind Marx's Hidden Abode: For an Expanded Conception of Capitalism', in *Critical Theory in Critical Times: Transforming the Global Political and Economic Order* (New York, 2017), 141–59; Paula Chakravartty and Denise Ferreira da Silva, 'Accumulation, Dispossession, and Debt: The Racial Logic of Global Capitalism – An Introduction', *American Quarterly*, 64 (2012), 361–85; Destin Jenkins and Justin Leroy, *Histories of Racial Capitalism* (New York, 2021).

[16] William J. Ripple *et al.*, 'What Is a Trophic Cascade?', *Trends in Ecology & Evolution*, 31 (2016), 842–9.

ecosystems in the past. What I find compelling about both the concept of accumulation and that of cascade, and what I contend makes them useful for better apprehending the nature of Empire's ecological impact, is that they both offer models for systems changing-over-time according to their own dynamics and momentum. In other words, they suggest explanatory narratives that do not grant individual actors causative roles.

Accumulation in colonial Myanmar took several different forms, but there were two that had the greatest impact on the country's elephant populations. One was the extractive teak industry, a mode of accumulation that took on an almost textbook form of 'accumulation by dispossession', as David Harvey has called it. Capital was accumulated by imperial firms forcibly bringing resources, peoples and places into capitalist relations with the backing and intervention of state power.[17] The other was the rice industry, where agriculturalists entered into the world market through their own volition, without necessarily entering into capitalist labour relations (i.e. being alienated from their means of production),[18] and, crucially, with the prospect for what Mahmood Mamdani has called 'accumulation from below' – that is, the opportunity to gain ownership of more land and cattle, and then purchase labour power and/or rent their property to make greater returns.[19] At the same time, elephants as a species offer us an opportunity to examine the cascade effects that likely resulted from the profound disruptions that their herds confronted as a result of their capture for timber extraction and the loss and fragmentation of their habitat on the rice frontier. They are renowned ecosystem engineers, spreading seeds, forging forest paths, discovering sources of water, and, as we have seen with regard to frogs, creating habitats.[20] Changes in their behaviours, ranges, habitats, diets and population size will have had myriad knock-on effects across the ecosystems of Myanmar.

During the late nineteenth century and into the early twentieth century, Myanmar became one of the world's biggest exporters of hardwoods. Teak was particularly desirable for its use in the production of ships, railway sleepers and luxury furniture.[21] The rapid development of the timber industry was a

---

[17] David Harvey, *The New Imperialism* (Oxford, 2005); Jim Glassman, 'Primitive Accumulation, Accumulation by Dispossession, Accumulation by "Extra-Economic" Means', *Progress in Human Geography*, 30 (2006), 608–25.

[18] Willem van Schendel, 'Origins of the Burma Rice Boom, 1850–1880', *Journal of Contemporary Asia*, 17 (1987), 456–72.

[19] Mahmood Mamdani, 'Extreme but Not Exceptional: Towards an Analysis of the Agrarian Question in Uganda', *Journal of Peasant Studies*, 14 (1987), 191–225. This accumulation could take illicit and corrupt forms; see Jonathan Saha, 'Paperwork as Commodity, Corruption as Accumulation: Land Records and Licences in Colonial Myanmar, c. 1900', in *Corruption, Empire and Colonialism: A Global Perspective*, ed. Ronald Kroeze, Pol Dalmau and Frédéric Monier (Basingstoke, 2021), 293–315.

[20] Herve Fritz, 'Long-Term Field Studies of Elephants: Understanding the Ecology and Conservation of a Long-Lived Ecosystem Engineer', *Journal of Mammalogy*, 98 (2017), 603–11; Gary Haynes, 'Elephants (and Extinct Relatives) as Earth-Movers and Ecosystem Engineers', *Geomorphology*, 157–158 (2012), 99–107.

[21] Arnold Wright, *Twentieth Century Impressions of Burma: Its History, People, Commerce, Industries and Resources* (London, Durban and Perth, 1910), 184–94.

vital motor in the expansion of capitalist and colonial relations in this often neglected corner of the Raj. Teak traders financed from Britain were vocal in lobbying Westminster and the Government of India to colonise the land-locked rump of territory governed by the once powerful Konbaung dynasty, mobilising their connections in both the press and in Parliament, as well as within Burmese communities.[22] Following the eventual annexation of upper Myanmar in 1885, they continued to inveigle the local government into inter-ceding on their behalf in the borderlands with Siam where colonial authority had not yet been securely established.[23] On the ground, the growing swathes of territory over which these firms were able to gain privileged rights, through favourable government leases, deprived substantial numbers of forest-dwelling peoples of their ancestorial access to forests and to the resources held therein. Extractive logging operations and the scientific management of forestry, them-selves frequently in tension with each other, came into conflict with the shift-ing subsistence farming of some indigenous Karen communities. This was a conflict in which imperial firms and the colonial state decisively held the upper hand. The imperial expropriation of timber laid the groundwork for anti-colonial grievances among hill populations.[24] Some of those displaced in the process entered the labour market as workers for the very timber firms threatening their communities' modes of subsistence, not least as elephant dri-vers.[25] In short, the timber industry reproduced, in an expanded form, unstable and conflictual social relations in Myanmar.

These social relations were not solely between humans. Vital to the indus-try were elephants. They were vital in two senses of the word. Elephants were essential to the labour processes of timber extraction and exportation. And elephants were also lively actors whose wilful undertakings and bodily needs shaped the industry itself. The instrumental benefits to exploiting elephants for the timber industry emanated from these innate mental and bodily capaci-ties. Asian elephants, while smaller than their African relatives, are, of course, famously powerful creatures, capable of dextrously manoeuvring heavy objects using their supple trunks. They also have prodigious stamina. When free to roam their habitats, they range over great distances across varied terrain. As

---

[22] Anthony Webster, 'Business and Empire: A Reassessment of the British Conquest of Burma in 1885', *Historical Journal*, 43 (2000), 1003–25; Alexandra Kaloyanides, 'Buddhist Teak and British Rifles: Religious Economics in Burma's Last Kingdom', *Journal of Burma Studies*, 24 (2020), 1–36.

[23] Jonathan Saha, *Colonizing Animals: Interspecies Empire in Myanmar* (Cambridge, 2022).

[24] Raymond L. Bryant, 'Fighting over the Forests: Political Reform, Peasant Resistance and the Transformation of Forest Management in Late Colonial Burma', *Journal of Commonwealth and Comparative Politics*, 32 (1994), 244–60; Raymond L. Bryant, 'Shifting the Cultivator: The Politics of Teak Regeneration in Colonial Burma', *Modern Asian Studies*, 28 (1994), 225–50; Raymond L. Bryant, 'Romancing Colonial Forestry: The Discourse of "Forestry as Progress" in British Burma', *Geographical Journal*, 162 (1996), 169–78; James C. Scott, *The Art of Not Being Governed: An Anarchist History of Upland Southeast Asia* (New Haven, 2009).

[25] Evidence of the preponderance of Karen men as elephant drivers can be found throughout the archives of the Bombay Burmah Trading Corporation. The following correspondence acknowledges their dependence on it by the 1930s: London Metropolitan Archives, hereafter LMA: CLC/B/207/ MS40475: 'Bombay Burmah Trading Corporation Limited: correspondence between branches and director for veterinary research relating to anthrax in elephants', 14 June 1938.

close-knit matriarchal herds, and as solo adolescent and adult males, they can cover areas of more than 3,000 square kilometres. They are also competent swimmers. Like humans, they are long-lived mammals, and have frequently been recorded living to over sixty years.[26] Their cognitive powers are recurrently compared to those of primates. Every passing year, new scientific studies incrementally add more evidence of their abilities, including the capacity for self-recognition and self-awareness.[27] They manipulate their environments for their own benefit. For instance, when injured they have been observed adopting behaviours to optimise their recovery.[28] They are known to independently use tools to manage parasites, regulate their temperature, and, with creative adaptations, access hard-to-reach sources of food.[29] But it is perhaps their attuned social skills that have been most critical in shaping their encounters with colonialism. Through visual and olfactory clues, they can distinguish between familiar and unfamiliar humans.[30] And they are also able to understand and respond to human social cues.[31] But quite apart from *Homo sapiens*, they have rich social lives within their own elephant communities. This shapes their psychology. They grieve, they breakdown.[32]

Bringing elephants into the labour process meant harnessing their capacities while severing individuals' social ties with their wild herds and recursively inflicting bodily pain. It was an unavoidably traumatic experience for the

[26] R. Sukumar, *The Asian Elephant: Ecology and Management* (Cambridge, 1992); R. Sukumar, *The Living Elephants: Evolutionary Ecology, Behaviour, and Conservation* (Oxford, 2003); T. N. C. Vidya and R. Sukumar, 'Social Organization of the Asian Elephant (*Elephas Maximus*) in Southern India Inferred from Microsatellite DNA', *Journal of Ethology*, 23 (2005), 205–10; R. Sukumar, 'A Brief Review of the Status, Distribution and Biology of Wild Asian Elephants *Elephas Maximus*', *International Zoo Yearbook*, 40 (2006), 1–8; Hannah S. Mumby *et al.*, 'Distinguishing between Determinate and Indeterminate Growth in a Long-Lived Mammal', *BMC Evolutionary Biology*, 15 (2015), 1–9.

[27] Joshua M. Plotnik *et al.*, 'Self-Recognition in the Asian Elephant and Future Directions for Cognitive Research with Elephants in Zoological Settings', *Zoo Biology*, 29 (2010), 179–91; Rachel Dale and Joshua M. Plotnik, 'Elephants Know When Their Bodies Are Obstacles to Success in a Novel Transfer Task', *Scientific Reports*, 7 (2017), 1–10.

[28] N. S. Manoharan *et al.*, 'A Case of a Lacerated Wound in an Asian Elephant (*Elephas Maximus*) and Its Cognitive Aptitude in Self-Healing', *Zoos' Print Journal*, 31 (2016), 7–8.

[29] Suzanne Chevalier-Skolnikoff and Jo Liska, 'Tool Use by Wild and Captive Elephants', *Animal Behaviour*, 46 (1993), 209–19; Benjamin L. Hart *et al.*, 'Cognitive Behaviour in Asian Elephants: Use and Modification of Branches for Fly Switching', *Animal Behaviour*, 62 (2001), 839–47; Kaori Mizuno *et al.*, 'Asian Elephants Acquire Inaccessible Food by Blowing', *Animal Cognition*, 19 (2016), 215–22.

[30] Emily J. Polla, Cyril C. Grueter and Carolynn L. Smith, 'Asian Elephants (*Elephas Maximus*) Discriminate between Familiar and Unfamiliar Human Visual and Olfactory Cues', *Animal Behavior and Cognition*, 5 (2018), 279–91.

[31] Oraya Ketchaisri, Chomcheun Siripunkaw and Joshua M. Plotnik, 'The Use of a Human's Location and Social Cues by Asian Elephants in an Object-Choice Task', *Animal Cognition*, 22 (2019), 907–15.

[32] G. A. Bradshaw, 'Not by Bread Alone: Symbolic Loss, Trauma, and Recovery in Elephant Communities', *Society & Animals*, 12 (2004), 143–58; G. A. Bradshaw and Allan N. Schore, 'How Elephants Are Opening Doors: Developmental Neuroethology, Attachment and Social Context', *Ethology*, 113 (2007), 426–36.

elephants and held considerable risks for the colonised human labour employed to capture, train and drive them. These dangers notwithstanding, the colonial regime was eager to facilitate the mobilisation of elephants. As British rule expanded into the territories of the Konbaung dynasty during the nineteenth century, colonial officials were quickly alert to the presence of seemingly innumerable herds of wild elephants.[33] They were also sensitive to the important symbolic role played by elephants within courtly cultures and within the Theravada Buddhist religious mores of many of their new subjects; although this did not necessarily mean that they had developed a particularly accurate or sophisticated understanding.[34] Crucially, as Sujit Sivasundaram has demonstrated in his landmark article on the topic, the East India Company had long been engaged with South Asian knowledges and practices of elephant-keeping and -capture.[35] The British regime thus arrived on the scene equipped with the requisite knowledge to appreciate the potential benefits to themselves of Myanmar's elephant population. Realising this potential was, however, beset with difficulties. Elephant thefts, enabled in no small part by the animals' unparalleled ability to traverse mountainous jungle,[36] were endemic to the borders of Myanmar throughout the late nineteenth century and into the mid-twentieth – indeed, elephant-smuggling over the border with Thailand remains a problem today.[37] But there were more immediate problems to be faced: first, the difficulties the colonial state confronted controlling elephants and arranging for their capture, and then large commercial timber firms' inability to maintain and reproduce their captive herds.

Using the Konbaung dynasty's sovereign claims to the right to wild elephants within its domain as a precedent, the British regime asserted that elephants were the property of the state.[38] This claim, however, was mostly fictive. To start with, the newly established bureaucracy in the southern, coastal regions of Myanmar following the 1852 Anglo-Burmese War struggled to hire elephant trappers. Burmese folk who had previously made their livelihoods capturing wild elephants were reluctant to continue in this line of work when tempted, instead, by the riches in prospect on the rice frontier. At least, they would not do so for the level of monetary inducement that the

---

[33] H. Falconer, *Report on the Teak Forests of the Tenasserim Provinces*, Selections from the Records of the Bengal Government, IX (Calcutta, 1852). See also National Archives of Myanmar, hereafter NAM: 1/1 (A) 35, 1853 File No. 35: 5 May 1852.

[34] Hiram Cox and D. G. E Hall, *Journal of a Residence in the Burmhan Empire, London 1821* (1971); Thomas Abercromby Trant, *Two Years in Ava: From May 1824, to May 1826* (1827); Howard Malcolm, *Travels in the Burman Empire* (Edinburgh, 1840); Kenneth R. H. MacKenzie, *Burmah and the Burmese* (1853); Henry Gouger, *Personal Narrative of Two Years' Imprisonment in Burmah* (1860).

[35] Sujit Sivasundaram, 'Trading Knowledge: The East India Company's Elephants in India and Britain', *Historical Journal*, 48 (2005), 27–63.

[36] Jacob Shell, 'Elephant Convoys beyond the State: Animal-Based Transport as Subversive Logistics', *Environment and Planning D: Society and Space*, 37 (2019), 905–23; Jacob Shell, 'Elephant Riders of the Hukawng Valley, Kachin State: Evasive Mobility and Vadological Geography', *Journal of Burma Studies*, 25 (2021), 261–98.

[37] Saha, *Colonizing Animals*, 158–61, 183–4; Chris R. Shepherd and Vincent Nijman, 'Elephant and Ivory Trade in Myanmar' (Kuala Lumpur: TRAFFIC, 11 December 2008).

[38] NAM: 1/1(A) 35, 1853 File No. 35: 5 May 1852.

state was willing to offer.[39] Moreover, elephants in the colony were not readily amenable to being controlled; officials were alarmed by herds of hundreds of elephants periodically wreaking destruction on freshly cleared agricultural lands, particularly as rice cultivation accelerated in the 1880s.

The booming rice industry developed alongside the growth of the teak industry and had direct effects on elephant populations. Like teak extraction, rice cultivation in Myanmar was of transnational importance. The rich alluvial soil provided fertile ground for the Ayeyarwady delta to undergo a dramatic transformation to become the largest rice-producing region in the world, having a ripple effect across the global cereal market. The white rice exported from Myanmar fed colonised labouring peoples (and some non-human animals) engaged in commodity production across the Empire, most notably in neighbouring Bengal. The delta was crucial to an interdependent network of food security established through and underpinning British imperialism.[40] The changes on the delta itself were profound, both socially and ecologically. While patterns of Burman peoples moving to cultivate rice at the frontiers of dynastic power predated British colonial rule,[41] from the 1850s what was still predominantly a mangrove-forested backwater at the margins of political power became a febrile hive of activity. Sparsely populated, isolated hamlets, hemmed in by the thick jungles and thickets of dense grass in the tidal delta, became enmeshed in an extensive tapestry of paddy fields, their populations growing fivefold to become thriving commercial hubs, connected by a busy riverine transport network to the bustling imperial port cities of Akyab (now Sittwe), Mawlamyine and Yangon.[42]

These social and environmental changes were materialised through the hard labour of pioneer cultivators – human, oxen and buffalo – most of whom migrated from the northern reaches of the country. Whilst uncultivated land was abundant and the agricultural frontier remained open, until the late 1920s, these migrants were able to claim their own plot and turn it into wet-rice paddy fields. The work this entailed was punishing. Thick forest needed to be felled, the undergrowth burnt, and the remaining dense network of roots dug out; it could take several years for the land to be in a suitable condition to be ploughed and planted. Even then, they were in a precarious

---

[39] NAM: 1/1(A) 278, 1857 File No. 7: 29 May 1857; 4 June 1857.

[40] Peter A. Coclanis, 'Distant Thunder: The Creation of a World Market in Rice and the Transformations It Wrought', *American Historical Review*, 98 (1993), 1050–78; Kathleen D. Morrison and Mark W. Hauser, 'Risky Business: Rice and Inter-Colonial Dependencies in the Indian and Atlantic Oceans', *Atlantic Studies*, 12 (2015), 371–92.

[41] Michael Adas, 'Imperialist Rhetoric and Modern Historiography: The Case of Lower Burma before and after Conquest', *Journal of Southeast Asian Studies*, 3 (1972), 175–92; Willem van Schendel, *Three Deltas: Accumulation and Poverty in Rural Burma, Bengal and South India* (New Delhi and Newbury Park, CA, 1991), 52–9; Michael W. Charney, 'Demographic Growth, Agricultural Expansion, and Livestock in the Lower Chindwin in the Eighteenth and Nineteenth Centuries', in *A History of Natural Resources in Asia: The Wealth of Nature*, ed. Greg Bankoff and Peter Boomgaard (Basingstoke, 2007), 227–44.

[42] *Imperial Gazetteer of India: Provincial Series, Burma Vol. 1: The Province; Mountains, Rivers, Tribes; and the Arkan, Pegu, Irrawaddy, and Tenasserim Divisions* (Calcutta, 1908), 350–5.

position. Flooding, wild animals and malaria were just some of the dangers that cultivators faced. This work was underpinned by heavy borrowing, mostly from local Burmese and overseas Indian sources, and misfortune could lead to them defaulting on their loan and losing their land to their creditor. But these risks were balanced by the prospect of accumulation, building on the success of the initial acquisition of land in order to acquire more, begin hiring labourers and renting to tenant-cultivators, and make greater returns. For many, though, this was not realised. In the main, primary producers did not retain the wealth generated through rice production,[43] and many agriculturalists were in a vulnerable position when the market went into crisis in the early 1930s. Precarity and poverty accompanied plenty.[44]

The ecological transformation was rapid, and from an elephant's perspective at least, profound.[45] Focusing in on one of the fastest-growing deltaic areas between 1880 and 1920, around the townships of Thôngwa and Myaungmya, the impact is pronounced. Correspondence in 1886 identified 230 elephants living in the local forests. They would frequently raid freshly cultivated paddy fields, destroying crops and jeopardising the livelihoods of these precarious cultivators. The still extensive tracts of *kaing* (sometimes referred to as elephant) grass rendered them elusive to those Karen and Burman peasants who appealed to the state to either set rewards for their destruction, or facilitate their capture; both permitted under the provisions of the recently introduced legislation for elephant protection.[46] However, just thirty years later, the local settlement report recorded that there were no longer any elephants left in the area. Elephants would occasionally visit by swimming across from the dwindling reserved forests in neighbouring districts, but they were now rare unwelcome visitors, rather than perennial and potent dangers.[47] While the occasional use of bounties to encourage the killing of some elephants,[48] and the issuing of licences to local elephant trappers, would have had some effect in reducing their numbers, the rapid deforestation

---

[43] It is challenging to distinguish clearly between those who were and were not engaged in cultivation, and so it may not have been the case that land was increasingly falling into the hands of non-agricultural landowners. Nevertheless, there was certainly greater social differentiation apparent on the rice frontier. See Asuka Mizuno, 'Identifying the "Agriculturists" in the Burma Delta in the Colonial Period: A New Perspective on Agriculturists Based on a Village Tract's Registers of Holdings from the 1890s to the 1920s', *Journal of Southeast Asian Studies*, 42 (2011), 405–34.

[44] Michael Adas, *The Burma Delta: Economic Development and Social Change on an Asian Rice Frontier, 1852-1941* (Madison, 1974), 39–124; Ian Brown, *A Colonial Economy in Crisis: Burma's Rice Delta and the World Depression of the 1930s* (2005), 10–13; van Schendel, *Three Deltas*, 1–36.

[45] As Michael Adas has argued, compared to some colonial agricultural frontiers the environmental change in rice frontiers was not as destructive, but he does not explore biodiversity at much length. Michael Adas, 'Continuity and Transformation: Colonial Rice Frontiers and Their Environmental Impact on the Great River Deltas of Mainland Southeast Asia', in *The Environment and World History*, ed. Edmund Burke and Kenneth Pomeranz (Berkeley, 2009), 191–208.

[46] NAM: 1/15(E) 43, 1886 File No. 12N: 27 Mar. 1886; 20 Nov. 1885.

[47] India Office Records, British Library, London, hereafter IOR: V/27/314/309: *Report on the Settlement Operations in the Myaungmya District, Season 1916-1919* (Rangoon, 1921), 16.

[48] NAM: 1/15(E) 701, 1891 File No. 66MS: 11 Aug. 1891; NAM: 1/15(E) 1290, 1894 File No. 1W-1: 31 Mar. 1894.

of the area to make way for paddy is likely to have been what displaced the local elephant populations.

Alongside allowing some shooting of elephants and licensing local trappers to catch them, the government explored the prospect of organising official kheddahs – of which more below – to solve two problems at once: to eliminate the problem of these rapacious elephants' raids while meeting growing demands for elephant labour.[49] By the late nineteenth century, the state's requirements for elephants became less important to military strength and administrative logistics due to improved infrastructure; although the use of elephants in wars and transportation continued, and continues, in Myanmar.[50] At the same time, elephants became more important, indeed indispensable, for commercial teak extraction. In the analysis of former employees turned historians of the Bombay Burmah Trading Corporation, the largest teak firm operating in Myanmar, the acquisition of large herds of working elephants was pivotal in enabling imperial companies to dominate logging. The ability to raise the capital to speculate in these giant workers gave the Corporation the edge when exploiting the increasingly hard-to-reach teak forests at the turn of the twentieth century.[51] Smaller Burmese outfits simply could not compete.[52]

The kheddah is a large stockade into which elephants are corralled after being chased down by humans armed with spears riding captive elephants. In contrast to the competing modes of capture, such as noosing or the use of pit traps, the kheddah could be used to seize scores of elephants in one go. But the method required considerable set-up costs and then the significant ongoing costs of maintaining a substantial staff of people and elephants. Fitfully and hesitantly, the Government of India was moved to sanction the establishment of kheddah operations in the colony in 1902, although the move was quickly exposed as an expensive, ill-fated folly. The scheme resulted in an appalling mortality rate, with roughly half the over 500 elephants captured in its first four years of operation dying of disease, neglect and trauma-induced breakdowns. To make matters worse, the superintendent, Ian Hew Warrender Dalrymple-Clark, was exposed in a dramatic court case as having adopted an alter ego, Mr Green, for the purposes of faking the deaths of elephants through forged paperwork, and selling them directly to timber firms, leaving the state out of pocket.[53]

The British regime, never entirely successful in realising its claim to Myanmar's elephants, left the capture of elephants mostly to colonised peoples through a licensing scheme. These arrangements enabled the large timber firms, such as the Bombay Burmah Trading Corporation, to establish

---

[49] NAM: 1/15(E) 43, 1886 File No. 12N: 20 Nov. 1885; 14 June 1885; NAM: 1/15(E) 690, 1891 File No. 66: 18 Apr. 1891; NAM: 1/15(E) 3159, 1908 File No. 2W-6: 23 Oct. 1908.

[50] Jacob Shell, 'The Enigma of the Asian Elephant: Sovereignty, Reproductive Nature, and the Limits of Empire', *Annals of the American Association of Geographers*, 109 (2019), 1154–71.

[51] B. H. Macaulay, *History of the Bombay Burmah Trading Corporation, Ltd., 1864-1910* (1934); A. C. Pointon, *The Bombay Burmah Trading Corporation Limited 1863-1963* (Southampton, 1964).

[52] Raymond L. Bryant, *The Political Ecology of Forestry in Burma, 1824-1994* (1997), 104.

[53] Saha, *Colonizing Animals*, 61–8.

considerable herds of captive elephants during the opening decades of the twentieth century. By 1914 the Corporation had amassed a herd of 1,753 elephants.[54] Between 1918 and 1941 they purchased a further 543 from elephant-capturing firms. Allowing for elephants transferred from Siam and animals born from their herd, as well as mortality, they operated with between 2,000 and 3,000 working elephants in the 1920s and 1930s.[55] Their smaller rival, Steel Brothers and Company, by way of comparison, had a herd of 1,507 elephants in 1934 and a further 365 calves.[56] Estimates for the overall number of timber elephants employed by the 1940s vary, but a figure of around 7,000, or 10,000 including calves, would seem plausible.[57]

The sexual reproduction of an elephant workforce from within herds, however, was not successful enough to maintain these herds or make up for deaths, in part because infant mortality among calves was high, and in part because firms were unwilling to cover the costs of 'unproductive' female elephants now employed in reproductive labour; although some modest schemes for training captive-born calves were trialled.[58] Recent studies also show greater reproductive ageing among captive elephants working in timber extraction in Myanmar, which may retrospectively explain some of the difficulties the firms encountered.[59] As a result, the majority of the nearly 10,000 working elephants of colonial Myanmar had been captured from the wild. This very likely tipped the demographic balance of wild to working elephants firmly in favour of the latter.

Elephants in Myanmar were caught between two modes of accumulation. The timber industry demanded their labour and was predicated upon the social reproduction of their captive state, a situation that could only be maintained at the expense of wild populations. Meanwhile, the expansion of the rice industry was enabled, not through improvements in agricultural techniques or technological advances, but by cultivating more and more land. The resulting deforestation meant significant habitat loss and fragmentation for elephant populations. These processes were compounded by hunting, both sanctioned and illegal, in spite of protective legislation; protections that in practice went little further than the paper they were drafted on.[60] Both the timber trade and rice cultivation in colonial Myanmar have been

---

[54] LMA: CLC/B/207/MS40473/002: Correspondence and notes, 30 Nov. 1914.

[55] LMA: CLC/B/207/MS40473/005: Correspondence between branches and notes relating to purchase, export and army hiring of elephants, 18 May 1948.

[56] Gordon Hundley, 'Statistical Record of Growth in the Indian Elephant (E. Maximus)', Journal of the Bombay Natural History Society, 37 (1934), 487–8.

[57] Khyne U Mar, 'The Demography and Life History Strategies of Timber Elephants in Myanmar' (Ph.D. thesis, University of London, 2002), 15.

[58] LMA: CLC/B/207/MS40473/004: Correspondence between branches and notes on stocks, accounts, purchases and transfer of elephants, 26 June 1933, 4 July 1933, 23 Aug. 1933, 5 Sept. 1933.

[59] Hannah S. Mumby et al., 'Elephants Born in the High Stress Season Have Faster Reproductive Ageing', Scientific Reports, 5, no. 13946 (2015), 1–11; Mirkka Lahdenperä et al., 'Capture from the Wild Has Long-Term Costs on Reproductive Success in Asian Elephants', Proceedings of the Royal Society B: Biological Sciences, 286, no. 1912 (2019), n.p.

[60] Saha, Colonizing Animals, 95–105, Vijaya Ramadas Mandala, 'The Raj and the Paradoxes of Wildlife Conservation: British Attitudes and Expediencies', Historical Journal, 58 (2015), 75–110.

framed by historians as tales of differential enrichment and impoverishment.[61] As we shall see, the ecological effects that cascaded from elephants' altered circumstances would suggest that a range of non-human creatures also numbered among those that were impoverished.

Identifying fraught and fractious modes of accumulation allows us to better understand the contingent structural constraints within which actors were living; what we might call an analytic of conjuncture.[62] The social reproduction of human and elephant labour power in the timber industry, and the expansion of rice cultivation across the Ayeyarwady delta, were the two modes of accumulation that became dominant in colonial Myanmar between 1880 and the 1920s. Attendant to these accumulations, and over this same time period, the elephant population decisively shifted from being predominantly wild to being mostly captive, and large herds of elephants disappeared from the deltaic regions of the country. If accumulation – as I hope to have shown – enables us to glean a fuller picture of this particular historical conjuncture, then the concept of 'cascade' allows us to conjecture on the resulting ecological impacts.

Pivoting from a conjunctural mode of analysis to one of conjecture, based on recent scientific literature, is a move that requires care. This is not least because of the dangers of reifying the results of ecological studies conducted in recent years and projecting their findings backwards onto a time when ecosystems were different. Such a move would miss the foundational point that, like all scientific endeavours, ecology was and is entangled in particular social relations and embedded in particular constellations of power.[63] In colonial and post-colonial contexts, this has meant that institutionalised knowledge-making practices, and the scientific validation of ecological research, have been predicated upon the simultaneous appropriation and marginalisation of indigenous understandings of ecosystems, as well the subordination and exclusion of colonised peoples within the academic discipline.[64] Natural history, the older, parent discipline of ecology, has now been shown to have played a constitutive role in the generation of gendered and racialised discourses that justified imperial hierarchies and bolstered colonial conquest.[65] Ecology, a term whose emergence in the mid-nineteenth century is largely coterminous

---

[61] Bryant, *Political Ecology of Forestry*; van Schendel, *Three Deltas*.

[62] Tania Li, *Land's End: Capitalist Relations on an Indigenous Frontier* (Durham, NC, 2014), 16–20.

[63] Donna Haraway, 'Situated Knowledges: The Science Question in Feminism and the Privilege of Partial Perspective', *Feminist Studies*, 14 (1988), 575–99; Gyan Prakash, *Another Reason: Science and the Imagination of Modern India* (Princeton, 1999); Shubhra Gururani and Peter Vandergeest, 'Introduction: New Frontiers of Ecological Knowledge: Co-Producing Knowledge and Governance in Asia', *Conservation and Society*, 12 (2014), 343–51.

[64] Nancy J. Jacobs, 'The Intimate Politics of Ornithology in Colonial Africa', *Comparative Studies in Society and History*, 48 (2006), 564–603; Sivasundaram, 'Trading Knowledge'.

[65] Sujit Sivasundaram, 'Imperial Transgressions: The Animal and Human in the Idea of Race', *Comparative Studies of South Asia, Africa and the Middle East*, 35 (2015), 156–72; Meena Radhakrishna, 'Of Apes and Ancestors: Evolutionary Science and Colonial Ethnography', *Indian Historical Review*, 33 (2006), 1–23; Londa Schiebinger, 'Why Mammals Are Called Mammals: Gender Politics in Eighteenth-Century Natural History', *American Historical Review*, 98 (1993), 382–411.

with high imperialism,[66] informed imperial conservation policies that often framed colonised societies and cultures as primitive and destructive, while granting privileged access to protected wildlife to white colonials and local notables, criminalising indigenous uses of the natural world.[67] All these are powerful reasons for historians to be wary in their engagement with ecology. Wary, I would emphasise, but not aloof.

The growth in environmental history, although not yet a decisive 'turn', as Julia Adeney Thomas has rightly warned, has resulted in an imperative to go far beyond merely tracing and deconstructing changing ideas about the environment in the past towards instead acknowledging, and taking account of, environmental factors in history.[68] As practitioners in an aligned subfield, animal historians have developed innovative approaches to uncovering the traces of non-human creatures that went largely unrecorded but were either implicitly present in texts or materially necessary for historical processes to have unfolded.[69] To supplement the evidence that can be found among the extant anthropocentric colonial-era archival materials that have survived the perpetual instability of imperialism and the struggles of decolonisation – archives that were, no less than contemporaneous ecological studies, structured by the racial logics of governing colonial states – it is imperative for historians to creatively engage relevant scientific disciplines.[70] To abstain from doing

---

[66] Anker, *Imperial Ecology*, 1–6; Donald Worster, *Nature's Economy: A History of Ecological Ideas* (Cambridge, 1994).

[67] William Beinart, 'Introduction: The Politics of Colonial Conservation', *Journal of Southern African Studies*, 15 (1989), 143–62; Peter Boomgaard, 'Oriental Nature, Its Friends and Its Enemies: Conservation of Nature in Late-Colonial Indonesia, 1889–1949', *Environment and History*, 5 (1999), 257–92; Robert Cribb, 'Conservation in Colonial Indonesia', *Interventions*, 9 (2007), 49–61; Peter Vandergeest and Nancy Lee Peluso, 'Empires of Forestry: Professional Forestry and State Power in Southeast Asia, Part 1', *Environment and History*, 12 (2006), 31–64; Peter Vandergeest and Nancy Lee Peluso, 'Empires of Forestry: Professional Forestry and State Power in Southeast Asia, Part 2', *Environment and History*, 12 (2006), 359–93; Shafqat Hussain, 'Sports-Hunting, Fairness and Colonial Identity: Collaboration and Subversion in the Northwestern Frontier Region of the British Indian', *Conservation and Society*, 8 (2010), 112–26; Alice B. Kelly, 'Conservation Practice as Primitive Accumulation', *Journal of Peasant Studies*, 38 (2011), 683–701; Ezra Rashkow, 'Resistance to Hunting in Pre-Independence India: Religious Environmentalism, Ecological Nationalism or Cultural Conservation?', *Modern Asian Studies*, 49 (2015), 270–301.

[68] Julia Adeney Thomas, 'Comment: Not Yet Far Enough', *American Historical Review*, 117 (2012), 794–803; Linda Nash, 'The Agency of Nature or the Nature of Agency?', *Environmental History*, 10 (2005), 67–9; Greg Bankoff, '"Deep Forestry": Shapers of the Philippine Forests', *Environmental History*, 18 (2013), 523–56.

[69] Sandra Swart, '"But Where's the Bloody Horse?": Textuality and Corporeality in the "Animal Turn"', *Journal of Literary Studies*, 23 (2007), 271–92; Etienne Benson, 'Animal Writes: Historiography, Disciplinarity, and the Animal Trace', in *Making Animal Meaning*, ed. Linda Kalof and Georgina M. Montgomery (East Lansing, 2011), 3–16; Brett L. Walker, 'Animals and the Intimacy of History', *History and Theory*, 52, no. 4 (2013), 45–67; Angela Cassidy et al., 'Animal Roles and Traces in the History of Medicine, c.1880–1980', *BJHS Themes*, 2 (2017), 1–23; Nancy K. Turner, 'The Materiality of Medieval Parchment: A Response to "The Animal Turn"', *Revista Hispánica Moderna*, 71 (2018), 39–67.

[70] Nicholas B. Dirks, 'Colonial Histories and Native Informants: Biography of an Archive', in *Orientalism and the Postcolonial Predicament: Perspectives on South Asia*, ed. Peter van der Veer and Carol Appadurai Breckenridge (Philadelphia, 1993), 279–312; Ann Laura Stoler, 'Colonial Archives

so does not allow the historian to avoid being tainted by the power relations at play in the production of scientific knowledge, since these power relations were often too pervasive and persistent to be confined to a particular field of study at a moment in time.[71] Instead, such an abstention allows the silences that imperialism helped to produce to continue to structure the histories that we write.[72]

There is now a growing body of ecological literature that focuses in on Asian elephants.[73] Engaging with this knowledge as a historian requires foregrounding the tentative nature of the research. This is knowledge that is liable to change – as the ecologists conducting these studies frequently and openly acknowledge. The truth-claims in this scholarship are hesitant and tentative, rather than absolute. They present as largely observational in nature, and are thus reflexively engaged with the spatial limits of their veracity and the necessary conditions for extrapolation.[74] Moreover, though, these are also studies conducted *after* the history tracked in these pages. But that this research has been produced at a new historical conjuncture does not invalidate its utility to the historian. To the contrary, it might be read as establishing a baseline for apprehending the historical role played by elephants at an earlier time when their numbers were far greater, their herds larger and their ranges considerably less encroached upon; a time of richer biodiversity, when the current mass extinction of creatures had not accelerated to the extent that it has in the last half a century. Ecosystems are dynamic and historically contingent, but the functional roles played by particular species within them are often resilient; a resilience that allows for the potential of environmental recovery through rewilding megafauna.[75] By identifying the roles played today by

---

and the Arts of Governance', *Archival Science*, 2 (2002), 87–109; Ricardo Roque and Kim A. Wagner, 'Introduction: Engaging Colonial Knowledge', in *Engaging Colonial Knowledge: Reading European Archives in World History*, ed. Ricardo Roque and Kim A. Wagner (2012), 1–32.

[71] Here I disagree with the approach taken by Peder Anker to limit the historical study of ecologies in imperial contexts to the development of knowledge. Anker, *Imperial Ecology*, 1–6. For counterpoints that bring in ecological knowledge, see Walker, 'Animals and the Intimacy of History'; Bankoff, '"Deep Forestry"'; Mahesh Rangarajan, 'Animals with Rich Histories: The Case of the Lions of Gir Forest, Gujarat, India', *History and Theory*, 52, no. 4 (2013), 109–27. For an expansive understanding of the place of scientific knowledge, see Isabelle Stengers, *Cosmopolitics* (2 vols., Minneapolis, 2010), I.

[72] Deb Roy, 'Nonhuman Empires'; Kalpana Ram, 'The Silences in Dominant Discourses', *South Asia: Journal of South Asian Studies*, 38 (2015), 119–30.

[73] Sukumar, *The Asian Elephant*; Sukumar, *The Living Elephants*.

[74] However, as social theorists of ecological knowledge have shown, it is better understood as emanating from deeply embedded relations with their subject matter, critiquing the pretence of objective observation. See Tim Ingold, 'Two Reflections on Ecological Knowledge', in *Nature Knowledge: Ethnoscience, Cognition, and Utility*, ed. Glauco Sanga and Gherardo Ortalli (New York, Venice and Berghahn, 2003), 301–11; Anna Tsing, 'Arts of Inclusion, or How to Love a Mushroom', *Manoa*, 22 (2010), 191–203; Vinciane Despret, *What Would Animals Say If We Asked the Right Questions?* (Minneapolis, 2016).

[75] Liv Baker and Rebecca Winkler, 'Asian Elephant Rescue, Rehabilitation and Rewilding', *Animal Sentience*, 5, no. 28 (2020), 1–20; Joris P. G. M. Cromsigt *et al.*, 'Trophic Rewilding as a Climate Change Mitigation Strategy?', *Philosophical Transactions of the Royal Society B: Biological Sciences*, 373, no. 1761 (2018), n.p.

Asian elephants in tropical forests like those of Myanmar, we can make reasoned conjectures on the cascade effects precipitated by British imperialism.

Let us start with their diets. Elephants are huge creatures and their digestive systems are not especially efficient. In the wild, they absorb up to only half the nutrients from the food that they consume. When mature, they eat around 100 kilograms a day.[76] When free to range and forage beyond the coercive control of human captors, their staple foods consists of a varied diet of grasses, tree bark, small twigs, and fruits.[77] To accompany this vegetation, they drink from streams and other bodies of fresh water. In the hot season they use their trunks to tap the ground and through the vibrations locate the water table, and then digging to expose the subsoil water, sate their thirst. Salt licks also supplement this diet, providing essential minerals that are otherwise insufficient in the greenery that they devour in great quantities. It is thought that they locate these through their extraordinary sense of smell.[78] These dietary habits have several 'downstream' effects within their ecosystem. Some of these stem from the mineral-rich nature of their dung, of which more shortly. Others emanate from the manner of their eating.

Their grazing prunes and thins the forest and grass, allowing more sunlight to reach the surface of the ground. This then facilitates the healthy growth of this plant life that, in turn, feeds other herbivorous mammals. The selective nature of their dietary choices also benefits other species. Elephants debark trees, breaking up the bark and loosening it, making it easier for several varieties of deer to eat. They also strip twigs of leaves, discarding this unwanted foliage on the ground for sambar, barking deer and the like to tuck into. Their maintenance of grasses and bush also has an indirect effect of supporting homeostasis in predator–prey relationships. In India and sub-Saharan Africa this has been shown to be a boon to big-cat populations, as well as to the quarry that they hunt. Their discovery of subsoil water and salt licks is also to the benefit of many of the creatures that they live alongside. Gaur, sambar and spotted deer share the salt licks exposed by elephants. Jackals, civets and wild boars drink from the pools of water created by elephants during the dry season, and peafowls and other jungle birds wash themselves in them. In these various ways, through their dietary habits alone elephants perform essential

---

[76] Kanchan Puri, Vishant Yadav and Ritesh Joshi, 'Functional Role of Elephants in Maintaining Forest Ecosystem and Biodiversity: Lessons from Northwestern Elephant Range in India', *Asian Journal of Environment & Ecology*, 9, no. 2 (2019), 3.

[77] Nitin Sekar and Raman Sukumar, 'The Asian Elephant Is amongst the Top Three Frugivores of Two Tree Species with Easily Edible Fruit', *Journal of Tropical Ecology*, 31 (2015), 385–94; Ahimsa Campos-Arceiz et al., 'Working with Mahouts to Explore the Diet of Work Elephants in Myanmar (Burma)', *Ecological Research*, 23 (2008), 1057–64.

[78] Puri et al., 'Functional Role of Elephants'; Balasundaram Ramakrishnan et al., 'The Role of Elephants in the Forest Ecosystem and Its Conservation Problems in Southern India', in *Indian Hotspots: Vertebrate Faunal Diversity, Conservation and Management*, ed. Chandrakasan Sivaperuman and Krishnamoorthy Venkataraman (Singapore, 2018), 317–43.

tasks in rendering forested environments more habitable for a range of smaller animals.[79]

Their dung is worth considering in its own right. As a result of their low absorption of nutrients, it is exceptionally rich and the piles of faeces left by their herds become micro-habitats for a range of creatures. In a pleasing contrast of what humans consider sublime and profane, elephants' poo is particularly alluring to butterflies. Some of the minerals found within elephant dung are thought to be essential to the reproductive health of male butterflies. Whilst the excrement remains wet, it attracts hosts of insects including termites, centipedes and, importantly, beetles. Unsurprisingly, the insectine clusters that congregate on dung piles draw the attention of birds and reptiles. Peafowl and skinks are known to lurk around elephant poo to feed on the feasting insect populations. But it is not only animal life that thrives around dung piles, they provide excellent conditions for fungi. The mushrooms that flourish as a result form part of the diets of some particularly charismatic fauna native to Myanmar, including sloth bears and star tortoise. However, the most far-reaching downstream effect of elephant dung is probably its role in seed distribution. Indeed, the passing of seeds through the elephant's digestive tract and back into the ecosystem does more than just spread seeds across wider terrains. The digestive enzymes the seeds encounter on their intestinal odyssey encourage germination, significantly increasing the likelihood of the seeds flourishing into mature plants.[80] A group of creatures that are intimately tied to this process of seed dispersal are dung beetles.

Dung beetles depend upon mammalian dung to reproduce. Different species do so in differing fashions. For instance, tunnelling dung beetles, as the appellation would suggest, dig narrow, vertical chambers in animal faeces within which they lay their larvae, which then hatch and feed off their habitat to grow and thrive. This tunnelling itself has the positive effect of moving nutrient-rich organic material to the upper layers of the soil. Aside from improving the richness of the earth, their tunnelling also helps to distribute seeds. Seeds that remain in the elephant dung, from the beetles' perspective, are effectively in the way. They are taking up real estate that could be occupied by their larvae, and so the beetles remove them from the dung and bury them to free up more space for their own kind to thrive. In so doing, they inadvertently protect the seeds from predators and pathogens, reduce seed clumping, and direct the dispersal of seeds to more favourable environments. Their role as 'secondary seed distributors' is worthy of note because of their dependence on mammal communities, and their population's vulnerability to threats caused by habitat modification. Although variegated by local ecological factors, overall studies suggest that high-intensity logging appears to significantly

---

[79] Ramakrishnan *et al.*, 'The Role of Elephants'; Craig J. Tambling *et al.*, 'Elephants Facilitate Impact of Large Predators on Small Ungulate Prey Species', *Basic and Applied Ecology*, 14 (2013), 694–701.

[80] Puri *et al.*, 'Functional Role of Elephants'; Ramakrishnan *et al.*, 'The Role of Elephants'; Ahimsa Campos-Arceiz and Steve Blake, 'Megagardeners of the Forest: The Role of Elephants in Seed Dispersal', *Acta Oecologica*, Frugivores and Seed Dispersal: Mechanisms and Consequences of a Key Interaction for Biodiversity, 37 (2011), 542–53.

reduce the amount of dung removed by dung beetles and the effectiveness of their distribution of seeds. They are also severely impacted by falls in mammal species, and have been identified as being depleted through the cascade effects resulting from game hunting.[81]

These observations enable us to think through the cascading impacts of accumulation in colonial Myanmar. Not only were their fewer wild elephants, roaming across more restricted terrain in smaller herds, but the nature of captivity would have had an impact on the creatures who otherwise benefited from elephants' dietary habits. In Myanmar, when working in camps in forests leased to imperial timber firms, elephants had a degree of freedom. At night, they were permitted to roam around the surrounding forest and forage for food, although in this they were frustrated by the fetters and chains attached to their legs to stop them from escaping entirely. Bells attached around their necks alerted their drivers to their locations when they needed to be recovered for work in the morning. As a result, the variety of their diets would have been more restricted than when free. This was recognised by the elephant management literature of the colonial era. What was referred to as the 'artificial' nature of their working lives required 'artificial' interventions into their diet. Burmese elephant drivers were required to procure fodder for their charges, and this was predominantly grass, a variety identified through an engagement with indigenous knowledge as *kaing*. Twigs and bark were deemed optional extras to give a bit of variance. But more artificial still were the sugary and salty foods dispensed to them, such as elephantine chapatis and jaggery sweets that were produced to meet the perceived needs of the labouring elephants, who were forced to work during the hours when in their days of freedom they would have rested and slept.[82] Their changed metabolism, expenditure of energy, and resulting stress from the hard labour of shifting teak required a more calorific diet, particularly during the hot season when elephants were less able to graze while they worked.[83]

Their limited mobility and changed diets would have had cascade effects. Firstly, the dung. Its content and quality would have been altered by the change in menu, and while it is difficult to know how this would have affected those insects who fed on it (let alone the creatures further along the chain that predated on them), it seems likely that the restricted range of vegetation and the addition of human-prepared supplementary meals would have reduced the

[81] E. Nichols *et al.*, 'Ecological Functions and Ecosystem Services Provided by Scarabaeinae Dung Beetles', *Biological Conservation*, 141 (2008), 1461–74; E. Nichols *et al.*, 'Co-Declining Mammals and Dung Beetles: An Impending Ecological Cascade', *Oikos*, 118 (2009), 481–7; Eleanor M. Slade, Darren J. Mann and Owen T. Lewis, 'Biodiversity and Ecosystem Function of Tropical Forest Dung Beetles under Contrasting Logging Regimes', *Biological Conservation*, 144 (2011), 166–74.

[82] George H. Evans, *Elephants and Their Diseases: A Treatise on Elephants*, 2nd edn (Rangoon, 1910), 16–22; G. Pfaff, *Reports on the Investigation of Diseases of Elephants* (Rangoon, 1940), 8–9; Jonathan Saha, 'Colonizing Elephants: Animal Agency, Undead Capital and Imperial Science in British Burma', *BJHS Themes*, 2 (2017), 169–89.

[83] Jonathan Saha, 'Do Elephants Have Souls? Animal Subjectivities and Colonial Governmentality', in *South Asian Governmentalities*, ed. Stephen Legg and Deana Heath (Cambridge, 2018), 159–77; Hannah S. Mumby *et al.*, 'Stress and Body Condition Are Associated with Climate and Demography in Asian Elephants', *Conservation Physiology*, 3 (2015), 1–14.

variety of nutrients that passed through the elephants' bodies. The fetters and chains would have meant that their dung was also spread over a much smaller range, and whatever defecations they produced during the day would have been located in areas affected by the near-constant disruption of logging. This would have limited the dispersal of seeds, particularly given the grass-based focus of the fodder, and disturbed the insect assemblages otherwise attracted to dung piles, as well as the birds and reptiles that used them as hunting grounds. The presence of humans in the vicinity of the dung would likely have discouraged visitations of cautious animals, such as sloth bears, who may have come in search of mushrooms. As already noted above, logging reduces the activity of dung beetles that would otherwise remove dung to more favourable sites and facilitate greater seed distribution, as well as more successful germination. As a result, the spread of vegetation that sustained deer and other ungulates would likely have been more limited through the mass conscription of elephants into the timber industry.

The provision of fodder to the elephant workforce, the tendency to establish elephant camps near bodies of fresh water for ease of hydration and ablutions, and the hobbling of elephants' mobility, would also have had knock-on effects. The vital work of elephants in finding and exposing subsoil water and salt licks would not have been done on the same scale, having a direct impact on the health of deer, wild boar and other small mammals. In considerable swathes of Myanmar, forests would have been left untended by elephants' grazing, pruning and thinning forest and grasses, a gardening role that helped stabilise deer and tiger populations;[84] both of which were also under threat from increased predation from humans. Finally, returning to the frogs with whom I opened this paper, the micro-habitats left in the wake of elephants' migrations would have been less extensive. There would have been fewer protected spaces for amphibians, along with some small mammals, to breed hidden from predators.[85]

The fate of Burmese elephants during colonial rule was not as apocalyptic as the advent of Empire proved for many other species in Myanmar: rhinoceros and crocodiles, for instance, saw their populations decimated to the thresholds of unsustainable levels.[86] Elephants were still endangered, but have survived in viable numbers. It has been posited by Thomas Trautmann that the continued utility of elephants in South and Southeast Asia may be the key to understanding why they have survived in the region, but have, for the most part, retreated from China.[87] Jacob Shell has gone further to suggest that the assemblages of humans and elephants apparent in Myanmar's border regions, as evasive modes of mobility and producers of subversive logistical infrastructures, might point the way to a more sustainable future in the context of climate

---

[84] Tambling *et al.*, 'Elephants Facilitate Impact of Large Predators on Small Ungulate Prey Species'.

[85] Platt *et al.*, 'Water-Filled Asian Elephant Tracks Serve as Breeding Sites for Anurans in Myanmar'; Robert M. Pringle, 'Elephants as Agents of Habitat Creation for Small Vertebrates at the Patch Scale', *Ecology*, 89 (2008), 26–33.

[86] Saha, *Colonizing Animals*, 83–105.

[87] Thomas R. Trautmann, *Elephants and Kings: An Environmental History* (Chicago, 2015); Mark Elvin, *Retreat of the Elephants: An Environmental History of China* (New Haven, 2004).

change and ecological disaster.[88] Nevertheless, the history of elephants contains multitudes. Creatures, such as dung beetles and frogs, who rarely make it into archival collections in their own right, were intertwined and implicated in the lives of Myanmar's forest-dwelling giants. The transformations in elephant demographics and behaviour wrought by their mobilisation for teak production, the destruction of much of their habitats, and widespread hunting, cascaded. We might not be able to reconstruct precisely what happened to those creatures who benefited from, even depended upon, the ecosystem engineering performed by elephants. But we can conjecture that life got harder and the margins for survival narrowed.

Animal history has opened up new interdisciplinary dialogues between the environmental and biological sciences, and the humanities. These dialogues have often taken place within one of two different conversations. One has been about the advent of the Anthropocene, the term deployed by a substantial number of scientists, social scientists and humanities scholars to connote a new geological epoch in which humans have become the single largest factor shaping the whole planet's ecology, and climate. The second conversation has concerned the benefits and pitfalls of the use of current scientific knowledge to aid our understanding of non-human creatures' actions and experiences in the past. Both of these conversations have been, in equal parts, inspiring and unsettling for historians; facilitating innovative approaches to researching and writing animal history, and also precipitating a broader conceptual and methodological crisis within the humanities.[89] These conversations are urgent and valuable, but there are others to be had alongside them. Another subject that animal history's interdisciplinary dialogue might broach, this paper suggests, is a discussion of the concepts that are used for explaining causation and change over time in different disciplines.

As I hope to have demonstrated, there are two particular concepts – one drawn from the humanities and social sciences, and the other from ecology – that are worth examining to open this new conversation: 'accumulation' and 'cascade'.

---

[88] Shell, 'Elephant Riders of the Hukawng Valley'.

[89] For an overview of the emergence of animal history and new directions in the field see Joshua Specht, 'Animal History after Its Triumph: Unexpected Animals, Evolutionary Approaches, and the Animal Lens', *History Compass*, 14 (2016), 326–36; for studies integrating historical research and scientific data to examine the Anthropocene, see Libby Robin and Will Steffen, 'History for the Anthropocene', *History Compass*, 5 (2007), 1694–1719; Robert Davis, 'Inventing the Present: Historical Roots of the Anthropocene', *Earth Sciences History*, 30 (2011), 63–84; Will Steffen *et al.*, 'The Anthropocene: Conceptual and Historical Perspectives', *Philosophical Transactions of the Royal Society A: Mathematical, Physical and Engineering Sciences*, 369 (2011), 842–67; for two very different approaches that draw on current scientific studies to write animal history, see Sam White, 'From Globalized Pig Breeds to Capitalist Pigs: A Study in Animal Cultures and Evolutionary History', *Environmental History*, 16 (2011), 94–120; Erica Fudge, 'Milking Other Men's Beasts', *History and Theory*, 52, no. 4 (2013), 13–28; and for some reflections on the challenges of these conversations, see Dipesh Chakrabarty, 'The Climate of History: Four Theses', *Critical Inquiry*, 35 (2009), 197–222; Thomas, 'Comment'; Ian Baucom, 'History 4°: Postcolonial Method and Anthropocene Time', *Cambridge Journal of Postcolonial Literary Inquiry*, 1 (2014), 123–42; Zoe Todd, 'Indigenizing the Anthropocene', in *Art in the Anthropocene: Encounters among Aesthetics, Politics, Environment and Epistemology*, ed. Heather Davis and Etienne Turpin (2015), 241–54.

The value of both of these concepts lies in their ability to offer causative expla-nations of change over time that do not rely upon there being knowing human agents consciously driving historical shifts.[90] As such, bringing these concepts together can move conversations on from the more abstract questions asses-sing the historiographical import of historians' engagements with environ-mental and biological sciences, to identifying interdisciplinary tools for explicating the dynamics behind specific environmental histories.[91] I hope that this paper has gone some way towards demonstrating the utility of both concepts in the case of elephants in Myanmar during the period of British colonial rule. These giant creatures became pivotal to the colony's timber industry, one of the most important sites for commercial forestry in the Empire.[92] They simultaneously had their habitats decimated and frag-mented by the unprecedented expansion of rice cultivation. Consequently, as frequently identified 'keystone species' and as well-acknowledged 'ecosystem engineers', the profound changes in the lives of Myanmar's Asian elephants would have had significant knock-on effects upon a range of other flora and fauna. Theirs is a history whose multispecies dimensions are more fully appre-ciated when conceptualised as having been caught up in accumulatory dynamics and cascade effects.

Acknowledgments. A version of this article was first presented as a Royal Historical Society lecture, read on 24 September 2021.

Funding statement. The research for this paper was made possible by an Arts and Humanities Research Council Early Career Fellowship (2014–15) and Follow-on-Funding (2017), as well as an Independent Social Research Foundation Mid-Career Fellowship (2019–20). I am extremely grateful for this support.

---

[90] For some of the key works that have influenced my emphasis on this approach to agency, see Nash, 'The Agency of Nature or the Nature of Agency?'; Vinciane Despret, 'From Secret Agents to Interagency', *History and Theory*, 52, no. 4 (2013), 29–44; Deb Roy, 'Nonhuman Empires'.

[91] Here I am responding in part to work that takes seriously the transformative implications of biological knowledge for the humanities. See Julia Adeney Thomas, 'History and Biology in the Anthropocene: Problems of Scale, Problems of Value', *American Historical Review*, 119 (2014), 1587–1607; Samantha Frost, *Biocultural Creatures: Toward a New Theory of the Human* (Durham, NC: Duke University Press, 2016).

[92] Wright, *Twentieth Century Impressions of Burma*, 184–94; Macaulay, *History of the Bombay Burmah Trading Corporation*; U Toke Gale, *Burmese Timber Elephant* (Rangoon, 1974); Bryant, *Political Ecology of Forestry*; Raymond L. Bryant, 'Branding Natural Resources: Science, Violence and Marketing in the Making of Teak', *Transactions of the Institute of British Geographers*, 38 (2013), 517–30; Saha, 'Colonizing Elephants'; David C. Wohlers, 'Prome, Burma – How a Village in Colonial Burma Became the Global Epicenter of Scientific Forestry and Impacted the Founding of the United States Forest Service', *Journal of Forestry*, 117 (2019), 515–24.

Cite this article: Saha J (2022). Accumulations and Cascades: Burmese Elephants and the Ecological Impact of British Imperialism. *Transactions of the Royal Historical Society* 32, 177–197. https://doi.org/10.1017/S0080440122000044

Transactions of the RHS (2022), **32**, 199–221
doi:10.1017/S0080440122000032

ARTICLE

The Contested Right of Public Meeting in England from the Bill of Rights to the Public Order Acts

Katrina Navickas

School of Humanities, University of Hertfordshire, Hatfield, Herts AL10 9AB, UK
Email k.navickas@herts.ac.uk

(Received 2 February 2022; accepted 13 February 2022)

Abstract

The 'right of public meeting' has historically been a key demand of extra-parliamentary political movements in England. This paper examines how public assembly came to be perceived as a legally protected right, and how national and local authorities debated and policed political meetings. Whereas previous histories have suggested that a 'liberal governance' dominated urban government during the nineteenth century, this paper offers an alternative framework for understanding the relationship between people and the state. It points to rights paradoxes, whereby the right of free passage and to 'air and recreation' often conflicted with the demand for the right of political meeting in challenges to use of public spaces. Local authorities sought to defend the rights of property against political movements by using the common law offences of obstruction and 'nuisance'. By the first half of the twentieth century, new threats of militant tactics and racial harassment by political groups necessitated specific public order legislation. Though twentieth-century legislation sought to protect certain types of assembly and protest marches, the implementation and policing of public order was spatially discriminatory, and the right of public meeting was left unresolved.

Keywords: Britain; public meetings; protest; public order

The 'right of public meeting' has historically been a key demand of popular political movements in Britain. The public meeting legitimated local elites within a constitutional process, but was also a site of contest, involving challenge to authority. All types of political associations in the eighteenth and nineteenth centuries claimed the legitimate right to hold meetings, alongside the rights of petitioning the monarch and Parliament and free speech, with reference to Magna Carta and the 1689 Bill of Rights. Perhaps even more than petitioning, participation in a public meeting was the most common experience that most of the population had of political debate and collective action before and indeed still after enfranchisement. Yet there was no legal right of public assembly in England and Wales until the Human Rights Act of 1998, which came into force in 2000. While the right of free speech was evident in case law by the late nineteenth century, precedents for the right of public assembly were much more intermittent, and still remain contested.[1] What Americans usually refer to as the law governing 'freedom of assembly' generally translates in the English context to the law of 'public order'.[2] Contemporary legal scholar A. C. Dicey recognised this ambiguity in his article 'On the Right of Public Meeting' in the *Contemporary Review* in 1889, published at the height of the crisis over the policing of socialist rallies in Trafalgar Square in London. Dicey concluded that there was no clarity, whether in common law, statute or legal precedent. Even if a meeting started out as lawful, that is with permission from the local authorities, a small breach of the peace would transform it into an unlawful assembly.[3] The debated distinctions between rights and liberties to meet are at the heart of the tensions stoked by political movements throughout this period.

This paper examines how public assembly and protest came to be popularly perceived as a legally protected right in England, and how government and local authorities debated and policed political meetings. It argues that these debates were an integral part of how the constitutional polity has developed since 1689, in ways that allowed for participatory but not democratic involvement by the unrepresented populace until the early twentieth century. This is by no means a narrative of democratising progress. It is rather a story of tensions, setbacks and intermittent repressive legislation and policing. I argue that the legal, statutory and police control of public meetings were driven by three paradoxes of English law: the first conflating rights with liberties; the other two that privileged common rights of air and recreation and free passage in public spaces over the liberty of public assembly. The article demonstrates how the peak of debates about the right of public meeting in England was reached when the government had delegated much of the decision-making back to local authorities and the police, but public order legislation had to be introduced centrally in response to new challenges of militancy and racial harassment in the early twentieth century.

Defining the public meeting

Public meetings took various forms, both official and unofficial. Formally constituted public meetings were held by a panoply of institutions, including the parish vestry, town council, the lord lieutenancy and county, and gatherings of ratepayers, or corporate guilds, and, after incorporation in the mid-nineteenth

---

[1] D. Mead, *The New Law of Peaceful Protest: Rights and Regulation in the Human Rights Act Era* (2010), 4.

[2] R. Vorspan, 'Freedom of Assembly: The Right to Passage in Modern English Legal History', *San Diego Law Review*, 34 (1997), 940 n. 67.

[3] A. V. Dicey, 'On the Right of Public Meeting', *Contemporary Review*, 55 (Apr. 1889), 508–27; Vorspan, 'Freedom of Assembly', 921–46, at 941.

century, increasingly town meetings. They usually followed an official process, called by a mayor or other official in response to a requisition from an (often specified minimum) number of 'respectable' inhabitants, usually to pass resolutions, sign a petition to Parliament or ratify an address to the monarch.[4] An 1857 House of Commons Select Committee, for example, reported that 'a public meeting should be a meeting lawfully called by the sheriff of a county or by the mayor of a borough, a meeting for the purpose of petitioning the Crown or either house of Parliament, a meeting of a town council, board of health or any public body'.[5] Though technically restricted to the membership of the body such as vestry members and ratepayers, in practice usually anyone could turn up, and entrance was only controlled in times of party political conflict.

Unofficial public meetings were called by acclamation or advertisement, and were just as mixed in their participation. The mass public meeting, held outside in town squares or marketplaces, or inside in civic or commercial buildings, often still abided by the ritual processes of an official meeting with speakers, committee, resolutions, amendments and voting. Open public meetings often shaded into other types of gatherings, like assemblies, demonstrations, electoral hustings and rallies.[6] Unlawful or tumultuous assembly was an offence under common law. Early modern legislation concerning public meetings aimed at preventing or restricting the practice of petitioning Parliament or the monarch. The 1661 Act against Tumultuous Disorders was intended to manage the huge volume of petitions that were taking up a significant proportion of parliamentary business, by limiting to twelve the number of persons who could present a petition. The 1689 Bill of Rights guaranteed the subject's right to petition, but the 1661 legislation ambiguously remained on the statute book and was invoked as late as 1817 during the 'March of the Blanketeers', when Manchester democratic radicals sought to stay within the rules to petition the Prince Regent. The 1714 Riot Act allowed magistrates to disperse tumultuous meetings by force with warning and was the main legislative tool used against public gatherings in the eighteenth century.[7]

An important shift in the form and purpose of public meetings occurred from the 1760s onwards. Emerging calls for parliamentary reform, and the populism of the agitation around renegade politician John Wilkes in 1768–9 created a new type of mass meeting. The pro-Wilkes crowds, independently of John Wilkes himself, appropriated and subverted official rites and processes of the county meeting and the electoral hustings.[8] From the 1790s onwards,

[4] See J. Innes, 'The Local Acts of a National Parliament: Parliament's Role in Sanctioning Local Action in Eighteenth-Century Britain', *Parliamentary History*, 17 (1998), 23–47.

[5] *Hansard's Parliamentary Debates* (hereafter *Hansard*), HL Deb., 13 July 1857, vol. 146, cc. 1363–6, https://api.parliament.uk/historic-hansard/lords/1857/jul/13/report-of-select-committee-presented.

[6] H. T. Dickinson, *The Politics of the People in Eighteenth Century Britain* (Houndmills, 1994), 103–5.

[7] M. Knights, '"The Lowest Degree of Freedom": The Right to Petition Parliament, 1640–1800', *Parliamentary History*, 37 (2018), 18–34, at 21–2; R. Poole, 'Petitioners and Rebels: Petitioning for Parliamentary Reform in Regency England', *Social Science History*, 43 (2019), 553–79, at 572.

[8] J. Rudbeck, 'Popular Sovereignty and the Historical Origin of the Social Movement', *Theory and Society*, 41 (2012), 581–601.

with the emergence of the first working-class democratic movement, these extra-official forms of public meeting were regularised. Radical delegate conventions and the 'mass platform' hustings sought legitimacy by taking the same forms of requisitioning, chair and resolutions, but were increasingly sites of conflict as the local authorities refused permission for them to be held. The Peterloo Massacre in Manchester on 16 August 1819 was the result of long-running tensions between the working-class democratic movement, local authorities and national government over what, and who, constituted a public meeting.[9]

Social movement theorist Charles Tilly saw the 'rise of the public meeting' (by which he meant the mass platform demonstration) as a key part of the democratisation of British politics. Tilly identified a key shift in what he termed contentious gatherings, away from an early modern mode of parochial and riotous collective action aimed directly at local figures of authority or relying on intermediaries to speak to power, to a less violent and more national and Parliament-focused polity by the early nineteenth century. His treatment of the public meeting and other categorisations of types of action, however, conflated official and unofficial meetings. His progression thesis moreover underestimated popular participation in town meetings before the 1760s while overestimating the dominance of the Parliament-focused public meeting by the 1830s.[10]

The 'new political history' in the 1990s suggested a more pessimistic but equally teleological trajectory. Gareth Stedman Jones, James Vernon and others considered the middle decades of the nineteenth century, in particular, as a battleground of ideas between emerging liberalism and more militant claims by radicals to represent 'the people'.[11] These historians strongly argued for constitutionalism as the populist discourse that subsumed, if not vanquished, the language of class that Marxist interpretations had previously identified as the politics of the people. Vernon saw in the pattern of public meetings and legislation to 1867 the 'fall of political man and closure of the constitution's radical libertarian democratic potential'.[12] He emphasised a marked decline in the power of the people to create their own politics. The new political history and urban historians attributed this decline to the emergence of a 'liberal governmentality' by the mid-nineteenth century. Patrick Joyce argued that the relationship between local elites and the state was dominated by a middle-class morality that was implemented through policing, sanitation and civic regulation schemes.[13] While his approach was influenced by

---

[9] M. Lobban, 'From Seditious Libel to Unlawful Assembly: Peterloo and the Changing Face of Political Crime c.1770–1820', *Oxford Journal of Legal Studies*, 10 (1990), 307–52.

[10] C. Tilly, 'The Rise of the Public Meeting in Great Britain, 1758–1834', *Social Science History*, 34 (2010), 291–9.

[11] J. Vernon, *Politics and the People: A Study in English Political Culture, c.1815–1867* (Cambridge, 1993); P. Joyce, *Visions of the People: Industrial England and the Question of Class, c.1848–1914* (Cambridge, 1991); G. Stedman Jones, *Languages of Class: Studies in English Working Class History, 1832–1982* (Cambridge, 1983).

[12] Vernon, *Politics and the People*, 336.

[13] P. Joyce, *The Rule of Freedom: Liberalism and the Modern City* (2011).

Michel Foucault, others drew from Norbert Elias's 'civilising thesis', whereby urban improvement likewise cemented the power of the middle-class and gentry elites over the streets.[14] Protest and popular politics was thereby controlled and regulated through municipal government and middle-class cultural hegemony in the city.

Studies of nineteenth-century popular politics have fragmented somewhat since the 1990s, examining individual political movements within a short time frame rather than across the whole period.[15] This paper encourages a return to a *longue durée*. One approach has been suggested by more recent work on petitions by Richard Huzzey, Henry Miller and Mark Knights among others.[16] They show how petitioning was a vital part of popular politics from the 1640s to the turn of the twentieth century. They also note a shift in how the right of petitioning Parliament was framed. Whereas earlier in the period, petitioning was claimed as an inherent right on its own, by the later eighteenth century there was, as Knights argues, an 'increasing tendency to view the right to petition as part of a group of mutually supporting rights, the most important of which were the right to assembly and the right to freedom of speech and print'.[17] I argue that the coalescence of the idea of the right to petition with a concept of the right of public meeting and free speech was an ongoing process of assertion of popular rights. Moreover, petitions were a major reason for many public meetings, but they were not the only purpose or result of them. There were many other types of political meeting and assembly, as we will see, that were just as integral to sustaining and contesting different relationships with the idea of the constitutional state.

This paper challenges the perceived extent to which the dominance of liberal elites resulted in diminished popular agency or class conflict. We need an alternative to both the optimistic trajectory charted by Tilly and the

---

[14] S. Gunn, *The Public Culture of the Victorian Middle Class: Ritual and Authority in the English Industrial City, 1840-1914* (Manchester, 2007)

[15] See for example R. Poole, *Peterloo: An English Uprising* (Manchester, 2019); Malcolm Chase, *Chartism: A New History* (Manchester, 2007).

[16] R. Huzzey and H. Miller, 'Petitions, Parliament and Political Culture: Petitioning the House of Commons, 1780–1918', *Past & Present*, 248 (2020), 123–64; M. Chase, 'What Did Chartism Petition For? Mass Petitions in the British Movement for Democracy', *Social Science History*, 43 (2019), 531–51; P. Loft, 'Involving the Public: Parliament, Petitioning and the Language of Interest, 1688–1720', *Journal of British Studies*, 40 (2016), 1–23; P. Loft, 'Petitioning and Petitioners to the Westminster Parliament, 1660–1788', *Parliamentary History*, 38 (2019), 342–61; H. Miller, 'Petition, Petition, Petition', in *Organising Democracy: Reflections on the Rise of Political Organizations in the Nineteenth Century*, ed. H. te Velde and M. Janse (2017), 43–61; H. Miller, 'Popular Petitioning and the Corn Laws, 1833–46', *English Historical Review*, 127 (2012), 882–919; B. Agnès, 'A Chartist Singularity? Mobilizing to Promote Democratic Petitions in Britain and France, 1838–1848', *Labour History Review*, 78 (2013), 51–66; P. A. Pickering, '"And your Petitioners, &c": Chartist Petitioning in Popular Politics, 1838–48', *English Historical Review*, 116 (2001), 368–88. Studies of petitioning from the empire include: *Native Claims: Indigenous Law against Empire, 1500-1920*, ed. S. Belmessous (Oxford, 2012); H. Weiss Muller, 'From Requete to Petition: Petitioning the Monarch between Empires', *Historical Journal*, 60 (2017), 659–86; K. O'Brien, *Petitioning for Land: the Petitions of First People of Modern British Colonies* (2018).

[17] Knights, '"The Lowest Degree of Freedom"', 32.

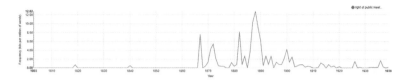

Figure 1 House of Commons debates, 1803–1939, frequency of the phrase 'right of public meeting', from *Hansard at Huddersfield* (2019), University of Huddersfield, https://hansard.hud.ac.uk

pessimistic model suggested by the 'new political history' that portrayed an increasingly exclusive and homogeneous political culture. Rather, the contests over the uses of public space for political meetings demonstrated the continuance of an independent radical tradition, and an active working-class politics separate from middle-class liberal discourse.[18] The paper draws upon the work of David Churchill, Christopher Hamlin and historians of nineteenth-century crime who challenge the model of liberal governance as structuring all relations between people and the state.[19] Rather, popular politics involved a more patchy and unfinished framework of policing and the law.

Debating the right of public meeting

There is a distinctive chronology to the debates around the idea of a right of public meeting. Using the text-mining tool of *Hansard at Huddersfield* we can track the use of the term in parliamentary debates from 1803 onwards (see Figure 1). The first instance of the term 'right of public meeting' was recorded in a House of Commons debate on 21 December 1819, on the Blasphemous Libel Bill, part of the Six Acts following the Peterloo Massacre. Lord Ebrington, a consistent supporter of the Whig opposition to the Tory government measures against popular radicalism, denounced the bill, claiming: 'Parliament had already restricted the right of public meeting.'[20]

The term 'right of public meeting' was already regularly employed in the constitutionalist discourse of popular radicalism. Political movements employed the rhetorical tropes of Magna Carta and the 1689 Bill of Rights to justify the right of public meeting. Yet the Bill of Rights only protected the right of petitioning the Crown, it did not guarantee the right of public assembly. Conventions and delegate meetings of parliamentary reformers and democratic radicals drew on the writings of James Burgh and other Whig calls on historical precedents in the Anglo-Saxon Witan, whose

---

[18] A. Taylor, 'Commons Stealers, Land-Grabbers and Jerry Builders: Space, Popular Radicalism and the Politics of Public Access in London, 1848–1880', *International Review of Social History*, 40 (1995), 383–407, at 394; M. Finn, *After Chartism: Class and Nation in English Radical Politics, 1848–1874* (Cambridge, 1993).

[19] D. Churchill, *Crime Control and Everyday Life in the Victorian City: The Police and the Public* (Oxford, 2017); C. Hamlin, 'Nuisances and Community in Mid Victorian England: The Attractions of Inspection', *Social History*, 38 (2013), 346–79.

[20] *Hansard*, HC Deb., 21 Dec. 1819, vol. 41, cc. 1414–45, https://api.parliament.uk/historic-hansard/commons/1819/dec/21/blasphemous-libel-bill.

representation was claimed to have been destroyed by William I and the so-called Norman Yoke. From the 1780s onwards, these historicist frameworks were combined with notions of absolute natural rights drawn from interpretations of John Locke's and Thomas Paine's constitutional writings (though of course these rights were overtly confined to the 'freeborn Englishman' and did not include women or indigenous colonial subjects).[21]

The 'Two Acts' passed in 1795 restricted popular political meetings and widened the remit of treason. The popular response was national, and divided into petitions for and against the legislation. The resolutions of hundreds of meetings of vestries, towns and counties were all collated in the compilation *The History of Two Acts*. Many of the petitions against William Pitt the Younger's measures liberally employed Whiggish rhetoric claiming the right to public discussion or meeting as protected by the 1689 Bill of Rights. Whether this was deeply felt ideology or more tactical in speaking parliamentary language to convince, it nevertheless entrenched the connection. For example, the Northumberland county meeting at Morpeth on 25 November 1795 unanimously passed three resolutions:

I. That the Bill of Rights is an essential component part of that original contract between the King and People, recognized and confirmed at the aera of the Revolution.

II. That the Freedom of Public Discussion and Petitioning for Redress of Grievances is one of the ancient, true and undoubted privileges of the People of England, ratified to them by the Bill of Rights.

III. That any attempt, directly or indirectly, to restrain or curtail the Freedom of Public Discussion is a violation of the Constitution, has a tendency to annul the Bill of Rights, and thereby to break the original contract between King and People.[22]

The 1817 and 1819 Seditious Meetings Acts, and the debates about the legality of the Manchester meeting that became the Peterloo Massacre, sought to draw a line between the officially called public meeting and the mass platform rally. The ultra-loyalist reaction to Peterloo was expressed in *An Inquiry into the Law Relative to Public Assemblies of the People* by Sir Codrington Edmund Carrington, chair of Buckinghamshire Quarter Sessions. Carrington melodramatically questioned the right of the people to use acclamation and consent to form a public meeting rather than go through the official channels of the requisition to the respectable local elites:

A Right, it seems, is claimed and exercised by those who style themselves Radical Reformers, to assemble the people, by *public* notification, upon any *public* occasion, at any time, in any place, and in any numbers; and to propose such subjects of petition, remonstrance, deliberation, or

---

[21] T. M. Parssinen; 'Association, Convention and Anti-Parliament in British Radical Politics, 1771–1848', *English Historical Review*, 88 (1973), 504–33.

[22] *The History of Two Acts* (1796), 300.

resolution, to the *acclamation and consent* of the assemblage thus brought together, as they may think fit.

In a country governed by law, with a Representative Body to watch over the interests of the people, have the Demagogues of the present day the right they so loudly assert, and so perilously exercise?[23]

By the time of the emergence of the Chartist movement in the late 1830s, the idea of the right was well established in radical discourse. William Lovett, secretary of the Chartist National Convention, was arrested and tried for seditious libel for his participation in the Bull Ring mass meeting in Birmingham in July 1839. At his trial, Lovett made an impassioned speech to the jury, proclaiming: 'an illegal and unconstitutional attack has been made on the right of public meeting; and be it remembered this right is broadly admitted and generally established by the fact of petitions emanating from such meetings being recognised by the legislature'. The counter-argument by the prosecution focused on the definitions set by the older seditious meetings legislation and common law: 'the meetings in the Bull Ring ... were not constitutional meetings; but tumultuous assemblies. The magistrates interfered with these meetings because they were called upon by the peaceable inhabitants to put them down.'[24] As crowds became more orderly and peaceful, authorities came to look upon the assembly itself – rather than its violence or seditious words – as the crime. The Seditious Meetings Acts, or more specifically trials of radicals arrested at mass demonstrations, had set the precedent that public meetings were seditious if they were judged by magistrates to cause 'terror to the respectable inhabitants'. Royal proclamations were issued against Chartist torchlit processions and meetings in the winter of 1838–9, but once they had expired, no further legislation was passed directly against political meetings. The somewhat amorphous and clearly class-based yardstick of fear among the well-to-do, whether the gathering was orderly or not, gradually replaced the more difficult-to-prove seditious libel spoken on the hustings as the reason given by authorities to refuse permission for mass meetings before they occurred and to disperse them by force if they took place.[25] Political meetings became a matter of local public order rather than national threats of sedition. This definition continued right through the nineteenth century. For example, in 1890 the Northampton magistrates sought to prevent a temperance meeting in the market square: their justification lay in a definition laid out by the Commissioners on the Criminal Code Bill of 1879: 'an assembly may be unlawful if it causes persons in the neighbourhood to fear that it will needlessly and without reasonable occasion provoke others to disturb the peace tumultuously'.[26]

---

[23] C. E. Carrington, *An Inquiry into the Law Relative to Public Assemblies of the People* (1819), 5, emphasis in original.

[24] *The Trial of W. Lovett ... for a Seditious Libel; ... at the Assizes at Warwick, the 6th of August, 1839*, 2nd edn (1839), 18.

[25] Lobban, 'From Seditious Libel to Unlawful Assembly', 345.

[26] *Return to an Address of the House of Commons*, 4 December 1890. Durham University Library, Earl Grey pamphlets collection: *Hansard*, HC Deb. 24 Jun. 1890, vol. 345, cc. 1807–21, https://api.parliament.uk/historic-hansard/commons/1890/jun/24/motionfor-adjournment.

The term 'right of public meeting' did not register regularly in parliamentary debates again until the 1866–7 Second Reform Bill. Radical movements continued to quote the constitutionalist idiom. As Antony Taylor has pointed out in his study of the reform agitation of 1866, most radicals preferred to employ the more elastic and less provable tropes of Anglo-Saxon freedoms rather than follow Reform League leader and lawyer Edmond Beales's more intensive approach of forensically challenging the specifics of the by-laws and current legislation that prevented them from meeting in Hyde Park.[27] With a couple of intervening peaks around the Fenian disturbances in Ireland in 1871 and 1882, the largest number of speeches debating or prominently mentioning 'the right of public meeting' took place in 1888 (forty-four in total), as did the greatest frequency of use of the term in debates. The Social Democratic Federation (SDF)'s challenge over the use of Trafalgar Square and other sites in the capital in the 1880s led to a proliferation of debate, publications, trials and legal judgements on whether the right of public meeting existed or had precedents.

London plays a central part in these debates and their historiography, particularly in the 1860s to 1880s.[28] The spaces of Trafalgar Square and Hyde Park naturally attract attention because they were the subjects of key parliamentary debates, legislation and policing. London's popular politics was unique spatially because of its direct connection to the centre of power. The Metropolitan police and special constables were under the centralised direction of the Home Office, unlike the systems of lord lieutenants and county constabularies outside the capital. Chartism in the 1840s and the Reform League in 1866–7, as Taylor points out, 'thus directly confronted the apparatus of central government in the seat of its authority'.[29] There were two key turning points in the London situation. First, an Act of 1877 authorised the Metropolitan Board of Works to control and manage parks and commons, and make by-laws, including against public meetings.[30] Second, the appointment of Sir Charles Warren as Metropolitan police commissioner in 1886 gave rise to a more militaristic form of policing, part of which was the enforcement of a ban on public meetings in Trafalgar Square, leading to what became known as the Bloody Sunday attack on the socialists in November 1887. The radical agitation in the capital was strongly confrontational. The socialists in particular sought to make these contests into class conflict rather than sticking to polite liberal discourse. Magna Carta or the Bill of Rights were hardly if at all cited in these debates, though Liberals regularly referred to the more generic 'constitution' in defending the right of meeting.

[27] Taylor, 'Commons Stealers', 390.

[28] L. Keller, *Triumph of Order: Democracy and Public Space in New York and London* (New York, 2010); I. Channing, *The Police and the Expansion of Public Order Law in Britain, 1829-2012* (2017); H. Awcock, 'The Geographies of Protest and Public Space in Mid-Nineteenth-Century London: The Hyde Park Railings Affair', *Historical Geography*, 47 (2019), 194-217; A. Davin, 'Socialist Infidels and Messengers of Light: Street Preaching and Debate in Mid-19th Century London', in *The Streets of London: From the Great Fire to the Great Stink*, ed. Tim Hitchcock and Heather Shore (2003), 165-71.

[29] Taylor, 'Commons Stealers', 387.

[30] Keller, *Triumph of Order*, 106.

The parliamentary response to the socialist and labour disturbances of the 1880s sought to define the status of public meetings once and for all, alongside more specific legislation relating to responsibility for managing public order in Trafalgar Square. Cunninghame Graham, the Liberal-turned-socialist MP for North West Lanarkshire, was one of those arrested for unlawful assembly in Trafalgar Square on Bloody Sunday. Upon his release from prison, he introduced the Public Meetings in Open Spaces Bill in the House of Commons on 13 July 1888.[31] The bill proposed an absolute and inalienable right of public meeting in open spaces that had been used for at least twenty years for that purpose. The local authorities could regulate such meetings in the spaces they controlled, but they could not be 'in restraint or prohibition of the general right of public meeting or freedom of speech'. The bill therefore was intended to be the first piece of legislation to actively recognise a general right of public meeting. It also associated it indelibly with another claimed right, that of freedom of speech.

The 1888 Public Meetings and the Trafalgar Square (Regulation of Meetings) bills failed to pass into legislation. The somewhat convoluted parliamentary debates about them also failed to resolve the question of the right of public meeting.[32] The result was that, rather than finally having definitive legislative guidelines on such rights, the police and local authorities were left on the ground 'using ambiguous and ill-defined powers under the breach of the peace doctrine' to marshal public assemblies.[33] This foregrounds a key point about the period from 1839 onwards, the reliance of the government on local authorities and delegating the decision-making on the ground to magistrates and chief constables of police, until 1908.

Contesting meeting sites

In a Commons debate of 12 May 1887, James Stuart, Liberal MP for Shoreditch-Hoxton in East London, was unsympathetic to the socialists' claims but attributed the problem of disturbances over the right of meeting to the fact that:

There is no town in England so badly off in regard to facilities for the holding of public meetings as London. Take Bradford with its great St George's Hall, capable of holding 5000 or 6000 persons and used as a large meeting place for the people of that town. Go to the East End of London and you'll find that probably the biggest hall is that of Shoreditch, which is only capable of containing 2000 persons.[34]

---

[31] *Hansard*, HC Deb., 13 July 1888, vol. 328, c. 1350, https://api.parliament.uk/historic-hansard/ commons/1888/jul/13/public-meetings-in-open-spaces-bill, Channing, *The Police and the Expansion of Public Order Law*, 121. The bill was preceded by an attempt to establish the right at common law, with a challenge by Edward Lewis, solicitor, to the Metropolitan police commissioner's prohibition: Ex Parte Lewis 1888 21 QBD 191.

[32] Keller, *Triumph of Order*, 136.

[33] Channing, *The Police and the Expansion of Public Order Law*, 122.

[34] *Hansard*, HC Deb., 12 May 1887, vol. 314, cc. 1746–70, https://api.parliament.uk/historic-hansard/commons/1887/may/12/public-meetings-metropolis-socialist.

The atheist Liberal MP for Northampton, Charles Bradlaugh, had made the same point in his article, 'On the Right of Public Meeting', in Annie Besant's freethought journal *Our Corner* in 1885.[35] In the debate on 'public meetings in the metropolis' on 1 March 1888, Lord Charles Russell, MP for Hackney South and Attorney General and Irish Home Ruler, repeated the point again, and advocated that the state should provide a dedicated and independent space or hall for political public meetings for Londoners.[36] That somewhat utopian idea obviously never came to fruition, but it is intriguing that it was proposed as a solution by the Gladstonian Liberals. In their studies of the socialist agitation of the 1880s, Edward Royle and Antony Taylor pointed to the spatial restrictions in the capital compared with industrial cities in the north, and reiterated Russell's and Bradlaugh's laments about the greater opportunity for public meeting outside the capital.[37]

Contests over the right to use public spaces and civic buildings for political meetings continued in most towns across Britain throughout the long nineteenth century. And Stuart's claims about Bradford do not entirely hold true. During the Manningham Mills woollen workers' strike of 1891, a monumental event in trade union history, strikers were allowed to hold rallies in St George's Hall, but not in the town hall, where 150 police were then stationed to prevent them assembling. In April 1891, a demonstration of around 6,000 people was held in Peckover Walks, a heavily populated street, to protest against the police authorities 'in their stringent regulations in regard to the public buildings of the town, and demands facilities for a free expression of opinion on all questions affecting the welfare of society'. A socialist town councillor brought a charge of assault against two policemen who had arrested him at Peckover Walks, but the magistrates dismissed the case, as 'they did not consider it necessary to decide whether the ground in question was a place on which there was a right of public meeting. Whether it was a highway or not, it was undoubtedly a place of public resort and the plaintiff was causing an obstruction by attempting to hold a meeting'.[38] Groups such as the unemployed, who could not afford to hire St George's Hall, met on a piece of waste ground on Morley Street, known locally as the Forum. In 1913, a man was prosecuted for obstruction on Great Horton Street nearby, and during the case the defence lawyer asked the magistrates to provide a legal site for open-air meetings, which reflected the continuing struggle, despite Stuart's and Bradlaugh's earlier claims about socialists' easy access to sites.[39]

A case study of Sheffield similarly illustrates the integral part that political meetings played in popular politics throughout the long nineteenth century, and the contested spaces in which the right was claimed. Records of 550 political meetings from 1788 to 1936 were text-mined and manually extracted

---

[35] C. Bradlaugh, 'On the Right of Public Meeting', *Our Corner*, 1 Nov. 1885, 258.

[36] *Hansard*, HC Deb., 1 Mar. 1888, vol. 322, c. 1880, https://api.parliament.uk/historic-hansard/commons/1888/mar/01/public-meetings-in-the-metropolis.

[37] E. Royle, *Radicals, Secularists and Republicans: Popular Freethought in Britain, 1866-1915* (Manchester, 1980), 285; Taylor, 'Commons-Stealers', 398.

[38] *Bradford Daily Telegraph*, 2 Mar. 1891; *Huddersfield Chronicle*, 16 Apr. 1891.

[39] *Shipley Times*, 3 Oct. 1913.

from a range of local and political newspapers, Home Office papers and council minutes.[40] Public meetings went on pretty much constantly throughout the nineteenth century. There was a peak during the Chartist agitation: 150 gatherings were conducted under the format of a public meeting (chair, requisition, resolutions) between 1839 and 1848. Twenty per cent of all the meetings were officially called by requisition and agreed by the master cutler, or mayor after the 1843 incorporation of local government. Seven and a half per cent were disallowed or prohibited by the authorities, and the status of the rest is unclear. The growing allowance of meetings held by advertisement or acclamation influenced the pattern. Requesting to the mayor to personally chair or convene the meeting, being refused, but proceeding because the authorities had not explicitly prohibited it from going ahead under other advertisement/chairing, were essentially the main narrative for most public meetings. The process of request, refusal and acclamation was almost ritualised in its frequency.

Only 18 per cent of the meetings were recorded as resulting in a petition or address. This finding tempers the conclusions of Richard Huzzey and Henry Miller about the centrality of petitions in nineteenth-century popular politics. It also challenges Tilly's progression thesis that contentious gatherings became predominantly centred on direct communication with Parliament.[41] Many public meetings were not aimed at effecting direct change in Parliament, and still sought either local redress, or were aimed at raising awareness and funds for international causes. For example, a public meeting at Sheffield Music Hall in September 1832 passed resolutions in support of the Polish nation and an address to the king calling on him to influence the Russian emperor to stop the cruelties against Poland; the meeting was led by Count Plater, 'a distinguished Polish nobleman'.[42] There were many meetings on the Eastern Question in the 1850s, convened by the political parties but where large numbers of varying opinions were represented.[43] Home Rule dominated the debates in the 1880s.[44]

Most open-air meetings of all kinds were held in Paradise Square. Its multi-party use was one of the more unusual features of Sheffield spatial politics compared with other industrial cities such as Manchester, where meetings were more geographically segregated between different civic sites. At a mass meeting in April 1848, Isaac Ironside, the firebrand Chartist and socialist local councillor, from the steps of the Freemasons' Hall on one side of the square, declared, 'this flight of steps belongs to the people – that this square

---

[40] Sources include: *Northern Star*; *Sheffield Times*; *Sheffield Register*; *Sheffield Iris*; *Sheffield Independent*; *Leeds Mercury*; *Peeps into the Past: Being Passages from the Diary of Thomas Asline Ward* (Sheffield, 1909); Home Office correspondence, 1791–1848, TNA, HO 40, 42, 52. Full database and sources available at https://historyofpublicspace.uk/political-meetings-mapper-2/political-meetings-in-sheffield.

[41] Huzzey and Miller, 'Petitions, Parliament and Political Culture'; Tilly, 'The Rise of the Public Meeting'.

[42] *Sheffield Independent*, 8 Sept. 1832.

[43] *Ibid.*, 1 Feb. 1851; *Halifax Courier*, 14 Jan. 1854.

[44] *Sheffield Daily Telegraph*, 3 Jan. 1888, 7 Feb. 1889.

belongs to the people'.[45] The square did not belong to the people: it was owned by the trustees of the Shrewsbury Hospital. Permission to use the square for meetings was required from the master cutler of the Cutlers' Guild, who dominated the local government of the town. Debates were less over the right of public meeting and more over its definition and who constituted and convened it. Party political tensions within the local elites, notably over the incorporation of the town, also shaped the occurrence of events. During the election of 1852, the *Sheffield Independent* commented on the difference between indoor and outdoor public meetings. Paradise Square was regarded as more open because a 'certain set' could not dominate the hosting of the meeting.[46] The square was the ve. 'e for Reform League demonstrations in 1867 and rallies of the unemployed in the 1880s.[47] The continued contests over the square show that middle-class disciplining and regulation of civic spaces in industrial cities was never accomplished, and indeed was rather encouraged by a party political system responding to the expanding franchise. In 1884, the Liberal Association requisitioned the mayor for a public meeting in Paradise Square to debate the County Franchise Bill. The mayor

> expressed his willingness to call a public meeting, but pointed out that Saturday afternoon was a most unsuitable day for a mass meeting in Paradise Square. In the first place, there were many shopkeepers and tradespeople of all kinds who could not possibly leave their places of business on a Saturday afternoon. Working men themselves might reasonably object to Saturday afternoon, when they usually went into the country on fishing and other expeditions, while a very large number were engaged with their wives attending to their shopping and other purposes. He supposed the requisitionists really desired to have a representative gathering – in fact, a town's meeting – and he therefore suggested that they should not select Saturday.

The mayor thus made the distinction between a public meeting and a truly 'representative' town's meeting. The Liberals debated the date but decided to hold it on Saturday regardless.[48]

The notion of public space being created through custom and usage became part of the justification for the right to public meetings in those sites. In July 1907, the *Sheffield Telegraph* ran an editorial, 'Paradise Square – is it a public meeting place?' reporting on conflict over who had the right to use the space. The Wesleyan Methodist Central Mission had been holding Sunday evening meetings in the square since 1906. In July 1907 they sought to hold an anti-gambling demonstration, and confusion arose over who owned the square and whether the meeting had been prohibited. The Shrewsbury Hospital trustees objected to the holding of the demonstration. The newspaper noted, 'meetings

[45] *Sheffield Independent*, 11 Apr. 1848.
[46] Ibid., 10 April 1852.
[47] Ibid., 7 May 1867; *Sheffield Daily Telegraph*, 16 Feb. 1886.
[48] *Sheffield Daily Telegraph*, 29 Mar. 1884.

of the Labour Party were similarly objected to and stopped some time ago'.[49] As with many privately owned urban areas, the common assumption arose that they were public spaces because they had historically been used for public meetings. The newspaper noted that because of this long history, 'people have got into the habit of referring to the place as if it were the public forum of the town'. But it warned, 'such meetings have been held in Paradise Square by permission and not as of public right. No right was ever acquired even by what the lawyers call long "user" for the very good reason that at least all the formal public gatherings held in the Square were the subject of a money payment to the trustees for the owners'. The Trustees had initially prohibited public meetings in the square, but this had been less of an issue due to falling demand for its use: 'One possible reason which we have heard alleged is the fact that after the electoral reform of 1884 political activity in Sheffield was decentralised. Each division has its own affairs to look after.'[50] This was not quite the full picture: although radicals used other spaces, the square continued to be used particularly for Conservative meetings. The newspaper noted the political shift in 1886: 'since the square ceased to be Radical and became Conservative it has been discovered ... that the "old forum" cannot afford room for more than 10,000'.[51] Hence the revival of public gatherings by the Methodists in 1906 was a novelty and caused conflict with the respectable occupants of the square who had not previously had to deal with the inconvenience.

Two paradoxes of common rights

From the 1860s onwards the right to public meeting was increasingly combined with or contradicted by two other established rights: the right to air and exercise in public spaces, and the right of free passage along the highway. These are what I term the 'parks paradox' and the 'highway paradox'. Edmond Beales's challenge to use Hyde Park before the Reform League riots was discussed in the conservative *Sheffield Independent* in 1864. The editor noted:

> Nobody wants to interfere with the right of Mr Beales's 'people' to hold open-air meetings; but unfortunately Mr Beales's 'people' want, or at least he says they do, to interfere with the rights of the people in general in the Parks. Unless listening to a speech of Mr Beales's can be fairly described as public recreation, the Parks are not kept up for him to address meetings in.[52]

This tension between liberties and rights came to frame the contests over use of open spaces well into the twentieth century.

---

[49] *Ibid.*, 23 July 1907.
[50] *Ibid.*, 23 July 1907.
[51] *Ibid.*, 20 Apr. 1886.
[52] *Sheffield Independent*, 17 May 1864.

The Victorian public parks movement was in part a philanthropic endeavour to preserve access to open spaces, but also enacted a form of enclosure and regulation of behaviour.[53] Emparkment immediately meant more restrictions on use through by-laws and internal policing by wardens. Kennington Common in London was enclosed and laid out as a park in 1852-3, likely as an indirect reaction to the mass Chartist demonstration there on 10 April 1848. All political gatherings were thereby against park regulations.[54] The royal parks prohibited political meetings, leading to the Reform League's agitation in 1866. The 1872 Parks Regulation Act reinforced the ban. In 1880, the indomitable agitator and commons preservationist John de Morgan led the legal challenge against the Metropolitan Board of Works's new powers to enforce by-laws against political meetings in their parks and commons.[55] Corporations and councils across the country quickly followed suit with their own by-laws and amendments to park regulations, although the extent was varied in that some chose to ban meetings entirely while others set out a process of requiring permission.[56] The parks issue therefore, through de Morgan in particular, became indelibly linked with access and free speech and the working-class movement against the enclosure of the last of the metropolitan commons and open spaces across the country.[57] The demonstrators, pulling up the newly laid railings, employed modes of resistance that do not fit the political schema of either Tilly's progression thesis or the new political history's emphasis on the dominance of liberalism in mid-Victorian popular politics. A compromise was enacted in the London parks in 1925, with specific sites being allocated for meetings. Public meetings at Kennington Park were relegated, however, to a spot outside the boundaries of the main park, on a small triangle of ground between the tramlines.[58] The local authorities realised that allowing the socialists and other groups to meet on the symbolic site of the Chartist meeting would be too incendiary.

Outside London, the Boggart Hole Clough case in Manchester was the most politicised and well-known contest over the parks, owing to the national attention drawn to the case by Keir Hardie and the Independent Labour Party (ILP). In 1895 the Manchester Corporation parks committee purchased Boggart Hole Clough, a wooded valley to the north of the city. Under an earlier by-law against nuisance, the council immediately prohibited the holding of public meetings there, and charged local ILP speakers with annoyance at the police court. Large demonstrations ensued, including a gathering of up to 50,000

---

[53] C. O'Reilly, *The Greening of the City: Urban Parks and Public Leisure 1840-1939* (2019).

[54] *The Era*, 22 Aug. 1852; Taylor, 'Commons-Stealers', 399.

[55] De Morgan v Metropolitan Board of Works, 1880 5 QBD 155.

[56] *The Clarion*, 18 July 1896, listed the councils that had prohibited public meetings in their parks, including Manchester, Salford, Liverpool and Birmingham.

[57] Taylor, 'Commons-Stealers', 401; M. Gorman, *Saving the People's Forest: Open Spaces, Enclosure and Popular Protest in Mid-Victorian London* (Hatfield, 2020); N. MacMaster, 'The Battle for Mousehold Heath, 1857-1884: Popular Politics and the Victorian Public Park', *Past & Present*, 127 (1990), 117-54.

[58] Plans of public meeting sites, 1938, London Metropolitan Archives (LMA), London County Council Parks Committee papers, LCC/PP/PK/053.

people to hear national ILP leader Ben Tillett in the park on 19 July 1896.[59] The legal cause against the corporation was taken up by a cross-labour alliance of ILP, socialists and the trades council. The contest was widely exploited by the labour movement for propaganda purposes. Keir Hardie summarised the challenge to use the park as 'a question of the rights of the citizen against the rights of the persons elected to do the business of the citizens'. Peter Gurney's study of the conflict followed Patrick Joyce's interpretation that this language represented populism.[60] I argue rather that it marked a distinctive working-class challenge to class relations and representation in both local and national government at a time of heightened class tensions.

Public parks were laid out later in Sheffield than elsewhere. The corporation allowed public meetings in its other parks, but only upon application. It was not until relatively late therefore that the SDF used the parks in Sheffield as their battleground.[61] During the 1908–9 election campaign, several SDF orators, including women, were arrested and fined for delivering public addresses in the parks.[62] *Justice*, the SDF newspaper, actively called for volunteers to break the by-laws by giving speeches. In July 1908, for example, Daisy Halling spoke in High Hazels Park, to a crowd that the newspaper alleged was about 8,000 people, and she was later charged and fined £3 at the police court.[63] A *Justice* editorial commented (in a reversal of Russell and Bradlaugh's earlier claims about London) that the conflict took place in

Metropolitan Parks, at Peckham Rye, the World's End, Dod Street and innumerable other places where we fought and won the right of free speech and of public meeting. We do not claim either that we have any right to cause an obstruction or to make ourselves a nuisance to anybody. But there is no more reason why meetings should not be held in the Sheffield parks than there is why they should not be held in similar places in London.[64]

Notably the contests were framed as being over 'free speech' more than the right of public meeting. In 1910 a new Parks Committee was formed by Sheffield Corporation. Applications for use of the parks were submitted regularly by labour and trades groups, socialists and the Women's Social and Political Union (WSPU), and most but not all were approved.[65] Free speech was also the cry of the SDF in the other battle over public space for use of public meetings, over the use of the streets. This issue became crucial as the form and sites of public meetings shifted by the later nineteenth century. Excluded from the parks by by-laws and from public halls by costly hire charges,

---

[59] P. Gurney, 'The Politics of Public Space in Manchester, 1896–1919', *Manchester Region History Review*, 11 (1997), 12–23, at 13.

[60] Gurney, 'The Politics of Public Space', 15; *Manchester Guardian*, 4 July 1896.

[61] *Labour Leader*, 3 July 1908.

[62] *Justice*, 20 June 1908.

[63] *Ibid.*, 4 and 25 July 1908.

[64] *Ibid.*, 27 June 1908

[65] Parks Committee minutes, 1910–29, Sheffield Archives, CA 981/1/1/1.

socialists, trades and unemployed groups used street corners as their meeting sites from the 1880s onwards.

The shift towards police using the common law offence of obstruction against protest assemblies was evident by the 1830s, when the secularist book-seller Richard Carlile was prosecuted for attracting large crowds outside his bookshop.[66] The 1835 Highways Act, section 72, gave police an extra tool for enforcing the right of free passage against obstruction. The number of tried cases does not represent the frequency of the use of obstruction, because the majority of cases were unreported, being tried at petty sessions, or did not reach court at all, simply being used by police to disperse a street activ-ity.[67] The legal opinion on Carlile's prosecution also instigated a distinction between stationary and moving crowds, which was to become even more sig-nificant as the century went on and processions were privileged above static assemblies on the street and highway.

In August 1843, Thomas Duncombe, radical MP for Finsbury, brought a motion before the House of Commons regarding a petition presented to Parliament by Chartists in Hull complaining about the actions of the police. The magistrates justified using police to disperse a Chartist meeting in the marketplace by arguing it was an obstruction of the highway under the 1835 Highways Act. Duncombe declared that the charge of obstruction was 'impos-sible, because the meeting took place in the market-place, where he under-stood meetings had frequently been held so late ago as 1842, when the Right Honourable Baronet (Sir Robert Peel) was carrying the Corn Bill through the house'. Sir James Graham ordered the Hull authorities to conduct an inquiry, but argued that although 'he was not disposed, on light grounds, to interfere with popular meetings', it was an obstruction because 'the market place was a square on which four streets abutted and ... was completely obstructed'.[68] In the later contests over the use of Trafalgar Square, the space was legally classified as a right of way, not a square. Court judgements on Cunninghame Graham after his participation in the Bloody Sunday distur-bances in 1887 determined that, under the Trafalgar Square Act 1844, the square was a thoroughfare and therefore the police were right to clear obstruc-tions, though the police commissioner's permanent ban on meetings in the square was not valid.[69]

The SDF now moved from squares to the street. Fining the SDF and other groups for holding lectures and meetings on street corners and in unlicensed halls became an increasingly common option for police and magistrates.[70] Dod Street in Limehouse in the East End was the key site of contest, with thousands of people assembling on the pavements, but there are significant examples from almost every town in Britain from the 1880s to 1914. Joseph Chatterton, the socialist electoral candidate for West Leeds, and two other SDF members were

[66] *Morning Post*, 18 Dec. 1834.
[67] Vorspan, 'Freedom of Assembly', 936.
[68] *London Evening Standard*, 5 Aug. 1843.
[69] Vorspan, 'Freedom of Assembly', 972.
[70] Royle, *Radicals, Secularists and Republicans*, 284–5.

tried for lecturing in the marketplace of Longton, Staffordshire, in September 1897.[71] Colne, Lancashire, saw a wave of cases against SDF speakers in 1894, the majority of which, however, were dismissed: 'the police have given the assurance that our comrades shall not be interfered with anywhere in Colne if they will keep off the side-walks'.[72] Questions were raised as to whether lecturers could obstruct a square as well as a highway, as at Trafalgar Square. In Birmingham, in 1908, the treasurer of the Unemployed Association was charged with obstruction for addressing a meeting in Chamberlain Square, the main civic area outside the town hall.[73] In Sheffield, local debate in 1905 centred on whether political and trades groups could continue to use the Monolith, a monument that had been erected for Queen Victoria for the 1877 Jubilee. As with the parks, the contest was framed in terms of free speech.[74] In early 1914, Sheffield city council prohibited the public meetings that had regularly been held at the Queen's Monument, ostensibly on safety grounds because of increased traffic. The decision was opposed by all the major activist groups – the Sheffield Trades and Labour Council, ILP, Socialists, Fabians, WSPU and Women's Labour League – who organised a mass procession and demonstration in March 1914.[75]

The offence of obstruction of the highway was used by the police against public gatherings for several reasons. It allowed the police wide discretionary powers within a vague and malleable concept, unlike previous specific definitions of open-air public meetings that the Seditious Meetings legislation had sought, and failed, to prevent. Moreover, it enabled the authorities to claim they were defending the common right of free passage, rather than discriminating against specific groups or behaviour.[76] Nuisance and annoyance are a key framework for understanding the reach, and attempts at urban ordering, of the later nineteenth-century state. Policing historians David Churchill and Christopher Hamlin have challenged older-established portrayals of Benthamite liberal governance of of the Victorian city. Rather than the Foucaudian channels of power that Joyce and Chris Otter saw as inherent in institutions of civic improvement and policing, they argue rather that liberal governance was patchy and incomplete within and between cities.[77] A key concern of all the debates, particularly over the use of public and civic space, was with the protection of private property. The role of property owners and ratepayers in defending their property was paramount, as opposed to the parallel emphasis on freedom to use the public highway.

Charles Bradlaugh, freethinker and instigator of much of the parliamentary debate about the right of meeting, naturally blamed the Salvation Army for fomenting the problem, in a piece in *Our Corner* in 1885:

---

[71] *Sheffield Evening Telegraph*, 3 Sept. 1897.

[72] *Justice*, 11 Aug. 1894.

[73] *Staffordshire Sentinel*, 14 Jan. 1908.

[74] *Sheffield Daily Telegraph*, 9 Feb. 1905.

[75] *Ibid.*, 9 Mar. 1914.

[76] Vorspan, 'Freedom of Assembly', 935.

[77] Churchill, *Crime Control and Everyday Life*, 100; Hamlin, 'Nuisances and Community'; A. Croll, 'Street Disorder, Surveillance and Shame: Regulating Behaviour in the Public Spaces of the Late Victorian British Town', *Social History*, 24 (1999), 250–68.

At street corners, religious bodies, Temperance advocates, Freethought speakers and others have for some 30 or 40 years habitually conducted their propaganda in the metropolis. The difficulties created by riotous opposition have been of late years enhanced by the outrageous proceedings of the Salvation Army.[78]

Precedents were set by legal cases involving the Salvation Army, whose parades were harassed by publicans' anti-temperance Skeleton Army in many towns, particularly on the south coast. An attack on a Salvation Army march at Weston-super-Mare, Somerset, resulted in a precedent-making legal case, Beatty versus Gillbanks in 1882, which authorized the processions to go ahead and the police to protect them against interruption.[79] These contests took place within a wider context of increasing regulation of street spaces. By the 1880s, proliferating regulations and by-laws controlled the way in which thoroughfares were used, by excluding sex workers, vagrants and other people regarded as undesirables, and keeping public spaces free from obstruction and dirt and other forms of pollution. As Constance Bantman's study of the policing of anarchists in London in the 1880s has shown, in this context political protest was recast as antisocial behaviour.[80] For example, in 1880, the shopkeepers of Westbar, Sheffield, complained to the town council about the state of the water pump. In the council debate, Mr Binney noted,

> he passed the pump several times on Sundays and there were a lot of idle characters assembled there. He believed the only useful purpose of the steps was as a platform for addressing the public. A chair would attain the same object and there would no longer be a standing nuisance.

Mr Bromley said 'it was not desirable in a thoroughfare like Westbar to have gatherings of a public character. Paradise Square was close by and was far more convenient.'[81] The result of these cases was that, firstly, marches and processions were increasingly distinguished from public meetings as separate, and secondly, there was more precedent for marches, as exercise of the right of passage along a highway deserved legal protection.

The public order acts

By the turn of the twentieth century, the emergence of new political movements using militant tactics raised different issues with regard to the right of assembly. The Salvation Army, and even the SDF, had been an easy target for police, but they were classed as a local public order problem rather than representing a threat to overturn the system. The militant activism of

---

[78] C. Bradlaugh, 'On the Right of Public Meeting', *Our Corner*, 1 Nov. 1885, 285.

[79] Vorspan, 'Freedom of Assembly', 950; Beatty v Gillbanks (1882) 9 QBD 308.

[80] C. Bantman, 'Anarchists, Authorities and the Battle for Public Space, 1880–1914: Recasting Political Protest as Antisocial Behaviour', in *Anti-Social Behaviour: Victorian and Contemporary Perspectives*, ed. S. Pickard (Basingstoke, 2014), 65–76, at 66.

[81] *Sheffield Daily Telegraph*, 15 Jan. 1880.

suffragettes, however, went much further than the street demonstrations of the socialists and trades unions.[82] Later, in the 1930s, the emergence of the fascist movement, with its provocative marching and large rallies, also stretched the capacities of the police and pointed to the need for new legislation, not least to deal with incitement to racist violence. The right of public meeting was tested to the limits of the law. This final section examines the background to the Public Order Acts in response to these movements' occupation of public space for meetings and demonstrations.

The WSPU developed the specifically disruptive tactics of interrupting public meetings and heckling speakers, which were countered by arrests for obstruction.[83] During Winston Churchill's election tour of northern England in December 1909, the suffragettes attempted to gain access to his public meetings. WSPU newspaper *Votes for Women* editorialised:

> The protests have been based on certain principles. If the women are allowed into the meetings, there to raise relevant issues, as Miss Dora Marsden did at Southport or to put questions, like Miss Gawthorpe at Manchester, then extreme measures of protest are not taken; but if the women are not allowed to make their protest by word of mouth, then other methods have to be brought into use. In Preston, for instance, no woman was allowed into the Public Hall ... hence local protesters attempted to address a meeting of protest outside the Public Hall, and for taking part in this three women were arrested.[84]

Rachel Vorspan notes how the novelty of the suffragette agitation in the history of obstruction law lay in their adoption of picketing, usually an industrial tactic, as a stationary street protest, especially outside the House of Commons. The government and courts treated picketing as functionally equivalent to a street meeting. The extension of public meeting to encompass picketing thus allowed 'the doctrine to expand to serve the government's interests'.[85]

The Public Meeting Bill was presented to Parliament in December 1908, by Conservative MP Lord Robert Cecil. The bill sought to create an offence of disorderly conduct at a public meeting by anyone intending to prevent the transaction of business.[86] The response of the Liberals to it was mixed, and centred on whether the measure would defend free speech at meetings or suppress it. The

---

[82] H. Miller, 'The British Women's Suffrage Movement and the Practice of Petitioning, 1890–1914', *Historical Journal*, 64 (2021), 332–56; L. E. Nym Mayall, 'Defining Militancy: Radical Protest, the Constitutional Idiom, and Women's Suffrage in Britain, 1908–1909', *Journal of British Studies*, 39 (2000), 340–71.

[83] *Manchester Evening News*, 17 Oct. 1905; Channing, *The Police and the Expansion of Public Order Law*, 171.

[84] *Votes for Women*, 10 Dec. 1909.

[85] Vorspan, 'Freedom of Assembly', 990.

[86] Channing, *The Police and the Expansion of Public Order Law*, 171; Hansard, HC Deb., 19 Dec. 1908, vol. 198, cc. 2328–43, https://hansard.parliament.uk/Commons/1908-12-19/debates. Henry Miller notes that Cecil however later defended some suffragettes at trials for obstruction. See *Votes for Women*, 3 Dec. 1909, 147, trial of Evelina Haverfield and Emmeline Pankhurst.

legislation marked a shift from the reluctance of nineteenth-century governments to pass specific legislation against particular protest groups in Britain, and their reliance on the discretion of local policing. The laws of obstruction were now seen as insufficiently effective against the perceived threat. The Public Meeting Act 1908 nevertheless did not solve the issue of the duties and actions of the police at such meetings, which varied across forces. The uncertainty led Liberal Unionist MP Austen Chamberlain to prevail on the home secretary to instigate a departmental committee. It concluded that it was unwise for the police to interfere with political meetings and therefore remained uncommitted to supporting legislation which would mandate them to do so.[87]

Following the First World War, rival meetings and marches held by the fascists and communists became the main public order issue of the day. The rise of the race question in the 1930s raised the necessity for more specific public order legislation against racially incited speech.[88] The battle of Cable Street between Jewish residents and police over the right claimed by Oswald Mosley's fascists to march through the East End of London in 1936 marked the peak of tensions, but again the government response was reactive rather than preventative. The 1936 Public Order Act, rushed through Parliament, enabled police to prohibit processions in advance, proscribed the wearing of political uniforms, and consolidated existing measures relating to threatening words and behaviour. However, it did not cover static public meetings.[89] Echoing earlier arguments, politicians in and out of government sought to use the legislation to protect political speakers and prevent organised public disruption of political meetings. The Act marked another reversal of attitudes towards processions compared with static meetings, the right to move compared with the right to assembly in one place. In April 1848, the Chartist mass meeting at Kennington Common had been allowed but the procession to Parliament was not; this was reversed by the 1880s and 1890s, with processions and parades by the Salvation Army and SDF being allowed, but not their gatherings on street corners, nor later the suffragette picketing outside public halls; the 1930s fascist and communist agitation led to new legislation specifically against marches and military-style drilling.

More problematic was the definition of public meetings held on private premises. The Committee on the Duties of the Police with respect to the Preservation of Order at Public Meetings 1909 noted, 'if a public building is hired or even lent to an association or other section of the public for the purposes of a meeting, it becomes in law for the time being a non public place'. This definition caused immense problems with the policing of Mosley's fascist rallies in the mid-1930s, notably at Earls Court, raising debates over whether the police had the right to enter and intervene.[90] The issue was not resolved

---

[87] *Departmental Committee on the Duties of the Police with Respect to the Preservation of Order at Public Meetings* (1909).

[88] J. Lawrence, 'Fascist Violence and the Politics of Public Order in Britain', *Historical Research*, 76 (2003), 238–67.

[89] Channing, *The Police and the Expansion of Public Order Law*, 139.

[90] Ibid., 92.

until the amendments to the Public Order Act 1936 in 1967 in response to race riots and hooliganism, which sought to extend the definition of 'public place' to include indoor privately owned venues such as 'dance halls, coffee bars, cafes, cinemas and bingo halls'.[91] Yet though the public order legislation was national, it was always patchily implemented as it depended very much on the proclivities of the individual police force on the ground. There was always a tension between the letter of the law and its practical implementation.

The Criminal Justice and Public Order Acts of 1986 and 1994 were spatially discriminative, again centred on the ongoing issue of policing the right of free passage along the highway, rather than the right of assembly. The Conservative governments aimed the legislation at specific groups seen to be a threat to the state who were obstructing the roads and occupying private land with vehicles: striking workers on flying pickets during the miners' strike of 1984–5; Gypsies, Roma and Travellers; New Age travellers holding raves; and environmental protesters campaigning against road building. The Acts created an offence of aggravated trespass, and gave local authorities and the police stronger powers to prevent and turn away convoys of travellers on the roads and encampments on both public and private land. They encapsulated the fact that the right to free passage of the public took legal precedence over the right of assembly, and that the government and police defined which people constituted 'the public' and which groups were excluded from that definition.[92] The right of public assembly was not defined in statute until the 1998 Human Rights Act. Later parliamentary and public debates, such as those about the Metropolitan police order against the environmental activist group Extinction Rebellion holding protests in any area of London in 2019, government restrictions on public gatherings under emergency health regulations during the Covid pandemic in 2020, and the passage through Parliament of the Police, Crime, Sentencing and Courts Bill in 2021 have again highlighted the tensions between the right of public meeting and policing of public order.[93]

Conclusion

How does this narrative change our picture of political participation in England during the eighteenth and nineteenth centuries? The evidence for public meetings demonstrates not a dominant liberal elite closing down constitutional discourse, but rather the continuity of well-established and personal modes of communication and participation in the political process. The contests over public meetings indicate that popular politics did not wholly fit a model of civilising elites in the later nineteenth century, nor a Foucauldian framework positing that

---

[91] Public Order Act 1936 revisions to deal with hooliganism, 1967, TNA, Home Office files, HO 325/7.

[92] R. Card and R. Ward, 'Access to the Countryside: The Impact of the Criminal Justice and Public Order Act 1994', *Journal of Planning and Environmental Law*, 6 (1996), 447–62.

[93] House of Lords and House of Commons Joint Committee on Human Rights, *The Government Response to Covid-19: Freedom of Assembly and the Right to Protest, Thirteenth Report of Session 2019–21*, 17 March 2021, https://committees.parliament.uk/publications/5153/documents/50935/default; Police, Crime, Sentencing and Courts Bill, 2021, https://bills.parliament.uk/bills/2839.

the Victorian state became so bureaucratised and controlling that it governed a 'society of strangers'.[94] Public meetings retained, and indeed were predicated on, personal party politics and direct challenges between activists and local elites who knew each other. The right of public meeting was defended as an integral constitutional right, firstly together with the right to petition, and then from the later nineteenth century onwards alongside the right of free speech. Working-class agency was more than evident in the setting-up of meetings, resolutions and counter-resolutions, and the creative development of a wider range of public meetings, including the convention and the 'mass platform' demonstration. The widening franchise sustained the vitality of public meetings and the demands for these rights. Though often conducted within a liberal discourse, this did not preclude genuine challenges to the system and other potentially more revolutionary forms of protest. London saw the most contests over public meetings and their sites that were debated in Parliament, but similar contests were enacted in every town across the country, and formed a crucial part of provincial political cultures, social hierarchies and local government.

The evolution of legislation and regulation regarding public meetings was often reactive in that it followed some perceived threat to the political elites, but it was patchy, and often left to the discretion of local officials. The state could never fully discipline or control its subjects, either through liberal governance or more repressive measures. The shift in policing to use of the common law of obstruction against meetings illustrated how local authorities and police pitted other rights against the demand for public assembly: the right of free passage along a highway, and of air and recreation in open spaces. This tension between different rights was exploited by police on the ground to provide them with discretion as a way of getting around official policy. The rights of property were spatialised in the defence of the right of free passage over the right of assembly. By the turn of the twentieth century, however, new threats of militant tactics and racial harassment by political groups necessitated specific public order legislation. Though this sought to protect certain types of public assembly and protest marches, the implementation and policing of public order was spatially discriminatory. The Home Office and police commissioners decided who formed the 'public' in public order and public space. The right of public meeting was left unresolved until the 1998 Human Rights Act and remains highly contested.

Acknowledgements. Acknowledgements to Sarah Lloyd, Richard Huzzey, Henry Miller and Mary O'Connor for their advice on an earlier version of this paper.

---

[94] Huzzey and Miller, 'Petitions, Parliament and Political Culture', 128.

Cite this article: Navickas K (2022). The Contested Right of Public Meeting in England from the Bill of Rights to the Public Order Acts. *Transactions of the Royal Historical Society* **32**, 199–221. https://doi.org/10.1017/S0080440122000032

Transactions of the RHS (2022), **32**, 223–239
doi:10.1017/S008044012200010X

Runaways London: Historical Research, Archival Silences and Creative Voices

Fahad Al-Amoudi[1], Kate Birch[2] and Simon P. Newman[3]*

[1]Creative and Life Writing, Goldsmiths University of London, London W14 8RD, UK, [2]Ink Sweat & Tears, London SW12 8DG, UK, and [3]Institute for Research in the Humanities, University of Wisconsin–Madison, 432 East Campus Mall, University Club Building, Madison, Wisconsin 53706, USA
*Corresponding author. Email spnewman3@wisc.edu

Abstract

This article explores how popular historical knowledge and understanding can be deepened by collaboration between historians, creative artists, and editors, publishers and those who support and develop the creative arts. Historical research into enslaved people who escaped in seventeenth- and eighteenth-century London reveals much about their enslavers but very little about the enslaved people themselves. However, archival gaps and silences can be imaginatively filled, and those who engage with the historically inspired creative work can explore the nexus of historical research and artistic creativity. In this article the authors (a historian and two members of the creative industry) detail how their 'Runaways London' collaboration developed, and how the work of poets and artists, premised on extensive historical research, deepens our understanding of race and slavery in British history, achieving something that is beyond the reach of historical research and writing alone.

Keywords: London; slavery; poetry; art

RUN away from his Master, a Negro Man Slave, named Will, and sometimes goes by the Name of George. Whoever will apprehend the said Negro, and bring him to John Fielding, Esq; in Bow-street, Covent Garden, shall receive two Guineas Reward. He is a tall stout black Man, had on when he went away a blue Flannel Jacket, grey Breeches, checked Shirt, red Woollen Cap, and a Hat, (a Sea Dress) he also took with him an old thin blue Coat.[1]

---

[1] *Public Advertiser*, 29 October 1757.

We know virtually nothing about the enslaved man named Will or George, other than the fact that in the autumn of 1757 he attempted to escape his enslavement in London. This short newspaper advertisement is quite likely the only surviving archival record of this man's existence, and it is one of many hundreds of similar notices published in British newspapers between the 1650s and 1780s. The 'runaway slave' newspaper advertisement was invented in London in 1655 and was utilised in the city for a half-century before spreading to the colonies where it would become the most ubiquitous evidence of resistance to slavery. These advertisements were at the heart of a research project funded by the Leverhulme Trust, and between 2015 and 2018 a team led by Newman located, transcribed and analysed these advertisements, eventually making them available in a searchable database. The first phase of the database features 836 advertisements from England and Scotland published between 1700 and 1779, and at present hundreds more from the period 1655–1780 are being processed for inclusion in the database.

The advertisements demonstrate that slavery's revolution in labour and race was as much a British phenomenon as a colonial one, and during the second half of the seventeenth century people in London, Bristol and elsewhere were intimately involved in the creation of racial slavery. Then and throughout the first three-quarters of the eighteenth century people of colour were brought into the British Isles by visiting colonists, merchants, government officials, ship captains, planters and other White Britons. Some came directly from West Africa, others from the Caribbean and North American colonies, and still more from the South Asian trading bases of the East India Company. Some were free or indentured, others were enslaved, and many were in a liminal state between freedom and slavery.[2]

---

[2] The legal status of enslaved people was unclear in England during the seventeenth and for much of the eighteenth century. At least one historian has concluded 'that slavery did not exist as an institution in England and Wales', while another suggested that Black people may have escaped because 'like their white counterparts, [they] did not always like their masters.' See Kathleen Chater, *Untold Histories: Black People in England and Wales during the Period of the British Slave Trade, c.1660-1807* (Manchester, 2009), 95; Susan D. Amussen, *Caribbean Exchanges: Slavery and the Transformation of English Society, 1640-1700* (Chapel Hill, 2007), 221. But most historians now agree that although quite different from Caribbean and American slavery, racial bondage in England was real and the enslaved were often vulnerable to a return to plantation slavery.

For scholarship on people of colour in the early modern British Isles see Miranda Kaufman, *Black Tudors: The Untold Story* (2017); Gretchen Gerzina, *Black London: Life before Emancipation* (New Brunswick, 1995); Catherine Molineux, *Faces of Perfect Ebony: Encountering Atlantic Slavery in Imperial Britain* (Cambridge, MA, 2012); Kim F. Hall, *Things of Darkness: Economies of Race and Gender in Early Modern England* (Ithaca, 1995); Imtiaz Habib, *Black Lives in the English Archives, 1500-1677: Imprints of the Invisible* (Aldershot, 2008); Amussen, *Caribbean Exchanges*; Folarin O. Shyllon, *Black Slaves in Britain* (Oxford, 1974); Norma Myers, *Reconstructing the Black Past: Blacks in Britain, 1780-1830* (1996); Peter Fryer, *Staying Power: The History of Black People in Britain* (1984); James Walvin, *The Black Presence: A Documentary History of the Negro in England* (1971); M. Dresser and A. Hann (eds.), *Slavery and the British Country House* (Swindon, 2013); D. Fraser, 'Slaves or Free People? The Status of Africans in England, 1550-1750', in *From Strangers to Citizens: The Integration of Immigrant Communities in Britain, Ireland and Colonial America, 1550-1750*, ed. R. Vigne and C. Littleton (Brighton, 2001), 254-60; V. C. D. Mtubani, 'African Slaves and English Law', *Pula:*

Many of the enslaved in Britain were children who were made to work in domestic service and, as Susan D. Amussen has observed, young Black male pages became 'an increasingly common accoutrement' of elite English women and men. Catherine Molineux has described these enslaved children as 'a form of social currency, consumed and displayed in a semiotic system of status'.[3] Working as a page, a gentleman's manservant, a lady's maid, a coach driver or even a carpenter, craftsman or sailor in Britain was very different from labour on colonial plantations. The nature and conditions of the work undertaken by these people of colour appeared very similar to that of White British servants, many of them children, and very different from the labour of enslaved Black people in the colonies. Britons commonly referred to enslaved domestic and household workers as servants, but this was in part due to the fact that during the early modern period the word servant could include slavery: Tyndale's scriptures, the King James Bible and the Geneva Bible seldom used the words slave or slavery, instead referring to the enslaved as servants.[4] Even the Israelites who escaped from slavery in Egypt were described as 'servants'. But appearances and language were deceptive and should not blind us to the experiences of enslaved people in Britain. Many were little more than children yet they had experienced the trauma of violent separation from family and community, the Middle Passage, and colonial plantation slavery. And they knew that they remained at the mercy of people who might easily take or send them to the hell of slavery in the plantation colonies, as happened to young men like Sambo (enslaved by Samuel Pepys) or Martin (enslaved by Robert Cunninghame Graham), both of whom were ripped from domestic service in Britain and sold into Caribbean slavery. Although some Black people in Britain were free, others were bound by the memory and the reality of colonial slavery, and their fear of being returned to the Caribbean, giving them strong motivations to escape. So real and so terrifying was this threat that one 'Negroe Servant' in England who was 'threatened by his Master, for some Misconduct, to be sent to the Plantations' responded by hanging himself in his owner's coal cellar.[5] (The Middle Passage from Africa and then sale of the enslaved in the Caribbean is represented in Figure 1.)

Botswana Journal of African Studies, 3 (1981), 71–5. We know far less about South Asians in seventeentth-century London, but there is a little more work in this field for the eighteenth century: see Emma Rothschild, *The Inner Life of Empires: An Eighteenth-Century History* (Princeton, 2011), 87–91, 291–9; and E. S. Filor, 'Complicit Colonials: Border Scots and the Indian Empire, c.1780–1857' (Ph.D. thesis, University College London, 2014), 205–14.

[3] Amussen, *Caribbean Exchanges*, 179; Molineux, *Faces of Perfect Ebony*, 31. For more on religion, civility and rank in racial relations in Britain see Roxann Wheeler, *The Complexion of Race: Categories of Difference in Eighteenth-Century British Culture* (Philadelphia, 2010).

[4] See Naomi Tadmor, *The Social Universe of the English Bible: Scripture, Society, and Culture in Early Modern England* (Cambridge, 2010), 82–118.

[5] 'Yesterday a Negroe Servant', *Derby Mercury* (Derby), 22 June 1753. For information about Sambo's fate see Claire Tomalin, *Samuel Pepys: The Unequalled Self* (New York, 2002), 177, 405–6; Arthur Bryant, *Samuel Pepys*, III: *The Saviour of the Navy* (Cambridge, 1938), 270. These events took place well after Pepys had ceased keeping a diary. For information about Martin, see Robert Cunninghame Graham to Angus MacBean, 24 March 1773, Letter Book 1772, Graham Papers, National Library of Scotland, Acc 11335/18, 41.

Figure 1 'Forgotten journey of the enslaved', @ Tasia Graham, *Runaways London*, 31.

One of the most significant and widespread forms of resistance to slavery was escape, and this occurred in the British Isles just as it did in the American and Caribbean colonies. The newspaper advertisements generated by these escapes in Britain were short, rarely longer than 100 words. They appeared alongside mundane notices for lost or stolen property (including dogs and horses), and for books, medicines and other items for sale, showing that the enslaved were readily accepted by readers and advertisers alike as yet one more form of property. They were written by and from the vantage point of enslavers, and the brief descriptions of people who had escaped and the clothing they wore often did not even include the name of the escapee. The advertisements are usually the only surviving records of the people who had escaped, yet they reveal very little about those seeking to free themselves. Newman has published a monograph and scholarly essays about these British freedom seekers, yet while we often know a great deal about enslavers, in many cases it has proved all but impossible to discover anything substantial about individuals who are little more than archival ghosts.[6] Historians of the enslaved in Britain, especially those who challenged their bondage by escaping, are, in Saidiya Hartman's words, 'forced to grapple with the power and authority of the archive and the limits it sets on what can be known, whose perspective matters, and who is endowed with the gravity and authority of historical actor'.[7] It is possible to tabulate broad numbers and patterns of gender, age, race and ethnicity, and on occasion to illuminate the cases of people for whom more records exist. But beyond these broad brush strokes the enslaved freedom seekers of early modern Britain can be only imagined, for almost every detail of these people and their lives has been lost.[8]

As he completed his book on freedom seekers in seventeenth-century London, Newman was eager to explore ways of having Black and South Asian Londoners creatively respond to his research, imaginatively filling in the gaps. Poetry and art can play a significant role in the decolonisation of the curriculum (both school and university) and a broader coming to terms with the reality and continued effects of slavery and colonialism. In collaboration with historians, and grounding their work in historical research, creative artists can help imagine lost histories in ways that broaden and deepen public understanding of a largely forgotten past. The violence and oppression of

---

[6] Simon P. Newman, *Freedom Seekers: Escaping from Slavery in Restoration London* (2022); Newman, 'Freedom-Seeking Slaves in England and Scotland, 1700–1780', *English Historical Review*, 134 (2019), 1136–68; and Newman with N. Mundell and S. Mullen, 'Black Runaways in Eighteenth-Century Britain', in *Britain's Black Past*, ed. G. Gerzina (Liverpool, 2020), 81–98. See also Newman, 'Escaping Enslavement in Eighteenth Century Scotland', in *The European Experience of Slavery*, ed. R. von Mallinckrodt (Berlin, forthcoming), and 'Sugar Planters and Freedom Seekers in Seventeenth-Century London', *Early American Studies* (forthcoming).

[7] Saidiya Hartman, *Wayward Lives, Beautiful Experiments: Intimate Histories of Riotous Black Girls, Troublesome Women, and Queer Radicals* (New York, 2019), xiii. Hartman has led the way in conceptualising the silence and violence of the archive with reference to enslaved Black people. See Hartman, *Lose Your Mother: A Journey along the Atlantic Slave Route* (New York, 2007), as well as Marisa Fuentes, *Dispossessed Lives: Enslaved Women, Violence, and the Archive* (Philadelphia, 2016), and the essays in a special issue of the journal *History of the Present* entitled 'From Archives of Slavery to Liberated Futures?', edited by B. Connelly and M. Fuentes, 6 (2016), 105–215.

[8] Recognising these gaps in the archive as an opportunity, the Runaway Slaves in Britain project team commissioned a graphic novel based on three Scottish advertisements. *Freedom Bound* was created with financial support from the Leverhulme Trust, the Economic and Social Research Council and the University of Glasgow, and it included research data accumulated about the three freedom seekers and their enslavers, as well as more advertisements, maps and other data. Each state secondary school in Scotland received thirty-five copies of *Freedom Bound*, and in many schools it has become part of teaching and learning about the slave trade and slavery. See W. Pleece, S. Khan and R. Jones, *Freedom Bound: Escaping Slavery in Scotland*, based on research by S. Newman and N. Mundell (Glasgow, 2018).

slavery is replicated in the archive in which the enslaved are silenced, and historians face enormous challenges in trying to reconstruct these histories in ways that do not replicate the power imbalances of the past. Poetry and art can creatively fill spaces of elision and silence, and working with young Black and South Asian creative artists promised to imaginatively fill some of the archival silences of those who resisted slavery in London, as well as enabling these creative artists to take ownership of their community's London history.[9]

In June 2020, as Black Lives Matter protests engulfed British cities in response to the murder of George Floyd a month earlier, Newman approached Birch, the publisher of Ink Sweat & Tears Press (IS&T). Birch and IS&T had worked with and published some of London's Black and South Asian writers and were about to set up an editing internship programme for poets from these communities and other ethnic minority groups.[10] Birch then discussed the idea of a publication of creative work about London's enslaved freedom seekers with several writers, including Mona Arshi and Rishi Dastidar, chair of Spread the Word, a London-based writer development agency. Committed to making literature 'more inclusive of all voices', Spread the Word has developed the ongoing Young People's Laureate for London scheme; the Complete Works (2008–10) a mentoring scheme for advanced Black and Asian poets; and the current Flight 1000 Associate scheme, funded by the Esmée Fairbairn Foundation and providing training and support for writers from diverse backgrounds to enter the publishing industry. Spread the Word was the ideal organisation to coordinate the project, and Birch then approached Ruth Harrison, its director.[11]

Newman, Birch and Harrison were then joined by Peggy Brunache, a Haitian-American lecturer in the history of Atlantic slavery and director of the Beniba Centre for Slavery Studies at the University of Glasgow. In a series of meetings, the four established the Runaways London project group, and they agreed to secure funding to commission work by young Black and South Asian poets and artists. The Runaways London project would then publish the poets' and artists' work as a book; commission a short film about the creation of these works; and make the book, the film and teaching materials for schools freely available online. Newman applied for and secured awards from the British Association for American Studies/United States Embassy Small Grants Programme, and the Economic and Social Research Council, Impact Acceleration Scheme. Brunache secured further funding from the University of Glasgow, and Birch solicited donations from private individuals within the City of London's insurance/reinsurance industry. Finally, Harrison made a successful application for significant funding from the City of London

---

[9] For consideration of the silence and violence of the archive and the need for creative approaches see Hartman, *Wayward Lives, Beautiful Experiments*, and *Lose Your Mother*; Fuentes, *Dispossessed Lives*; Connelly and Fuentes (eds.), 'From Archives of Slavery to Liberated Futures?'; and Sunny Singh, 'Writing about Minoritised People', https://twitter.com/ProfSunnySingh/status/1423335297245454345, 5 August 2021.

[10] *Ink Sweat & Tears*, https://inksweatandtears.co.uk, accessed 26 March 2022.

[11] Spread the Word, https://www.spreadtheword.org.uk/about-us, accessed 15 March 2022.

Corporation – Central Grants Programme. Altogether the project leaders secured about £35,000. As the project developed, Birch contacted the director of the Museum of London, Sharon Ament, and then Finbarr Whooley (director of Content) and Glyn Davies (head of Curatorial), and this enabled the planning of a launch event at the museum's Docklands site, home of the *London, Sugar & Slavery* permanent exhibit. More events were projected, to be organised after publication of the creative work and film.

Newman then set about translating his research into a portfolio of materials for the 'creatives', the writers and artists. This included primary sources and a brief historical analysis of London and England in the seventeenth and eighteenth centuries, of how slavery worked in the British Isles, and how free and enslaved people of colour lived in the capital. The completed dossier included several case studies, each beginning with a single advertisement for a freedom seeker and then developing contextual information about the enslaver, other people mentioned in the advertisement, the nature of the London locations specified in the text, and whatever could be surmised about the freedom seekers themselves.

Many of the freedom seekers identified in seventeenth- and eighteenth-century advertisements were children or young adults, and the Runaways London project team agreed that it was appropriate to seek to commission young Black and South Asian artists and writers (under the age of thirty). Harrison at Spread the Word began by approaching two poets: Momtaza Mehri, 2018 Young People's Laureate for London, and Gboyega Odubanjo, a published poet and editor of the highly regarded *bath magg*. At the same time Harrison approached the illustrator Olivia Twist, whose work has explored overlooked narratives and documented social history. All three were enthusiastic and were commissioned to produce work for the project. Spread the Word then issued an Open Call for applications from emerging poets and artists in May 2021.

Some applicants made clear that they felt drawn to the project because it not only resonated with their racial heritage but with the otherness that they were feeling as queer and non-binary people. What united almost all of them was the fact that they were unaware or barely aware of the presence of enslaved Black and South Asian people in Britain in seventeenth- and eighteenth-century London. But despite that, applicants repeatedly articulated their strong sense of commitment to the project and the need for this history to become centre stage with a focus on the colonisation, oppression and commodification of the enslaved in this period of London history. The applicants made it very clear that this was not just about the past, and that their growing awareness of this history and the work they were producing clearly resonated with their own experiences in present-day London and Britain. In June 2021 Birch and Harrison shortlisted and then interviewed the finalists, eight writers and three artists, before selecting the poets Memoona Zahid, Oluwaseun Olayiwola and Abena Essah, and the illustrator Tasia Graham. With Mehri, Odubanjo and Twist, the team of seven 'creatives' was complete.

After several initial Zoom meetings between all of the creatives and the project team, the latter realised that given the difficult and emotive subject, less formal meetings and discussions might be better and more productive for the creatives. Several of the creatives contacted Newman to discuss and ask questions about his research, and many of them met with Brunache. Al-Amoudi had joined the project team (he was then working as the IS&T editing intern). As someone of African descent, and as both a history graduate and a writer, he was well positioned to become the primary contact for the creatives. He set up Zoom meetings where he would introduce the session and then leave the writers and artists to discuss the project among themselves. From this point, Al-Amoudi became the creatives' main point of contact.

As they delved into the research materials for Runaways London, none of the writers were surprised by the 'depth and pervasiveness of human horror', to quote emerging poet Olayiwola.[12] The dehumanisation of freedom seekers, the erasure of their indigenous identities, and the persistent threat of plantation slavery was nothing new to the artists, but they were able to ask questions of the sources, of the silence within, that aren't usually asked and are even more rarely answered in traditional historical research and writing. An academic essay can analyse what is there but can, at best, only speculate on the shape of what is missing. For example, the creatives referred often to physical violence being inflicted on enslaved servants in London even though there is no direct historical evidence to prove that this took place, although it surely did occur. Violence by masters and mistresses against the White servants and apprentices who dominated London's workforce 'was a regular event in early modern society', and Samuel Pepys and his wife were typical in their habitual beatings of young servants. Given that extreme violence against enslaved people was routine on slave ships and in the colonies, and that violent chastisement of White servants was routine in England, it seems reasonable to assume that the enslaved in seventeenth- and eighteenth-century London faced violent abuse, despite the lack of surviving archival evidence.[13]

A poem or an artistic work is a break in that archival silence that grabs its reader or viewer by the collar and demands their attention. A poem or an image is urgent and has the freedom to imagine what was and what could have been. The writers and artists took this approach to the project and imagined the lives that eluded historians hampered by archival silences, while recognising the limits of what can never be known. They asked what happened, who it happened to and when it happened, but crucially they asked, 'but how did it feel?'[14] The reward of imaginative historical work by creatives includes the ability to find an emotional resonance with the reader as

---

[12] Oluwaseun Olayiwola to Kate Birch, 21 January 2022.

[13] S. D. Amussen, 'Punishment, Discipline, and Power: The Social Meanings of Violence in Early Modern England', *Journal of British Studies*, 34 (1995), 1–34, at 13. For more on servants and apprentices in London's population see Newman, *Freedom Seekers*, 8–12; Ann Kussmaul, *Servants in Husbandry in Early Modern England* (Cambridge, 1981); Ilana Krausman Ben-Amos, *Adolescence and Youth in Early Modern England* (New Haven, 1994). For more on violence against servants see Tim Meldrum, *Domestic Service and Gender 1600-1750: Life and Work in the London Household* (Harlow, 2000), 92–3; and G. T. Smith, 'Expanding the Compass of Domestic Violence in the Hanoverian Metropolis', *Journal of Social History*, 41 (2007), 42–7.

[14] Olayiwola to Birch, 21 January 2022.

well as an intellectual one, so that historians, curators, institutions and the general public are collectively engaged in a project to better understand our past.

The Runaways London project deals with harrowing stories of chattel slavery, domestic servitude and the violent recapture of Black and South Asian young people. Though the daily realities of these freedom seekers are unknown and there is fertile ground to reimagine their lives, should we be doing that work? Odubanjo asked these questions throughout this process as he grappled with the implication of writing from an incomplete archive and what the repercussions could be:

> The process reaffirmed to me the idea that violence and violent acts don't exist in a vacuum; these things don't just happen once without further impact. Removing them [the enslaved] from their homes was a violence; enslaving them was another; their names were taken from them, their children; and, although we try to honour them today, that violence continues as we mine their lives for meaning.[15]

It is that last sentence that resonated most with the group. Was it fair to the freedom seekers that we rhetorically exhume their bodies, their lives and evoke their likeness, imagining their stories for meaning in the present, for social gain, even for financial gain? Saidiya Hartman, Marisa Fuentes, Jessica Marie Johnson, Jennifer Morgan and other historians of the Black Atlantic have all recognised that the archive itself is part of the problem, erasing enslaved Black and South Asian people as conscious and feeling individuals, often reducing them to a statistical presence in account books and similar records. How can we tell impossible stories, Hartman asked, and she proposed that historians should strain against the limits of the archive by undertaking what she termed 'critical fabulation', to imagine what cannot be verified. The result is 'a history of an unrecoverable past; it is a narrative of what might have been or could have been; it is a history written with and against the archive'.[16] The artists involved in the project were hyper-aware of their position relative to those of the people they were writing about and what it meant to write humanity back into a space where humanity had been excised, all in a fashion shaped by and resonating with the impact of present-day events and concerns. Essah's, Olayiwola's and Mehri's poems all demonstrate this. Essah's narrative poem, 'Nothing's Changed', ruminates on the concept of Black bodies being hunted by authority in both eighteenth- and twenty-first-century contexts by showing young people who are chased by slave-catchers and then later fleeing imprisonment by the police.

---

[15] Gboyega Odubanjo to Kate Birch, 11 November 2021.

[16] Saidiya Hartman, 'Venus in Two Acts', *Small Axe*, 26 (vol. 12, issue 2), June 2008, 10, 11, 12. Fuentes, *Dispossessed Lives*; J. M. Johnson, 'Markup Bodies: Black [Life] Studies and Slavery [Death] Studies at the Digital Crossroads', *Social Text*, 36, issue 4 (2018), 57–79; Jennifer L. Morgan, *Reckoning with Slavery: Gender, Kinship, and Capitalism in the Early Black Atlantic* (Durham, NC, 2021).

Whoever should bring him back
shall be rewarded with three guineas.
Tall and sturdy negro boy.
Black male with a history of violence.
Call the metropolitan police
if you see this dangerous suspect[17]

Essah also took it upon themselves to comb through the research for marginalised narratives within the Black community:

Moreover, as a queer non-binary person it was important for me to queer up the research. Precolonial queer ancestry is rich within the African continent and this fact should be widely known. Thus, telling a queer love story between two people of Ghanaian and Nigerian heritage not only gave me the chance to explore indigenous cultures and religions but it also allowed me to explore the truth – that queerness was and is a beautiful and common reality within the African continent.[18]

The creatives' work aligned with Hartman's injunction to paint as full a picture as possible of the lives of their subjects, 'straining against the limits of the archive ... [and] enacting the impossibility of representing the lives' of enslaved Black Londoners.[19] Mehri asks the difficult question of what happened to those who sought and found their freedoms. What challenges did they face in seventeenth- and eighteenth-century London? What discriminations and barriers did they encounter as they entered the 'ever-mushrooming' city? Georgian London was hardly the most accepting or safe culture for vulnerable groups. Even though there was a burgeoning population of free Black and South Asian people in the city, members of this community faced institutional discrimination and hostility. Black and South Asian Londoners often had to deal with poverty, exclusion, a lack of social mobility and the risk of being kidnapped and sent into plantation slavery. From 1731 onwards, Black people were forbidden to learn trades, were not entitled to wages or poor law relief and were frequently subject to unjust imprisonment.[20] Mehri's poems suggest that it is one thing to no longer be bound, but it is another to have legal and financial freedoms. The impetus of her lyric sits comfortably between our own contemporary context and those of the freedom seekers:

---

[17] Abena Essah, 'Nothing's Changed,' in *Runaways London: For the Enslaved Freedom-Seekers of the 17th and 18th Centuries*, ed. Fahad Al-Amoudi and Kate Birch (2021), 54–5. Hartman and others have warned against attempting 'anything as miraculous as recovering the lives of the enslaved or redeeming the dead', and Gayatri Spivak demonstrates not only that the subaltern cannot speak but that to pretend that they can reflects our own hubris. See Hartman, 'Venus in Two Acts', 11; G. C. Spivak, 'Can the Subaltern Speak?' in *Marxism and the Interpretation of Culture*, ed. C. Nelson and L. Grossberg (1988), 271–313.

[18] Essah, introduction to poems, in *Runaways London*, 48.

[19] Hartman, 'Venus in Two Acts', 11.

[20] Gerzina, *Black London*, 19.

... From here, the water is a blanket of possibility. Risk is gloriously circumstantial. Shorn of livery & lace, I inhale the fugitive smog, few possessions to weigh down this inconspicuous uniform of tatters. Mine, all mine ...[21]

This is where Mehri and Essah derive just some of the power of their verse. Overlaying contemporary concerns with the hopes, fears and realities of the past lights a fire of urgency in the work. In response to the question 'why should we resurrect freedom seekers?', they answer unequivocally that it is because their challenges are ours, that the effects of colonialism and slavery can be felt today.

The creatives' work was infused by their desire to problematise the language of the archive and the violence – both physical and psychological – it continues to purport. The source material itself placed Black and South Asian people in the same linguistic and physical plane as advertisements for items of clothing, job advertisements and other miscellaneous items in newspapers. It was a shocking and blunt statement that enslavers – with the support of newspaper editors – viewed Black and South Asian people as nothing more than chattels; and the lack of a challenge to this narrative risks reproducing this injustice. The writers underwent the work of celebrating the freedom seekers' humanity but in doing so they also challenged the established marginalisation of these figures. This was perhaps the riskiest element to the work and placed the writers in the most peril from a number of different interest groups. Odubanjo's poem, 'Proprietor Rap', showcases this most clearly. The poem was an exercise in satire that dexterously used the contemporary hip hop semantic field and syntax to problematise the language of the advertisements and the vocabulary of enslavers:

might just spend a boy on a necklace
sell a boy for a pipe of madeira   come
by him   come and buy a boy split
the booty spin the yarn take the boy
as gospel   my assets have assets
my boy has the painted-callico
with the buttons   call him a steal[22]

Once again, his blurring of the modern with the historical created the dimension of urgency that gave the poem its impetus, and his choices in language heightened our understanding of how currency was placed on human life. Crucially, though, Odubanjo's poem was a persona poem, placing him directly in the mindset of those who exploited Black slave labour. It is an exemplary exercise in sensitivity and pathos, where the language of the poem invites you to engage critically in how strange the source material is, how different

---

[21] Momtaza Mehri, 'Bankside, Breaking', in *Runaways London*, 13.
[22] Odubanjo, 'Proprietor Rap', in *Runaways London*, 25.

the morality of enslavers is to our own, and how parody accentuates the grief we feel for lives perpetually changed by the slave trade.

Other writers challenged what was missing in the language of the archive rather than what was present. We have already seen how daring Essah was in bringing desire and same-sex love to the source material that was notably devoid of agency. Olayiwola and Zahid made this the central theme of their writing, taking risks in form and voice to create work that brought new dimensions of agency to the freedom seekers' lives. Olayiwola worked primarily through the mind and body to explore the idea of unfreedom in a metaphysical sense. There is an intimacy in his poetics that exhibits a different kind of risk, one that dares to access the intensely personal thoughts and emotions of people whose interior lives are completely unknown to historical researchers:

> O to be inside that flight,
> to be damaged beyond the instinct of return –[23]

Where the body was a vehicle towards freedom in other writers' work, in Olayiwola's work it became an extension of the same force that sought to oppress freedom seekers, evoking a line from Mehri's opening poem from the book, 'We are a remembering people'.[24] Like Essah and Olayiwola, Zahid also took the risk of showing us a love story between two young freedom seekers. What made her approach unique was the choice to write a long poem that played with the white space on the page, space that both reflected the absence of information in the archives and gave the reader appropriate moments to pause and revel in moments of memory, longing and tenderness:

> whilst ripping out blades of grass she prayed –
>   around her neck the brass weighed like a promise
> ready to be broken
>   the sky   a whirlpool spinning out god's answer:
>   Run[25]

In her artistic works Graham 'went deep into the experience' of the freedom seekers, putting herself 'in the eyes of these people', something she found 'quite hard'. It was important that her work was done 'delicately', that it did not 'romanticise trauma'.[26] Her illustrations look back to where the freedom seekers were coming from, their initial capture, enslavement, their daily lives and attempts at escape, but also look forward to their future, their place in the world and the conflict between African culture and the enslaved self. The free woman in Graham's final illustration now has to:

---

[23] Olayiwola, 'Once', in *Runaways London*, 45.

[24] Mehri, 'Bankside, Breaking', 13.

[25] Memoona Zahid, 'A Possible Entrance into the Moon', in *Runaways London*, 70.

[26] Tasia Graham, panel discussion at *Runaways London* launch, Museum of London Docklands, 21 October 2021.

face the idea that she may be Black-British, but she is not viewed as a citizen due to the colour of her skin, nor does she identify with the culture she once had. This illustration depicts the confusion and the loss of African identity, that many Black-British people face today with a loss in their culture and who they really are, through the effects of slavery.[27]

Graham's point was borne out by a conversation broadcast on London-born David Lammy's LBC talk radio programme in March 2021, during which a caller insisted that Lammy was not entitled to describe himself as English 'Because you're African Caribbean!' Lammy took issue with this, and ended the conversation by lamenting 'How is that here in England you can only claim that Englishness effectively ... if you are White?'.[28]

Twist, conversely, chooses to highlight all that is strong and positive about these freedom seekers: 'I kind of wanted to shift focus. In my practice, I use drawing as a tool to demonstrate worth.'[29] Like her fellow creatives, Twist reclaims their humanity, celebrates their resilience, glories in the fact that these young people slipped away down the same roads where her community lives, works and goes to school: 'Time and time again we are reminded of how we seem to have a knack for finding the small glimmer of joy, and fanning that.'[30] While the poets explore the imagined inner lives of London's enslaved people, the artists in their bold and confident work demanded that viewers acknowledge and accept the Black and South Asian presence in London, both past and present.

A common theme emerges from the writers and artists beyond their subject matter. They are all in the early stages of their careers and they took risks with form, structure and voice in order to ask difficult questions of the historical source materials. Their creative engagement with that data involved raising the question of whether such investigation is appropriate, and thereby encouraging readers, audiences and potentially students to consider that issue. The creatives' approach to the Runaways London project was successful in challenging the language of an archive filled with the words and actions of enslavers, and responding creatively within a space of violent elision. Al-Amoudi and Birch then worked to craft the creative work together with historical data and advertisements furnished by Newman and Brunache to give readers a fuller sense of context. It would be easy for readers to get lost in poetry and artwork that takes some knowledge for granted, so it was necessary for the editors to give the reader as many tools to understand the poetry and artwork as possible without asking the artists to explain themselves. Ultimately, the editors added some of the advertisements and contemporary images of London on the inside covers and throughout the anthology.

---

[27] Tasia Graham, Introduction to artwork, in *Runaways London*, 30.
[28] David Lammy speaking with Jean, LBC (Leading Britain's Conversation), 29 March 2021, https://www.lbc.co.uk/radio/presenters/david-lammy/david-lammy-schools-caller-who-tells-him-hes-not-english, accessed 13 December 2021.
[29] Olivia Twist, panel discussion at *Runaways London* launch.
[30] Olivia Twist, Introduction to artwork, in *Runaways London*, 60.

Location is of huge importance to the project; part of the surprise for a prospective reader or perhaps for students engaging with this would be the little-known information that slavery existed in London. It was therefore crucial that the anthology emphasised the areas of the city where freedom seekers would have found community, where they lived and where they escaped. Similarly, the advertisements placed before each writer's and artist's chapter (and on the inside covers) provided context to the figures they referenced in the work and allowed the reader into the world of the archive that the artists were working from. Reproduction of these advertisements is inherently problematic: as Marisa Fuentes has suggested, 'violence is transferred from the enslaved bodies to the documents that count, condemn, assess, and evoke them, and we receive them in this condition.' If we read an advertisement in which an enslaved child is described wearing a metal collar upon which the enslaver's name and address was engraved, we reimagine and symbolically reinscribe the violent dehumanisation of that enslaved child. Yet in most cases these advertisements – however deeply problematic they may be – are the only surviving evidence of the very existence of the enslaved people they described. As Ann Laura Stoler has suggested, we can read 'along the archival grain' and read much more in and through these advertisements than might be seen at first glance, helping return Black life, agency and culture in part through an archive that has all but erased it. The challenge facing us in this collaborative project was to balance the inherently problematic nature of the advertisements for freedom seekers with the fact that they were vital to our objective of imagining the real people behind the perfunctory, crass and often racist language used by enslavers to describe them. We worked with the poets and artists in 'subverting the discourse of the runaway ad[vertisements] and the gaze' of the enslavers who created them, thereby 'shift[ing] the epistemological weight of the archival document'.[31]

The organisation of the illustrations, expertly crafted by Twist and Graham, was placed specifically so that the art and the poetry supported each other in their affirmation of the humanity of the people behind the advertisements. Odubanjo's final poem, which explores the relationship between plantation slavery and slavery in London, immediately precedes Graham's illustrated narrative of a young woman of African descent being forcibly taken from her home and made to endure the Middle Passage (see Figure 1).[32] Similarly, Essah's final poem, which describes a Black Ball, supports Twist's illustration of a London Black-owned tavern which hints of the present as well as the past.[33] (See Figure 2.) The anthology is prefaced by an explanatory historical introduction by Newman and Brunache, and each poet and artist begins

[31] Fuentes, *Dispossessed Lives*, 5, 29; Ann Laura Stoler, *Along the Archival Grain: Epistemic Anxieties and Colonial Common Sense* (Princeton, 2008). For more on this issue see, for example, Hartman, *Lose Your Mother* and 'Venus in Two Acts'; Johnson, 'Markup Bodies'; S. Smallwood, 'The Politics of the Archive and History's Accountability to the Enslaved', *History of the Present: A Journal of Critical History*, 6, no. 2 (2016), 118–32.

[32] Odubanjo, 'Cousin', in *Runaways London*, 27; Graham, 'Forgotten Journey of the Enslaved', in *Runaways London*, 31.

[33] Essah, 'Bra Fie: For Sabinah', in *Runaways London*, 56–7; Twist, 'Black Owned Taverns', in *Runaways London*, 61.

Figure 2 'Black Owned Taverns', @ Olivia Twist, *Runaways London*, 61.

their own section with a personal reflection on the sources and their creative work. But rather than explaining their work, these introductions enabled the creatives to illuminate the ways in which their own understandings of and reaction to historical research inspired them to explore and imagine particular people, places and themes.

The importance of location to the artists, made clear in Graham's representation of work and escape in London in Figure 3, was further emphasised with the film. This was coordinated by Tom MacAndrew (programme manager at Spread the Word) who also looked after the teaching resources and the project launch. Ashley Karrell of Panoptical produced *Runaways London*, featuring Brunache, Odubanjo and Essah, all filmed on location in the City of London.[34] Like the anthology, the film combines the historical references

---

[34] The film, a pdf of the book, and the teaching resources are all available at https://www. spreadtheword.org.uk/projects/runaways, accessed 15 March 2022.

Figure 3 'Escaped, captured and repeated', @ Tasia Graham, *Runaways London*, 33.

with the poems and the illustrations themselves. Brunache gives the context, Essah and Odubanjo provide the framework of their creative approach. There are images of the actual ads but these are also read aloud, their words typed across the screen to give emphasis. All five poets read their work, sometimes over Graham and Twist's striking illustrations, sometimes over images of the skyline and buildings of the City, an area that emerged from and thrived on the international commerce of the Restoration period that included human beings as commodities. Views of the Royal Exchange and Lloyd's of London all reference this time, and even subtle hints of a compromised past are seen with film of the Jamaican Wine House on the site of the original Jamaican Coffee House (where enslaved people were bought and sold, and which was often mentioned in the runaway advertisements as the place to which they could be returned for a reward by any person who had recaptured them). A shot of the East India pub is a lingering shadow of the vast sway of the East India Company.

The project was launched in October 2021 at the Museum of London Docklands, featuring readings and discussions of their work by the creatives, and follow-up events included a similar event hosted by Lloyd's of London in March 2022. The venue was particularly appropriate given that the original Lloyd's Coffee House was often specified in advertisements as a location to which recaptured freedom seekers could be taken.

The trauma inherent within these seventeenth- and eighteenth-century advertisements can easily reach out and touch us today. The work of young, early-career Black and South Asian creatives in grappling with this history is nothing if not courageous. They rejected the easy choice of reproducing the content of fragmentary archival records, instead choosing to challenge those records and daring to imagine their histories. This is not work that historians can do easily, although it cannot happen without the foundations of historical research and knowledge. The collaboration between historians, literary editors and young creatives helped fashion 'a history of an unrecoverable past', providing glimpses 'of what might have been'. The work of the creatives fashioned a 'history written with and against the archive', expanding the historical consciousness and awareness of people across society.[35]

---

[35] Hartman, 'Venus in Two Acts', 12.

Cite this article: Al-Amoudi F, Birch K, Newman SP (2022). Runaways London: Historical Research, Archival Silences and Creative Voices. *Transactions of the Royal Historical Society* **32**, 223–239. https://doi.org/10.1017/S008044012200010X